REVOLUTIONARY TIMES

Ireland 1913–23: The Forging of a Nation

REVOLUTIONARY TIMES

Ireland 1913–23: The Forging of a Nation

MIKE CRONIN & MARK DUNCAN

MERRION PRESS

First published in 2024 by
Merrion Press
10 George's Street, Newbridge
Co. Kildare, Ireland
www.merrionpress.ie

© Mike Cronin and Mark Duncan, 2024

978 1 78537 484 5 (Hardback)
978 1 78537 485 2 (Ebook)

A CIP catalogue record for this book is available from the British Library.

All rights reserved. No part of this publication may be reproduced, stored in a retrieval system, or transmitted, in any form or by any means (electronic, mechanical, photocopying, recording or otherwise), without the prior written permission of both the copyright owner and the publisher of this book.

Typeset in Avenir Next 9/14 pt and Cambria 9/12 pt

Front cover image: Crowds surround prisoners recently released from British prisons in 1917. Courtesy of the National Library of Ireland.
Back cover image: Who Fears to Speak of Easter Week? Courtesy of the National Library of Ireland.

Printed in Dubai.

Merrion Press is a member of Publishing Ireland.

CONTENTS

Introduction vii

List of Abbreviations xv

1913 1

1914 35

1915 73

1916 111

1917 147

1918 185

1919 223

1920 263

1921 297

1922 335

1923 375

Further reading 410

List of illustrations 413

Acknowledgements 414

INTRODUCTION

THIS BOOK has its origins in an online project, *Century Ireland*, a historical newspaper that told the story of the events of Irish life throughout the period covered by the Irish Decade of Centenaries. The website ran for more than a decade and still remains fully accessible online (www.rte.ie/centuryireland). However, there is ample evidence to suggest that, even after a decade of feasting on the fruits of fresh scholarship and newly released archives, the appetite for histories of the Irish revolutionary period remains as strong as ever, and so it seemed a good idea to translate something of the essence of the work in which we have been involved into book form.

But how do you squeeze an online project that encompassed thousands of articles, including more than a dozen exhibitions and thematic galleries, and hundreds of film and audio features, into the borders of a book format? The answer is, of course, that you don't. What this book seeks to do, in its structure, form and design, is to capture the website's essence in print, taking the years 1913 to 1923 as its time frame, a period in Irish history dominated by such major events as the Dublin 'Lockout', the passage of the Irish Home Rule Bill, the outbreak and prosecution of the First World War, the 1916 Easter Rising, the conscription crisis, women's suffrage, the War of Independence, partition, the Anglo-Irish Treaty, the Civil War and the accession of the new Irish Free State into the League of Nations. Taken together, these defining developments formed the spine of the so-called Decade of Centenaries, the term applied by the Irish government to its extensive programme of commemorations that involved ceremonies, projects and initiatives of various kinds and of varying scale that were often as much locally organised and community-focused as they were state-led and nationally inclined.

INTRODUCTION

The book is structured around each of the years covered by the Decade of Centenaries, and each chapter seeks to explore a single year in depth by including a timeline of major and noteworthy events, together with contemporary-styled reportage of historical news stories. To explain and contextualise what was happening and to draw upon the latest historical research, each chapter is supplemented with two short essays that address and reflect upon a particular theme. Individual chapters then close with imagery from a commemorative event that took place during the 2013-23 period.

These essential elements also provided much of the core content of the *Century Ireland* project, which launched in May 2013 as a partnership between Boston College, RTÉ, the National Library of Ireland, the National Archives of Ireland and other cultural institutions, with funding from the Department of Tourism, Culture, Arts, Gaeltacht, Sport and Media. The book spans the entirety of the commemorative decade and allows dominant political and other considerations to be covered alongside the humdrum realities of everyday experience. This approach is less about avoiding contested narratives of the past – an impossible task – and more about allowing for multiple and complicated narratives, as stories from the news cycle invariably broaden the lens onto everyday events, such as sport and leisure activities, new trends and fashions, extreme weather incidents, debates around the provision of housing, and much, much more.

We were encouraged in our approach by a commemorative programme that reached far beyond the discipline of history and was all the more creative and vital for it. Through cultural performance, art projects and the exploration of the experiences of previously marginalised groups, the Decade of Centenaries brought about a new understanding of social conditions in Ireland, the role of women in Irish society, and the impact of the First World War on the home front and on those Irish men and women serving at the front lines. In the steering of this broad, multidisciplinary approach, successive Irish governments were greatly helped by the guidance provided by its own Expert Advisory Group (EAG) on Centenary Commemorations, established in 2012 to 'advise the Government on centenary commemorations of major events'. The chair of this Advisory Group, Maurice Manning, stated that the group, to which a number of professional historians were appointed, would 'seek to set a tone that is inclusive and non-triumphalist, ensuring authenticity, proportionality and openness'.[1] Crucially, too, the EAG advised that the period of commemorations should not be used to 'contrive an ahistorical or retrospective consensus about the contemporary impact and legacy of divisive events'.[2]

INTRODUCTION

The Decade of Centenaries, History and the Contemporary Context

What people were and weren't willing to commemorate or contemplate went to the very core of the commemoration conundrum for those who saw in the centenaries an opportunity for emphasising a 'shared history' and the furthering of reconciliation on a politically fractured island. After all, as historians were often at pains to point out, commemoration is never simply a question of honouring or remembering the past. Rather, it is, as Laura McAtackney has noted, 'the deliberate act of remembering an aspect of the past, at a particular time and place, as a symbolic act in the present'.[3] Whatever ways the history of the 1913–23 period was presented and commemorated, therefore, it would be understood and consumed in the almost constantly shifting contexts of the contemporary. If there was a somewhat self-satisfactory feel to the first phase of the Decade of Centenaries, it may well have been that it occurred against the backdrop of a harmonious and seemingly strengthened Anglo-Irish relationship, of peace and stability in Northern Ireland, and at a moment that coincided with Ireland regaining the economic sovereignty it had lost to the troika of the International Monetary Fund, the European Central Bank and the European Union in the course of the economic crisis that erupted in 2008. The second phase of the Decade of Centenaries was always going to navigate more hazardous historical terrain, most obviously in the form of how the divisive experiences of partition and the Civil War might be marked. But it also took place amidst the damaging fall-out from the UK's referendum vote to leave the European Union in June 2016, just eight days before Europe's political leaders, including the Irish president, gathered in France to mark the centenary of the Battle of the Somme.[4]

Brexit, an ostensibly English nationalist project, swung a wrecking ball at the relative stability delivered by the Good Friday Agreement and the key understandings that underpinned it. The effects were most obviously felt within Northern Ireland, but Anglo-Irish relations also entered a new phase of volatility as the Irish government moved to defend its vital national interests – the retention of an open border on the island of Ireland and a shoring up of Ireland's position within the single European market – as the UK government sought to negotiate the terms of its EU exit. It was all a far cry from 2012, when Taoiseach Enda Kenny and British Prime Minister David Cameron issued a joint statement declaring that the relationship between the two countries had 'never been stronger or more settled, as complex or as important, as it is today'.[5] In the commemorative context, the lengthy post-Brexit wrangling exposed, above all else, the still unsettled nature of this relationship and the enduring legacy of a partition settlement, upon which the negotiations around Irish border issues helped shine a renewed spotlight. The marking of the centenary of partition would nevertheless prove a mostly muted affair. This was largely attributable to the spread of Covid-19 in 2020 and the ensuing series of 'lockdowns', which led to shuttered schools, colleges and businesses, and to the clearing of entire calendars of cultural and other activities.[6] In the North, where differing perspectives on the past can too easily be mapped neatly onto divergent visions for the political future, historian Caoimhe Nic Dháibhéid suggested that the pandemic 'provided, perhaps, a welcome distraction from full-throttle commemoration wars'.[7]

And yet, to hardly anybody's great surprise, the Decade of Centenaries still threw up its fair share of commemoration controversies. There was the #wakingthefeminists social media response to the announcement of the Abbey Theatre's male dominated Rising anniversary, which kick-started its own revolution of sorts by forcing a serious interrogation, at levels of both policy and practice, of power relations and gender equality throughout Irish theatre and the arts more generally.[8] There was the repeated vandalism that forced the removal of a necrology wall in Glasnevin Cemetery erected to remember all those who died in the Irish revolution – Irish and British, combatants and civilians – and inspired by the example of the Ring of Remembrance at Ablain-Saint-Nazaire in France, which simply remembers soldiers from all sides killed in the First World War.[9] Then, in 2021, there was the mini furore that erupted over a decision by President Michael D. Higgins to decline an invitation to a multi-denominational Christian church service in Armagh, organised for the Anglican St Patrick's Cathedral and styled as a 'service of reflection and hope to mark the centenary of the partition of Ireland and the formation of Northern Ireland'. In doing so, Higgins, who felt the invitation had been framed in a manner that was not politically neutral, found himself accused by the DUP's Jeffrey Donaldson of being a 'united Ireland champion rather than a leader of reconciliation' – the two, needless to say, are not necessarily inimical – and criticised by former Taoiseach John Bruton, who considered it a lost opportunity to recognise 'present constitutional realities, while pointing the way to a more hopeful future'.[10] It was, nonetheless, a remarkably popular decision in the south, where 68% of respondents to an *Irish Times* opinion poll defended the decision by a president who had been a central figure in official centenaries ceremonies throughout the decade. For their part, the organisers of the Armagh religious service expressed disappointment at the 'polarised public commentary' that followed the president's non-attendance at an event where the very polarising history of partition was itself dutifully acknowledged. Speaking to an audience that included senior Irish and British government representatives, if not the two heads of state hoped for, the Derry-born Roman Catholic Primate of All Ireland, Eamon Martin, remarked upon the contemporary currency of partition as a 'symbol of cultural, political and religious division'.[11]

If only in its diminished form, the Armagh church service did go ahead. But in the years and decades to come, might it be, as Sara Dybris McQuaid and Fearghal McGarry have suggested, that it is the commemorations 'that did not occur' that will be considered those of most significance or interest to the historically curious?[12] Should this prove to be the case, then pride of place may well be afforded to the ill-fated proposal to hold a commemorative event for the Royal Irish Constabulary (RIC) and the Dublin Metropolitan Police (DMP) in January 2020. Influenced by the ferocity of the political and online reaction, and in the heightened political atmosphere of an impending general election, the proposal was dropped by a somewhat chastened government. The severity of the backlash led Fine Gael leader Leo Varadkar to later suggest that the country had 'lost its way' in relation to the conduct of commemorations and to urge a return to the practice of 2016 where, he said, ceremonies had been 'non-partisan. We commemorated what happened, sought to understand it, contextualise it, learn from it.'[13] For historian Diarmaid Ferriter, a member of the EAG, the uproar over the planned commemoration of the pre-independence police forces, and their associations with the loathed forces of the Black and Tans and Auxiliaries, who were in the vanguard of opposing the Irish separatist struggle in 1920 and 1921, illustrated the need for government to 'tread carefully' when it came to emotive issues where there was a need to guard against 'distortion and simplification'.[14]

In the long term, perhaps the most effective antidote against impulses towards the simplifying and propagandising of the past will be the open access provided to the extraordinary archival records of the revolutionary generation. Perhaps the more access that is provided to the raw materials of history, the more appreciation there will be not only of the idealism and heroism that undoubtedly animated it, but also of its complications and messy realities. If, as Professor Anne Dolan has ventured, 'history's job is to make it harder to be so certain and so shrill', then the more light that is cast on the varied lived experiences of those involved the better.[15] For that reason, the most enduring legacy of the Decade of Centenaries is likely to be the resourcing of libraries and archives across Ireland to invest in the extensive digitisation of material relating to the 1913-23 period and to make it widely and freely available to researchers, academic and otherwise. Included amongst this material are the remarkable – and vast – records of the Military Archives, whose ongoing digitisation and public release of the Bureau of Military History (1916-21) witness statements, together with the Military Service Pensions Collections, have already helped transform scholarship on the revolutionary decade and the lives and afterlives of those who participated in it. And these are only just beginning. The monumental scale of archival and public heritage endeavours is such that their surfaces have barely been scratched, and so they will continue to inspire new research, drive different lines of enquiry and fuel fresh perspectives on this defining period – and the decades that followed – long after the commemorative spotlight has shifted elsewhere.

This book has benefited enormously from such work as has already been undertaken in these areas, and what we offer here is an array of historical material from the period 1913-23, as well as contextual essays explaining the main themes that emerged during the commemorative period. The historical understanding of the interlinked and multifaceted series of events that took place in Ireland, and beyond, during this decade has become highly nuanced as archival material has become available and historical practices have widened in their approach. After the fiftieth anniversary of the Rising in 1966, the Department of External Affairs published *Cuimhneachán, 1916-66: A Record of Ireland's Commemoration of the 1916 Rising*. In his foreword the Taoiseach of the day, Seán Lemass, concluded that the book would serve as a 'tangible reminder of the pleasure it gave us to recall, fifty years afterwards, the stirring events of 1916'.[16] The material offered here shows how the appreciation of Ireland's history has broadened out so that the past is more than a single, stirring event.

ENDNOTES

1. *The Irish Times,* 7 March 2012.
2. Diarmaid Ferriter, '1916 in 2016: Personal reflections of an Irish historian', *Irish Historical Studies*, vol. 42, no. 161 (2018), p. 161.
3. www.rte.ie/brainstorm/2021/0921/1248033-why-commemoration-is-controversial-even-if-we-feel-it-shouldnt/.
4. *The Irish Times*, 2 July 2016, www.irishtimes.com/news/world/europe/leaders-unite-for-100th-anniversary-of-the-battle-of-the-somme-1.2707a625.
5. Joint statement by Enda Kenny and David Cameron, 'British Irish Relations, the Next Decade', 12 March 2012, www.gov.uk/government/news/british-irish-relations-the-next-decade.
6. See Mark Simpson, 'NI 100: How was Northern Ireland's centenary marked?', 30 December 2021, www.bbc.com/news/uk-northern-ireland-59669635.
7. Caoimhe Nic Dháibhéid, 'Historians and the Decade of Centenaries in modern Ireland', *Contemporary European History*, vol. 32, iss. 1, pp. 21–6.
8. Mary McAuliffe, 'Commemorating Women's Histories during the Irish Decade of Centenaries', *Éire-Ireland*, vol. 57, nos 1 & 2 (Spring/Summer 2022), p. 249; Helen Meany, 'Waking the Feminists: the campaign that revolutionised Irish theatre', *The Guardian*, 5 January 2018, www.theguardian.com/stage/2018/jan/05/feminist-irish-theatre-selina-cartmell-gate-theatre.
9. *The Irish Times*, 4 February 2022, www.irishtimes.com/news/ireland/irish-news/glasnevin-memorial-wall-to-be-discontinued-after-repeated-vandalism-1.4793707.
10. Quoted in Stephen O'Neill, 'Wherever Green is Orange', *Éire-Ireland*, vol. 57, nos 1 & 2 (Spring/Summer 2022), p. 309; also *The Irish Times*, 17 September 2021, www.irishtimes.com/news/politics/president-higgins-suggests-bruton-should-withdraw-criticism-1.4677055.
11. *Irish Independent*, 21 Sept 2021, www.independent.ie/irish-news/politics/church-group-regrets-service-to-mark-ni-partition-led-to-polarising/40886407.html; also The Journal.ie, 21 Oct 2024, www.thejournal.ie/ni-event-amagh-5580013-Oct2021/.
12. Sara Dybris McQuaid and Fearghal McGarry, 'Politics and Narrative in Ireland's Decade of Commemorations', *Éire-Ireland*, vol. 57, nos 1 & 2 (Spring/Summer 2022), p. 24.
13. *The Irish Times*, 16 December 2020, www.irishtimes.com/news/ireland/irish-news/leo-varadkar-says-we-have-lost-our-way-in-the-decade-of-centenaries-1.4438436.
14. *The Irish Times*, 13 February 2020, www.irishtimes.com/news/ireland/irish-news/did-the-ric-commemoration-controversy-impact-on-election-2020-1.4172768.
15. 'Paper by Professor Anne Dolan – Machnamh 100', 3 December 2020, https://president.ie/en/media-library/speeches/paper-by-professor-anne-dolan-machnamh-100.
16. Department of External Affairs, *Cuimhneachán, 1916–66: A Record of Ireland's Commemoration of the 1916 Rising* (Department of External Affairs, Dublin: 1966), p. 11.

LIST OF ABBREVIATIONS

DMP	Dublin Metropolitan Police
DORA	Defence of the Realm Act
FAI	Football Association of Ireland
FOIF	Friends of Irish Freedom
GAA	Gaelic Athletic Association
GPO	General Post Office
ICA	Irish Citizen Army
IFA	Irish Football Association
IFU	Irish Farmers' Union
ILP&TUC	Irish Labour Party and Trades Union Congress
INTO	Irish National Teachers' Organisation
IOC	Irish Olympic Committee
IPP	Irish Parliamentary Party
IRB	Irish Republican Brotherhood
IRFU	Irish Rugby Football Union
ITGWU	Irish Trade and General Workers' Union
IWFL	Irish Women's Franchise League
IWWU	Irish Women Workers' Union
LFA	Leinster Football Association
NSPCC	National Society for the Prevention of Cruelty to Children
RIC	Royal Irish Constabulary
RUC	Royal Ulster Constabulary
UIL	United Irish League
USC	Ulster Special Constabulary
UUC	Ulster Unionist Council
UVF	Ulster Volunteer Force
WSPU	Women's Social and Political Union

1913

'Scores of well-fed metropolitan policemen pursued a handful of men, women and children running for their lives before them. I saw a young man pursued by a huge policeman, knocked down by a baton stroke, and then, whilst bleeding on the ground, batoned and kicked.'

Count Casimir Dunin Markievicz in a letter to *The Freeman's Journal*
1 SEPTEMBER

1913

1 JAN
A house on Nelson Street in Limerick catches fire, resulting in the death of a young girl.

1 JAN
Sir Edward Carson suggests an amendment to the Home Rule Bill that excludes Ulster. The bill is rejected by the House of Commons.

3 JAN
Nationalists propose proportional representation for the Irish Senate as part of the Home Rule Bill.

△ **3 JAN**
The Duke of Abercorn, James Hamilton, dies of pneumonia.

6 JAN
The Sailors' and Firemen's Union demand higher wages for their workers at the Dublin docks.

Home Rule Bill Wins Approval from House of Commons
— *Now for the Lords*

London, 17 January – The Home Rule Bill, a bill allowing for the self-governance of Ireland through an individual Irish Parliament, passed through the House of Commons yesterday. The bill was bolstered in Parliament by the Nationalist Party, led mostly by Mr John Redmond. The Unionist Party, however, vehemently disagreed with the bill and tried to both amend and defeat it throughout its journey in the Commons. The bill passed by a vote of 367 to 257.

The Unionist Party, composed primarily of the men of Ulster, worked to amend the bill to exclude the Ulster region from the area of governance under the bill's newly created Irish Parliament. This amendment, proposed by Sir Edward Carson, was defeated by a majority of 97. In the final vote on the bill, the only 16 Irishmen to oppose it in the Commons all came from Ulster. With the most fervent opposition to Ulster's inclusion coming from Carson, several speeches were given both before and after the passing in the Commons to create resistance in the region.

'Who's Afraid?' Home Rule and the Parliament Act, Punch, *15 January 1913.*

REVOLUTIONARY TIMES 1913–23

Other amendments to benefit Ulster's interests occurred throughout the debates. The bill creates two legislative houses, a Senate and House of Commons. With the House being the lower, yet larger, body proposed, with 164 members, and the Senate with only 40 members, the Unionists attempted to increase the number of men in the Senate to 100 to help protect their minority rights. This is due to the provision that if any bill is passed within the lower body that fails to pass the Senate, a joint sitting of the houses would follow where the number of men in the Commons would easily outvote the Senate. The Unionist amendment failed, however, as did the amendment to exclude Ulster in its entirety.

Sailings Cancelled as Strike Action Hits North Wall Schedule

Dublin, 30 January – The workers of the City of Dublin Steam Packet Company at North Wall went on strike today, suspending service. The strike came without notice to the company and involves over 100 men. The company was forced to cancel sailings for the day as a result of the sudden turn of events.

The strike began as a result of the foremen refusing to join the Irish Transport and General Workers' Union, of which all the other men are members. It is reported that the union called the men out of work after they started their normal shift at 7.30 a.m. It is likely that the men did not want to strike themselves but are following union orders. The company states that the men are paid well and without grievance to such rates, focusing the reason for the strike entirely on the foremen's choice to not join the union. The strikers have yet to make a statement.

Flooding Threatens Midlands as Waters Rise to Highest Level Since 1879

Banagher, 3 February – The midlands have been experiencing flooding as water levels have continued to rise over the past few weeks. Eight weeks ago, the level of the Shannon at Banagher was five feet above the minimum needed in the river for navigation purposes. The waters have gradually risen since last month with the exception of one day that was followed by a double rise the next.

1913

6 JAN
An inquiry into conditions at a Dublin workhouse is opened after workers complain of being provided with sour milk and poor food.

7 JAN
Peace discussions between Turkey and the Balkan states are suspended after failure to come to an agreement.

7 JAN
Queen's Island Unionist Club adopts a resolution reaffirming their will to exclude Ulster from the Home Rule Bill.

13 JAN
Edward Carson combines a number of militia groups that will form the basis of the Ulster Volunteer Force (UVF).

16 JAN
The Home Rule Bill is read for the third time in the House of Commons, passing by a vote of 367 to 257.

16 JAN
A Unionist Women's Protest is held against the Home Rule Bill in Dublin, as is a unionist demonstration in Belfast, where shots are fired.

16 JAN
The Irish Protest Committee forms to protest the introduction of religious belief into Irish politics.

REVOLUTIONARY TIMES 1913–23

1913

17 JAN
An all-Ireland meeting is convened by the Lord Mayor of Dublin to discuss the crisis caused by new restrictions by Minister Runciman on the cattle trade.

17 JAN
An amendment is added to the Franchise Bill in the House of Commons excluding Irish women from gaining suffrage.

20 JAN
Irish concerns about restrictions on the cattle trade are introduced to Parliament, but the policy remains unchanged owing to a concern with preventing disease.

30 JAN
The Home Rule Bill is rejected in the House of Lords by a vote of 326 to 69.

30 JAN
Over 100 labourers at the City of Dublin Steam Packet Company at North Wall go on strike.

31 JAN
The Ulster Unionist Council (UUC) officially announces the establishment of a paramilitary body, the UVF, as part of the ongoing unionist campaign against Home Rule.

Last weekend was affected by consistent hail, rain and snow, with no longer than a half-hour of dryness. The already rising water levels have now gained immense proportions, greatly harming the area. Melting snow in the hills has compounded the flood risk, causing gushing torrents from all outlets on their way into the valley of the Shannon. All roads, both public and private, were impassable for a considerable time due to the melt.

The entirety of the low-lying valley is submerged, with only high fences able to be seen above the water. This has been the highest flood on record since 1879.

Suffragettes' Hunger Strikes and Hunger Strikes Bill

Dublin, 28 February – Suffragists Margaret Cousins and Margaret Connery were yesterday released from prison after serving a one-month sentence. The women were imprisoned for breaking windows in Dublin Castle as a protest to the removal of Irish women from the Franchise Bill in the House of Commons. This bill, which would provide the right to vote to women of the United Kingdom, now excludes women in Ireland. Barbara Hoskins, also imprisoned in Tullamore, was released earlier this month, on the 8th; however, Mabel Purser remains in Tullamore jail for an additional month due to default of bail.

The four suffragettes, Margaret Connery, Mabel Purser, Barbara Hoskins and Margaret Cousins, who were imprisoned in Tullamore jail and went on hunger strike in protest against their conditions.

During the second week of their imprisonment, the women engaged in hunger strikes in order to receive better treatment. While Mrs Hoskins was in poor health upon release earlier in the month, Mrs Cousins and Mrs Connery were in good health as the strike ended prior to their release.

As suffragist demonstrations continue, Parliament has been working on a solution to stop the issue of hunger strikes by the imprisoned suffragists. On 28 March, Mr Reginald McKenna introduced a bill in the House of Commons in an effort to prevent further hunger strikes. This legislation allows for the temporary release of prisoners engaging in the strikes to regain their health before re-imprisoning them to finish their sentence. Formally the Prisoners (Temporary Discharge for Ill Health) Act, but nicknamed the 'Cat-and-Mouse' Bill, it provides an alternative to force-feeding the strikers or allowing them to die.

Ireland's Population Continues to Fall, but at a Slower Rate – Census Confirms

13 March – The results of the most recent census in Ireland have begun to appear. The census took place on 2 April 1911, and results are arriving in patches nearly two years later. Although smaller pieces have been released already, the complete census for Ireland has now reached the House of Commons.

The population of Ireland has continued to decline. In 1901 the population was 4,458,775 and in 1911 it went down to 4,390,213. Although still a decrease, this is the smallest decrease that Ireland has faced in 72 years – since the famine. In the preceding decade, the population decreased by 5.23%, but only by 1.54% this decade. The results also depict a trend of increase in town populations and a decrease of rural populations as more Irish move towards urban areas.

Suffragette Convicted of Defacing Sculpture of John Redmond

Dublin, 8 May – An Irish suffragette, Geraldine Manning, told a court in Dublin today that she would not pay the 25 shillings fine imposed on her for defacing a statue.

Ms Manning (40) had been convicted by the court of daubing green paint across a bust of John Redmond, the leader of the Irish Parliamentary Party. She was protesting against the failure of the party to support a Women's Franchise Bill in the House of Commons. This bill – which would have given voting rights to six million women across the United Kingdom – was defeated by 47 votes.

A scrap of paper left by Ms Manning on the pedestal on which the bust of Mr Redmond rests, read: 'Why didn't you get us votes for women, Mr Redmond? A traitor's face is no adornment to our picture gallery!' The bust

1913

3 FEB
Fighting between Turkey and the Balkans continues as the nations fail to negotiate a peace at talks in January, restarting the war.

3 FEB
After a weekend of storms, the midlands suffer severe flooding resulting in fuel shortages and property damage.

8 FEB
The House of Commons begins to negotiate solutions to problems in the Irish cattle trade, including a decrease in time restrictions between trades.

10 FEB
John Redmond visits Waterford for the opening of a new bridge. He gives a rallying speech discussing the Home Rule Bill and how Ireland will soon succeed in attaining this goal.

11 FEB
After undergoing a hunger strike, suffragists incarcerated in Tullamore jail for breaking the windows of Dublin Castle in protest at the removal of Irish women from the Franchise Bill are granted the same privileges as male political prisoners.

12 FEB
Turkey appeals to the powers of Europe to intervene in peace negotiations between it and the Balkans.

1913

15 FEB
Ireland defeat England 2–1 at Windsor Park in their British Home Championship football clash, with two goals from Billy Gillespie, a native of Donegal, who played professionally for Sheffield United.

18 FEB
Pembroke Urban Council requests funds for building working-class housing, and an inquiry begins.

▽ **19 FEB**
The **Midland Great Western Railway Company** passes a resolution requesting that the government remove restrictions on the cattle trade and end the crisis that has dogged the movement of cattle between Ireland and Britain as they show a clean bill of health for all cattle.

was on display as part of an exhibition of sculpture at the Royal Hibernian Academy on Lower Abbey Street. The court heard evidence from Edward Ryan, an attendant at the Academy, that he had followed Ms Manning as she fled from the building down Abbey Street and into Marlborough Street.

Ms Manning, who was accompanied in court by members of the Irish Women's Franchise League, smiled as she entered the dock and said in response to the imposition of the fine, 'I will not pay.'

Cartoon published in The Irish Citizen *mocking John Redmond's failure to support the Women's Franchise Bill.*

Working for a Sober Ireland

15,000 people attend Temperance rally in Monaghan

Monaghan Town, 2 June – 'The people of Ireland should be sober from end to end and look with contempt on the man who over-indulged,' the Lord Mayor of Dublin, Lorcan Sherlock, told a huge Temperance rally in Monaghan town yesterday.

The Lord Mayor told the cheering crowds that he saw a new Ireland being constructed in the next twenty years and that the means to attain their own salvation was about to be thrust upon the Irish people: 'Ireland will start in competition with other nations with a great deal of leeway to make up, and if we want to hold our own, it is not half-Ireland or three-quarters Ireland we want sober, but all of Ireland.'

The Lord Mayor's words were cheered by the 15,000 people who had gathered from all 40 of the parishes of the vast diocese of Clogher, which stretches across the counties of Monaghan, Louth, Fermanagh, Tyrone, Armagh and Donegal.

The entire event was organised by a local priest, Fr James McNamee, who proposed a resolution – adopted by all – 'discountenancing the use of intoxicating drinks at wakes, funerals, sports, harvesting operations, and calling upon parents and others to inculcate Temperance principles in the youth of Ireland'.

Roger Casement Says Poverty in Connemara is 'worst in civilised world'

Dublin, 13 June – Roger Casement has spoken of his sorrow at the scenes of poverty and distress he witnessed on a recent visit to Connemara.

Mr Casement was knighted for reports into human rights abuses in South America and has previously written a report documenting evidence of cruelty and mutilation of natives in the Congo. Speaking of the conditions in Connemara, he said, 'I have nowhere seen, even in the most primitive regions, a population housed as many of these people are, or battling for existence with a soil so incapable in itself of supporting human life.' These were, he said, 'the most-miserably situated rural communities that any civilised country holds today'.

Evidence for this misery lay all around. At the infant school in Carraroe, Mr Casement was met by a local priest, Fr Healy: 'When I visited a few days ago there were 160 infants on the rolls – little boys and girls alike clad, or half-clad, in homespun skirts. Many were absent because they had no clothes.'

Fr Healy said that, at a cost of 1d per day, a meal could be provided for all such children to ensure they were fed before going home to hungry

Casement wrote of the dire living conditions he witnessed in rural Galway.

1913

27 FEB
After completing a one-month sentence in Tullamore jail, suffragists Margaret Cousins and Margaret Connery are released from jail.

10 MAR △
King George V opens the new session of Parliament, the second of his reign. Five suffragists are arrested while trying to present a petition to the King upon his entrance to the building.

13 MAR
Results from the 1911 census begin to appear, revealing that Ireland has had its smallest population decline since the Great Famine.

15 MAR
Ireland are defeated at home by Scotland in their final British Home Championship football match and finish bottom of the table.

1913

17 MAR
A ship leaves North Wall for the first time in seven weeks, despite the ongoing strike of workers from the Sailors' and Firemen's Unions.

17 MAR
John Redmond gives a speech in London stating that Home Rule is not dead and that Ireland only needs to wait a few months for the bill to pass in the House of Lords.

25 MAR
A Unionist demonstration attended by over 30,000 people takes place in Belfast.

26 MAR
The Dublin Steam Packet Company begins negotiations with the strikers of the Sailors' and Firemen's Unions.

28 MAR
'Hunger Strike' legislation is introduced in Parliament that would allow for the temporary and conditional release from jail of those in poor health due to hunger strikes. They would be re-imprisoned after regaining their health.

29 MAR
Linfield defeat Glentoran 2–0 to win the Irish Cup final in front of 20,000 spectators at Celtic Park in Belfast.

homes. When a previous donation to the school had allowed for bread to be provided at lunchtime, attendance had increased to 150 per day.

Want of education is compounded by want of employment, and the only answer seems to be emigration: 'America has been, and is, the great relieving officer of Connemara.'

Mr Casement concluded, 'It might be said that a considerable area, inhabited by many thousands of people, lies on the verge of chronic famine and that many households, penned in animal shelters, dwell in dread of recurrent sickness.'

Home Rule Bill Rejected by House of Lords

London, 15 July – 'Will English troops be ordered at the dictation of John Redmond to shoot down loyal men who wish to remain part of the United Kingdom?' asked Lord Londonderry in the House of Lords in London today.

Speaking in a debate on the Government of Ireland Bill that would grant Home Rule to Ireland, Lord Londonderry said that the opponents of Home Rule in Ulster were drilling as an army because 'they were determined not to sacrifice their birthright, not to submit, vulgarly speaking, to being kicked out of the Empire, and they were determined to oppose it, if necessary, by force of arms'.

Lord Londonderry's trenchant speech came as the House of Lords rejected the Government of Ireland Bill for the second time. Instead, the Lords supported an amendment proposed by Lord Lansdowne that the House should decline to consider the bill until 'it has been submitted to the judgment of the country'. The margin of defeat was substantial, with Lord Lansdowne's amendment winning by 302 votes to 64, a margin of 238. In proposing his amendment, Lord Lansdowne, the leader of the Unionist peers, said that the Home Rule Bill was detestable in principle, pernicious in its leading features, and inexcusable in the circumstances in which it was brought forward. He particularly objected to the treatment of Ulster, saying that it would make Ulster subject to 'a disloyal majority'.

Industrial Unrest Spreads as Strike Action Hits Factories and Farms

Dublin, 14 August – A settlement of the six-week Dublin coach-builders' strike has not resulted in the anticipated return to work.

A deal recently negotiated between the employers and the employees may yet unravel because of a failure to take account of the demands of unskilled workers represented by the Irish Transport and General Workers'

Dublin's electrified tram system was heavily used and profitable. With over 95km of active line, it played a vital role in the commercial and social life of the city.

Union (ITGWU). The employers claim that they had considered the position of these men and decided to increase the salary of the unskilled hands, despite not receiving any demands from them during the negotiations. These demands have now been presented but, coming in the wake of the negotiated settlement, the employers have not only refused to accede to them, they have decided to post in each factory a notice to the effect that without the labourers' return to work, the establishment would be closed down and the skilled men paid off.

Meanwhile, the dispute at the Dublin United Tramways Company (DUTC) appears no closer to resolution. If anything, both the workers and directors appear to be steeling themselves for a more serious stand-off.

The directors of the DUTC are believed to have considered their options should their workers decide on strike action, with reports that they will import men from England to work the trams. *The Irish Worker* has gone so

1913

31 MAR
After many years of public discussion, the possibility of a highway connecting Dame Street and Henry and Mary Streets is proposed and finances are discussed by citizens interested in the project.

31 MAR ▽
J.P. Morgan, the American financier, dies.

"I Like a Little Competition"—J. P. Morgan

2 APR
After a second reading of the Hunger Strike Bill, only 43 members of the House of Commons vote against it.

14 APR
The Pembroke Urban Council secures funds for their housing scheme for the working class.

REVOLUTIONARY TIMES 1913–23

1913

19 APR
The strikers from the Sailors' and Firemen's Unions reach an agreement to return to work during negotiations with the Dublin Steam Packet Company and will return to work on 21 April.

21 APR
The *Aquitania*, the world's largest ship, is launched from Glasgow.

24 APR
The Hunger Strike Bill is read for a third time, passing by a margin of 224 to 56, despite the small opposition's illustration of its harshness during debate.

25 APR
The Portrush branch of the UVF stages a route march and series of exercises. This is the first time that *The Irish Times* mentions the UVF.

27 APR
Belfast, presently the largest city in Ireland, celebrates its tercentenary as a municipality.

3 MAY
The go-ahead is announced in the House of Commons for an underwater cable that will link the Irish phone system directly to that of Britain. The work will take three months and will vastly improve the speed and quality of calls between the two islands.

far as to allege that Mr William Martin Murphy is behind efforts to induce employers to lock out their workers, believing self-preservation to be his primary motivation. 'Every dog and devil, thief and saint is getting an invitation to come and work for the Dublin Tramway Company,' the paper has reported. 'Every man applying is asked, "Do you belong to Larkin's Union?" If so, there is no employment.'

In the face of this mounting pressure, the resolve of the workers appears strong. One of the tramway conductors has suggested that the 'fight will be a walk-over or a very stiff one'.

As it is among tramway workers, so too it remains among farm labourers in parts of north Co. Dublin. Industrial unrest continues unchecked, with some 200 farm labourers involved in strike action that could have serious repercussions for harvesting operations. Responsibility for organising the labourers is attributed to the ITGWU, which, *The Freeman's Journal* reports, has been active, with mixed results, in the districts of Santry, Coolock and Cloghran.

William Martin Murphy, chairman of the Dublin United Tramway Company.

Bloody Sunday in Dublin

One man dead, hundreds injured as police baton charge crowds in the capital

1 September – Dublin succumbed to heavy rioting for the second day in a row after police baton-charged crowds gathered on Sackville Street. Already being described as 'Bloody Sunday', yesterday's disturbances followed a series of violent clashes in and near the city the day before, and they signal a serious escalation of the conflict between employers and trade unions arising out of the strike of the Dublin tram workers, which began on 26 August.

What triggered yesterday's appalling scenes was the public appearance and subsequent arrest of the trade union leader Mr James Larkin at the Imperial Hotel on Sackville Street. As Larkin, who was acting in defiance of a proclamation prohibiting any such meeting, was being led away to the police station, there was an indiscriminate wielding of batons by the police on the crowds who gathered on Dublin's main thoroughfare. The heavy-handed police action left many injured and requiring hospitalisation.

1913

After the arrest of trade union leader Jim Larkin, the DMP mounted a series of violent baton charges against striking workers gathered on Sackville Street and elsewhere. The police used their batons freely against the protesters and many were seriously injured.

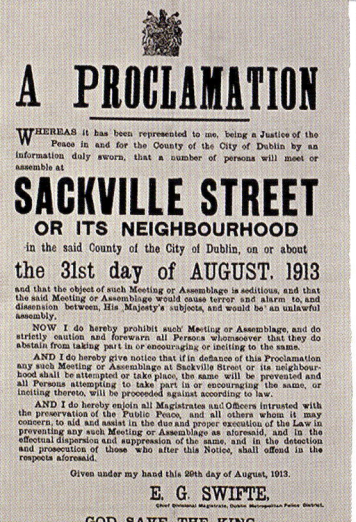

Today, in a letter published in *The Freeman's Journal*, Count Casimir Dunin Markievicz has stated that the violence perpetrated on the crowd was vicious and unwarranted. There had been, he stressed, no attempt to rescue Larkin and no breach of the peace. The excesses of the police were the equal of the events of Bloody Sunday in St Petersburg, he added. 'Scores of well-fed metropolitan policemen pursued a handful of men, women and children running for their lives before them. I saw a young man pursued by a huge policeman, knocked down by a baton stroke, and then, whilst bleeding on the ground, batoned and kicked, not only by this policeman, but by his colleagues lusting for slaughter. I saw many batoned people lying on the ground, senseless and bleeding.'

REVOLUTIONARY TIMES 1913–23

1913

8 MAY
Geraldine Manning, suffragette, is convicted of defacing a sculpture of John Redmond on display at the Royal Hibernian Academy. She is sent to prison for refusing to pay a fine. Manning targeted the sculpture because the Home Rule leader had voted in Parliament against women's suffrage.

16 MAY
An outbreak of typhus affects areas around Carraroe, Gorumna and Lettermullen. The disease has been a constant problem in south Connemara over the past two decades.

△ **4 JUN**
The Irish horse Aboyeur wins the Derby at odds of 100–1. The race is overshadowed by the suffragette **Emily Davison** stepping in front of the King's horse, Anmer, at Tattenham Corner on the Epsom course. She dies from her injuries on 8 June.

Count Markievicz described the scene as a 'complete triumph for the police' and a 'Bloody Sunday for Ireland'.

Another witness to the riot was Mr Handel Booth, the Liberal MP for Pontefract, who likewise saw little justification for the brutality of the methods deployed.

Yesterday's rioting followed similarly ugly scenes in the capital the day before. Trouble flared early on Saturday afternoon when trams were attacked in Ringsend. Motormen and conductors were jeered by strike supporters and the glass on a number of carriages was smashed. The police intervened with a series of baton charges and by making a number of arrests. At one point, a tramway official jumped onto the road, drew a revolver and threatened the crowd.

Later on Saturday, the focus of the disorder moved to the city centre.

In all, Saturday's violence resulted in 320 people being treated at Jervis Street Hospital, but the most serious casualty was a 33-year-old labourer from Spring Gardens, off the North Strand, who died on Sunday morning from injuries sustained in the riots on Saturday.

The city remains in a state of high tension and the Lord Mayor of Dublin has said that he will be seeking an immediate public inquiry into the general conduct of the police over the last two days. In the face of growing criticism, however, Mr Harrell, Assistant Commissioner of the Dublin Police, has claimed that reports of police misbehaviour have been exaggerated.

Tragedy in Dublin as Tenements Collapse
Children among the dead in Church Street disaster

Dublin, 3 September – There were horrific scenes on Dublin's Church Street last night as bodies – injured, maimed and deceased – were picked from the rubble of two collapsed tenement buildings.

The houses, numbers 66 and 67, came crashing down at 8.45 p.m, and by the early hours of the morning, following a frantic and exhaustive rescue effort, four dead bodies had been retrieved from the ruins.

Number 66 fell first, enshrouding the street in a cloud of dust and debris. Inside the house lived five families and 25 people. One of them, who had been situated at a window and became aware that something was up, raised an alarm just before the building gave way.

For many, it was too late. In the neighbouring number 67, which contained a similar number of families, residents, on hearing the roar and crash of falling masonry next door, made a dash for the street and escaped before their own their home came tumbling down after them. They all escaped.

The victims were taken to Richmond Hospital, where four were later confirmed to have died. The youngest of the deceased has been named as

1913

A photo essay of the tragedy appeared on the front page of the London based Daily Sketch *as news of the Church Street collapse reverberated throughout the United Kingdom.*

four-and-a-half-year-old Elizabeth Sammon. Her brother, Hugh (17), who was among those out of work in connection with the dispute at Jacob's, also perished, having returned to one of the houses in an attempt to save his younger sister.

In addition to the two Sammon children, Nicholas Fitzpatrick, an unmarried man, was also killed. The fourth fatality is a woman, but such was the disfigurement caused to her that so far it has been impossible to accurately identify her.

7 JUN
Customs officials in Dublin seize a large consignment of rifles at the port which were thought to have been bought by the UVF.

13 JUN
Roger Casement says, after a recent visit to the region, that the levels of poverty in Connemara are the worst in the 'civilized world'.

19 JUN
In a speech to Home Rule supporters in Glasgow, John Redmond declares that 'the cause of Home Rule is in a triumphant position. Nothing can dislodge it and the modern King Canute had better give up his attempts to order the tide not to flow.'

6 JUL ▽
Douglas Hyde reiterates his belief that the Gaelic League should build Irish culture and the language and should not be used for political purposes.

REVOLUTIONARY TIMES 1913–23 13

1913

7 JUL
The Home Rule bill passes in the House of Commons by 352 votes to 243.

12 JUL
40,000 attend a Twelfth of July celebration in Belfast and hear Edward Carson condemn Home Rule.

15 JUL
The Home Rule Bill is defeated in the House of Lords by 302 votes to 64.

△ **17 JUL**
The Irish aviator **Alexander William Hewetson** is killed when his private plane crashes on Salisbury Plain.

17 JUL
Businessman William Martin Murphy adds his weight to the campaign opposing the construction of an art gallery spanning the River Liffey to house the paintings of Sir Hugh Lane. Murphy said he did not believe anyone in Dublin supported the plan.

This death-toll may still rise, of course, as by 1 a.m. there were believed to be about 20 people still unaccounted for.

The search and rescue effort continued into the early hours of this morning. It was led by units from the Dorset Street and Tara Street fire brigades, which arrived on the scene accompanied by two ambulances. In attendance, too, were Capuchin Fathers attached to the Father Mathew Church, together with a body of about 50 Dublin Corporation employees who, armed with picks, shovels and crowbars, began the laborious work of clearing away the amassed debris.

They toiled in the most difficult and dangerous of conditions, their efforts hampered by darkness and the inadequacy of the lanterns and candles held aloft by willing helpers.

A Relief Fund has been established in the offices of *The Freeman's Journal*, to which sympathisers are being asked to contribute a shilling of their money.

Provisional Government for Ulster Formed in Belfast

Belfast, 27 September – Sir Edward Carson today conducted a review of the Belfast Divisions of the Ulster Volunteer Force at the Balmoral Showgrounds, which lie on the outskirts of Belfast. *The Belfast Telegraph* has reported that 12,000 men, drilled and efficient, took part in the event.

Perhaps the most striking aspect of the Balmoral spectacle was the unfurling of a new flag, emblazoned with a red hand and stars of each county of the new state of Ulster. Although Sir Edward Carson made no reference to the flag in his speech, it follows a decision earlier this week to establish a Provisional Government for Ulster.

That decision, taken at a meeting of unionists in the Ulster Hall in Belfast, is planned to take effect as soon as the Home Rule Bill is passed by the House of Commons.

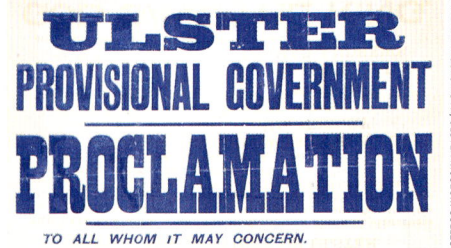

The 500 men present in the Ulster Hall passed a motion effectively giving control of such a government to the Ulster Unionist Council, led by Sir Edward Carson.

His speech opened amidst extraordinary cheering and shouting. He said that he now bore a responsibility that he felt had never fallen to any other man: 'Our duty is to guide and direct into the proper channels the methods of resisting this Home Rule Bill, if the government persist in forcing it upon us, and that is exactly what we are trying to do by setting up a Provisional Government.'

Churchill Proposes Partition of Ireland

Dundee, 9 October – Winston Churchill, the Liberal Party MP, has used his annual visit to his constituency at Dundee in Scotland to promote the idea of 'the temporary absence of the representation of Ulster' when Home Rule is introduced to Ireland next year.

Mr Churchill continued, 'Our bill is not unalterable, and the procedure of the Parliament Act renders far-reaching alterations possible.'

Noting the determined and sincere opposition of Sir Edward Carson and other unionists to Home Rule, he continued, 'It is obvious that the claim of North-East Ulster for special consideration for herself is a very different claim from the claim to bar and defer Home Rule and block the path of the whole of the rest of Ireland.'

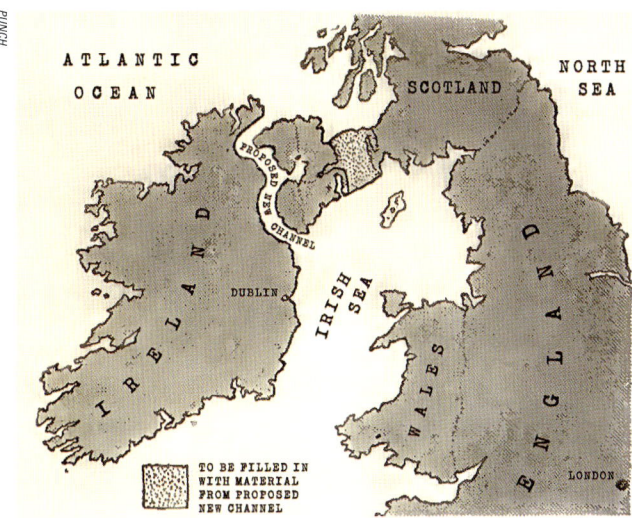

'*The problem of divided Ireland solved by a simple feat of engineering – if Scotland make no objections.*' Punch *magazine offers a tongue-in-cheek suggestion for how the border proposed by Winston Churchill might be created.*

1913

1 AUG △
Michael Moran of the Royal Dublin Golf Club retains his Irish Professional Golf Championship title, played at Portmarnock.

5 AUG
Thomas Whelan is fined one guinea by the courts for having organised a cock-fighting contest in June at Camla, Co. Monaghan, attended by 400 people.

15 AUG
Messrs Cook's Dublin manager announces that the numbers of summer tourists arriving into Ireland are some of the highest on record, with visitors from Britain and the US being especially notable.

17 AUG
Roscommon defeat Galway in the semi-final of the Connacht Senior Hurling Championship. Owing to the withdrawal of Sligo and Mayo, Roscommon claim their one and only provincial hurling title.

REVOLUTIONARY TIMES 1913–23   15

1913

21 AUG
The Dublin Committee for the Prevention of Infantile Mortality claims that the high infant death rate in Dublin is largely attributable to ignorance on the part of mothers. Every year 11,000 babies are born, of which 660 die before reaching their first birthday.

26 AUG
The Lockout begins in Dublin.

30 AUG – 1 SEP
Disturbances and riots break out in Dublin arising from the Lockout.

31 AUG
Bloody Sunday in Dublin as strikers come under attack from members of the DMP. Two are killed and hundreds injured.

2 SEP
Two tenements collapse on Church Street in Dublin, killing seven people.

3 SEP
Dublin employers led by William Martin Murphy pledge to repudiate James Larkin's ITGWU.

7 SEP
A large gathering of striking workers and their supporters in Dublin demand free speech, the right to trade union membership and an inquiry into police brutality.

'It is a claim which, if put forward in sincerity, not as a mere wrecking manoeuvre, could not be ignored or brushed aside without full consideration by any government.'

Mr Churchill's proposal was immediately rejected by Irish Parliamentary Party MPs. Speaking in London, John Dillon said, 'The whole idea of lopping off part of Ireland is unworkable, and so grotesque that I am sure the government will never dream of it.'

Archbishop Attacks 'export of Irish children'

23 October – The Archbishop of Dublin, Dr William Walsh, has launched a bitter attack on the proposed scheme to have the children of workers affected by the Lockout moved to England where they will be cared for by English families.

Archbishop Walsh set out his 'consternation' at the idea and, speaking directly to the mothers of the children, said, 'I can only put it to them that they can be no longer held worthy of the name of Catholic mothers if they so far forget their duty as to send away their little children to be cared for in a strange land, without security of any kind that those to whom the poor children are to be handed over are Catholics, or indeed are persons of any faith at all.'

The danger to the relocated children's spiritual well-being as depicted in an Irish Independent *cartoon wasn't the only concern of Dr Walsh. He also feared that youngsters who experienced a higher standard of living wouldn't want to return to the slums.*

Acting on the Archbishop's instructions, Dublin priests intercepted the first group of children who were due to be brought to England. There were remarkable scenes as some 50 children were being prepared for the journey by rail and ship to England. The children had been brought by Ms Dora Montefiore, the suffragist and socialist, to Tara Street Baths to be washed before the journey.

Led by Fr Landers and Fr McNevin, a crowd of 200 people gathered at the baths to protest. Addressing the crowd, Fr Landers said that if people in England genuinely wished to help, they should send over money so the children could stay with their parents.

In light of the protests, about 35 children returned to their homes with family or friends.

Strikers Urged to Join New Citizen Army

Strikers 'take a leaf from Carson's book'

Dublin, 19 November – A new body – the Irish Citizen Army – has been founded in Dublin.

The new army is recruiting from the ranks of the strikers engaged in the current Lockout in the city.

At a public meeting outside Liberty Hall in Beresford Place in Dublin, James Connolly noted that Orangemen have already ordered a supply of

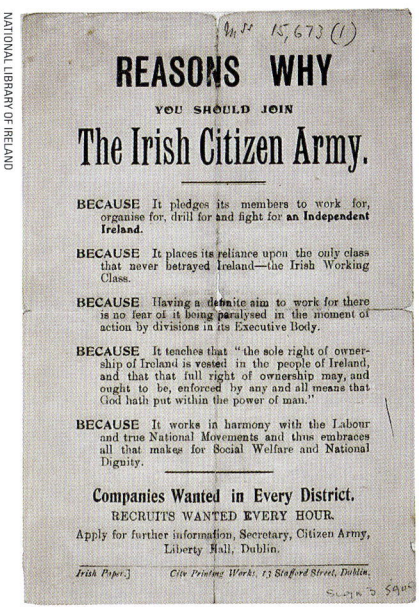

A pamphlet urging striking workers to join the Irish Citizen Army co-founded by union leader James Connolly.

1913

8 SEP
A poem about the events in Dublin by W.B. Yeats is published, titled 'September 1913'.

17 SEP
In Newry, Sir Edward Carson announces that an Ulster Provisional Government will be formed should Home Rule be implemented.

24 SEP
The UUC approves Carson's plan and designates that its standing committee will be the 'central authority' for the Provisional Government, which will be headed by Carson.

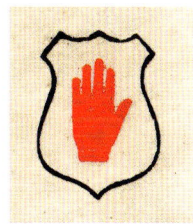

27 SEP △
12,000 members of the UVF parade at the Royal Ulster Agricultural Society showgrounds in Belfast in opposition to Home Rule.

27 SEP
The *Hare*, a ship chartered by British trade unionists to bring food to striking workers in Dublin, docks on the Liffey.

1913

4 OCT
The Central Council of the Gaelic Athletic Association (GAA) agrees to purchase a stadium at Jones' Road in Dublin from Frank Dineen for £3,500; they will later rename the stadium Croke Park.

5 OCT
Canon Patrick Sheehan, a founder of the anti-Redmondite All-for-Ireland League in 1910 and a prolific author, dies.

6 OCT
An official report states that workers who are locked out of work should not have to pledge not to join the ITGWU before they are re-employed.

△ **7 OCT**
George Russell (Æ) publishes an open letter 'To the masters of Dublin' in *The Irish Times* in response to the Dublin Lockout.

16 OCT
A major parade in Dublin in support of striking workers and the ITGWU is held.

19 OCT
The writer Emily Lawless dies in London.

rifles: 'We have not done so yet ... but we want our men to be trained and drilled, so that when it comes to a pinch they will be able to handle a rifle.'

Supporting the formation of the Irish Citizen Army, Connolly said, 'We mean to have a regular establishment for majors, captains, sergeants and corporals, for we mean to defend our rights as citizens, and any man who means in the future to become a member of the Transport Union must be prepared to enrol himself in our citizen army.' He continued, 'Stand up and throw the upper classes off your back, and by stopping the wheels of industry you will make these people recognise the great power that you possess. Our rebellion is against the employing classes, so that we shall have our rights, and to that end we mean to fight until victory crowns our flag.'

Connolly concluded by saying that Captain Jack White would lead the army and train the men who enlisted. He also said that they had offers from other officers to help do the same.

White, originally from Co. Antrim, is a former officer in the British Army who fought in the Boer War. He has recently been involved in support of the Home Rule cause and spoke beside Sir Roger Casement at the pro-Home Rule meeting organised at Ballymoney.

White is reported to have suggested the idea of a citizen army and to have spoken of the benefits of drilling workers, particularly in light of the way they have been attacked by police.

Drilling for the Citizen Army is to take place at Croydon Park in Clontarf

Irish Volunteers Founded in Dublin

Dublin, 25 November – An Irish Volunteers army was founded at a meeting in Dublin today. Up to 7,000 people attended the meeting at the Rotunda Rink, with the crowds overflowing into the Rotunda Gardens.

In a manifesto, the new 'Irish Volunteers' set out their object as 'to secure and maintain the rights and liberties common to all the people of Ireland'. They swore to drill and to build a disciplined army, but to use it only for defensive and protective purposes, and not to seek to dominate.

The meeting was presided over by Eoin MacNeill, a professor at UCD and a leading member of the Gaelic League. Prof. MacNeill opened the meeting by saying that action and not words was the point of their presence: 'The whole country has long been thinking, long deliberating, on the right course of action to be taken, and is there any Irishman worthy of the name that has not come to the conclusion that the action we are now proposing was the right action to take?'

Prof. MacNeill continued, 'To win and to preserve our just rights, our

1913

Óglaig na hÉireann
Irish Volunteers.

A PUBLIC MEETING
For the formation of **IRISH VOLUNTEERS**
and the enrolment of men,
WILL BE HELD IN THE
LARGE CONCERT HALL,
ROTUNDA,
ON
TUESDAY, NOV. 25
At 8 p.m.
EOIN MacNEILL, B.A., will preside
All able-bodied Irishmen will be
eligible for enrolment.

GOD SAVE IRELAND.

CURTIS, PRINTER, 12 TEMPLE LANE, DUBLIN.

The attendance at the meeting to form the Irish Volunteers, chaired by Prof. Eoin MacNeill, was drawn from every section of Irish nationalism including members of the Gaelic League, the Ancient Order of Hibernians and Sinn Féin.

rights as Irishmen, our rights as an Irish nation, three things above all are required: courage and vigilance and discipline.'

Last night's meeting came against the backdrop of further suggestions in England that some compromise could be worked out that would exclude Ulster from the remit of the Home Rule parliament promised for Dublin. This proposition has been rejected out of hand by nationalists.

In recent weeks groups of men had begun to form themselves into Volunteer groups in Dublin and in Athlone, while Prof. MacNeill had published an article entitled 'The North Began', which laid the basis for last night's meeting.

Amongst the other speakers at the meeting was the school headmaster, Patrick Pearse, who declared that the Irish Volunteers did not spring from any differences of opinion between Irish people; rather it had its roots, he insisted, in something that all Irishmen shared: the love of Ireland.

21 OCT
In a letter to *The Freeman's Journal*, Archbishop William Walsh of Dublin denounces a plan to evacuate the children of striking Dublin workers to Britain.

24 OCT
A meeting of Protestants hostile to Ulster unionist resistance to Home Rule takes place in Ballymoney, County Antrim.

27 OCT
Imprisonment of Labour leader James Larkin for use of seditious language.

1 NOV
Eoin MacNeill's article 'The North Began' is published in the Gaelic League's paper *An Claidheamh Soluis and* advocates for the formation of a nationalist equivalent to the UVF.

1 NOV
Trade unionist James Byrne, who had been arrested for his role in the ongoing Lockout crisis, dies in prison after a hunger strike.

3 NOV
Kilkenny defeat Tipperary at Croke Park to win the All-Ireland Senior Hurling Championship.

1913

10 NOV
The Dublin Volunteer Corps enrols 2,000 men and promises to preserve the civil and religious liberties of Protestants who live outside Ulster in the event of Home Rule being enacted.

19 NOV
The Irish Citizen Army (ICA) is established at the Antient Concert Rooms, Dublin.

25 NOV
The Irish Volunteers launch at the Rotunda Rink, Dublin.

28 NOV
At a unionist meeting at Dublin's Theatre Royal, Andrew Bonar Law declares that if Home Rule is introduced, Ulster will resist and that such resistance would have the support of his Conservative Party.

28 NOV
Suffrage campaigner Hanna Sheehy Skeffington is imprisoned after she is found guilty of striking a policeman while protesting against the presence of Bonar Law in Dublin.

4 DEC
The importation of military weapons into Ireland is prohibited by Royal Proclamation.

Ban Imposed on Arms Imports to Ireland

MacNeill declares the right of every nationalist 'to bear arms'

6 December – A Royal Proclamation was last night published in *The London Gazette* prohibiting, under the provisions of the Customs Consolidation Act, 1876, the importation of arms and ammunition into Ireland.

This significant new development comes less than a fortnight since the formation of the nationalist Irish Volunteers and following months of mass demonstrations by the unionist Ulster Volunteer Force.

There have been contrasting reactions to the prohibition across the country. For the most part, the Ulster unionists seem unfazed. Along with signalling an acceptance on the government's part that their willingness to take up arms in opposition to Home Rule was no mere bluff, there is also a sense that the ban comes too late to thwart their ability to mount an effective resistance. There is an apparent belief within unionism not only that they are already sufficiently well-armed, but that the prohibition will prove impractical to implement. For even when the free importation of arms of recent months is ended, secret gunrunning is likely to take its place.

The reaction of the men behind the newly established Irish Volunteer movement has been far less relaxed. For them, the measure is at once repressive and objectionable. Interviewed by the *Irish Independent*, Professor Eoin MacNeill, a member of the new body's Provisional Committee, described the proclamation as 'a very strange' and 'very curious one at this time'.

Prof. MacNeill defended the right of Irishmen of all political views to bear arms, adding that no grouping in Ireland had called for a law of this kind to be introduced. 'We take it for granted that the application of a special law of this kind to Ireland has the opposition of Nationalist opinion now as in all former times. Irish Nationalists cannot change their tune in order to allow an English Government to deal with the Orangemen, and we have quite sufficient confidence in our fellow countrymen to bear arms at any time … We are against the suggested proclamation regarding bearing arms for Ulster. We say that every Irishman has the right to bear arms.'

MacNeill's views were echoed by Mr Laurence J. Kettle, a fellow member of the Provisional Committee of the Irish Volunteers, who claimed that the movement had already enrolled 5,000 members.

Prof. Eoin MacNeill.

Ireland Celebrates Christmas after Busy Business Period

26 December – Ireland celebrated Christmas Day yesterday with religious ceremonies throughout the country. In the capital, the Pro-Cathedral was the setting for a solemn High Mass at both 6 o'clock and 12 o'clock, the latter presided over by Dr Walsh, the Archbishop of Dublin, and attended by the Lord Mayor and members of the Corporation.

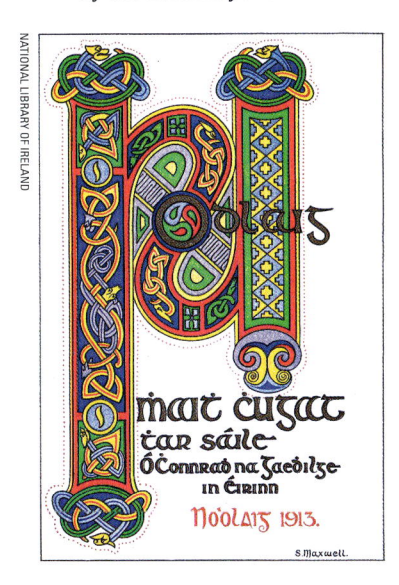

Across the city, devotions began with the celebration of Holy Communion from 8 a.m. in St Patrick's Cathedral, the service commencing with the entrance of a choir singing 'O Come all ye faithful'. The sermon was preached by the Dean of St Patrick's, who remarked on how the 'principle of the Christian divine life was radically different from that of the world's view of greatness'.

Meanwhile, in hospitals across the city, special efforts were made to brighten the lot of those unfortunate enough to be away from family and home for the festive period. Balancing the working demands of the hospital with the Christmas spirit was no easy task in Jervis Street, where the accident department was busy throughout the day. However, many of those presenting did so with trivial injuries, quite a number of which resulted from burns sustained in the course of cooking the Christmas dinner.

Conradh na Gaeilge Christmas card.

For many businesses and those who staff them, the Christmas festivities bring to an end a period of intensive activity. For those working in the postal service, in particular, the countdown to this Christmas brought unprecedented pressures.

If the shops of the city have been humming with activity, it is nothing to what has been going on in the postal depots. The sheer volume of postal traffic is underlined by the numbers involved. On one single day, 20 December, the RMS *Olympic* brought 212,000 letters and newspackets, with 1,949 registered letters. In addition, 290,000 letters, 9,000 newspackets and 3,245 registered letters were brought by the *New York* passenger liner, while the *Empress of Ireland* also offloaded 130,000 letters and 4,000 newspackets.

This year's foreign mail has been the heaviest in history.

1913

8 DEC
Speaking in Preston, James Larkin, who was released from jail in November, denounces the role he believes British trade unionists played in breaking the Dublin strikes.

14 DEC
Kerry defeat Wexford to win the All-Ireland Senior Football Championship in front of 17,000 spectators.

14 DEC
A meeting is held in Cork to organise a city corps for the new Volunteer movement. The meeting is presided over by J.J. Walsh and addressed by Eoin MacNeill.

22 DEC
The North of Ireland Football Club (an Ulster rugby club) announces that it is abandoning its games to allow its players to practice military drill more frequently with the UVF.

30 DEC △
Irish-born polar explorer **Ernest Shackleton** announces he will begin an expedition in October 1914 to become the first person to cross the Antarctic.

Remembering 1913
a hundred years on

Over 20,000 people gather on O'Connell Street to watch a re-enactment of the events of Bloody Sunday 1913. The event was organised by the Irish Congress of Trade Unions. The role of union leader Jim Larkin was played by the actor Ger O'Leary, and he proclaimed, in the role of Larkin, that 'the bosses of Dublin are using starvation as their weapon, but they will fail as all tyranny will fail'. The performance ended with a recreation of the violent police baton charge against the protesters.

31 August 2013

REVOLUTIONARY TIMES 1913–23

'Why can't you get us votes for women …?'
– Suffrage and Irish Politics

'HOW DARE YOU come to Kingstown when women are being tortured in prison and subjected to injustices!' These words were shouted by Hanna Sheehy Skeffington in the direction of the Earl of Aberdeen, the Lord Lieutenant of Ireland, in July 1913. Aberdeen was addressing the opening of a fete staged to raise money for a new working men's club in the People's Park in Kingstown when Sheehy Skeffington interjected. She was quickly seized by a detective and removed from the park.

Sheehy Skeffington was a leading voice in the Irish suffrage movement and had been a founder member of the Irish Women's Franchise League (IWFL) in 1908. Demands for women's suffrage did not begin with the founding of the IWFL, as the North of Ireland Society for Women's Suffrage had been formed in 1872, and the Dublin Suffrage Association was established in 1876. However, the IWFL was different in that it was a far more radical movement and echoed the militancy of the Women's Social and Political Union (WSPU), which had been established by Emmeline Pankhurst and her daughters in Britain in 1903. The IWFL also differed from its predecessors in the fact that many of those involved in the movement believed that the advancement of suffrage was tied to the cause of Irish nationalism.

The complexity for the IWFL, in terms of advancing its argument for suffrage, was that the leadership of the IPP, in particular John Redmond and John Dillon, was firmly opposed to votes for women. It was not simply a question of tactics – they believed that Home Rule was the primary objective for Ireland following the 1910 general election – but that they were opposed to women's suffrage as a matter of principle. Dillon famously stated in 1912 that 'women's suffrage will,

'… women's suffrage will, I believe, be the ruin of western civilization'.

I believe, be the ruin of western civilization'. Herbert Asquith, the prime minister after the 1910 election, also opposed women's suffrage on principle.

Faced with the opposition of the government, which effectively blocked any advancement of the suffrage cause within Parliament, the campaign for women's votes became ever more radical. In Ireland the target of such radicalism was not only the government, in the form of Asquith's Liberal Party, but also, and more directly, the IPP and its leadership. On 13 June 1912, eight women, including Sheehy Skeffington, were arrested after they smashed windows in Dublin Castle as a way of highlighting the suffrage cause. The judiciary throughout this period were particularly harsh on suffragettes who appeared before them, and these women, for an act of petty vandalism, were sentenced to imprisonment terms of between one and six months, to be served in Mountjoy Prison.

In July 1912 Asquith travelled to Dublin to address a Home Rule meeting alongside John Redmond at the Theatre Royal. Francis Sheehy Skeffington, Hanna's husband, attended the meeting and demanded votes for women before being ejected. At the close of the meeting Asquith and Redmond left in a carriage but were attacked by two British suffragists, Mary Leigh and Gladys Evans. The two women were sentenced to five years' hard labour in Mountjoy for throwing an axe at Asquith. Once in prison, they went on hunger strike and were joined by the women of the IWFL, who were serving their sentences after their attack on the windows of Dublin Castle. Both Leigh and Evans were force-fed while in prison, during August and September 1912. Force-feeding of suffragettes was unusual in the Irish context, and the treatment of Leigh and Evans, both their harsh sentences and the enforced feeding, was seen as a message from the authorities to Irish suffragettes not to escalate their own campaign.

THE MAJESTY OF THE LAW.
Punch *magazine, March 1913.*

Despite this, by 1913 the Irish women's campaign had intensified. In March a bust of John Redmond that was on display at the Royal Hibernian Academy was vandalised with paint by Geraldine Manning. Manning refused to pay her fine when she appeared in court and was sent to prison. In November Hanna Sheehy Skeffington was again arrested after trying to present suffrage pamphlets to Conservative Party leader Andrew Bonar Law and unionist leader Edward Carson when they were in Dublin. She was sent to Mountjoy and immediately went on hunger strike for five days, at which time she was released under the terms of the Prisoners (Temporary Discharge for Ill Health) Act, 1913. This Act was used frequently in Ireland as the Lord Lieutenant had made it clear that there should be no force-feeding of Irish women in Irish prisons. As a result of her arrest, Sheehy Skeffington was sacked from her teaching job.

The position of the IWFL, indeed of the whole suffrage movement in Ireland, was highly complex. While their cause – the right to vote – was clear-cut, the competing political claims on the island around the national issue caused problems. Many women stood behind their respective national positions, arguing for the primacy of either Home Rule or the continuation of the Union, and they believed that, in the context of a rapidly overheating political crisis, the issue of suffrage could wait. Relationships with Pankhurst's WSPU were strained over this issue, as the British organisation's view was that suffrage must come first, before any other issue. Christabel Pankhurst made her feelings clear by stating: 'No votes for women, no Home Rule.' In 1913 and early 1914 the WPSU, believing that the Home Rule leadership could not be moved on the suffrage issue, targeted unionist politicians in their campaigning. In the spring of 1914 a militant campaign led to arson attacks on unionist-owned buildings in Belfast that resulted in the arrest of two WSPU activists, Dorothy Evans and Midge Muir. They appeared in court and, charged with possession of explosives, Evans made clear the contradictions in contemporary Irish politics in the way women were treated. Quite reasonably, she asked why James Craig was not also appearing in court charged with arming the UVF? The two women were convicted of possessing arms. Evans was sent to Tullamore jail, where she went on hunger strike, and was released in late July.

In late summer 1914 the First World War began. The IWFL opposed the war but, in the context of war-time mobilisation, ceased its radical activities in the name of suffrage. With women across Ireland already split on the issue of whether the suffrage issue or the national question should come first, the formation of Cumann mBan in April 1914 added a further radical voice to the mix. The women of Cumann mBan would play a critical role in the Rising of

> **Many women stood behind their respective national positions, arguing for the primacy of either Home Rule or the continuation of the Union.**

1916 and were outspokenly militant and republican in thought and action. In response to this organisation's emergence, the suffragette newspaper, *The Irish Citizen*, dismissed its members as 'slave women' who were subservient to the republican ideology of the Volunteers. However, after her husband, Francis, was executed by an errant British officer during the Rising, Hanna Sheehy Skeffington threw her weight behind the republican party, Sinn Féin, and by 1917 was a member of its executive.

At the end of the war the political landscape in Ireland had shifted completely. Home Rule was dead and the radical republican vision of Sinn Féin was in the ascendant. The 1918 general election was fought by a newly enlarged electorate under the terms of the Representation of the People Act. Under this Act, the electorate in Ireland had increased from 697,337 in 1911 to 1,936,673, and this growth included all women over the age of thirty who met a property qualification. While this was far from the votes for all women for which suffragettes had campaigned, the national context had also been transformed. The 1918 election was the last fought with Ireland as a whole remaining part of the Westminster system. So, while women in Ireland over thirty and with the requisite property did vote, they, like most of the nationalist population, switched their votes to Sinn Féin.

When Dáil Éireann was formed in January 1919 around the Sinn Féin MPs who refused to take their seats in Westminster, only one woman, the imprisoned Countess Markievicz, had been elected (only two women had stood for election in Ireland). After the subsequent War of Independence had ended, and twenty-six counties of Ireland achieved a substantial measure of control over their own affairs, the Dáil drew up the Constitution of the Irish Free State in 1922, which would allow all citizens over the age of twenty-one to vote in future elections 'without distinction of sex' (a step not taken by the British until 1928).

The campaign that had raised awareness of the suffrage question had been fought in the face of many objections, much harassment, and under a legal system that convicted Irish women for militancy in their cause while turning a blind eye to the militancy of Irish nationalist and unionist politics of the time. And despite winning the vote, the conservative and Catholic guiding principles that came to guide Ireland from the mid-1920s meant that women's rights were still restricted. In August 1921 Countess Markievicz had become only the second woman in the world to become a government minister. After the split over the issue of the Anglo-Irish Treaty, Markievicz left the government. It would not be until 1979 that another woman would sit in an Irish government Cabinet.

People, Poverty and Politics

John Cooke was not a professional photographer. He didn't belong to any of the big commercial operators who spanned what was said to constitute a 'photographic mile' on both sides of Dublin's River Liffey, stretching from Grafton Street on the southside to Sackville Street on the north. Cooke nevertheless took his camera to parts of the city where commercial photographers, with businesses built on the sale of portraiture and postcards with scenic views, seldom strayed. In the autumn of 1913 Cooke, as Honorary Treasurer of the National Society for the Prevention of Cruelty to Children (NSPCC), visited some of Europe's worst slums alongside fellow NSPCC officials, and found everywhere 'something to condemn'. The photographs he took – of decaying tenements, of squalid living conditions and ill-clad children – were submitted in evidence to a Dublin housing inquiry, which had been established in the aftermath of the collapse of tenement buildings in Church Street in September 1913 in which seven people were killed. Among the dead were three young children and an adult woman whose body was discovered in a distressing state beneath a mountain of fallen masonry by a member of Dublin Fire Brigade. 'She was crushed into a pulp,' the fireman recalled. 'The head and face was flattened out and the body was bruised, squashed, and mixed up with the bricks and mortar and broken splinters.'

When the housing inquiry undertaken by the Local Government Board published its report the following February, Cooke's tenement images were presented as an appendix, picture proof of a grim reality where 87,305 people lived in just 5,322 houses, many of them deemed 'unfit for human habitation'.

… a grim reality where 87,305 people lived in just 5,322 houses, many of them deemed 'unfit for human habitation'.

PEOPLE, POVERTY AND POLITICS

The grim reality of living conditions in Dublin's overcrowded and poverty-stricken tenements were captured in the photographs taken by John Cooke in the autumn of 1913.

Included in these numbers were over 20,000 families who lived in just a single room. How might such conditions be improved? The report urged, amongst other measures, the construction of new houses on 'virgin soil' on the outskirts of the city, maintaining that it was only by dealing adequately with the housing crisis that the heavy death rate among Dublin's working classes – higher than any of the other major population centres in the then UK - could be seriously reduced. Improvements were therefore urgently required, but the intervention of the First World War and the subsequent separatist struggle and Civil War, meant that little progress was immediately made. So meagre, indeed, were the advances that, just over a decade later, another report would decry Dublin's housing situation as nothing less than a 'tragedy'.

The tension building between employers led by William Martin Murphy and union organised workers is illustrated in this 1912 Ernest Kavanagh cartoon.

The dismal dwellings of Ireland's urban poor evoked widespread sympathy, but when it came to their working life and struggles for better pay and conditions, a broad base of support was less easy to discern. On the contrary, the rise of labour activism after the emergence of the ITGWU in December 1908 attracted downright hostility from some, not least from a group of Dublin employers led by William Martin Murphy, whose many business interests included ownership of the *Irish Independent* and chairmanship of the Dublin United

Tramways Company. It was Murphy's decision to sack tram-workers suspected of membership of the James Larkin-led ITGWU that precipitated strike action by tram drivers and conductors in August 1913, events spiralling into a general 'lockout' by hundreds of employers of up to 25,000 laid-off workers, the latter drawing support from, amongst others, British trade unionists.

While the lockout ended in defeat for workers in early 1914, the employers' victory was a pyrrhic one. Over the decade that followed, trade unionism would only strengthen, helped in part by UK legislation intended to prevent industrial disputes during the First World War by compelling employers to enter arbitration with trade unions. Soaring Irish trade union membership – the ITGWU ballooned from 5,000 to 120,000 members between 1916 and 1920 – was also partly a measure of the increased bargaining power of workers during the war and their constant struggles to keep pace with rapidly rising living costs. Food prices, for example, were estimated to be 189% higher in February 1917 than they had been in September 1914. The impact was such as to cause campaigner and historian Mary Hayden to complain that the weekly wages paid to some working women in Dublin did not even provide enough to 'buy them proper food, if they required no clothes and slept in the streets'. Startling as it was, this was not an unreasonable assertion. Remarking on the wage demands that drove labour unrest across society in March 1917, even the Inspector General of Police felt obliged to concede that it was 'obvious in that in existing circumstances the old rates are totally inadequate'.

> … the weekly wages paid to some working women in Dublin did not even provide enough to 'buy them proper food, if they required no clothes and slept in the streets'.

The efforts of the trade union movement were successful to an extent. Labour historian Niamh Puirséil has observed that almost 'every section of the workforce secured wage increases' during the war years, even if they continued to trail the rate of inflation. Organised labour also flexed its muscle in the wider political sphere, most emphatically when, in the form of a general strike, it weighed into the campaign of passive resistance that, in the spring and early summer of 1918, defeated British government plans to introduce conscription to Ireland. Later, during the Irish War of Independence, a similarly motivated general strike was called in support of hunger-striking republican prisoners in Mountjoy Prison, while railway workers pursued a more long-running action – lasting from May to December 1920 – by refusing to operate trains carrying British military and munitions of war, a defiance that seriously undermined the British effort to stifle the Irish insurgency. The rise of trade unionism, especially in the years from 1918 to 1921, was notable for its geographical spread, with, notably, the proliferation of ITGWU branches across all parts of the country excluding Ulster.

Of course, Ireland was still a predominantly agricultural society, but the Irish countryside had undergone something of a social revolution in the previous two decades. Emigration, sustained since the famine of the mid-nineteenth century, continued to drain the land of people, but the lot of the Irish rural dweller had improved in some significant respects. Housing for tens of thousands of agricultural workers had been greatly improved as a consequence of the 1906 Labourers Act, while a series of land reforms that started in the late nineteenth century, designed to mollify a nascent Irish nationalism, had allowed for eleven million acres to be transferred from landlord to tenant ownership by 1914. However, while the beneficiaries were many, a significant cohort remained locked out of land ownership, and when the First World War simultaneously halted land purchase and closed off the option of emigration, rural Ireland became, in the words of historian Terence Dooley, 'a prison of the malcontented'. While farmers fared well from high wartime prices for cattle and produce, the lust for land persisted among those still without. Occasionally, and particularly in counties like Clare and Galway, the resultant frustrations found expression in agrarian agitation: the non-payment of rent, cattle drives and the intimidation of landowners to force sales.

> ... a 'large number of terrified landowners came beseeching the Dáil Government for protection'.

Such rural tensions did not abate with the end of the First World War. Agrarian agitation would flare-up spectacularly in 1920 – again mostly in the western counties of Connacht – at a time when the Royal Irish Constabulary (RIC) was in effective retreat from rural barracks as a new, local war intensified. More agrarian outrages were recorded in 1920 than for any year since 1882, and in the absence of local policing, a 'large number of terrified landowners', Kevin O'Shiel later recalled, 'came beseeching the Dáil Government for protection'.

Dáil Éireann was the parliament established by the Sinn Féin movement that had displaced the IPP in the political affections of Irish nationalist voters in the 1918 general election. The newly elected republicans had pledged to deny the right of the British government to legislate for Ireland and did this by establishing a rival assembly and underground administration. However, when the Dáil voted to ratify the Anglo-Irish Treaty of December 1921 and the republican movement split, the fall-out required the new Provisional

Government to embark on an already onerous project of state building in tandem with an economically destructive civil war. Before it did, this Provisional Government found the means to donate £1,000 to Saor an Leanbh, an Irish arm of Save the Children, to support famine relief in Russia. In doing so, Arthur Griffith, President of the Dáil, referenced Ireland's own experience of famine and its need to 'recognise that the claims of suffering humanity do not stop short at national frontiers'. This was not meant to deflect from the serious need that existed within Ireland itself, and Saor an Leanbh was also fundraising to relieve distress in Connemara, where inspectors dispatched by the new government had found families on the verge of starvation.

Want was not confined to the west, however: poverty was widespread and it drove a surge in demand for charitable services. Early in 1922, for instance, St Vincent de Paul reported that the problem of homelessness was such that admissions to its night shelter had climbed to a record high of 30,361 the previous year, more than double its yearly average and fuelled by high unemployment. The number of free meals the Catholic charity provided similarly spiked, up from 26,801 in 1920 to 47,607 in 1921. The role that Church charities and religious bodies would occupy in the newly independent, twenty-six county state would only increase as, to quote historian Lindsey Earner-Byrne, 'limited welfare provision was pruned and depleted to survive the economic reality of political independence'.

It was true that the Civil War added considerably to the financial burden of the nascent Irish Free State and constrained any room for budgetary manoeuvre, but ideology too played its part in compounding the problems of poverty and driving dependence on Church charities. Nowhere was this more obvious than in the decision in 1924 to cut by a shilling a week the old age pension, a truly transformative piece of British social legislation from 1908 that had been enthusiastically embraced in Ireland. The Free State Minister for Finance, Ernest Blythe, defended the pension cut on the basis of fiscal prudence – the books needed balancing and the pension was by far the largest welfare expense of the state – but there was no denying how deeply unpopular a measure it was or that it had a disproportionately damaging impact upon the poor. The government could, and did, counter that there were no good choices available to them. 'There are certain limited funds at our disposal,' Blythe's ministerial colleague, Patrick McGilligan, informed the Dáil during a debate on unemployment some months later. 'People may have to die in this country and may have to die through starvation.'

WELL MET!

GREAT BRITAIN JOINS HER ALLIES IN THE FIELD.

1914

'... his Majesty's Government declared to the German Government that a state of war exists between Great Britain and Germany as from 11 p.m. on August 4, 1914.'

Official statement from the British Foreign Office
4 AUGUST

1914

▽ **7 JAN**
Patrick Pearse addresses the first meeting of the Irish Volunteer branch of Gorey, Wexford, and tells the audience that nationalists should arm themselves to counter the unionist threat.

12 JAN
For Ireland's Sake, a new film produced by the Kalem Film Company of New York, is released in the United States.

17 JAN
Edward Carson inspects a parade of the East Belfast Regiment of the UVF.

17 JAN
Thomas Harten, a free labourer working for a coal merchant in the city, is beaten to death on Eden Quay in Dublin. It is believed he was attacked because he was working in defiance of the ongoing labour strike in the city.

Open Warfare in Dublin City

12 January – 'It was open war and as dangerous as a battlefield,' Inspector Campbell of the Dublin Metropolitan Police explained, as the Commission of Inquiry into the conduct of the police at the strike disturbances in August and September opened in the Four Courts in Dublin.

The principal incidents that led to the establishment of the commission took place on the last weekend of August 1913, when rioting took place across Dublin.

Further testimony from the police described scenes all across the city, from Ringsend to Marlborough Street and far beyond, as 'fierce and appalling'. It was claimed that police were met with a fusillade of bricks, jam-pots, pokers, sewer pipes, bottles and frying pans from the balconies of houses.

A succession of police witnesses told the tribunal that they had been attacked repeatedly by strikers and their supporters, and had had no option but to defend themselves.

Labour leaders in Dublin have boycotted the inquiry and yesterday staged a series of street meetings in opposition to its proceedings.

Newspaper sketches of some of the main protagonists who featured in the inquiry.

REVOLUTIONARY TIMES 1913–23

1914

Inspectors Purcell and Freeman (left to right) were among the police witnesses to testify before the Dublin riots inquiry along with Superintendent Quinn who was in charge of the infamous baton charge.

18 JAN
Dublin transport workers return to work after the lockout and labour dispute that had begun in 1913.

24 JAN
John Redmond tells a meeting in his home constituency of Waterford that talk of an impending civil war in Ireland is ridiculous.

Drogheda is the Driest Place in Ireland

13 January – The lowest rainfall in Ireland in the past year was recorded at Drogheda, Co. Louth, where total rainfall for 1913 reached just under 28 inches. By contrast, the highest rainfall recorded in Ireland was at Caragh Lake in Co. Kerry, where it exceeded 87 inches in the course of the year.

The wide disparity of rainfall illustrates once again the great difference in precipitation between the southwest of Ireland and the east coast. All of the lowest recordings of rainfall were at locations along the east coast, while all of the highest were in the south and west of the country.

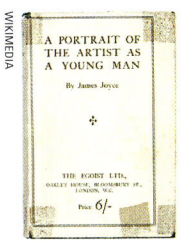

FEB ▷
James Joyce's ***A Portrait of the Artist as a Young Man*** begins serialisation in *The Egoist*.

A view of Drogheda port in the early 1900s. The town recorded the lowest rainfall in Ireland in 1913. The monthly meteorological report showed that rain fell on just thirteen days in July that year.

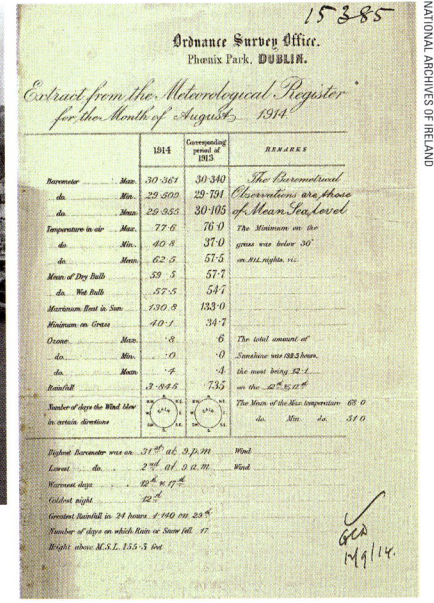

REVOLUTIONARY TIMES 1913–23

1914

4 FEB
A staging of **George A. Birmingham**'s comedy *General John Regan* at Westport town hall is interrupted when the crowd storms the stage in protest at the 'stage Irishness' of the play. A riot ensues and 20 men are arrested.

14 FEB
Ireland lose the first international rugby match of the season to England at Twickenham. The game was attended by King George V and British Prime Minister H.H. Asquith.

20 FEB
A Fethard-on-Sea lifeboat capsizes in service, after being struck by a wave in rough seas off the Co. Wexford coast. Nine crew lose their lives.

21 FEB
Lady Gregory outlines the objectives of the Abbey Theatre's new School of Acting in an interview with *The Freeman's Journal*.

Dublin is a Gigantic Factory for Making Criminals

26 January – The slums of Dublin 'may be regarded as a gigantic factory for the production of criminals to fill the jails, of paupers to be supported at the expense of the public rates, and of sick patients to be nursed and medically treated in the numerous hospitals, for the support of which constant appeals are being made,' said the lawyer S. Shannon Millin at a meeting of the Statistical Society in Dublin last night.

Mr Millin endorsed the words of the late Recorder of Dublin, who had previously stated, 'The current history of Dublin is a tale of two cities, a city of splendour and a city of squalor.'

Aware of the dangers posed to young boys living in tenements, Fr Benvenutus of St Mary of the Angels, Church Street, established the Catholic Boys' Brigade. It aimed to 'suppress vice and evil habits of every kind amongst them, especially evil speaking, evil conduct, the use of tobacco to a certain age & c.'

Redmond: Talk of Civil War Is Absurd

26 January – 'You are on the eve of a great change in the public life of Ireland,' John Redmond MP has told a huge nationalist rally in his home constituency of Waterford.

Mr Redmond said that twice already the Home Rule Bill has passed through the House of Commons in London by majorities of more than 100 votes: 'All the powers of wealth, privilege and bigotry beat against the Bill in vain. Every appeal to prejudice, to ignorance, to party passion, to race hatred, and to religious bigotry has been made, and has failed.'

He continued, 'Never in the history of these countries has any great reform encountered such powerful and vindictive opposition, and emerged with less damage from the ordeal.'

Despite this opposition, Mr Redmond expressed his absolute confidence in the delivery of Home Rule legislation this year. Failure to do so would be to restore the House of Lords veto, restore Tory rule, and it would, Mr Redmond insisted, condemn the Liberal Party to utter impotence, dishonour and extinction.

Mr Redmond also dismissed as 'absurd' all talk of civil war, and he downplayed the threats of the Bill's Ulster unionist opponents.

More than 25,000 people crowded into the city to hear Mr Redmond speak, with observers comparing it to the great Parnell rally at the same site in 1881.

A sample spread from the Local Housing Board of Ireland's report into the miserable conditions of Dublin's slums. The stark photographs included in the 53-page publication were taken by John Cooke and W.J. Joyce.

Fourteen Dublin Corporation Members Own Tenement Houses

18 February – The report of the Dublin Housing Inquiry has revealed that 14 sitting members of Dublin Corporation own tenement houses in the city. Several members of the Corporation own more than a dozen houses each, while ten own up to three houses each.

One member, Alderman Corrigan, owns 19 tenement houses and a further 13 smaller houses across the city. Several of these houses – all of which are rented out – are classed as being unfit for human habitation and incapable of being rendered fit for such habitation.

1914

25 FEB
Sir Hugh Lane defeats Walter Strickland in an election of governors and guardians to become the new director of the National Gallery of Ireland.

26 FEB
HMHS *Britannic*, designed as the third and largest Olympic-class ocean liner, is launched at the Harland & Wolff shipyard in Belfast. Its construction had been delayed due to modifications made following the sinking of *Titanic*.

1 MAR
The Department of Agriculture confirms three outbreaks of foot-and-mouth disease in Co. Cork. Movement of animals in or out of the impacted areas is prohibited.

9 MAR
Prime Minister Asquith proposes to allow the Ulster counties to hold a vote on whether or not to join a Home Rule Parliament in Dublin. Nationalists reject the idea.

1914

△ **14 MAR**
Ireland draws 1–1 with Scotland in their final Home International soccer fixture in Belfast. Prior defeats of Wales and England leave Ireland as table-toppers, the first time they win outright the British Home Championship tournament.

17 MAR
To mark St Patrick's Day, John Redmond sends a gift of a pot of shamrock to the White House. President Woodrow Wilson spends the day with a sprig of the shamrock in the buttonhole of his jacket.

20 MAR
The Curragh incident or mutiny. British Army officers at the Curragh Camp resign their commissions rather than face being ordered to take action against Ulster unionists resisting if the Home Rule Bill is passed into law. The government backs down and all the officers are reinstated.

Alderman Corrigan, as well as other members of the Corporation, also received a rebate of taxes despite the fact that the houses do not meet basic living standards. In one of the houses, the drains are not properly trapped or ventilated, and the house is filthy; in another, there are no toilet facilities in the house or in the backyard, and tenants are forced to go to their neighbours' houses to use the toilet.

The report, completed by a departmental committee appointed by the Local Government Board of Ireland, was initiated following the collapse of two tenement buildings on Church Street on 2 September 1913. Seven people, including three children, died in the incident.

Throughout, the report is clear in its opinion that until the housing problem is dealt with there will be no adequate reduction in Dublin's 'heavy' death rate.

Fresh Foot-and-mouth Outbreaks in Cork

2 March – The Department of Agriculture has confirmed three outbreaks of foot-and-mouth disease in Co. Cork.

The outbreaks have occurred at Ballynacourty, near Kinsale, at Ballinacrusha near Queenstown, and at Douglas. The department has now prohibited the movement of all animals out of – and within – the scheduled radius of 15 miles from the infected farms.

Strident disinfection measures were introduced to try to halt the spread of the disease beyond the affected areas. The infected animals were slaughtered on site and their carcasses carefully prepared before being disposed of in large pits.

The movement of all farm animals in and around Cork city has also been prohibited as it is understood that it was from that city that the infected animals recently came. All animals suspected of infection have been destroyed.

A statement released by the Department of Agriculture asserts that the source of infection is most likely to be drovers and dealers who have recently been in Birkenhead Port in the north of England, where several cases of foot-and-mouth disease have been detected.

The export trade of cattle between Ireland and Britain has now ceased and there are also restrictions on the movement of animals in the counties of Dublin, Kildare and Wicklow.

Asquith Proposes the Temporary Partition of Ireland

Carson Rejects Proposed Compromise

10 March – The Prime Minister, Herbert Asquith, has announced his revised plans for the introduction of Home Rule for Ireland.

Such was the interest in the debate in the House of Commons that the attempts of MPs and observers to secure a place in the chamber or in the galleries were said to resemble the crush outside the gates of a football ground before an important match.

Mr Asquith told parliament that he did not expect his proposals to be received with enthusiasm, but he asked that they be given deliberate and dispassionate consideration. He said that if the Home Rule Bill were introduced unchanged there would be violence and civil strife in Ulster, while if it were not introduced at all, there would equally be disastrous consequences in the rest of Ireland.

It was these hazards, he said, that had led him to a compromise: between the dates of the passage of the Home Rule Bill and the actual establishment of a Home Rule Parliament in Dublin, each of the counties of Ulster may vote upon the question of exclusion for a period of six years.

After six years, any counties that had voted to opt out would only be forced to come into the administration of the parliament in Dublin with the consent of the majority of the electors of the United Kingdom.

The Conservative leader, Andrew Bonar Law, immediately rejected the proposals, saying that they had caused in him a feeling of grave disappointment.

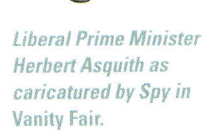

Liberal Prime Minister Herbert Asquith as caricatured by Spy in Vanity Fair.

1914

2 APR
Cumann na mBan is formed as an auxiliary of the Irish Volunteers at a meeting in Wynne's Hotel, Dublin. Agnes O'Farrelly chairs the meeting.

6 APR
The second reading of the Home Rule Bill passes at Westminster.

7 APR
Police in Connemara seize stills and an estimated 100 gallons of poitín on Gorumna Island.

10 APR
Newspapers note that Good Friday 1914 marks the 900th anniversary of the Battle of Clontarf. There are no public events.

11 APR △
Mrs Pat Campbell stars in the leading role as George Bernard Shaw's *Pygmalion* is performed for the first time in London.

1914

15 APR
The 47th annual meeting of the Irish National Teachers' Organisation (INTO) opens in St Columb's Hall, Derry.

24–25 APR
In a major act of gunrunning, 25,000 rifles and over 3 million rounds of ammunition from Germany land at Larne, Bangor and Donaghadee for use by the UVF in its fight against Home Rule.

6 MAY
The House of Lords rejects, by a 44-vote margin, a Women's Enfranchisement Bill to afford women the right to vote in parliamentary elections.

12 MAY
Revolver shots are fired from the crowd at a junior soccer match in Belfast involving Linfield and Springfield Amateurs.

△ **19 MAY**
Frederick James Walker, a motorcycle racer from Kingstown, is killed at the Isle of Man TT races when his bike collides with a wooden barrier.

Sir Edward Carson also rejected the scheme as unacceptable. He said that the men of Ulster would never agree to sacrifice their friends in the south and west. The leader of Ulster unionism nevertheless welcomed acceptance of the principle of Ulster exclusion but insisted that what Ulster did not want was a sentence of death with a stay of execution.

Cumann na mBan founded in Dublin

2 April – A new organisation of Irish women has been founded today at Wynn's Hotel in Dublin.

Cumann na mBan is dedicated to advancing the cause of Irish liberty by organising Irish women to that purpose. It is also dedicated to assisting the arming and equipping of a body of Irishmen for the defence of Ireland.

The meeting was chaired by Agnes O'Farrelly, who asked whether the women of Ireland should stand idly by while the most sacred things in life were at stake.

Cumann na mBan flyers listed weapons training along with first aid skills as part of its core activities.

Miss O'Farrelly, a lecturer in Irish at UCD, said that they had come to the meeting to declare for the integrity of the nation and for the inalienable right to self-government. They did not want a divided Ireland, she said, and neither did she want some temporary settlement that would lead to years of uncertainty.

She continued by saying that the first duty of the women present was to give their allegiance and support to the men who were fighting for the cause of Ireland, whether in the British House of Commons or at home in Ireland organising the Volunteers.

Miss O'Farrelly was criticised by another speaker, Mary Kettle (wife of Professor Tom Kettle, the former MP), for referring to the Irish Parliamentary Party 'in a sneering manner'.

Other women who spoke at the meeting were Countess Markievicz, Mrs Dudley Edwards, Mrs Wyse Power and Miss Gavan Duffy.

Low Pay of Irish Schoolteachers Condemned

16 April – Irish national schoolteachers are poorly paid in comparison to their counterparts in other countries, the annual congress of the Irish National Teachers' Organisation was told today in the Guildhall in Derry.

Salaries in Scotland are much in advance of those in Ireland and the same is true for England. The congress also heard that the Education Board in Ireland was entirely out of touch with national sentiment and that it was in no way representative of Irish public interests.

Schoolchildren with their teachers in the west of Ireland.

1914

28 MAY ▽
Erskine Childers and **Darrell Figgis** travel to Hamburg to negotiate the purchase of arms for the Irish Volunteers.

31 MAY
Reports suggest that as many as 130,000 men have joined the Irish Volunteers in the seven months since the organisation was established.

9 JUN
Nine students from Trinity College Dublin appear in court and are fined following their arrest for an attack on a cab driver, as well as an attack on the offices of the IWFL. The two incidents occurred on the occasion of the annual 'Trinity Day' festivities.

11 JUN
It is reported that four people were killed when a fire engulfed an undertaker's on Lower Gerald Griffin Street in Limerick city.

1914

12 JUN
At the sports day at St Enda's School, President of the Gaelic League Douglas Hyde praises the school's principal, Patrick Pearse. He states that men like Pearse 'are bringing back the consciousness of belonging to a nation'.

15 JUN
James Joyce's *Dubliners*, a collection of 15 short stories depicting life in Dublin during the early 20th century, is published in London.

23 JUN
A Government of Ireland Amending Bill is introduced to the House of Lords to allow the counties of Ulster to vote on whether they wish to join a Home Rule Ireland. The Lords passes the Bill on 14 July.

25 JUN
Addressing the National Catholic Total Abstinence Congress, Father J.A. Cullen, SJ, urges the future Home Rule Parliament to reject the evil of drink.

28 JUN
Archduke Franz Ferdinand, heir to Austro-Hungarian throne, and his wife, the Duchess of Hohenberg, are assassinated in Sarajevo.

4 JUL
A Cavan man is fined 20 shillings, *The Anglo-Celt* reports, for cruelty to a cat. The animal was found tethered in a field so it would act as a scarecrow.

Ulster Unionists Import Guns at Larne

25 April – Ulster unionists have landed a huge consignment of arms and ammunition at the ports of Larne, Donaghadee and Bangor. More than 25,000 rifles and up to 3 million rounds of ammunition are said to have been brought in by shipments that arrived under the cover of darkness.

The cover for the gunrunning was a meticulous and elaborate scheme that involved the mobilisation of Ulster Volunteers all across the province, ostensibly for test purposes. While police were busy monitoring the mobilisation, the arms were brought ashore.

The town of Larne saw intensive activity from 9 p.m. last night as all approaches were patrolled by Ulster Volunteers. When the shipment was landed, up to 600 cars and lorries, escorted by members of the Ulster Despatch Riders' Corps, began the work of distributing the rifles and ammunition across Ulster.

The SS Fanny *returned to Germany after leaving a cargo of rifles in Ulster.*

The Illustrated London News' *extensive coverage of the arms landing included dramatic illustrations of how the 25,000 rifles and 3 million rounds of ammunition were unloaded and transported from Larne to safehouses under the cover of darkness.*

It was almost dawn before the entire shipment had been landed and distributed. A coastguard is reported to have suffered a heart attack during the operation.

The response of the government has been to send General Sir Nevil Macready to take military charge of the Belfast district. Prime Minister Asquith has said that the government will take, without delay, appropriate steps to vindicate the authority of the law and protect officers and servants of the King, as well as His Majesty's subjects.

The response of Irish nationalists to the gunrunning is awaited with interest. However, in the *Irish Worker* newspaper, Jim Larkin has compared the manner in which Ulster unionists are being treated with that of the previous treatment of Irish nationalists: 'Why were the men of '67 proscribed, sentenced to long and torture-filled years of penal servitude – banished forever from their native land for actions identical with the actions of Carson, Craig, and the Ulster lieutenants?'

Redmond Proclaims the Death of the Act of Union

26 May – John Redmond has declared that the Act of Union between Great Britain and Ireland is now dead.

The leader of the Irish Parliamentary Party said that the assembling of an Irish Parliament, under the provisions of the Home Rule Bill, was now as certain as the rising of tomorrow's sun. Mr Redmond was speaking yesterday after the third reading of the Home Rule Bill in the House of Commons had ended with a majority of 77 votes in favour of the government.

Mr Redmond said, 'Today's division marks the death, after an inglorious history of 114 years, of the Union of Pitt and Castlereagh. That Union, the cause of Ireland's poverty, misery, depopulation and demoralisation – the cause of famine, insurrection and bloodshed, and of the disloyalty of the Irish people

THE FIGHT FOR THE BANNER.

While Redmond and Carson play tug of war for control, John Bull stands in the background and remarks, 'This tires me. Why can't you carry it between you? Neither of you can carry it alone.'

1914

10 JUL
The unionist Provisional Government of Ulster, chaired by Edward Carson, holds a special meeting at the Ulster Hall, Belfast. The meeting resolves to complete 'our arrangements to resist by every means in our power every attempt to impose the authority of any Home Rule Parliament on Ulster'.

21 JUL △
The Buckingham Palace conference, called in an attempt to end the nationalist and unionist dispute over **Home Rule**, is opened by the King.

23 JUL
A coroner's court in London hears of the death of 33-year-old Dr Patrick Henry Black at the Windsor Hotel. Although a teetotaller, Black, who had previously practised at Dalkey in Dublin and at the Rotunda and St Vincent's Hospitals, was a known user of cocaine and it is ruled he had taken an overdose.

REVOLUTIONARY TIMES 1913–23

1914

24 JUL
The Buckingham Palace conference ends in failure as neither nationalists nor unionists see a way to break the impasse.

26 JUL
The yacht *Asgard* is sailed into Howth by Erskine and Molly Childers. They land 900 rifles and 26,000 rounds of ammunition for use by the Irish Volunteers. British troops are moved into Dublin city centre in an attempt to stop the Volunteers from moving the weapons into the city. As crowds gather at Bachelors Walk, the soldiers open fire, killing three. A fourth man dies later from bayonet wounds.

28 JUL
The First World War begins when Austria-Hungary declares war on Serbia.

throughout the world – is dead and its place is to be taken by a new union, founded on mutual respect and goodwill between the two islands. And to be followed, I firmly believe, by the history of peace, prosperity and goodwill between the two islands.'

Mr Redmond has promised co-operation and friendship with the opponents of Home Rule, but prospects for conciliation appear as remote as ever.

The leader of the Conservative Party, Andrew Bonar Law, described the proceedings in the House of Commons as 'a contemptible farce'. He said they always knew that the government had the power to push through their bill, but in doing so they have deprived themselves of all moral authority.

Mr Bonar Law concluded, 'The final act in this drama will be played, not in the House of Commons, but in the country – and there, Sir, it will not be a farce. It is to the people that we appeal.'

Redmond Moves to Take Control of the Irish Volunteers

10 June – John Redmond has moved to take control of the Irish Volunteers.

In a letter published in the press today, Mr Redmond says that it is vital that the Volunteers – whose membership has now reached 140,000 since its foundation in November 1913 and is estimated to be growing at more than 5,000 per week – fall into step with the Irish Parliamentary Party.

He writes: 'Any attempts to create discord between the Volunteer Movement and the Irish Party are calculated, in my opinion, to ruin the Volunteer Movement, which, if properly directed, may be of incalculable service to the national cause.'

Advertisements such this one for Fallon's outfitters were in response to the growing demand for military uniforms and equipment as the Volunteer movement caught the imagination of young Irish men. An indication of the growing militarisation of the country is this list of individuals authorised by the King to conduct drilling in Ireland.

Mr Redmond acknowledges that he was initially hostile to the establishment of the Volunteers, noting that up to two months ago he felt that its establishment was 'premature'.

This was no longer the case: 'The effect of Sir Edward Carson's threats upon public opinion in England, the House of Commons and the government; the occurrence at the Curragh Camp; and the successful gun-running in Ulster vitally altered the position.'

Mr Redmond said that at that point the Irish Party took steps to inform its supporters to join the Volunteers and the result was that the movement had spread 'like a prairie fire' and would soon include all the nationalists of Ireland.

The result of this, he continued, was that the leadership of the organisation now needed to be reconstituted. He noted that the present leadership committee was 'Provisional', with all of its 25 members residing in Dublin.

Patrick Pearse is Reviving the Nation

12 June – 'For want of proper education, people in this country had forgotten that they had a country – but men like Patrick Pearse and schools like St Enda's are bringing back again the consciousness of belonging to a nation,' said Douglas Hyde, the President of the Gaelic League, during a speech at a sports day held today at St Enda's School in Dublin.

Mr Hyde said that Irish people would not accept England, and yet they had seen in Ireland for many years only an imitation of England.

He said that Mr Pearse was trying to change that through his school: 'His philosophy is the philosophy of all who are concerned with the creation of what might be called an Irish Ireland, as distinct from an imitation English Ireland.'

Hyde was presenting prizes at the sports day in Rathfarnham. The event was attended by past and present pupils and their families.

Pearse wanted St Enda's to have an 'Irish standpoint and atmosphere', based on inspirational teaching and freedom for the individual student.

1914

△ **1 AUG**
Ernest Shackleton departs London on board the *Endurance* at the start of his attempt to cross the Antarctic. Accompanying Kildare-born Shackleton are Kerryman Tom Crean and Cork-born Tim McCarthy.

1 AUG
Days after the Howth gun-running, a smaller shipment of arms and ammunition bound for the Irish Volunteers is landed at Kilcoole, Co. Wicklow.

3 AUG
Germany declares war on France as its troops hurry through Belgium on the way to Paris.

3 AUG
John Redmond tells the House of Commons: 'The government may withdraw every one of their troops from Ireland. I say that the coast of Ireland will be defended from foreign invasion by her armed sons.'

REVOLUTIONARY TIMES 1913–23

1914

4 AUG
Great Britain declares war on the German Empire and its allies.

4 AUG
With war erupting in Europe, President Woodrow Wilson proclaims American neutrality – the US must, he says, be 'impartial in thought as well as in action'.

△ **5 AUG**
Co. Kerry-born **Horatio Herbert Kitchener** – Lord Kitchener – is appointed British Secretary of State for War. He immediately initiates a massive recruitment drive through the raising of a series of volunteer 'new armies'.

6 AUG
HMS *Amphion* is sunk by a minefield off the Hook of Holland. 150 men are killed including 20 Irish. They are the first Irish casualties of the First World War.

Franz Ferdinand Assassinated in Sarajevo

28 June – Archduke Franz Ferdinand, heir-presumptive to the crowns of Austria-Hungary, and his wife, the Duchess of Hohenberg, have been shot dead in the city of Sarajevo in Bosnia today.

Passing through the streets in a motorcade, the Archduke was shot when the car in which he was travelling slowed at one point.

An assassin forced his way through the crowd and fired two shots into the car. One of the rounds struck the Archduke in the throat, severing a large artery. The second entered the Duchess's side. Both died within minutes of being wounded.

A Serbian, Gavrilo Princip, was immediately arrested at the scene and is said to have confessed.

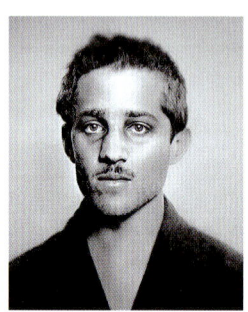

The shooting of Archduke Franz Ferdinand (top) and his wife by Gavrilo Princip (bottom) sent shockwaves throughout Europe and further afield. Princip's act was illustrated in La Domenica del Corriere, *an Italian weekly newspaper.*

48 REVOLUTIONARY TIMES 1913–23

1914

Gunrunning at Howth!
Irish Volunteers land hundreds of guns and ammunition

26 July – There were sensational scenes in the seaside village of Howth, Co. Dublin today when the Irish Volunteers successfully landed hundreds of guns and a considerable amount of ammunition.

Shortly after midday an ordinary yacht, the *Asgard*, sailed into the harbour at Howth and soon afterwards about 1,000 members of the Irish Volunteers appeared on the pier. Half of the Volunteers formed a cordon to prevent access to the pier, while the remainder began to pass rifles and boxes from the yacht.

Some of the arms were distributed to Volunteers, while the remainder were placed in motor cars and driven away.

The Howth gunrunning had clear precedent in the successful gunrunning undertaken by the Ulster Volunteers at Larne last April, when more than 25,000 rifles were landed and dispersed across Ulster.

A woman who was on holidays at Howth has given a graphic description of the event: 'I was on the head of the East Pier about noon when I noticed a white-painted yawl of at least 50 tons, smartly kept, and steered by a lady.

'Turning around I saw at least a couple of hundred men running for all they were worth towards the pier from the direction of the railway station. While they were running up the pier the hatches of the yawl were opened. Some of the men from the pier jumped down and handed up to their comrades Lee-Enfield rifles.'

Mary Spring Rice and Molly Childers on board the Asgard during the gunrunning voyage.

Three People Shot Dead by British Soldiers on Bachelors Walk

27 July – Three Dubliners were shot dead yesterday by British soldiers at Bachelors Walk in Dublin.

Mary Duffy (50), Patrick Quinn (46) and James Brennan (18) were killed when soldiers fired on a crowd who were throwing stones and abusing the King's Own Scottish Borderers as they returned to barracks. More than 30 other people are in hospital, some with serious injuries, including men who were bayoneted by the soldiers.

The incident at Bachelors Walk came in the wake of the successful gunrunning which took place at Howth by the Irish Volunteers earlier in the day.

8 AUG
The Defence of the Realm Act (DORA) is introduced, giving the government sweeping powers in Britain and Ireland including censorship of the press and the suppression of activities deemed to threaten or interfere with the defence of the nation.

10 AUG
Representatives of Irish rugby clubs meet at Lansdowne Road for the purpose of 'forming a Rugby Football Volunteer Corps'.

15 AUG
Wartime censorship of the press, under the terms of the DORA, begins.

1914

An artist's interpretation of the chaotic scenes at Bachelors Walk when three civilians were killed by troops using live fire and bayonets against a jeering crowd. A fourth victim died some weeks later. Dubliners' revulsion at the slaughter was reflected in the massive crowds that thronged the city's streets for the subsequent funerals.

21 AUG ▽
The 10th (Irish) Division of the British Army is established, consisting of battalions from across Ireland. It is the first of three new army divisions raised from Ireland during the war and is led by Galway-born **Lt Gen. Bryan Mahon**.

As hundreds of Volunteers were coming back into the city along the Howth Road, they found their way blocked by two cordons of police and by soldiers from the King's Own Scottish Borderers.

William Harrell, the Assistant Commissioner of the Dublin Metropolitan Police, ordered his men to attempt to disarm the Volunteers. In the ensuing scuffle shots were fired, while the police used batons and soldiers used their bayonets. Less than 20 guns were captured, with the remainder being spirited away by the Volunteers.

Later, as the soldiers marched back into Dublin City, they were pursued by a hostile crowd, who hurled abuse and, occasionally, missiles. At Bachelors Walk, the soldiers charged at the crowd with bayonets and a series of volleys was fired, resulting in death and injury.

The House of Commons has since been told that Sir John Ross, the Chief Commissioner of the Dublin Metropolitan Police, has resigned, and that Assistant Commissioner Harrell has been suspended pending an inquiry.

Europe at War!

11 August – The major powers in Europe are now at war, with reports of heavy fighting on several fronts.

Battles between French and German troops around Altkirch have resulted in up to 100 French troops being killed or wounded, with more casualties on the German side.

From Belgium come reports of intense battles all along a line stretching from Liège to Tongres. And in Bosnia a major battle between Austrian and Serbian troops is hourly expected, while fighting between both armies has continued in Serbia for more than ten days now.

German troops are also massing close to the Dutch border, with the neutrality of Holland now in question.

In Britain, Prime Minister Herbert Asquith has announced that a new army of 100,000 men is to be formed under Lord Kitchener. All reservists have now been called up and recruitment to fight in Europe has now reached at least 3,000 men each day across Britain.

The events of the past ten days have transformed life in Europe, with a series of war declarations and invasions bringing one country after the next into the war.

The tensions that flared spectacularly after the assassination of Archduke Franz Ferdinand on 28 June, leading Austria-Hungary to declare war on Serbia at the end of July, have proven impossible to contain.

The alliances between various powers – rooted in a complex mesh of power, trade, geography and ethnicity – have demolished all optimism that diplomacy could resolve the dispute.

The rapidity of events has taken most observers by surprise, but what is now clear is that the war is now between all of the major powers in Europe, with the exception of Italy, which has declared itself neutral.

Members of Belgium's Garde Civique (civil guards) in their distinctive leather top hats forming a defensive line on a road outside Liège.

1914

22 AUG ▽
The first UK engagement in the European war is made by the **4th Royal Irish Dragoon Guards**. They encounter several German cavalrymen on patrol near Mons and Irish-born Corporal Edward Thomas has the distinction of firing the British Army's first shot in the war.

22 AUG
The *Anglo-Celt* reports that a special court in Enniskillen has charged George Acheson with wounding another man by stabbing him with a pitchfork. The court hears that the Acheson 'had taken a lot of drink' when attending a funeral on the day of incident.

23 AUG
Heavy fighting at the Battle of Mons involves the Royal Irish Regiment. In the first day of fighting, 21 of the regiment's officers and men are killed – the first Irishmen of the war to die in the land conflict.

1914

▽ **23 AUG**
Lt Maurice Dease, an Irishman serving with the British Expeditionary Force at Mons, dies while using a machine gun to pin down advancing German forces. For his bravery he is awarded the first Victoria Cross of the war.

3 SEP
Edward Carson urges members of the UVF to enlist and 'go and help to save your country and to save your Empire'.

6–12 SEP
The First Battle of the Marne sees British and French forces counter-attack along a 300km front to bring a halt to the German offensive in France.

10 SEP
The first German military prisoners of war to be interned in Ireland arrive for detention at Richmond Barracks, Templemore.

On the one side are Germany and Austria-Hungary, and on the other are Russia, Serbia, Britain and France. Other smaller countries are allied to these powers and the scale of the conflict is such that all countries will most likely be drawn into battle.

Irish Soldiers Involved in Fighting at Mons

25 August – The first battle between the German and British armies has ended with the British inflicting heavy casualties on the Germans before being forced to retreat.

Amongst the Irish soldiers fighting at Mons were members of the 4th Royal Irish Dragoon Guards, some of whom may be amongst the casualties.

The battle at Mons is part of a series of battles taking place along a long frontier where Allied troops are seeking to resist the advance of the German Army.

Despite the retreat, the British Army claims success in preventing the French Army from being outflanked. This was achieved, even though it was heavily outnumbered. The Secretary of State for War, Lord Kitchener, sent a message of support to the soldiers engaged at Mons: 'Congratulate troops on their splendid work. We are all proud of them.'

The British Expeditionary Force arrived in France on 14 August and reached Mons on 22 August.

A painting by war artist William Barnes Wollen (1857–1936) titled 'Our "Little Contemptibles"', shows the British Expeditionary Force in one of the early engagements around Mons.

An armed UVF guard at a training camp. Carson calls on such men to join the war effort: 'England's difficulty is not Ulster's opportunity. England's difficulty is our difficulty.'

Ulster Volunteer Force to Form Separate Division in the British Army

September – The Ulster Volunteer Force is to be given its own division within the British Army.

A meeting of the Ulster Unionist Council was told yesterday by Sir Edward Carson that negotiations with the War Office had produced a scheme that he could recommend for acceptance.

'If we get enough men from the Ulster Volunteer Force, they will go under the War Office as a division of their own – and if we get enough, they can go as two or more divisions.'

Carson urged all Ulster Volunteers to enlist now in the British Army: 'Go and help save your country! Go and help to save your Empire! Go and win honour for Ulster and for Ireland.'

The meeting also saw a pledge from Sir Edward that Ulster unionists were fully committed to fighting for the Empire, but that they would be determined to reassert their opposition to Home Rule once victory was assured.

Redmond Urges Irish Volunteers to Join the British Army

21 September – John Redmond, the leader of the Irish Parliamentary Party, has called on members of the Irish Volunteers to join the British Army.

He said, 'Go on drilling and make yourself efficient for the work, and then account for yourselves as men, not only in Ireland itself, but wherever the firing line extends in defence of right, of freedom and religion in this war.'

1914

11 SEP ▽
Lord Kitchener authorises the formation of a second Irish New Army – the **16th Division**. Lt General Sir Lawrence Parsons will later be appointed to take command.

"EVERYWHERE AND ALWAYS FAITHFUL"
16th (Irish) Division.

14 SEP
Owing to the war, and with the exception of those involving schoolboys, the Irish Rugby Football Union (IRFU) decides on the cancellation of all matches for the rest of the year.

18 SEP
The Government of Ireland Act receives Royal Assent, but is suspended for the duration of the war.

20 SEP
In a speech at Woodenbridge, Co. Wicklow, John Redmond calls on members of the Irish Volunteers to go 'wherever the firing line extends'.

24 SEP
The Irish Volunteers split between those who follow Redmond's call to fight in the war, and a more radical faction, led by Eoin MacNeill, who dismiss the conflict as an imperial dispute and stay at home to defend Ireland.

1914

25 SEP
At a meeting at the Mansion House to encourage men to join the war effort, addresses are made to the audience by Redmond as well as Prime Minister Asquith.

28 SEP
The Irish Neutrality League is formed with James Connolly as president.

▽ **2 OCT**
German spy **Carl Hans Lody**, who had been operating in Britain since the start of the war, is arrested at the Great Southern Hotel, Killarney. He is returned to London, found guilty of espionage, and executed on 6 November.

'Presenting the Colours'. John Redmond and the Maryboro Volunteers in Woodenbridge, Co. Wicklow.

Mr Redmond made the comments yesterday in the village of Woodenbridge, where he was attending a parade of the East Wicklow Volunteers, having travelled overnight from London.

He told the Volunteers, 'Remember this country is in a state of war, and your duty is two-fold. Your duty is, at all costs, to defend the shores of Ireland from foreign invasion. It is a duty more than that of taking care that Irish valour proves itself on the field of war, as it has always proved itself in the past.'

Mr Redmond was clear that the duties of the Volunteers extended far beyond Irish shores: 'It would be a disgrace forever to our country, and a denial of the lessons of her history, if young Irishmen confined their efforts to remaining at home to defend the shores of Ireland from an unlikely invasion and shrinking from the duty of proving upon the field of battle that gallantry and courage which have distinguished your race all through its history.'

He set out the reasons for war: 'The interests of Ireland as a whole are at stake in this war. This war is undertaken in defence of the highest principles of religion, morality and right.'

Mr Redmond has also urged the establishment of an 'Irish Brigade' within the British Army – one that would be officered by Irishmen – but there has not yet been a positive response from the British government.

Irish Volunteers Split Over Redmond's Recruitment Plea

Founders of the movement call for the establishment of a 'National Government' in Dublin

25 September – Tensions within the Irish Volunteers have flared into open view with the announcement that all John Redmond's nominees

A poster outlining Redmond's position.

have been removed from the ruling committee.

The announcement came in a statement from 20 members of the governing committee that is highly critical of Mr Redmond. Issued by the founder of the Irish Volunteers, Prof. Eoin MacNeill, the statement condemns Mr Redmond for his call on Irish Volunteers to join the British Army.

'He has declared it to be the duty of the Irish Volunteers to take foreign service under a government which is not Irish,' the statement reads. 'He has made this announcement without consulting the Provisional Committee, the Volunteers themselves, or the people of Ireland, to whose service alone they are devoted.'

The statement was laced with bitterness at the manner in which Mr Redmond had assumed control over the Volunteers three months ago when it was a proven success, having initially opposed its establishment and operations.

Ultimately, the immediate establishment of a national government was demanded by Prof. MacNeill and his fellow signatories, amongst whom were P.H. Pearse, Bulmer Hobson, Éamonn Ceannt, Thomas MacDonagh, Seán Mac Diarmada and Liam Mellows.

A split in the Volunteers now appears inevitable and a battle for control of the nationwide organisation is already underway.

Gaelic League Promises to Abstain from Politics

12 October – The Gaelic League will rigorously abstain from all connection with politics and from all discussions of politics, except inasmuch as they relate directly to the Irish language.

This commitment came in a motion passed at a meeting of the Gaelic League in Dublin on Saturday night. It was proposed by Douglas Hyde, who said that such a commitment was important now more than ever.

The meeting of the Coiste Gnótha of the Gaelic League had earlier heard a plea from J.J. O'Kelly that the members of the League should 'remain at home and do their part for their native country'.

1914

5 OCT
The *Irish Independent* publishes a letter by Sir Roger Casement protesting against Irish involvement in the war.

12 OCT
The Irish Neutrality League holds its first public meeting, in Dublin.

18 OCT
The Royal Navy's Grand Fleet takes shelter in Lough Swilly, while Scapa Flow is secured against submarine attack.

18 OCT
Clare easily overcome Laois, 5–1 to 1–0, in the All-Ireland Hurling Championship final at Croke Park. It is Clare's first ever All-Ireland title.

A poster promoting a language collection for the Gaelic League in 1913. The organisation was keen to reaffirm its commitment to be a non-political entity.

1914

19 OCT
The start of the First Battle of Ypres as French, Belgian and British forces clash with the German Army. Neither side achieve a significant breakthrough and they settle into the trench warfare that characterised the remainder of the war on the Western Front.

25 OCT
The first convention of the 'original section of the Irish Volunteers' is held at the Abbey Theatre, Dublin. Held in private, and with Eoin MacNeill presiding, 170 delegates attend.

◁ **28 OCT**
Authorisation for the formation of the 36th (Ulster) Division is given. The division comprises large elements of the pre-war UVF and follows extensive unionist lobbying and recruitment.

31 OCT
Roger Casement arrives in Germany.

1 NOV
Refereed by Harry Boland, the All-Ireland football final between Kerry and Wexford ends in a draw. Twenty-six special trains are laid on for a fixture that draws 15,000 spectators to Croke Park.

This motion was objected to by a Waterford delegate who said that the Gaelic League should avoid taking sides in political issues.

It was then that Douglas Hyde put his counter-motion, which was accepted by the meeting.

Police Seek Early Closing Time for Dublin Pubs

3 November – Police in Dublin today made an application to the courts to have the closing time of Dublin's pubs, clubs and hotels set at 8 p.m. every evening.

The application was made before the Recorder of Dublin at the City Sessions in Green Street Court by the Chief Commissioner of Police William Davies.

In moving the application, the Solicitor General of Ireland, James O'Connor, said that it was one to which the War Office and the Executive Government in Ireland attached great importance.

Mr O'Connor informed the court, 'The order was essential for the preservation of the efficiency of the troops, who are about to be engaged in a life-and-death struggle with the enemy.'

Tim Healy KC, representing the Licensed Grocers' and Vintners' Association, noted that officers in barracks were free to drink away after

A military procession makes its way down Parkgate Street in Dublin past a public house. The police move to have Dublin's pubs close at 8 p.m. every evening was supported by James O'Connor, the Solicitor General, who stated that the earlier closing time was 'essential for the preservation of the efficiency of the troops'.

8 p.m. and that the officers' mess closed only when the officers decided to go to bed: 'Inside the barracks it is recreation, and outside it is drunkenness.'

The court heard also that the average number of soldiers drunk on any given day on Dublin's streets was between 300 and 500.

'Santa Claus' ship docks in Dublin

24 December – Sixty-three enormous cases of Christmas presents from the children of the United States to the Irish children of soldiers and sailors serving in the British forces were today distributed from the Mansion House in Dublin.

Some 2,500 parcels were handed out to children and their families, despite fears that the adverse weather would prevent the toys, clothes and food being given out.

The presents were brought to Dublin by an American steamship, the *Jason*, which has been dubbed the 'Santa Claus ship' in some Irish newspapers. The ship had earlier docked at various European ports leaving her cargo of gifts for families of the combatants of the belligerent nations. That the project was strictly neutral is apparent from the fact that German children also received gifts donated in America.

The Irish share of the consignment was handled by officials of the Local Government Board based at the Mansion House in Dublin.

Volunteers packing presents into crates for their voyage across the Atlantic in the USS Jason, *a navy supply ship.*

1914

29 NOV
In the All-Ireland football final replay, in front of 20,000 spectators, Kerry defeat Wexford by three points.

1 DEC △
Willie Redmond, brother of IPP leader John Redmond, declares his intention to join the war effort.

18 DEC
After three months' training in Aldershot, England, the 16th (Irish) Division arrives in France.

27 DEC
Sir Roger Casement agrees to assist the establishment of an 'Irish Brigade' to be recruited from Irish prisoners of war held in German custody.

Remembering 1914
a hundred years on

President Michael D. Higgins attends Glasnevin Cemetery to lead a ceremony to dedicate the Cross of Sacrifice, which remembers those who fought and died during the First World War. The Cross of Sacrifice was a joint initiative by the Glasnevin Trust and the Commonwealth War Graves Commission, the latter represented on the day by Britain's Prince Edward, the Duke of Kent. The unveiling of the Cross of Sacrifice was marked by the attendance of colour parties from the Defence Forces and the British Army.

31 July 2014

REVOLUTIONARY TIMES 1913–23

'... the headlong avalanche of death and victory'
Ireland and the First World War

IN HIS POSTHUMOUSLY published *The Ways of War* (1917), Thomas Kettle wrote about serving as a soldier in the First World War. He recounted the view, at night-time, from the trenches: 'Over there in front across No Man's Land there are shell-holes and unburied men. Strange things happen there. Patrols and counter-patrols come and go. There are two sinister fences of barbed wire, on the barbs of which blood-stained strips of uniform and fragments more sinister have been known to hang uncollected for a long time.' Kettle's writing captured the ways that the war was fought, and how men endured the long periods where nothing happened, long hours in flooded, rat-infested trenches before 'the brief ecstasy of assault, the flash of bayonets, the headlong avalanche of death and victory'.

Kettle, an academic, writer and barrister by profession, who had served as the IPP's MP for Tyrone East between 1906 and 1910, had volunteered for military service after the outbreak of the war, serving as a junior officer with the Royal Dublin Fusiliers alongside men whose spirit and courageous deeds he made sure to record. In a last letter to his brother on the eve of his own death, Kettle wrote, 'I have never seen anything in my life so beautiful as the clean and so to say radiant valour of my Dublin Fusiliers. There is something divine in men like that.' Killed near Ginchy, France, on 9 September 1916, Kettle's body was buried in an unknown grave and his name subsequently listed on the gateway for the missing dead of the Battle of the Somme at the imposing Edwin Lutyens-designed Thiepval Memorial.

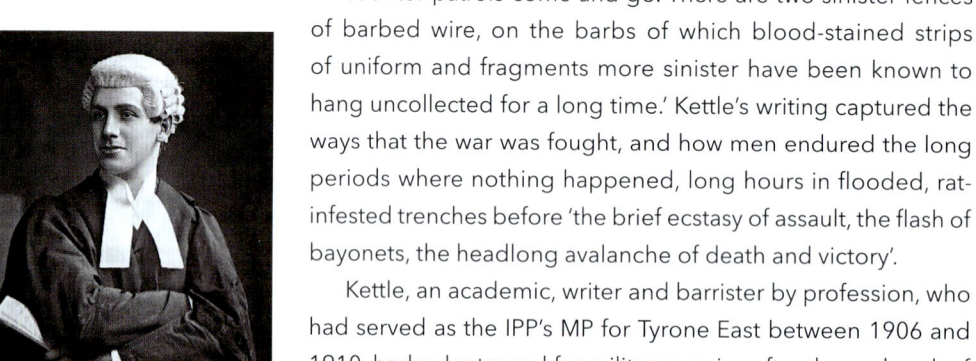

A photograph taken in 1905 of Tom Kettle in his barrister's wig and gown.

'... THE HEADLONG AVALANCHE OF DEATH AND VICTORY'

Kettle's death in France occurred less than a month after the Easter Rising in Dublin. As a Home Rule nationalist, Kettle had little sympathy for the insurrection, yet he felt outrage at the brutality of the British response, which included the killing of his brother-in-law, the pacifist Francis Sheehy Skeffington. The Rising and its aftermath fed Kettle's disillusionment with the war and his understanding of how his wartime service would be remembered when set against that of the executed rebel leaders. Where the latter would, Kettle predicted, go down in history as heroes and martyrs, he was destined to be recalled as nothing more than a 'bloody British soldier'. However, in that – as in his death – Kettle was far from alone. More than 200,000 Irish served in uniform during the First World War, and between 30,000 and 35,000 would die doing so.

The descent into war in the summer of 1914 had not been anticipated. Although the preceding decades had witnessed a build-up of political tensions in Europe, with the emergence of two powerful alliance blocs and the rapid expansion of rival armies and armaments, the escalatory sequence of events that led to major conflagration began with the assassination on 28 June 1914 of Archduke Franz Ferdinand, heir to the Austro-Hungarian throne, and his wife, by a Bosnian-Serb nationalist in Sarajevo. In the weeks that followed, Europe's military and political leaders made a series of decisions that turned a local conflict into a European-wide, and later global, war.

When Britain declared war on Germany on 4 August, there were already 28,000 Irishmen serving in the British Army, and a further 30,000 reservists ready for immediate call-up. Unlike in Britain, where conscription was introduced in early 1916, compulsory military service was never extended to Ireland during the war. So why, even if not quite at the same rate as Britain, did so many volunteer to serve? The reasons are varied: many were undoubtedly motivated by a sense of opportunity or excitement, or, as David Fitzpatrick demonstrated, by the 'attitudes and behaviour of comrades', others by the prospect of a wage and lots more by a sense of patriotic duty. For the unionist population, such patriotism was straightforward, as they considered themselves British and sons of empire. Once London had

A recruitment poster celebrating the valour of Macroom's Michael O'Leary, one of 37 Irishmen to be awarded the Victoria Cross during the course of the war.

decreed that Home Rule would not be enacted for the duration of the war, Edward Carson was able to publicly commit his followers, particularly those in the UVF, to the formation of the 36th Ulster Division.

For nationalists the position was more complex, but in his Woodenbridge speech, IPP leader John Redmond told his followers 'that it is their duty, and should be their honour, to take their place in the firing line in this contest'. As Redmond presented it, the war was a moral matter and as much about Irish interests as those of Britain. It would, therefore, be a 'disgrace' to Ireland and her traditions and history if Irishmen confined themselves only to the defence of their own shores. It was a controversial and divisive call: for a start, it catalysed a split in the Irish Volunteers. And while a majority sided with Redmond – assuming the new name of 'National Volunteers' – a significant minority didn't. Pacifists, too, would oppose the war as an imperial contest in which Ireland should have no part, a perspective shared by the labour leader, James Connolly. Writing in the *Irish Worker* just days into the war, Connolly expressed fears that not only would Europe's working class end up slaughtered for the 'benefit of kings and financiers', but that the 'misery and suffering' that would be visited upon the Irish people would be 'simply incalculable'.

Despite such warnings, Irishmen proceeded to serve in all branches of the army, navy and air force, and in all theatres where the war was fought. Many Irish-born men who had emigrated fought the war wearing Australian, Canadian, New Zealand, South African and United States uniforms. Some 4,300 Irish women also volunteered for service and were particularly active in nursing at home and on the front line – forty-three of them were killed. The majority of Irishmen were concentrated in three volunteer divisions of the British Army: the 10th Irish Division, the 16th Irish Division and the 36th Ulster Division. The 10th Irish Division landed at Gallipoli in April 1915 and would later serve in Macedonia, Egypt and Palestine. The 16th Irish Division was active on the Western Front throughout the war and suffered heavily at the battles of Messines and Passchendaele in 1917. The 36th Ulster Division also fought on the Western Front and was particularly involved in fighting during the Battle of the Somme, in which the division suffered catastrophic casualties. Almost 2,000 members of the division would die on the first day of the Somme campaign on 1 July 1916, their extraordinary loyal sacrifice becoming an essential tenet of Ulster Protestant and unionist identity. As the historian and playwright Philip Orr has observed, 'a sacrifice had been made which would surely tie Ulster to the Empire for good, banishing any thought of "Dublin rule" from the minds of British politicians, at least as far as the north of the island was concerned'.

Three Irish Guards taking a well-earned rest from carrying duckboards near Ypres in 1917.

Whether unionist or nationalist, the experiences of Irish servicemen during the war were not dissimilar. There were many outstanding acts of heroism, and the Victoria Cross was awarded to thirty-seven Irish-born soldiers, including the first of the war to Westmeath-born Maurice Dease, killed in the Battle of Mons just two weeks after hostilities had begun. Thousands of men died at the hands of the enemy, but many were killed by their own side, in accidents or through illness. Thousands of others returned to Ireland permanently disabled or disfigured, or else with mental trauma that would blight the rest of their lives. Of those men who flouted military discipline and deserted because they could no longer face the fighting, twenty-eight from Ireland were executed by military authorities. These included James Crozier, an eighteen-year-old from Belfast, who had been underage when he enlisted in September 1914 and was executed for desertion on 27 February 1916 after enduring a hard winter on the Somme. Crozier's colonel would write how at the appointed time of execution 'a volley rings out – a nervous volley it is true, yet a volley. Before the fatal shots are fired I had called the battalion to attention. There is a pause, I wait. I see the medical officer examining the victim. He makes a sign, the subaltern strides forward, a single shot rings out. Life is now extinct.'

While the wartime fighting never extended to the Irish landmass, there were significant civilian deaths. The waters around Ireland were patrolled by German U-boats, which regularly attacked military, merchant and civilian vessels. On 7 May 1915, for example, the large ocean liner *Lusitania* was attacked and sunk off the Cork coast: 1,193 of the ship's 1,960 passengers and crew were killed. The sinking of the *Lusitania*, en route from New York to Liverpool, provoked international outrage and hardened public attitudes against Germany, including in the neutral United States, 128 of whose citizens were among the *Lusitania*'s dead. This sinking did not lead to America's entry into the war, but the resumption of unrestricted German submarine warfare in 1917 (the tactic had been modified following American protests at the loss of civilian lives on the *Lusitania*) was a key factor. The impact of the American decision of April of that year was immediately visible in Ireland: within weeks, half a dozen destroyers had entered Queenstown (now Cobh) harbour, the start of an influx that saw over ninety warships and 8,000 sailors based in the coastal town by late summer.

By then, the First World War still had more than a year to run. The end finally came with an armistice signed just outside Paris in the early morning of 11 November 1918. On demobilisation, Irish war veterans, many physically and mentally scarred, returned to a country that had been politically transformed. Where, on the eve of the war, the political divisions on the island had centred on the issue of Home Rule, Irish nationalist sentiment had in the two years since the Easter Rising transitioned towards support for Sinn Féin and full Irish independence. Sinn Féin's rise was cemented by, inter alia, its dominant

Germany retaliated against the British blockade across the North Sea and English Channel, which cut off its food and war supplies, by deploying a policy of 'unrestricted U-boat warfare'. Her submarines prowled the Atlantic torpedoing any ship they encountered. This 1916 illustration shows one such attack on a merchant ship.

showing in the 1918 election, and by the establishment of the first Dáil and the start of the IRA's military struggle against the British administration in Ireland in 1919. According to historian Emmanuel Destenay, hundreds, and possibly as many as a thousand, First World War veterans joined the IRA campaign between 1919 and 1921. Significant though this number was, it still only represented a small fraction of veteran experience. So what of the others?

For soldiers returning to Ulster, especially those of a unionist persuasion, the reception reflected gratitude for their imperial service, which was marked with annual acts of commemoration, notably on 11 November and 1 July – the former a day of remembrance shared across the United Kingdom, the latter a day to specifically remember those who fell at the Somme. Such commemoration was undoubtedly political, especially that relating to the 36th Ulster Division and the Somme, which, as Neil Jarman has noted, was 'introduced into Orange mytho-history as a contemporary equivalent to 1690'. In contrast, those Irishmen returning from military service to Southern Ireland found their war-service record at odds with a new political climate and soon to be overshadowed by the service records of very different – republican – veterans' groups. Even so, and notwithstanding the difficulties the veterans experienced, including instances of discrimination, commemoration of the First World War was a familiar feature of life in the Irish Free State throughout the 1920s and 1930s: in 1924, for instance, 20,000 war veterans paraded through the streets of Dublin in front of crowds that ran into the tens of thousands. And this was not a one-off demonstration: similar, well-attended parades were also held in other Irish cities, poppies were widely worn, and community-driven and funded public war memorials were erected in many towns and cities throughout those decades.

At Islandbridge in Dublin, albeit at a deliberate remove from the city centre, an impressive Irish National War Memorial Gardens was completed in 1939. It was there, in 2016, after decades of renewed consciousness-raising of Ireland's First World War experience by a dedicated cohort of academics and journalists, that the Irish state's centenary commemoration of the Battle of the Somme was held and President of Ireland Michael D. Higgins laid a wreath. Significantly, this Irish commemorative event was not held on the anniversary of the Somme campaign's commencement, but a week later. That is because on 1 July the Irish President had been in Thiepval to participate in an international commemorative ceremony, as part of which, beneath a memorial to the missing that bore his name, the last letter written by Thomas Kettle was read aloud to the large attendance of dignitaries and relatives.

The Winning and Losing of Irish Home Rule

IN CORK AT least, it was a New Year's Eve with a difference. On 31 December 1913, to welcome what was already being widely proclaimed as 'the Home Rule year', a concert was staged at the City Hall, after which a procession involving several hundred cyclists, torchbearers and representatives of various public bodies was led through the principal streets of the city. Festivities finished on the Grand Parade, where, at a 'National Monument' erected several years earlier, large crowds joined in the singing of 'A Nation Once Again'. The sheer spectacle of it all, the press reported, was met with general 'enthusiasm and rejoicing', which 'testified in a remarkable fashion to the demand of the people of Cork for Self-Government'. This demand for Home Rule had been the driving ambition of the IPP for the previous forty years and its delivery was now, finally, widely anticipated.

Nationalist confidence in the apparent imminence of Home Rule was grounded in two errant convictions: firstly, a faith in the capacity of Prime Minister Herbert Asquith to deliver for an Irish Party upon which his British Liberal government had become electorally dependent in the wake of the Westminster general election of 1910; secondly, a sense that Ulster unionist militancy was something of a bluff and that Edward Carson and his followers would reconcile themselves to Irish Home Rule once it became a reality. This downplaying of the strength of unionist resistance occurred in defiance of mounting evidence from late 1910 onwards that Ulster unionism was mobilising in opposition to Home Rule on a vast and unprecedented scale. Twice before – in 1886 and 1893 – the prospect of Home Rule had been scuppered at the parliamentary stage, the intervention of the House of Lords being required in 1893 to defeat a bill that had passed

> 'All means' extended to the use of force – or at least the very serious threat of it.

through the House of Commons. However, by the time the third Home Rule Bill was introduced to the same Commons in April 1912, the Lords' veto had been replaced by mere powers of delay and it was this that galvanised Ulster unionist reaction, as well as that of their Tory allies. Conservative Party leader Andrew Bonar Law travelled to the Balmoral showgrounds outside Belfast that April to pledge, before a crowd of 100,000 unionists, his support for Ulster's Home Rule opposition, clarifying months later that there was 'no length of resistance' unionists could go to with which he could imagine himself finding fault.

(LEFT) *Much of the Catholic merchant class were staunch Home Rule supporters and would often combine their commercial promotions with political messages. The striking example above, c. 1910, shows a green flag with a harp flying proudly over the Irish Houses of Parliament in Dublin.*

(RIGHT) *A 1912 Anti-Home Rule 'stamp' sold for a penny to raise funds for the Unionist cause.*

But how far were unionists from the north-east prepared to go? In September 1912 nearly half a million of them, Protestant Ulstermen and women, signed either the Ulster Solemn League and Covenant or an accompanying 'Women's Declaration', the former containing a commitment to use 'all means which may be found necessary to defeat the present conspiracy' that was the proposed Home Rule Parliament in Dublin. 'All means' extended to the use of force – or at least the very serious threat of it. In January 1913 opposition to Home Rule took a turn towards organised paramilitarism when the UVF was founded.

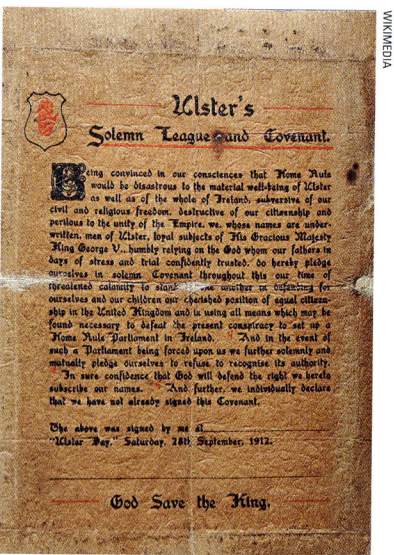

28 September 1912: Sir Edward Carson signing the Ulster Solemn League and Covenant in Belfast City Hall on what was deemed 'Ulster Day'. Conscious of the propaganda value of the moment, Carson pauses for the camera at a table draped in the Union Flag, silver pen in hand and surrounded by major unionist figures such as James Craig (to his left), who masterminded the impressive event.

Organisationally modelled on British military structures and supported by a significant body of retired British officers, 'Carson's army' – as the UVF became known – held rallies and drilled openly with rifles. The accompanying rhetoric was defiant and frequently fiery to the point of incendiary. Observing from Dublin was an impressed Eoin MacNeill, professor of early Irish history at UCD: 'a wonderful state of things has come to pass in Ulster,' he wrote in *An Claidheamh Soluis* in November 1913, his article acting as catalyst for the creation (without the backing of the IPP leadership at first) of a rival force of Irish Volunteers, which, in turn, gave impetus to the foundation the following April of its female auxiliary, Cumann na mBan.

... its opponents could no more stop Home Rule than the 'shrieking of the winter wind can stop the blooming of the flowers of June'.

The militarisation of Irish society that had begun with Ulster's unionists had now extended to nationalist Ireland. Even if much of it was for show rather than real effect – an expression primarily of political sentiment – extra-parliamentary agitation fast became a popular complement to traditional parliamentary

SECOND THOUGHTS.

Mr. John Redmond. "FULL SHTEAM AHEAD! (*Aside*) I WONDHER WILL I LAVE THIS CONTRAIRY LITTLE DIVIL LOOSE, THE WAY HE'D COME BACK BY HIMSELF AFTHERWARDS?"

John Redmond, a favourite target of Punch, *is once again mocked for what is seen as his inability to convince Ulster unionists that their future interests are best served with Home Rule.*

methods. And yet, notwithstanding this escalation, in the early weeks of 1914 John Redmond was breezily proclaiming his belief in the unstoppability of Home Rule, telling his Waterford constituents that Asquith was as 'firm as a rock' and that its opponents could no more stop Home Rule than the 'shrieking of the winter wind can stop the blooming of the flowers of June'.

Such certitude was totally misplaced. The British government had, since 1912, been considering potential opt-outs from Home Rule for Ulster, and in March 1914 Asquith formally announced plans to temporarily – for a period of six years – exclude Ulster from the provisions of the legislation. This pleased nobody. Carson denounced the temporary nature of the opt-out as a 'mere stay of execution', although both he and Bonar Law accepted that the principle of partition had been conceded.

Asquith's difficulties were compounded by an 'incident' at the Curragh army camp in March 1914 that raised doubts about the ability of his government to enforce its policy in Ireland. Although no orders were disobeyed (as none were given), more than fifty officers made explicit their unwillingness to undertake military operations to face down Ulster unionist militancy, which would find its most impressive expression on 24–25 April when the UVF brought ashore, without hindrance and principally in Larne, approximately 25,000 rifles and three million rounds of ammunition. It was a spectacular, morale-boosting exercise, yet the gunrunning succeeded only in turning what historian Alvin Jackson says was a largely unarmed force 'into a badly armed force'. The Irish Volunteers, soon to come under John Redmond's control and balloon into a mass force of its own, were even more poorly equipped but delivered a propaganda coup of their own when openly importing arms into Howth in late July. In contrast to the impassiveness of the response in Ulster, they were met with British Army resistance, an intervention that ended tragically when a battalion of the King's Own Scottish Borderers killed four civilians on Bachelors Walk after being taunted on their return to the city about their failure to stop the Volunteers.

Concerned at the spiral of events, which could lead to a 'dire calamity', King George V convened a four-day conference at Buckingham Palace from 21 July, attended by the leaders of Irish nationalism and unionism, as well as Asquith and Bonar Law. Essentially, this conference addressed what Asquith identified as the two principal outstanding issues that prevented the safe passage of Home Rule: firstly, the area of Ulster to be excluded, and secondly, the duration of this exclusion. No compromise or resolution was reached, and the failure of the conference effectively signalled the exhaustion of political efforts to resolve the looming crisis.

In the end, the outbreak of European war in early August 1914 did what all manner of political manoeuvring had failed to do. It averted the threat of civil strife in Ireland. Indeed, the most immediate and remarkable consequence of Britain's declaration of war on Germany was its pacifying effect on Irish life, as revealed in the confidential police reports that poured into Dublin Castle. A number of these told of a cooling of tensions. In Co. Tyrone, for instance, war abroad was credited by police with working a 'revolution' in party feeling at home as antagonism towards Germany forged an unlikely unity between opposing Volunteer forces.

The war had another effect, however. In an effort to sideline the Irish question and ensure IPP backing for the recruitment drive, the British government moved at speed to place the Home Rule Act on the statute books. After decades as a key cleavage in British party politics, and after months of rising tensions with mobilising private armies, the third Home Rule Bill passed through the House of Commons in about seven minutes. 'I feel', Asquith wrote, 'as if a great weight were off my chest.' It is easy to understand why: although the Bill had been passed, it was accompanied by the Suspensory Act, which ensured that Home Rule would not come into effect until an indefinite date 'not being later than the end of the present war'. Crucially, too, the passage of the Bill came with assurances from Asquith to unionists that coercion of Ulster was a course a British government 'would never countenance or consent to'.

For Irish nationalists, the outcome was wholly anticlimatic. What should have been a moment of triumph and vindication for John Redmond and his IPP turned out to be anything but. Home Rule had been delivered but not realised. The Act was on the statute books, but not in force. The absence of implementation, of something to show for the years of high politicking in Westminster, left Redmond and his colleagues exposed and vulnerable. Constitutionalism passed, in the words of historian Charles Townshend, 'into a kind of suspended animation', which, after all the heightened expectation of delivery, invited ridicule from the party's opponents. The party lost its raison d'être and Redmond's unequivocal support of Irish recruitment to the British war effort – he urged that Irishmen go 'wherever the firing line extends' in a speech at Woodenbridge, Co. Wicklow on 20 September – catalysed a split within the Irish Volunteers. Part of the membership, albeit less than 13,000 of a 170,000-strong force, chose to continue under Eoin MacNeill's leadership in determined opposition to Irish involvement in the war.

While the majority of Volunteers heeded Redmond's call, Irish expectations of the war would soon jar with their actual experience of it. The anticipated short war never materialised and the more protracted it became, the more it fed a growing sense of Irish disillusionment. The longer it continued, too, the more marginal Redmond and Irish considerations became to British politics, a reality copper-fastened by the creation of a coalition government in May 1915 that ended the parliamentary arrangement whereby the IPP had been required to prop up the Liberal government of Asquith. Over a year later, after Irish separatists had mounted an insurrection in Dublin and proclaimed a republic, a Royal Commission took evidence from Augustine Birrell, the Chief Secretary of Ireland. For Birrell, the appointment of the coalition cabinet with Edward Carson in its ranks 'seemed to make an end of Home Rule, and strengthen the Sinn Féiners [the political group which would, erroneously, come to be identified with the Rising] enormously all over the country'. A transformation of Irish political life was in train.

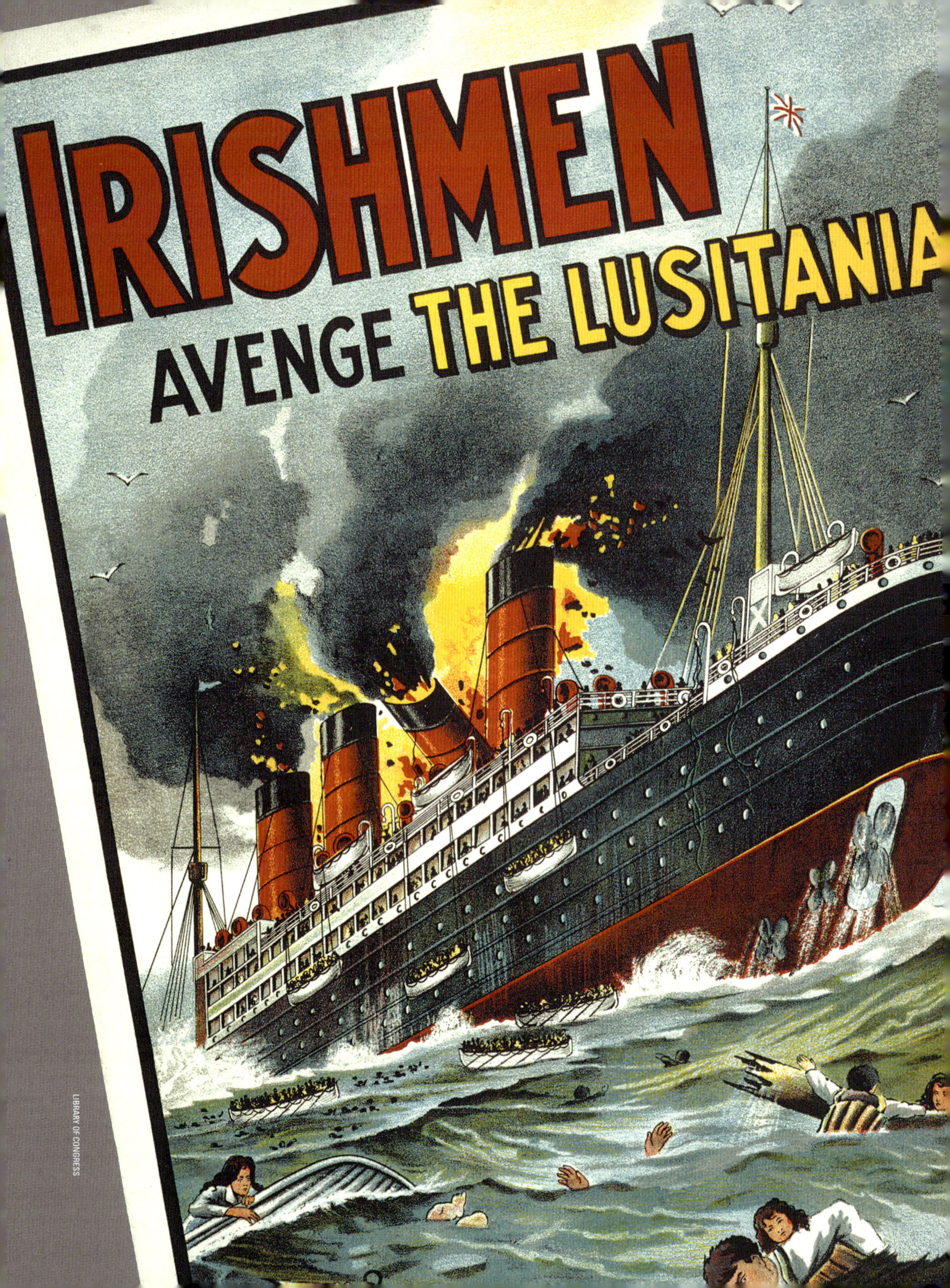

LIBRARY OF CONGRESS

1915

'Travellers intending to embark on the Atlantic voyage are reminded that a state of war exists between Germany and Great Britain ... and that travellers sailing in the war zone on ships of Great Britain or her allies do so at their own risk.'

Notice from the German government published in forty US newspapers
1 MAY

1915

The Kaiser is Coming!

January – All along the eastern seaboard from Cork to Antrim, residents have been warned by the authorities to be prepared for German raids and even invasion.

In case of emergency, people should be ready to immediately head inland and bring with them all cattle, horses, motor cars, bicycles, agricultural implements and other articles that might prove serviceable to the enemy. Further instructions have been given to destroy all petrol, hay and animal fodder in the event of evacuation.

These instructions have been criticised by P.J. O'Neill, the chairman of Dublin County Council and an extensive farmer at Kinsealy: 'The notion of advising people if an attack were made to destroy their crops and to send their cattle and what belongings they could remove into the wilderness without accommodation for themselves or their cattle is futile.'

Suggestions that the Germans might be about to invade have also been met with a certain scepticism across the country.

When a meeting of the Dungannon Urban Council debated the proper steps to take in the event of invasion, it was suggested by one member,

Propaganda depicting the Kaiser as a bloodthirsty pirate helps stoke fears.

---

6 JAN
Lieutenant David Williamson from Co. Tyrone writes to his family to tell them of an extraordinary truce at the front on Christmas Day: 'There was a sort of truce arranged today (Christmas Day) between some of our fellows and the Germans in front of them. Although the regiments to right and left kept firing spasmodically all day, the others went across and they and the Germans exchanged tobacco, and talked and sauntered about between the two lines of trenches.'

6 JAN
'For my part, I am fighting for Ireland', the poet, university lecturer and former Irish Party MP Tom Kettle tells a recruitment rally in Drogheda. He added that he would 'rather see this war through as a sixth-rate soldier than a first-rate man of letters'.

10 JAN
A pastoral letter entitled 'Patriotism and Endurance' by Cardinal Mercier from Belgium is translated and read to Irish Mass-goers. Following the publication of the pastoral, Cardinal Mercier is kept under house arrest and guarded by the German military.

Alexander Patterson, that watchmen should be appointed to provide some instrument of alarm to people: 'By having watchmen, the townspeople would not be caught napping in case of invasion.' His suggestion was greeted with amusement by his colleagues on the council.

At Cavan Quarter Sessions a boy was charged with the larceny of three cattle. He had been told by some men that the Kaiser was coming to Ireland and that he had better hide the cattle from him. At their instigation, the boy was driving the cattle along a back road when he was intercepted.

U-boat Attacks in the Irish Sea

January – Three British trading ships have been sunk in the Irish Sea by a German submarine.

The submarine U-21 sank the *Ben Cruachan*, the *Linda Blanche* and *Kilcoan* along the Mersey–Belfast route. The sinkings are part of the concerted German attempts to cripple British trade.

U-21 is the submarine that sank the British light cruiser *Pathfinder* early in September last year, which resulted in the loss of 259 lives. It is a vessel of some 800 tonnes, with four torpedo tubes, and includes anti-aircraft weapons as well as traditional guns.

The sinking of the merchant vessel *Ben Cruachan* was a particularly curious affair. Quartermaster Inglis, one of crew members, reported that

1915

13 JAN
A massive earthquake in the Avezzano region of central Italy leaves approximately 30,000 people dead.

19 JAN △
The first German Zeppelin raids on England's east coast see the Norfolk towns of **Great Yarmouth** and King's Lynn bombed.

23 JAN
According to local reports the collapse of the fishing industry in Donegal is causing people along the coast severe distress. The discontinuance of herring fishing and the postponement of the proposed marine works at Burtonport for the duration of war has left some families on the brink of starvation.

Sightings of U-boats in the Irish Sea and the British Channel became more frequent as the Imperial German Navy ramped up its activities.

1915

31 JAN
Alderman John Clancy, who died six days after being elected Lord Mayor of Dublin, is buried in Glasnevin Cemetery.

4 FEB
Dublin Chamber of Commerce presents William Martin Murphy with a portrait painted by William Orpen. The Chamber pays tribute to Murphy's leadership role in combating the 1913 labour strike in Dublin.

△ **4 FEB**
Cheering breaks out in the House of Commons after MPs are informed of the suspension of **Sir Roger Casement**'s pension. It follows reports that Casement was 'practically a prisoner' in Berlin, where he had gone to solicit support for a rebellion in Ireland.

4 FEB
Germany declares the waters surrounding Great Britain and Ireland to be a war zone and that enemy shipping in the area would be sunk without warning.

---

the German submarine appeared beside the steamer as they headed for Larne. The crew of 23 were put into boats, which were then ordered alongside the submarine.

The commander of the submarine requested that the captain of the *Ben Cruachan* hand over the ship's papers and logs. He continued, 'Our skipper told him the papers had been left aboard the vessel and the skipper was ordered to accompany a German officer and two sailors and secure the papers.'

Once the papers had been handed over, the Germans placed a mine aboard the vessel. There was then a violent explosion and the ship sank, stern first, with the bow up in the air.

The submarine's commander expressed regret for his actions but said, 'War is war!' He expressed a hope that the crew of the *Ben Cruachan* would be picked up quickly and that the weather would not worsen too greatly. The captain and the commander shook hands and saluted each other.

U-21 then submerged and disappeared. It has since been seen at various locations around the Irish Sea and – amongst other things – unsuccessfully chased the mail steamer *Leinster*. Several shipping companies have now suspended sailings across the Irish Sea.

New Lord Lieutenant for Ireland

22 February – Lord Wimborne, the new Lord Lieutenant of Ireland, made his first public appearance on Saturday when he visited the Dublin Castle Red Cross Hospital.

Accompanied by his officials and leading physicians, he visited each of the wards of the hospital and conversed with several patients. Lord Wimborne commended the staff on the manner in which they were treating wounded soldiers.

Earlier this week, the new Lord Lieutenant had arrived by ship from England and was received by the Under-secretary for Ireland, Sir Matthew Nathan, at Kingstown Harbour. He was subsequently sworn in at a ceremony at Dublin Castle in front of a large attendance of Privy Councillors, state officials and other invited guests. The oath of allegiance and the official oath were administered by Sir E. O'Farrell and the Sword of State

Ivor Churchill Guest Wimborne, 1st Viscount Wimborne, known as Lord Wimborne.

was handed to the new viceroy. At that moment, a salute of 15 guns was fired from the Phoenix Park, followed by three further salutes of 21 guns apiece.

Last week the country bade farewell to Lord and Lady Aberdeen. The couple travelled along a preorganised route from the entrance to Dublin Castle to Westland Row station. The streets were adorned with bunting and were lined with cheering crowds. A guard of honour was provided by the 5th Battalion of the Royal Inniskilling Fusiliers and the 7th Battalion of the Royal Dublin Fusiliers.

From Westland Row, they took the train to Kingstown, where they boarded the *Connaught* and set sail to the sound of Carriglea School Band performing 'God Save the King'.

Launched in December 1914, Arthur Griffith's biweekly newspaper attempted to circumvent DORA, which forbade new propaganda writing, by simply reprinting articles from other sources.

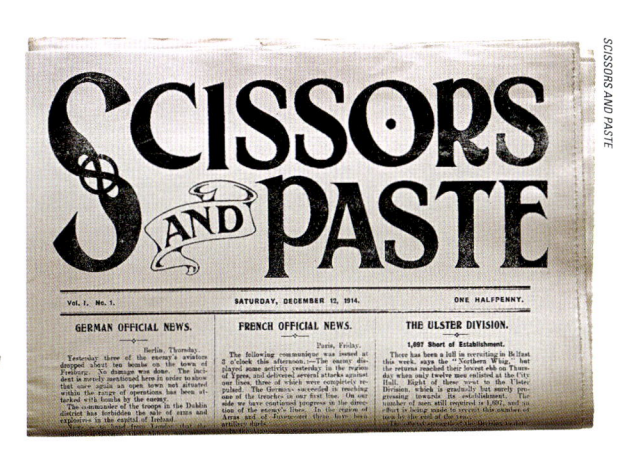

British Authorities Suppress a Further Nationalist Newspaper

2 March – British military authorities today raided the offices of the *Scissors and Paste* newspaper on Middle Abbey Street.

The paper, run by Mr Arthur Griffith, is the successor to the Sinn Féin newspaper, which had previously been suppressed. The premises of P. Mahon at Yarnhall Street, where the paper is printed, were also raided.

Both raids were carried out at around 3.30 p.m. At Yarnhall Street, Captain Atkinson, assisted by ten colleagues – including a superintendent, a sergeant and an inspector – proceeded to seize copies of the paper and assorted paperwork. A large crowd gathered outside to watch as the police, with assistance from Mr Mahon's staff, dismantled the machinery to ensure that no further printing could take place.

At the editorial offices on Abbey Street, the police read a warrant under the Defence of the Realm Act and warned that no further publications of the newspaper would be permitted.

1915

5 FEB
A new playground opens at the top of Constitution Hill in Dublin, beside the Broadstone terminus of the Midland Great Western Railway. The vacant land was given by the railway company and transformed into a playground by men employed by the Mansion House Committee for Relief of Distress.

17 FEB
The new Lord Lieutenant of Ireland, Lord Wimborne, arrives in Ireland. His first public appearance will be at the Dublin Castle Red Cross Hospital.

20 FEB △
It is reported that **William Archer Redmond**, IPP MP for East Tyrone and son of party leader John Redmond, has joined the Cadet Corps of the Irish Brigade at Fermoy. It is expected that he will receive a commission in the 6th Battalion of the Royal Irish Regiment.

1915

2 MAR
British military authorities raid the offices of the *Scissors and Paste* newspaper on Dublin's Middle Abbey Street. Run by Arthur Griffith, the paper is a successor to the Sinn Féin paper previously suppressed by the military.

7 MAR
'We shall never consent to divide this island or this nation and we shall never consent to allow any section, clique, or faction to rule the people of Ireland', IPP MP John Dillon tells a review of Irish Volunteers in Belfast.

8 MAR
William Gough enters a police barracks in Belturbet and confesses to murdering his wife, Rose Anne. Pointing to his stained clothes, he says, 'This is her blood on me.'

15 MAR
Catholic, Presbyterian and Methodist Church leaders in Ireland sign a petition to British Prime Minister H.H. Asquith calling for immediate action against the abuse of alcohol in Ireland. The petition states that 'drink is doing more damage in the war than all the German submarines put together'.

There were also arrests in other parts of the country as police sought to suppress any manifestation of dissent against the war effort.

In Wexford, a journalist from the *Enniscorthy Echo*, James Bolger, was arrested at the newspaper's offices and brought to Dublin. The charge against him was failure to disclose information about ammunition and explosives that were present in the house in which he lodged.

St Patrick's Day Celebrated

18 March – A large reception was held in London yesterday to honour Ireland's patron saint, St Patrick. It was held in the Oak Room of the Hotel Cecil and was followed by a concert in the Grand Hall.

The huge crowd heard John Redmond say that without the war the event would have been a celebration of Irish political triumph – but that triumph had merely been delayed.

Mr Redmond continued, 'We are witnessing the enactment of a great tragedy. The shadows of suffering and of death hover over our land. The issues at stake at this moment are the liberty and civilisation of the world and, in a very special way, the existence of small nationalities.

'We have met here tonight to celebrate St Patrick's Day by a demonstration of sympathy and support for Belgium, that gallant little land,

Cardinal Bourne, Catholic Archbishop of Westminster, was present at the St Patrick's Day reception in the Hotel Cecil. The Prelate, whose mother Ellen was Irish, is shown here presenting shamrocks to members of the Irish Guards.

which has done more, and suffered more, than any other country in this great struggle for human liberty.'

Mr Redmond concluded by paying tribute to those Irishmen currently fighting for the British Army.

Across Ireland, festivities were also held to mark St Patrick's Day. In Galway five bands led a large parade through the city. There were a few cases of drunkenness, but the city remained quiet.

Another public procession passed through Drogheda, led by a local band playing patriotic songs. Those who marched included representatives of the Volunteers, the GAA, trade unions and the Ancient Order of Hibernians.

In Limerick, the holiday saw many people wear the shamrock – including soldiers stationed in the city.

New Tourist Agency for Ireland

22 April – A new body to promote Ireland as a tourism destination was founded at a meeting of representatives from all over Ireland at the Mansion House in Dublin yesterday.

In spite of the ongoing global war, the Tourist Organisation Society of Ireland was launched, and it hopes to build on the tourism development conference held in Cork several weeks ago.

The meeting heard confirmation from the managers of all the leading Irish railway companies that there is no intention to withdraw or curtail any of the excursion services in Ireland.

Bundoran, Co. Donegal and its fine beach was highlighted by the Lord Mayor of Dublin as one of the many attractive destinations in Ireland where people from Britain could holiday.

1915

28 MAR
The 'shameless drinking of the wives and mothers of soldiers at the front' is condemned at a temperance meeting held on Dublin's Church Street.

31 MAR
About 400 people clash with police at a farm at Lisduff, Co. Galway. It follows the recent purchase of the farm by a family from Loughrea.

5 APR
Jack Johnson, champion since 1908, loses his world heavyweight boxing title to the unfancied Jess Willard after a 26-round fight in Havana, Cuba.

13 APR
The Marchioness of Aberdeen criticises the failure to provide adequate playgrounds for children in Ireland at the annual meeting of the Women's National Health Association.

1915

21 APR
The Tourist Organisation Society of Ireland is founded at the Mansion House to promote Ireland as a tourism destination.

24 APR
Several hundred Armenian intellectuals are arrested and later executed by the Ottoman authorities. This marks the start of what becomes known as the 'Armenian genocide'.

25 APR
Allied Forces launch an attack on the Ottoman Empire at the Gallipoli peninsula – it is part of a campaign to take control of key strategic positions around the Dardanelles Strait separating Asia from Europe.

6 MAY
170 dockers on Dublin's south quays take strike action in a dispute over wages.

7 MAY
RMS *Lusitania* is sunk off south coast of Ireland by a German U-boat with the loss of more than 1,000 lives. The *New York Herald* condemns the attack as a 'deliberate, cold-blooded, premeditated outrage'.

A view across the cask yard at St James's Gate Brewery, owned by Guinness, one of the many Irish breweries and distilleries that were concerned about the proposed taxes.

While it is likely that the tourism trade from America is essentially lost for the duration of the war, it is hoped to attract tourists from Britain who find themselves shut off from the continent of Europe. Ireland should also prosper from the fact that it has proved immune, thus far, to Zeppelin raids.

The Lord Mayor of Dublin, who opened proceedings, made particular reference to the beauty of Wicklow, Killarney, the Blackwater Valley, and the northwest region, including Connacht and Donegal, saying that if these areas were properly advertised they would certainly attract visitors from England and Scotland.

The new organisation has received messages of support from leading public representatives and societies.

Proposed Ban on Drink

1 May – 'Drink is doing more damage in the war than all the German submarines put together', the Chancellor of the Exchequer, David Lloyd George, told the House of Commons yesterday as he promoted the British government's proposal to dramatically increase the taxes on alcohol.

Among the proposed changes is a doubling of the tax on whiskey, with similar increases on wine and beer.

Mr Lloyd George said that there were reports from all the chief centres of armaments that avoidable loss of time was mostly attributable to excessive drinking. 'There has always, in peacetime, been a good deal of time lost through excessive drinking. But we can afford it then, we cannot now.'

1915

The leader of the Irish Parliamentary Party, John Redmond, said that the proposals were opposed by every party in Ireland. He said that Ireland was prepared to do her duty and make every sacrifice for the war, but that the proposed taxes would destroy, root and branch, a great Irish industry.

Reaction among publicans was one of dismay. One publican told the press: 'The additional impost means the wiping out of the distilling trade and the disemployment of many hands. In fact, I would prefer that we licensed traders were closed up forthwith.'

Public meetings have been planned for across Ireland as fears grow that the proposals will cost thousands of jobs. More than 5,000 men are employed in brewing in Dublin alone, many more are employed in distilleries, while barley growers are also certain to be affected.

There were also views expressed in the drinks industry in Ireland that the increase in taxation was rooted in Mr Lloyd George's personal beliefs. One representative said, 'It would appear to me that Mr Lloyd George is at present a wholesale temperance reformer. You cannot make England sober by penalising Ireland.'

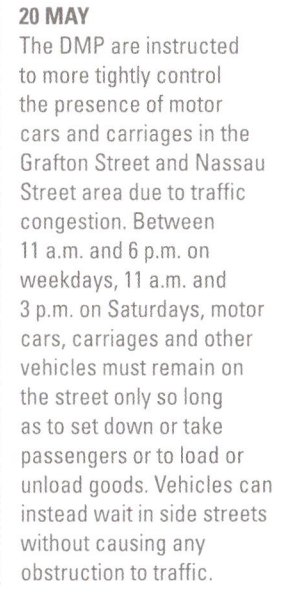

20 MAY
The DMP are instructed to more tightly control the presence of motor cars and carriages in the Grafton Street and Nassau Street area due to traffic congestion. Between 11 a.m. and 6 p.m. on weekdays, 11 a.m. and 3 p.m. on Saturdays, motor cars, carriages and other vehicles must remain on the street only so long as to set down or take passengers or to load or unload goods. Vehicles can instead wait in side streets without causing any obstruction to traffic.

Shockwaves across an ocean – The New York Times *carries news of the appalling loss of life, including many Americans.*

23 MAY ▽
Italy joins the Allies by declaring war on Austria-Hungary.

Lusitania Sunk!

8 May – More than 1,300 lives are feared lost after the *Lusitania* was hit by a torpedo off the south coast of Ireland yesterday.

The famous Cunard Steamship Company ship was 12 miles off the Old Head of Kinsale in Co. Cork, en route for Liverpool from New York, when it was torpedoed by a German submarine shortly after 2 p.m. The torpedo exploded inside the ship and sent fumes all over. There was something of a panic on board the ship, while the crew sought to maintain order and launch the lifeboats.

1915

24 MAY
Members of the Irish Volunteers, as distinct from the pro-Redmond National Volunteers, who gather in Limerick are set upon by a group of women. Female relatives of soldiers serving at the front throw a volley of stones at the men who were trying to board a train. The women celebrate their attack by dancing in the street.

25 MAY
A new coalition government is formed in the UK. Asquith remains as prime minister and unionist leader, Sir Edward Carson, becomes attorney general.

31 MAY
The abnormally high mortality rate of children in Dublin is considered at a conference on child welfare held in the theatre of the Royal Dublin Society. The numbers of deaths of children in the first quarter of the year have risen from 144 per 1,000 to 181 per 1,000. General fears are expressed that the summer months would see the numbers climb still higher.

9 JUN
US Secretary of State William Jennings Bryan resigns in a dispute with President Wilson over the contents of a diplomatic note to Germany.

The immediate aftermath of the sinking as envisaged by the artist William Lionel Wyllie in his painting The Track of the Lusitania.

The ship sank extremely quickly; it disappeared some 18 minutes after being hit.

A wireless message from the *Lusitania* was received in Queenstown harbour at 2.15 p.m. asking for assistance. All available tugs and steam trawlers set out immediately to rescue as many passengers as possible. Rescue efforts were aided by almost perfect sea conditions, with the weather beautifully fine and a light southeast wind blowing. Some passengers managed to clamber into lifeboats, and these were taken on board local vessels. It is estimated that some 600 people may have escaped the ship.

The survivors were brought to hotels, boarding houses and family homes. Many were dazed and in shock, as well as shivering from the dampness of their clothing.

Although the lifeboats on the *Lusitania* had room for some 2,600 people, and early reports suggest there were only 2,000 on board; the speed at which the ship sank would have left it impossible for all aboard to have escaped.

At the Cunard offices in Liverpool a huge crowd assembled and besieged the staff with anxious enquiries as to the fate of their friends and relations. There were distressing scenes as people of all classes scrambled for the news, which was published on the windows of the offices by staff.

Amongst those believed to be lost is Sir Hugh Lane, director of the National Gallery in Dublin.

1915

First Reports from Gallipoli

19 May – Stories of the brutal battles for Gallipoli have reached Ireland as the first letters to soldiers' families arrived home. The grim and deadly nature of the experiences of the Royal Dublin Fusiliers is all too clear from reading these first-hand accounts.

The Fusiliers had left their ship in the Dardanelles on Sunday 25 April, at 5 a.m., as a naval bombardment of Turkish positions got underway.

Irish soldiers were in small boats making their way towards land when they came under fire, as the testimony of one private recalled: 'About one and a half miles from shore the enemy's shells started to burst around our boats, doing a lot of damage. As we got closer bullets started to whiz around us, killing several men in our boats. I had my right arm scorched in two parts by bullets, but I was one of the lucky ones.'

The men were stuck in their boats attempting to head for the beach: 'Machine guns galore were playing on us from a trench unseen at the bottom of the cliff, not 100 yards from us.'

Bullets and other ammunition were sprayed all around: 'Before I knew where I was, I was covered with dead men. I was simply saturated all over with blood. When they pulled these poor fellows off me they were all dead, and the poor fellow under me was dead. The boat was awful to look at, full of blood and water.

'There must be very few of our battalion left now. We were the first to land, and, with the Munsters, we lost very heavily. Almost all the officers were killed or wounded, I believe. I never wish to see such a bloody sight again. I don't mind fighting, but to be in an open boat and powerless is another thing.'

19 JUN
Owing to the continued occupation of their grounds by the British military, the Royal Dublin Society announces the cancellation of the Horse Show for the second year running.

20 JUN
Two female teams from Dingle travel by trawlers across the bay to Caherciveen to play 'friendly' matches against local opposition. Reporting on the games the following week, *The Kerryman* also notes that a Caherciveen 'Ladies' Hurling Club is now in full swing' and 'colleens' elsewhere are encouraged to follow their example.

Many of the officers of the 1st Battalion of the Royal Dublin Fusiliers were killed or injured while storming the beaches at Gallipoli.

REVOLUTIONARY TIMES 1913–23

1915

Redmond Declines British Cabinet Position

May – The leader of the Irish Parliamentary Party, John Redmond, has declined to accept a role in the new coalition government formed in London. Mr Redmond was rumoured to have been offered the position of postmaster general.

His decision to refuse a cabinet position was announced at a meeting of the party in the Mansion House in Dublin. A resolution approving of his action was unanimously passed. Mr Redmond's position is considered to be in strict adherence with Irish nationalist tradition and policy.

The party agreed that it will support the new government, just as it had the old, albeit on the understanding that it is in place only for the duration of the war and that it does not deviate from the existing policy on Ireland.

Fears were expressed in certain Irish quarters, however, that the presence of Sir Edward Carson, the leader of the Ulster unionists, at the heart of government might spell doom for Irish nationalists.

The new UK coalition government will continue to be headed by the Liberal leader Herbert Asquith, but will also include several Conservative ministers, including Andrew Bonar Law, who has been appointed colonial secretary. The ending of the Liberal administration was hastened by the crisis of the war and recent revelations about shell shortages in the field.

A letter from Asquith to Redmond, sent after Redmond's decision not to take part in the coalition government: 'I hope you do not need to be assured how highly I treasure the memory of the work which we have done together in the past, and how unshaken and unshakeable is my confidence, not only in the justice, but in the certain success of our common cause.'

The Conscription Threat

June – The new Minister for Munitions, David Lloyd George, has delivered a wide-ranging speech in Manchester in which he said that the government would introduce conscription if it became necessary to do so.

Mr Lloyd George said, 'If the necessity arose I am certain that no man of any party would protest. I don't talk about it as if it were anti-democratic.

△ **29 JUN**
Cork-born Fenian **Jeremiah O'Donovan Rossa**, a veteran member of the Irish Republican Brotherhood (IRB), dies in New York. His body will be returned to Ireland for burial.

1 JUL
The Irish Times reports that a meeting of the Gorey Board of Guardians has been informed about a large number of unmarried girls entering the workhouse to give birth. The same meeting is told that some 40% of marriages in Co. Wexford were 'marriages of necessity'.

12 JUL
Traditional 'Twelfth' celebrations are muted owing to the absence of so many Orangemen on war service.

We won and saved our liberties in this land on more than one occasion by compulsory service.

'France saved the liberty she had won in the great revolution from the fangs of tyrannical military empires purely by compulsory service.

'It has been the greatest weapon in the hands of democracy many a time for the winning and preservation of freedom.'

Mr Lloyd George did say, however, that it would be a mistake to resort to conscription unless it were absolutely necessary and that he believed that point had yet to be reached. His comments did not prevent the spread of rumours that compulsory military service was to be introduced, and the matter was discussed at length at a meeting of the Irish Parliamentary Party in the House of Commons in London.

The meeting – presided over by party leader John Redmond – saw unanimous support for a motion proposed by John Dillon. That motion made clear that the party was 'opposed to compulsory military service' and that any attempt to introduce it would be met with 'our vigorous resistance'.

The motion also argued that the existing system of voluntary recruitment had produced magnificent results and that any attempt to undermine it was 'scandalous and treacherous'.

Lusitania Bodies Found

Cork, 22 June – 'Going down with *Lusitania*. Mr. McManus. Goodbye.' So read a message that was inside a bottle that washed up at Carthy's Cove near Youghal, Co. Cork yesterday.

Debris from the sunken vessel continues to wash up on the south and west coasts of Ireland. Meanwhile, several bodies picked up off the Aran Islands have been buried at Kilronan, the main village on Inis Mór.

1915

18 JULY
The semi-final of the Munster senior hurling championship between Cork and Limerick is abandoned in Thurles after players and supporters engage in a free fight. Four minutes from the end of the game trouble erupts as Limerick's John Mackey and Cork's P. Nagle come to blows, at which point some of the 14,000 spectators invade the pitch and join the fight. The match is abandoned.

22 JUL
A monument to the memory of 'innocent civilians slain by British soldiers' on Bachelors Walk in July 1914 was prohibited, the House of Commons is told, because it was likely to cause disaffection to the King and damage war recruitment.

Queenstown (Cobh) played host to the largest official burial ceremony of Lusitania's *casualties. On 10 May the mass funeral of 145 unidentified victims took place following a special Requiem Mass in St Colman's Cathedral. The procession was flanked by huge numbers of people to the Old Church Cemetery where the remains were buried in three large pits dug by soldiers and marines.*

1915

25 JUL
Over 16,000 climb Croagh Patrick's Reek in Co. Mayo, the largest crowd to attend the **annual pilgrimage** for several years. Masses are celebrated continuously from 8 a.m. to noon at three altars in the oratory at the mountain summit.

29 JUL
Douglas Hyde resigns as President of the Gaelic League. In a letter read to the League's Ard-Fheis in Dundalk, Hyde claims the workload involved had affected his health.

1 AUG
The funeral of Jeremiah O'Donovan Rossa in Dublin draws enormous crowds onto the streets. The graveside oration is delivered by Patrick Pearse.

6 AUG
Members of the 10th (Irish) Division land at Suvla Bay in Gallipoli. The division will suffer huge losses in the campaign that follows.

A dispute has arisen in Galway after more victims of the *Lusitania* were buried at Killeany. At the Galway Board of Guardians meeting, it was recorded that Mr O'Flaherty, a local government official, said that he had been told by the parish priest, Fr Farragher, that he had no right to bury the bodies in consecrated ground as there was no evidence the victims were Catholic. Fr Farragher further stated that he would have to write to the Bishop, and that the bodies would probably have to be exhumed.

Mr O'Flaherty said that he informed Fr Farragher that he did not know what denomination the bodies were, but that he had no other place to bury them. He continued that he had seen Protestants buried in Catholic cemeteries in Inishnee and in Galway.

The meeting noted that the victims of the *Lusitania* were all human beings and that they deserved appropriate treatment, such as that provided by Mr O'Flaherty.

VC Winner Comes Home

Cork, 24 June – Sergeant Michael O'Leary, who received the Victoria Cross from King George V this week, has arrived back in Dublin to a warm reception.

Sergeant O'Leary travelled home to Cork and was received with great enthusiasm at Limerick Junction, Cork and Macroom train stations. In a series of brief comments in Dublin, Sergeant O'Leary displayed his Victoria Cross and said, 'It does not look much, but it stands for something, and I shall always treasure it.'

In respect of the future conduct of the war, Sergeant O'Leary said, 'What we want is shells, more shells, and more shells. If we get them we will get

Sergeant O'Leary on leave in Inchigeela chatting with his father, Daniel, and two friends.

the Germans on the move and beat them, but they are too well fortified for us to beat them in trench warfare.'

The reports from France that Sergeant O'Leary had been killed in the course of bitter fighting in France have left him particularly anxious to see his parents. He said that such reports must have upset them.

He agreed that the fighting around Cuinchy had been intense but did not want to describe the combat in which he killed eight German soldiers.

Sergeant O'Leary is on seven days' leave.

Munitions Work for Ireland?

29 July – Ireland is ready and willing to play her part in providing material for the war effort, the House of Commons heard today.

T.P. O'Connor, the Irish nationalist MP, said the government must ensure that Ireland got a full share of munitions work, both on patriotic and commercial grounds.

Illustrated London News *image of women in a Scottish munition works making shells.*

Mr O'Connor highlighted the scale of Mr Lloyd George's ambition for delivering munitions. He continued by saying that it was clear the resources available in Ireland were much larger than had been imagined or suspected by the government. He appealed to Mr Lloyd George to treat Ireland the same way he had other parts of the United Kingdom and to rely on local assistance and local direction.

Mr Lloyd George, the Minister for Munitions, said that he has plans to establish a central office in Dublin to oversee engineering operations in Ireland. He added that the engineering resources of the island were currently being surveyed and they would soon be in a position to say precisely what role Ireland would fulfil.

1915

11 AUG
A monster fish – known as a barracuda – is caught off the Blasket Islands, Co. Kerry. The fish is more than nine feet in length and is furnished with a breastplate of armour more than two inches thick. The tail is like that of a shark and its dorsal fin retracts into its body like a periscope while it attacks its prey.

13 AUG
It is reported that the number of people 'insane under care' in Ireland is 25,180. According to a newly published report of the Inspectors of Lunacy in Ireland, this is double the number recorded in 1880.

15 AUG
Lt Michael Fitzgibbon, 7th Battalion, Dublin Fusiliers, is killed in action on the Gallipoli Peninsula. A 29-year-old law student when he enlisted, he was the son of John Fitzgibbon, IPP MP for South Mayo. Another son of the MP, John, is killed by a shell in France in 1918 while serving as a chaplain.

19 AUG
The Belfast-built White Star Liner SS *Arabic* is struck by a German torpedo four miles from Cape Clear. The ship sinks in ten minutes with the loss of 44 lives.

1915

21 AUG
Bohemians Football Club organises entertainment and refreshments for more than 100 wounded and disabled soldiers at Dalymount Park. Music is provided by the band of the 3rd Battalion, Royal Irish Regiment.

△ **23 AUG**
Irish newspapers report that former US President **Theodore Roosevelt** is strongly urging America to join the fight against Germany.

1 SEP
Exhibits at the National Museum of Ireland are damaged after a wall collapses at its building on Kildare Street, Dublin.

4 SEP
An inquest into the death of Lieutenant Ewen Henry Cameron (33), on a train in Co. Wicklow hears that the young man had taken his own life. Cameron, the son of the well-known doctor Sir Charles Cameron, locked himself into a toilet compartment and shot himself. He was an officer in the 7th Battalion of the Royal Dublin Fusiliers.

Mr Lloyd George also said that the Irish role may not necessarily be turning out shells: 'So far as I am able to see from the reports I have had up to the present, there are parts of Ireland which would be very useful in turning out fuses or some other component parts of the shells, although they could not turn out the whole of them.'

Hyde Resigns from Gaelic League

30 July – Douglas Hyde has resigned as president of the Gaelic League. The shock resignation was announced at the Gaelic League's Ard-Fheis in Dundalk, Co. Louth, yesterday.

A letter from Dr Hyde said that he could not allow his name to be entered into the presidential election due to ill health and the amount of work the position required.

Dr Hyde noted that when he looked back on the work that had been done over the last 40 years, it almost looked to him a miracle. He said that he had done his best for the organisation and that it was a cause of great sorrow to him that he had decided against remaining as president.

Dr Hyde said that he left his best wishes to the delegates and that his heart would remain in the work as much as it was on the first day, and that he would continue to support the cause of the Gaelic League.

The sense that the Gaelic League is becoming increasingly politicised was confirmed with the election to its Coisde Gnótha (governing body) of John McDermott and John Hegarty. Mr McDermott is a well-known figure in advanced nationalist circles who is currently in prison as a result of charges brought under the Defence of the Realm Act, while Mr Hegarty was recently in court charged with the possession of guns and explosives in Enniscorthy, Co. Wexford.

Dr Hyde had previously spoken out against this apparent politicisation of the Gaelic League and it is believed that this was a contributory factor in his decision to step down as president.

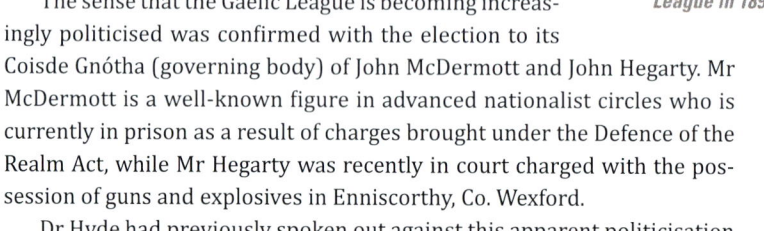

Dr Douglas Hyde, who wrote under the pen name An Craoibhín Aoibhinn, co-founded the Gaelic League in 1893.

O'Donovan Rossa Funeral Takes Place

Dublin, 1 August – Patrick Pearse, the schoolteacher and Irish-language activist, delivered a stirring oration at the graveside of the late Jeremiah O'Donovan Rossa at Glasnevin cemetery.

In the course of his speech, Mr Pearse paid homage to O'Donovan Rossa's unrepentant Fenianism and to Ireland's 'dead generations' of men who fought for freedom. He laid out a vision of Ireland as 'not free merely, but Gaelic as well; not Gaelic merely, but free as well'.

Mr Pearse claimed, 'The seeds sown by the young men of '65 and '67 are coming to their miraculous ripening today.'

He concluded, 'They think that they have pacified Ireland. They think that they have purchased half of us and intimidated the other half. They think that they have foreseen everything, think that they have provided against everything; but the fools, the fools, the fools! They have left us our Fenian dead, and, while Ireland holds these graves, Ireland unfree shall never be at peace.'

The funeral of O'Donovan Rossa will be remembered as one of the most striking nationalist demonstrations ever witnessed in Dublin. Special trains brought thousands of people from all parts of Ireland, while people also travelled from England and the United States. The remains of the Fenian leader had previously lain in state at City Hall for several days.

Patrick Pearse delivering his stirring oration at the graveside of O'Donovan Rossa.

Soldier's Wives a Drunken Menace in Dublin?

Dublin, 29 August – Claims that the wives of soldiers and sailors serving in the war are repeatedly drunk have been vigorously contested in Dublin.

Since the beginning of the war it has become commonplace to assert that female dependents have used the separation allowance they are being paid to indulge their desire for drink. It is regularly assumed – usually without enquiry – that every woman seen drunk on the streets or leaving a public house is the wife of a soldier or a sailor.

1915

6 SEP △
Bulgaria joins the Central Powers after signing an alliance treaty with Germany. It enters the war the following month.

9 SEP
David Lloyd George, the British Minister of Munitions, tells a Trade Union Congress in Bristol that Britain will lose the war without the co-operation of the trade unions.

3 OCT
The Irish Times reports on the 'methodical massacre' of Armenians by Turkish forces. The previous week the same newspaper published claims that at least 450,000 Armenians had already been killed, with a further 600,000 rendered homeless or exiled.

1915

12 OCT
Edith Cavell, a British nurse working in German-occupied Belgium, is shot by firing squad after being found guilty of assisting Belgian, British and French soldiers to evade German capture.

15 OCT
A conference on recruitment at the vice-regal lodge in the Phoenix Park decides that a new Department of Recruiting in Ireland is to be established. Lord Wimborne, the Irish Lord Lieutenant, will act as director.

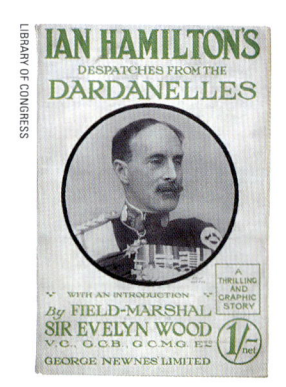

△ **16 OCT**
Sir Ian Hamilton is removed as commander of the Dardanelles Expeditionary Force in charge of the Gallipoli campaign. His replacement, Sir Charles Carmichael Monro, immediately recommends the evacuation of the British troops from the peninsula.

'The Demon Drink' as illustrated in Punch

THE ENEMY'S ALLY.

There are almost 50,000 women in Dublin in receipt of separation allowances, and the number of such women who are charged with drunkenness does not exceed a half-dozen per week.

It is certainly the case that there are many drunken women in Dublin, but an investigation has revealed that there has been little increase in this tendency since the beginning of the war. It is conceded, however, that the women who drank freely before the war are now indulging more heavily than ever.

Similarly, the Society for the Prevention of Cruelty to Children has reported no increase in the number of women reported for neglect of their children.

Successful Year for Irish Tourism

October – The Irish Tourist Organisation Society has hailed the success of tourism across the island over the past year.

The society was set up early in 1915 with the ambition of promoting tourism in Ireland by helping local tourism centres advertise the attractions of their districts.

A public subscription was undertaken and a sum of more than £200 collected. This sum has been used to stimulate interest in various parts of Ireland, often by means of getting newspapers to highlight the beauties of an area. To this end, some 254 newspaper columns – often accompanied by photographs – appeared in the Irish press over the last six months, extolling tourist resorts in Ireland.

This campaign has been at least partly responsible for the increase in tourist traffic, according to the society.

Evidence to support this claim comes from all across the island. W.J. Cunningham, the town clerk of Portrush in Co. Antrim, said his town 'had been visited by very many from Dublin and the south on account of advertisements inserted by the Council in the Dublin and Cork papers and the work of the Society'.

The town clerk of Kingstown, J. Sherlock Vaughan, agreed, saying, 'I made inquiries from the principal hotels and boarding houses in Kingstown, and am informed the season so far has been exceptionally good; in fact, in some of the establishments it is the best season they have had for years.'

Similar reports of successful seasons have come from Kilkee in Co. Clare and Youghal in Co. Cork.

Cork Man Writes Home from Gallipoli

8 October – Captain A.J.D. Preston of the 6th Battalion, Royal Dublin Fusiliers wrote a letter to his father in Co. Meath on the morning of 15 August 1915. That afternoon, Captain Preston was killed in action.

In his final letter, Captain Preston wrote of the action that he had seen at Suvla Bay, of the fierce fighting that raged all around, and of the men who lost their lives. He wrote of their landing on the shore at 4.30 a.m., with gunshots all around, and of marching two miles along the coast under heavy fire to get behind some cliffs.

They rested on their first evening near a hillock, which had been the scene of a heavy fight that morning. They spent some time burying the bodies of about 100 Turks and a good number of their own side.

The following day there was a ferocious battle:

'During the day we lost twelve officers, and we believe six of these to have been killed, including the second in command, and some 350 men. As I was marching back a bullet struck the ground not an inch in front of my toe.

'The snipers are extraordinary; they sit in the trees, and you never know where the bullets are coming from … Our doctor was dressing wounded under a tree when the man got hit from overhead. They found two snipers in the next tree: they didn't take them prisoners!'

Captain Preston's battalion was part of the 10th (Irish) Division which landed during the second major offensive on Gallipoli in August 1915.

1915

19 OCT
The resignation of Sir Edward Carson from the British Cabinet is made public. Carson later explains that his decision was 'actuated by no personal or party motives' and that he had always acted 'in the interest of my country'.

23 OCT △
Cricketer **W.G. Grace**, 67, dies of a cerebral haemorrhage at home in England. He is described as 'the greatest and most attractive figure that ever appeared on the cricket field'.

24 OCT
The All-Ireland hurling final is played at Croke Park, with Leix (Laois) defeating Cork to win their first-ever title. The final scoreline is 6–2 to 4–1.

1915

1 NOV
Mary Hayden, Professor of Modern Irish History in UCD, co-founds, along with Mary Louise Gwynn, the Irish Catholic Women's Suffrage Society.

2 NOV
A Corkman is prosecuted for exhibiting and distributing indecent photographs on Patrick Street in the city.

4 NOV
Angelo di Lucia, a 30-year-old Italian who ran an ice-cream business in Sligo, is sentenced to death for killing his wife in December 1914. Also convicted is Jane Reynolds, a young woman who worked as a servant in the di Lucia household. The death sentences are later commuted to penal servitude for life.

13 NOV
The Pavilion in Kingstown, a distinctive large wooden structure built in 1902 to accommodate 3,000 people, is destroyed by fire.

29 NOV
A report prepared by the Chief Inspector of Irish Industrial Schools and Reformatories states that the children committed are in a 'poor and badly nourished condition' and many are victims of neglect.

Leix are All-Ireland Hurling Champions

25 October – Leix have won the All-Ireland hurling championship for the first time, defeating Cork, who were strong favourites.

Leix were beaten by Clare in the 1914 final and their success on this occasion was a tribute to the manner in which they trained for the game – and indeed for the entire championship.

All yesterday morning it had threatened rain, and that rain duly arrived before the game started – and it fell in torrents. Leix were better prepared for the rain than Cork and appeared on the field wearing their overcoats. On top of that, the Leix team brought resin to put on their hurleys to improve the grip; Cork did not do this.

History makers – in dreadfully wet conditions, Leix (Laois) overcame a slow start against pre-game favourites Cork to capture the Leinster county's first All-Ireland title.

At the appointed time, the referee, William Walsh (who 'controlled the game in a masterful way, giving satisfaction to all') called in the two captains and spun the hurley. The Cork captain, Sheehan, correctly chose on which side the hurley would fall and directed that his team would defend the city end of the pitch.

Walsh threw in the ball to start the match at 2.54 p.m. and Cork started as if to justify their position as favourites, scoring three early goals. Leix settled midway through the half, however, and scored two goals of their own, as well as two points. They trailed by just one point at the interval.

The match was won in the early minutes of the second half. As the rain worsened to a downpour, Leix scored three quick goals and, despite a late rally by Cork, when the final whistle was blown the score stood at Leix 6–2 (20 points), Cork 4–1 (13 points).

One observer of the game noted that he was 'lost in admiration at one of the most magnificent battles that had ever been played in the final … Every stroke of the hurley was like an electric shock, while the ball shot here and there and everywhere with lightning-like speed.'

Major Storm Hits Ireland

Dublin, 13 November – A storm of almost unprecedented severity swept Ireland yesterday.

For 24 hours howling gales from the northeast drove rain in torrents, causing flooding and widespread damage to property. Across the country, miles of telegraph poles were blown down.

Houses had walls blown in and roofs blown off. Roads were flooded as rivers overflowed their banks, the sea pushed past sea walls, and drains were unable to cope with the scale of rainfall. Boats were smashed from their moorings and lost to the sea.

Memories of storms past: an uprooted tree near Kells, Co. Meath, following a storm c.1900.

In several places – including Nenagh, Co. Tipperary – the heavy rain was followed by a snowstorm. Two men in the county were found dead by the side of the road, and a similar tragedy was witnessed in Wexford.

In Dublin, more than two and a half inches of rain fell before 9 p.m. and the velocity of the wind reached 60 miles per hour. Trams and railways ceased running and, at the height of the storm, even walking across O'Connell Bridge proved impossible. Suburbs from Drumcondra to Ballsbridge were flooded as rivers burst their banks, leaving many houses under water.

Kingstown was left in darkness when the gasworks was flooded. There were similar scenes in Cork, where almost all electric and gas lights were extinguished.

Calmer conditions followed the storm, but fears of flooding remain and warnings have been issued for all parts of the country, with people being advised to take extreme care.

1915

6 DEC
After mounting criticism of his military strategy, Field Marshal Sir John French resigns as commander-in-chief of the British Expeditionary Force in France and Flanders. He is replaced by Sir Douglas Haig.

7 DEC
Woodrow Wilson makes his State of the Union address and defends America's policy of neutrality. 'We have stood apart, studiously neutral. It was our manifest duty to do so.'

10 DEC △
The Irish Times hails **Francis Ledwidge** as a 'new voice in poetry in Ireland' and a 'minute observer, a very mirror of nature'. Meath-born Ledwidge enlisted with the Royal Inniskilling Fusiliers in October 1914 and was involved in the Gallipoli campaign during 1915.

14 DEC
Patrick Pearse and Prof. Eoin MacNeill address a large anti-conscription rally in Dublin's Mansion House.

Remembering 1915
a hundred years on

Anu stage *Pals: The Irish at Gallipoli* at Collins Barracks. The play told the story of a group of young Irishmen who volunteered to fight in the war and found themselves in April 1915 trying to stay alive as part of the force that launched an assault on the beaches of Gallipoli. The play was site specific – Collins Barracks, formerly the Royal Barracks, was the place from where the 7th Battalion of the Royal Dublin Fusiliers had departed for Gallipoli in 1915. D Company of the 7th Battalion, the Pals in the play's title, was made up of rugby players from the IRFU who had volunteered for the army together.

3 February–30 April 2015

REVOLUTIONARY TIMES 1913–23

Life During Wartime
–The Irish Home Front

WRITING IN THE *Irish Citizen* on 7 August 1915, Hanna Sheehy Skeffington observed that 'women are coming into their own in a good many ways: war and its exigencies have helped destroy many cherished male prejudices about them'. The war transformed the roles that women played in Irish society and would, in part, lead to the introduction of limited women's suffrage in 1918. The changes on the home front were many and varied, but from the outbreak of war the transformed situation was immediately noted.

On the day that the German Empire declared war on Russia in August 1914, Emily Wynne, a fabric designer living in Glendalough, Co. Wicklow, began a home-front diary. Four days later, on 5 August, with Britain now having entered the conflict, she wrote: 'Willie Eager returning from work in Arklow reports great excitement over two Germans captured there (probably completely innocent individuals!) and that two war ships were guarding Kynoch [munitions factory]. Johnson [a local shopkeeper] said he would have to shut up tomorrow or the day after, being completely sold out and prices in Arklow said to be enormous. A sack of 2lbs of flour ordered by us on Saturday said to cost 6s/7d now is charged 9s/4d.'

'Willie Eager returning from work in Arklow reports great excitement over two Germans captured there …'

Wynne captured the feeling of exhilaration and fear in the first days of the war, as well as the instant wartime pressures that arose in the form of sharp price rises and anxieties around food scarcity. The sense of upheaval and of a people entering the unknown was palpable. None of this was particular to Ireland, of course. Rather, in common with neighbouring Britain, historian Catriona Pennell has observed how the 'immediate impact of the outbreak of the war was characterized by disruption and dislocation'. This was evident everywhere, most obviously in the rapid mobilisation of Irish-garrisoned British troops – between 30,000 and 40,000 of them in 1914 – who filled the trains in garrison towns and caused congestion around the major ports of exit. Throughout that hectic first week of war, an employee at the Dublin Port and Docks Board power station recalled working almost continuously as troops started arriving from all parts of the country – by train, on horse and on foot.

(LEFT) **A 1915 recruitment poster produced in Dublin to appeal to a young man's sense of camaraderie and adventure. It features a large number of soldiers smiling and raising their caps in a welcome to potential new recruits. Naive messaging such as this disappeared as word of the reality of war filtered home from the front.**

(BELOW) **Campaigns to tempt farmers away from the land had very little success, due in part to a wartime spike in the cost of agricultural produce.**

One of those departing soldiers was Walter Denny, who told of Dubliners singing and cheering the troops on the quayside and presenting them with parting gifts of buns, cigarettes and chocolates. However, this was not a universal Irish reaction, and for those not part of the initial military exodus the onset of war signalled the beginning of a new domestic reality. On 7 August 1914 the Westminster Parliament passed the Defence of the Realm Act, under which a raft of government regulations were introduced to limit the lives of those who saw out the war not on a battlefield but at home. The powers accorded to the British state were draconian: in order to secure the 'public safety and defence of the realm', the government deployed these DORA regulations (which were updated on several occasions) to do everything from restricting pub opening hours to curbing freedom of expression in the form of press censorship. In

Once a man was confirmed dead, his next of kin were informed of the terrible news. The families of officers were notified by telegram but for the families of enlisted men the news arrived more slowly, via a copy of Army Form B 104–82 sent in the post. This example was sent from the Infantry Records Office, Cork, to Mrs A. Green, informing her of the death of her son Harold Green, Royal Irish Regiment, from wounds received in action on 22 August 1918.

December 1914, for instance, the DORA was used to suppress a series of Irish newspaper titles – *The Irish Worker, Sinn Féin, Irish Freedom* and *Éire-Ireland* – that were deemed seditious and damaging to the British military recruitment drive. Copies of offending titles were stripped from newspaper shelves, and in some cases printers were raided and their machinery dismantled. If the purpose of these actions was to silence the more radical Irish voices, their success was short-lived. No sooner were certain newspapers quashed than others sprang up in their place. Throughout 1915 a new 'mosquito' press emerged to rail against recruitment and pre-emptively challenge any threat that conscription might be introduced to Ireland. These small newspapers also criticised John Redmond's IPP and the mainstream press, whose 'diseased imagination', James Connolly charged in December 1915, had 'lured thousands of Irishmen to their destruction'.

While Ireland was not a setting for any First World War fighting, the destructive realities to which Connolly referred were evident to all in the broken figures of the injured and disabled soldiers who were visible in most Irish towns, their presence a chilling reminder to families with enlisted sons and brothers of the perils associated with serving at the front. So too were the lengthy lists of the dead published in newspapers and the steady flow of letters – telegrams in the case of officers – that the War Office sent to inform families of the deaths of their loved ones. These were not the only fatalities of the war, of course. To those killed fighting abroad could be added those killed in Irish waters after Germany launched a submarine campaign against Allied shipping. Irish ports

Posters such as this, a common sight throughout the country, played a major role in the recruitment drive by using plain language to provide detailed information on soldiers' pay and the benefits of the separation allowances scheme.

such as Queenstown were vital in fighting against the threat of German U-boats, and from 1917 the ships of the Royal Navy were joined by those of the US Navy after the United States entered the war. This influx created quite the stir. 'Our men had much more money than the native Irish boys, and could entertain the girls more lavishly at the movies and ice cream stands,' the US naval commander, William S. Sims, later recalled. 'The men of our fleet and the Irish girls became excellent friends: the association, from our point of view, was a very wholesome one …' From the church pulpits of Cork and elsewhere, the view was somewhat different, and a measure of moral panic was apparent in the concerns publicly expressed over interactions between the American visitors and local women, who, at one point, were reminded by a special conference of Cork priests of their duty to uphold the 'fair fame of Irish womanhood for purity'.

Across many combatant countries, birth rates fell during the First World War. The Irish experience conformed to this trend, though the rate of decline – 11% – was less than that in England, Scotland and Wales, and significantly less than that in Belgium, France or Germany. In Ireland's case the marriage rate was largely unaffected, but the removal of 200,000 servicemen for the war period would have had the effect of restricting the opportunity for the necessary marital relations. The wives of those servicemen deployed overseas were given a separation allowance by the War Office as a means of welfare support – 12s 6d per week for the wife of a private or corporal, topped up with 5s extra for each child. The impact on many working-class families in urban areas, whose men had previously been labourers or unemployed, was considerable: in some cases it resulted in an actual increase in household income and afforded women a greater degree of control over their domestic sphere.

Nevertheless, the separation allowance came with no end of controversy, as newspapers readily reported on incidences of working-class women spending their money on alcohol and being arrested for drunken behaviour. Class and gender prejudices informed this coverage, and the extent of female drunkenness was undoubtedly exaggerated, yet it still had the effect of fuelling demands from the Catholic Church and other sources for restrictions to be placed on the sale of alcohol amidst concerns about, among other things, child welfare and women's sexual behaviour. More broadly, as Fionnuala Walsh has written, the experience of separation women in Ireland was illustrative of a 'social morality' that home-front communities helped forge during the war, where 'the surveillance of state and society confined women to narrowly defined codes of behaviour. Private behaviour became a matter of public concern.'

In the wake of the Easter Rising in 1916, however, it was the public rather than the private behaviour of the separation women that attracted comment. Numerous witness statements delivered to the Bureau of Military History recall the verbal abuse and jeering that was directed at rebels in the wake of the Rising by 'separation women' outraged at the participants' disloyalty during a time of war and fretful that the disruption might threaten the payment of their allowances. To an extent, the women's reaction underscored a critical economic fact – that the First World War was, as Padraig Yeates has noted, generally 'good for Dublin. Living standards rose and mortality rates fell as money flowed into the tenements in separation payments to soldiers' wives.'

Beyond the tenements, middle-class Irish women assumed a vast array of voluntary roles, busying themselves with everything from charitable fund-raising to assisting refugees (3,000 fleeing Belgians arrived in Ireland in the autumn of 1914), and gathering and dispatching food, clothing and other items to Irish servicemen on the front lines. Women also volunteered in large

Poster outlining that the way a housewife dealt with rising food prices and widespread shortages mattered not just to her own family but to the war effort as a whole.

numbers for nursing duties, a remarkable 5,688 of them signing up with the joint committee of the Red Cross and St John's Ambulance Association.

The National Shell Factory at Parkgate Street, Dublin, was the first and largest state-built munitions plant in Ireland with others opening in Cork, Limerick, Galway and Waterford during the course of the war. It was staffed in the main by women who, despite a low basic wage, were able to earn up to 60 shillings a week, which was more than most male manual workers earned.

In the workplace, as in the charitable sphere, the war created opportunities for women, however temporary, that would not otherwise have existed. For instance, munitions factories, such as Mackie's in Belfast or Kynoch's in Wicklow, employed hundreds of women, while, by 1918, 1,426 of the 2,148 employees of the five state-run shell factories were also women. The bulk of new economic openings, nevertheless, fell to men who, in the absence of conscription and the outlet of emigration, were still in sufficient supply to fill the majority of employment gaps left by enlisted servicemen.

The one sector of the economy where few gaps opened up was also the largest. More than half of all occupied males on the eve of the war were involved in agriculture, and recruiters repeatedly remarked upon the reluctance of Irish farmers and farm labourers to enlist. The family nature of farming had much to do with this, as did the wartime boom, which meant there was ample work available as an alternative to joining up. As international competition reduced and demand soared, 'agricultural production flourished', historian David Fitzpatrick observed, 'to a degree unknown since the Napoleonic wars'. The prices commanded for livestock and crops rose sharply, and there was a rapid increase, as a result of compulsory regulations, in the amount of land devoted to tillage. For all that, concerns over food supplies were constant, and complaints were routinely aired about profiteering retailers and milk and food producers. Fuel was also hard to come by, the problem of supply compounded by Ireland's reliance on imports. With merchant shipping engaged in the war effort and prone to German attack, stocks of coal often fell low, forcing the authorities to cut back on the central power supply, as a consequence of which shops and businesses often had to close early.

Theatres and music halls played an important role in boosting the morale of the general public. A variety of stars, such as the ever popular singer/songwriter Percy French, maintained a gruelling and exhausting performance schedule throughout the war years. Horseracing also thrived.

Amidst all this hardship, Irish people continued to seek out opportunities for fun and distraction, for recreation and entertainment. But where would they find it? For many social and cultural bodies, the war forced a consideration as to whether it was possible, or even appropriate, to continue their activities. In sport, both rugby and soccer authorities decided to suspend their top-flight fixtures for the duration of the war. The GAA, in contrast, did not. Horse racing, apart from a government-enforced break during 1917, also continued and, even though not all racetracks remained operational, attendances and gate receipts were remarkably healthy at those that did. At Baldoyle, for instance, the average daily attendance at race meetings by 1918 stood at 6,960, a significant jump from its 1914 daily average of 3,577. The cinema, a new attraction at the start of the war, was also highly popular, with people attending to see newsreels showing footage from the front or to entertain themselves with the latest cinematic offering. Music halls and theatres continued as popular recreational outlets, and major days of celebration, such as Christmas Day or St Patrick's Day, while more muted than in peacetime, were still celebrated.

In keeping with the political landscape of the country, the Irish home-front experience was transformed by the events of Easter 1916. While there was no disruption to the separation payments or higher rates of employment and income – these continued through to the Armistice of 1918 – the Rising did usher in significant changes. For those living in Dublin, the physical destruction of the central shopping and business district reshaped their urban space, and the ongoing war meant that reconstruction was slower than it might otherwise have been. Widespread arrests and imprisonments in the months following the Rising also meant that many families lost their breadwinner, without the compensatory cushion of a separation allowance. In practical terms, the immediate application of martial law, first in Dublin and later across the whole country, meant that no one was allowed to be outside their home between 8.30 p.m. and 5 a.m. Trams in Dublin stopped running from 7 p.m., and all theatres and places of entertainment were compelled to close at 8 p.m. All pubs were shut too, and while off-licences were allowed to remain open, they could only sell groceries. Censorship of postal services was also introduced, and a more conspicuous and intrusive military presence, particularly in the capital, took hold. In the short-term, therefore, the effect of the British response to the Rising was to limit the day-to-day lives of many Irish people. In the long-term, however, the effect was even more dramatic and ensured that demobilised soldiers returned to a very different country to the one from which many of them had departed at the outset of the war. The Ireland to which they returned not only had to grapple with the multiple legacies of the First World War but would soon become a theatre of war itself.

'The slaughter was dreadful … The water was red with blood'
–The Irish at Gallipoli, 1915

MAJOR GUY NIGHTINGALE was a professional soldier and had served in India and Burma before 1914. He arrived in Gallipoli on the first day of the land campaign, 25 April 1915, with the 1st Battalion, Royal Munster Fusiliers. His battalion was among the first to land on Turkish soil, having disembarked, under fire, from the SS *River Clyde*. At the end of the first day of fighting he wrote a two-page letter to his mother, which informed her that 'the Dublins and ourselves have been formed into one regiment. We both left England 1000 strong, and now together we are 8 officers and 770 men! … It has certainly been a tough job. The heaps of dead are awful, and the beach where we landed was an extraordinary sight the morning they buried them.'

The high casualty rate suffered by the Allied forces on the first day of the Gallipoli landings was not part of the military plan. This was supposed to be a quick victory that would change the course of the First World War. The plan was hatched after it became clear to the Allies in late 1914 that there would be no speedy resolution in mainland Europe. The Western Front had become static, and a costly trench war had begun. So, in November 1914, Winston Churchill, then First Lord of the Admiralty, suggested that if a new front was opened up against the Ottoman Empire (which he considered the weakest of the enemy powers), the Germans would have no choice but to move troops east to assist their allies. This in turn would weaken the German forces on the Western Front and hopefully lead to an Allied victory. Churchill also believed that a decisive strike against Turkey would bring Bulgaria and Romania into the war on the Allied side.

Initially the Allied attack on the Dardanelles was meant to be a naval-only operation. On 18 March 1915 the Royal Navy mounted a major attack against

In April 1915 the 7th Battalion Royal Dublin Fusiliers left the Royal Barracks (now Collins Barracks) for Basingstoke in England. They would be ordered to Gallipoli on 27 June and arrive on the peninsula on 7 August. They fought at Chocolate Hill and Kizlar Dagh before being withdrawn at the end of September having suffered heavy casualties.

Turkish defensive positions around Gallipoli. The aim was straightforward: to remove Turkish strongholds where their artillery was stationed and, once this had been achieved, to allow the minesweepers to work unhindered in clearing the waters. However, the attack was a disaster. While some damage was done to the strongholds, four ships struck a major placement of mines and were either badly damaged or sunk. In all, nearly 700 naval personnel lost their lives that day.

After the failure of this naval offensive, and with criticism that the fleet assembled consisted of older ships that weren't fit for purpose, the naval campaign was called off. The British, nevertheless, believed that the objective of that campaign – taking Turkey out of the war – was still a very good idea. Lord Kitchener decided that ground forces would, instead, be used to take out the Turkish inland strongholds and artillery. Once that had been done, minesweepers could be safely employed and the Dardanelles taken.

General Sir Ian Hamilton was placed in charge of the land campaign. His forces, expected to be between 70,000 and 80,000 strong, would be made up of Australian and New Zealand troops (ANZACs), as well as some from Britain and France. With the ANZACs in basic training in Egypt, and the British and French troops elsewhere in Europe, it took time for Hamilton to gather his army.

'THE SLAUGHTER WAS DREADFUL … THE WATER WAS RED WITH BLOOD'

The time lag between the end of the naval campaign and the start of the land assault, originally planned for 23 April, gave the Turks time to strengthen their defensive positions.

The Turks were under the command of a German officer, Otto Liman von Sanders. An awareness of where the Allies were most likely to land on the peninsula and the best positions for defence were largely dictated by a young Turkish officer, Mustafa Kemal, who was familiar with the area having fought there during the earlier Balkan Wars. The Turks had some 60,000 troops ready on the Gallipoli peninsula awaiting the Allied arrival.

The Allied assault on Gallipoli began on the morning of 25 April, with troops landing on six beaches. The northern beaches were the focus of the Australian and New Zealand troops, and that zone became known as ANZAC cove, while the southern beaches, the focus of British and French forces, became the Helles zone. The landings were made by troops packed into rowing boats, or, as at V Beach where the Irish battalions were concentrated, from a grounded ship (the SS *River Clyde*), from which the troops ran ashore via ramps. While two of the landings were made with little Turkish opposition, the landings at V and W beaches and at ANZAC cove were met by intense Turkish fire. At V and W beaches, the Allied troops suffered casualty rates of 60% to 70% on the first day. Much of this was attributable to the hazardous topography the Allies were required to negotiate. Entry to the peninsula was described as a 'death-trap' by one Dublin Fusilier, who, though injured, lived to tell the tale. Hit by a bullet in his side as he clambered from a boat, Private L. O'Byrne would claim that of 100 men who entered the sea with him, only twenty reached the shore. 'The slaughter was dreadful,' he later recalled. 'The water was red with blood.'

The experience of Guy Geddes of the Munster Fusiliers was much the same. Landing at V Beach that same day, he wrote that evening in his diary of the terror that had subsequently unfolded: 'beached at 6.25 as Dublins came in line – ghastly machine-gun fire & rifles opened on them & they were slaughtered. [At] 6.45: Henderson & I disembarked. Men mowed down & drowned owing to packs & lighter breaking away. Had to swim for it, awful tide. 6.30 pm Poor Jarrett killed just after. Pollard killed – many wounded. Came back with wounded to *Clyde* at 8.30 pm, transferred to trawler. Disgraceful show – with horribly wounded men on board.'

> 'Every one of us knows of some Irish mother or wife bereaved, some Irish household darkened, as the price of landing at Suvla Bay.'

'THE SLAUGHTER WAS DREADFUL ... THE WATER WAS RED WITH BLOOD'

For the Allies, the first day of the campaign had been a disaster. While all the beaches had been secured, little progress inland had been made. With the Turkish forces occupying high ground above the beaches, their positions largely remained secure.

The next few months saw various Allied and Turkish attempts to gain the upper hand, but the campaign effectively stalled and the fighting came to resemble the static trench warfare of the Western Front. During the summer months, the hot conditions and the constant struggle to supply enough fresh drinking water to Allied troops meant that conditions at Gallipoli were awful. Large numbers of troops, on both sides, succumbed to a dysentery epidemic that spread across the peninsula in the late summer.

Turkish forces had dug in before the invasion of the peninsula by the allies in April 1915, with gun batteries placed on heights above the landing beaches. Of the 130,000 troops who would die during the Gallipoli campaign, the Turks suffered the highest losses, losing 86,692 men.

One major attempt to gain the upper hand was made on 6 August, with an assault on the Turks via a landing at Suvla Bay. The landing was successful, and fighting continued throughout August as the Allies attempted to progress inland. However, despite a massive build-up of troops, the August offensive ultimately failed and saw an appalling loss of life. These landings had included a group of Irishmen who were all rugby players from the Dublin area. They had enlisted together and formed D Company. Perceived to be socially superior to other units of the Royal Dublin Fusiliers, they were referred to as the 'toffs among the toughs'. In the seven weeks at Gallipoli these rugby 'pals' suffered a 70%t casualty rate, and only seventy-nine men remained alive when they departed the peninsula. Indeed, the overall catalogue of losses at Gallipoli cast a large shadow back home. As one newspaper editorialised in mid-September 1915: 'Every one of us knows of some Irish mother or wife bereaved, some Irish household darkened, as the price of landing at Suvla Bay.'

After the landings at Suvla Bay the Connaught Rangers were involved in the last major battle of the campaign, the attempt to take and control Hill 60. The strategy failed, and on the first day of the attacks the Rangers suffered 198 casualties. The fighting on Hill 60 and the loss of the Connaught men dominated the headlines in the Irish press during August 1915. Such was

'THE SLAUGHTER WAS DREADFUL … THE WATER WAS RED WITH BLOOD'

the impact of the struggle on the popular consciousness at home that a new terrace being built at Croke Park became known as Hill 60. The terrace would, in the 1920s, be renamed Hill 16, when the remembrance of dead patriots became favoured over those who had died in Gallipoli.

With stalemate in Gallipoli by the autumn of 1915, and little apparent sign of any potential victory, Allied commanders decided on a withdrawal. As it transpired, the evacuation would be the single most successful part of the whole campaign. Between early December and 9 January 1916, nearly 40,000 troops and tonnes of equipment were successfully taken off the peninsula.

In all, the Gallipoli campaign lasted just over eight months. As a military operation it was a complete failure for the Allies. For the Turks, however, Gallipoli stood out as a great victory, and their hero of the campaign, Mustafa Kemal, would become the nation's president in 1923. In contrast, the campaign ended the military career of General Sir Ian Hamilton and led to the demotion of Winston Churchill from the position of First Lord of the Admiralty. More generally, as the historian Gary Sheffield has written, the experience of soldiers at Gallipoli was 'above all the fear of death and wounding, the strain of combat, and of course the awful sights and sounds produced by 20th-century industrialised warfare'. This was warfare of a kind that came at an estimated cost of 130,000 human lives, with approximately 4,000 Irish soldiers among them.

Unlike, for instance, in Australia, where the exploits of the ANZACs became a central part of the national narrative, the experiences of the Irish at Gallipoli have largely been forgotten, overshadowed by the political changes brought about by the 1916 Rising and the ensuing revolutionary struggle. But it wasn't simply this turn in Irish history that led to the absence of Gallipoli from the collective national memory. The Irish story at Gallipoli was also largely sidelined in the official British narrative. In January 1916, just three months before the Easter rebellion, and some months after he had been relieved of his responsibilities in Gallipoli, General Sir Ian Hamilton belatedly delivered his official dispatch of what had happened and why. The Irish newspapers had expected it to do 'tardy justice' to the contribution of Irish regiments, whose heroism, military qualities and sacrifice they believed had gone unacknowledged. By not doing so, or at least not doing so in emphatic enough fashion, the official dispatch served only to heap Irish grievance upon Irish loss. The failure to accord proper recognition to Irish soldiers was a folly too far and an insult too many. In her 1919 memoir, *The Years of the Shadow*, Irish writer Katharine Tynan, who had friends among the 10th Division who perished at Suvla, wrote: 'For the first time

East Mudros Military Cemetery, Greece, containing a small fraction of the graves of Allied soldiers killed in the Gallipoli campaign.

came bitterness, for we felt that their lives had been thrown away and that their heroism had gone unrecognised.'

For those lives that had not been 'thrown away', the mere fact of bearing witness to the bloodbath at Gallipoli had profound and devastating personal consequences. So traumatised, for example, was twenty-two-year-old Jasper Brett, a former Irish rugby international who had lost many friends fighting on the peninsula, that he committed suicide in February 1917, stepping in front of a train as it ran through a tunnel between Dalkey and Killiney. As for Major Guy Nightingale, who had written to his mother after the initial landing, his end was no less harrowing. Nightingale shot himself with his service revolver on 25 April 1935, the thirtieth anniversary of his arrival at Gallipoli, having suffered from alcoholism and depression, and having never come to terms with what he had witnessed there. Today, more than a century after the Gallipoli campaign concluded, its grim legacy remains etched in a landscape that still bears the marks of trenches and artillery bombardments. More obviously, however, its legacy is evident in the many memorials and the forty-four separate war cemeteries that span a peninsula where, owing to the character of the fighting and the complexity of recovering bodies, no known grave could be identified for the vast majority of soldiers killed – Irishmen among them.

WHO FEARS TO SPEAK OF EASTER WEEK?
1798 REBEL
1916 VOLUNTEER
General Post Office, DUBLIN
Liberty Hall DUBLIN
PADRAIC H. PEARSE
ROGER DAVID CASEMENT
JAMES CONNOLLY
POBLACHT NA H EIREANN
THE PROVISIONAL GOVERNMENT
IRISH REPUBLIC
TO THE PEOPLE OF IRELAND
FIANNA FÁIL
THE IRISH VOLUNTEERS
Who fears to speak of Easter week? who blushes at the
name? When cowards mock the patriot's fate, who hangs his head for shame? He's
all a knave, or half a slave, who slights his country thus. But a
true man, like you man, will fill your glass with us. He's
all a knave, or half a slave, who slights his country thus. But a
true man, like you man, will fill your glass with us.
Some on the shores of distant lands
Their weary hearts have laid,
And by the stranger's heedless hands
Their lonely graves were made;
But, though their clay be far away
Beyond the Atlantic foam—
In true men, like you, men,
Their spirit's still at home.
The dust of some is Irish earth;
Among their own they rest;
And the same land that gave them birth
Has caught them to her breast.
And we will pray that from their clay
Full many a race may start
Of true men, like you, men,
To act as brave a part.
They rose in dark and evil days
To right their native land;
They kindled here a living blaze
That nothing shall withstand.
Alas! that Might can vanquish Right—
They fell and passed away;
But true men, like you, men,
Are plenty here today.
THOMAS MACDONAGH
MICHAEL O'HANRAHAN
F. SHEEHY-SKEFFINGTON
JOSEPH M. PLUNKETT
J. J. HEUSTON
THE O'RAHILLY
SEAN McDERMOTT
THOMAS J. CLARKE
JOHN MACBRIDE
EDMOND KENT
CORNELIUS COLBERT
EDWARD DALY
COUNTESS DE MARKIEWICZ
St Stephen's Green, DUBLIN
Four Courts DUBLIN
THE IRISH REBELLION OF 1916 AND ITS MARTYRS
ERIN'S TRAGIC EASTER
© The Devin-Adair Company
F. Frigney

1916

'Irish men and Irish women: in the name of God and of the dead generations from which she receives her old tradition of nationhood, Ireland, through us, summons her children to her flag and strikes for her freedom.'

Patrick Pearse reading from the Proclamation of the Irish Republic
24 APRIL

1916

▽ **1 JAN**
The 1st Battalion, **Royal Dublin Fusiliers**, is evacuated from Gallipoli eight months after it first landed. Of the original 1,012 men who had landed on V Beach in April 1915 only 11 remained to take part in the retreat.

10 JAN
All remaining Allied forces are evacuated from Gallipoli. In all 83,000 men were evacuated after the decision to abandon Gallipoli was made in November 1915.

13 JAN
It is reported that a proposal by a Cork cinema owner that they be allowed to open for public screenings on Sundays was turned down by the city council.

14 JAN
The Lord Lieutenant's 'Report on Recruiting in Ireland' is published. It concludes that by the end of October 1915, 126,339 Irishmen had enlisted.

Unionists Condemn Exclusion of Ireland from Conscription

Westminster, 5 January – The decision by the British Cabinet to exclude Ireland from compulsory military service that is to be applied across Britain has been bitterly condemned by unionists.

A meeting of unionist MPs in the House of Commons was chaired by Sir Edward Carson and passed a motion saying that the exclusion of Ireland was 'an insult and humiliation to the loyal and patriotic population of the country, and an abandonment of the principle of equality of sacrifice in time of war on the part of His Majesty's subjects in the United Kingdom'.

The Executive Committee of the Irish Unionist Alliance had earlier unanimously adopted a motion claiming that any decision to exclude Ireland from conscription would be 'a national disgrace'.

The Irish Unionist Alliance went on to say that there should be no differentiation between Ireland and any other part of the United Kingdom in this matter.

Initial drafts of the Military Service Bill had included Ireland but were met with extensive lobbying by the Irish Parliamentary Party, which has repeatedly confirmed its absolute rejection of conscription.

Ultimately, the arguments of Mr Redmond and his colleagues swayed the government to exclude Ireland from the Bill.

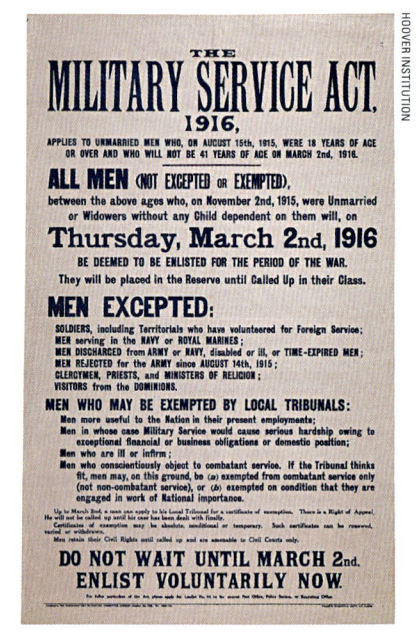

Poster explaining the Military Service Act 1916, which saw the introduction of conscription in Britain.

Exhibition of Irish Toys in Dublin

Dublin, 12 January – An exhibition of Irish toys opened this week in Dublin at St Stephen's Green.

The aim of the exhibition is to demonstrate the various toys that can be made in Ireland, which previously had to be imported from Germany and Austria. Exhibitors came from every province in Ireland.

Stuffed papier-mâché dolls were exhibited by the Sisters of Charity on

Lower Gardiner Street and on Seville Place, where a large number of girls were engaged in work before Christmas. They were unable to meet the demands for their products and are now going to try and organise on a more extensive scale.

The Irish Toy Industry Ltd, based in Belfast, exhibited a selection of Dometo interlocking blocks that are used in puzzles and in model-building. Another exhibitor from Dublin, T.F. Orr, showed working models of a steamer, a battleship, a railway engine and other mechanical toys.

As well as the exhibition, there were lectures on how the toy industry might be developed. Its potential as an employer of women was emphasised.

Redmond: Do Your Duty and Enlist in the British Army

Westminster, 19 February – John Redmond, leader of the Irish Parliamentary Party, has renewed his calls for Irishmen to join the British Army in a manifesto published today.

During this emotional appeal, he said, 'For the first time in history, we have today a huge Irish army in the field. Its achievements have covered Ireland with glory before the world and have thrilled our hearts with pride.

'You are under no compulsion save that of duty. In the name of honour, justice and religion, in the name of common gratitude, and in their own highest self-interest, I appeal to the young men of Ireland who are still available to form reserve battalions and to commence their training.'

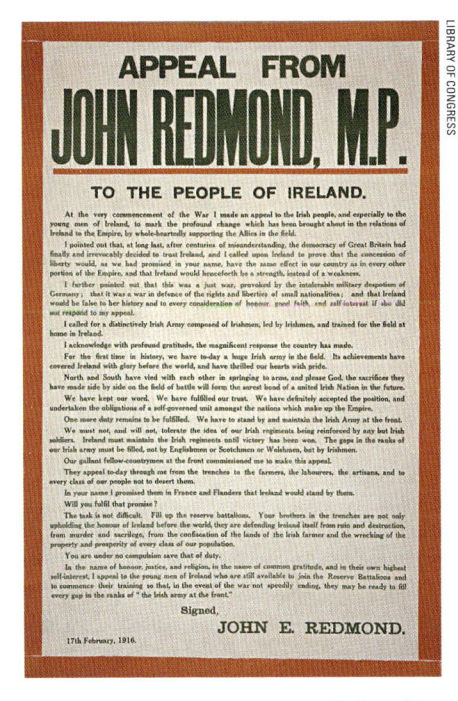

A poster containing the text of John Redmond's appeal to the Irish to join the British Army.

He challenged Irishmen 'to mark the profound change which has been brought about in the relations of Ireland to the Empire by wholeheartedly supporting the Allies in the field … After centuries of misunderstanding, the democracy of Britain had finally and irrevocably decided to trust Ireland.'

1916

15 JAN
The Irish Times supports John Redmond's demand for an investigation into the failed campaign by the Allied forces in Gallipoli. 'The parents and friends of the men of the Tenth Division have a right to know the truth', it editorialises.

27 JAN
Conscription is introduced to Britain by the Military Service Act. This applies to unmarried men aged 18–41 from 2 March and to married men in the same age bracket from April/May. The Act does not extend to Ireland.

3 FEB
Writing from France, Captain William Redmond, a brother of the IPP leader, describes the experience of war in a letter to the Bishop of Killaloe, Reverend Dr Fogarty: 'The shelling was terrific and the division suffered some losses. The day before we came out the enemy began to celebrate the Kaiser's birthday, and we were shelled without ceasing for 24 hours.'

9 FEB
It is reported that William Martin Murphy's Dublin United Tramways Company, which had been at the heart of the lockout dispute in 1913, increased its profits, in its most successful trading year ever, by £124,516.

1916

Flag flown from the Princes Street corner of the GPO from Easter Monday until after the surrender, when it was taken as a regimental trophy by the Royal Irish Regiment.

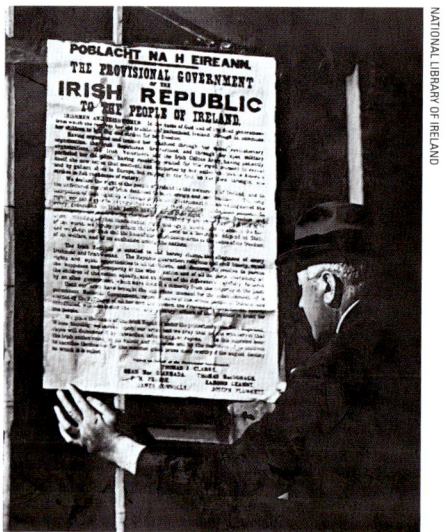

Dr Edmund J. McWeeney inspecting the Proclamation of the Irish Republic on the railings of St Stephen's Green in Dublin city on Easter Monday.

10 FEB
A major recruitment meeting, the first since the announcement of conscription, at Dublin's Mansion House is addressed by John Redmond and Lord Wimborne.

14 FEB
John Redmond is re-elected chairman of the IPP at a meeting in Dublin.

28 FEB
Addressing noon Mass in Cork Cathedral, Fr Matthew appeals to the people of the city to 'support women who traffic in vice and trade in sin'. Fr Matthew says that 100 such women were currently receiving mercy in the Magdalen Asylum run by the Sisters of Charity: 'these poor things … have been received to penitence'.

Fighting in Dublin as Irish Republic is Proclaimed!

Dublin, 24 April – Since early morning members of the Irish Volunteers and the Irish Citizen Army have been moving around Dublin and taking control of key city centre buildings.

At the General Post Office, where these rebels are headquartered, Patrick Pearse emerged at the front of the building at 12.45 p.m. and read the Proclamation of the Republic. This document has been distributed about the city and copies pasted onto walls. The Proclamation is an assertion of the Irish Republic as a sovereign, independent state. Two Irish flags have also been hoisted above the GPO.

Rebels have taken up positions in St Stephen's Green, and during the late morning and into the afternoon entered the South Dublin Union, Jacob's Biscuit Factory, Boland's Mills and the Mendicity Institution.

There has been violence during the day, and the rebels appear to be armed. Reports are emerging that a policeman was shot near City Hall, another near St Stephen's Green, that a man was killed outside the Shelbourne Hotel, and a youth was seriously wounded at the Magazine Fort in Phoenix Park.

Fighting between the rebels and British forces has been fierce at times, particularly around City Hall and the South Dublin Union. It is reported that British forces are moving into the city, and that more troops have been called on to move into Dublin from the Curragh.

As darkness falls the picture is still very confused and fast-moving. It is unclear what the rebels hope to achieve, or how swift and sustained the military response will be. There are reports that looting has begun in some parts of the shopping districts of the city and that fires are breaking out in some buildings in the Sackville Street area.

Martial Law for Dublin

Dublin, 26 April – A proclamation was announced yesterday by British authorities that places the city and county of Dublin under martial law. The proclamation was issued by Lord Wimborne, the Lord Lieutenant and General Governor of Ireland.

The proclamation states that 'all persons found carrying arms without lawful authority are liable to be dealt with'. It also states that the martial law decree will last for one month from the date of the proclamation, despite the press and military assuming the unrest will not last very long. It warns peaceable subjects to avoid dangerous areas or anywhere in vicinity of the military, and to stay within their homes as much as possible.

Further martial law restrictions were released today. These include a curfew from 7.30 p.m. to last until 5.30 a.m., restricting all people from leaving their houses unless under written permission of the military, and reaffirming that all persons seen carrying arms outside of the police or military are liable to be fired upon. These clarifications of the restrictions came from the Irish Command Headquarters, signed by Major General L.B. Friend.

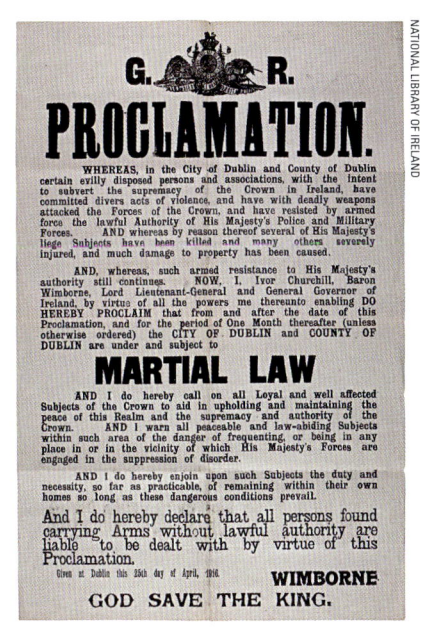

Poster issued on 25 April announcing that the Lord Lieutenant-General had introduced Martial Law throughout Dublin city and county for one month.

1916

29 FEB
The Derry Feis opens in the city and will run for a week. The Feis had been co-founded by Ambrose Ricardo, whose love of music inspired him to launch the annual contest.

7 MAR
Mark McDonagh is imprisoned for leading an Irish Volunteers march through an army recruitment meeting in Co. Galway.

9 MAR
At 6 p.m., Germany declares war on Portugal, which enters the nation onto the side of the Allies.

10 MAR
German offensive attacks continue in Verdun but are repulsed by the French. This ends the second phase of the battle of Verdun.

20 MAR
A crowd attacks Sinn Féin's Tullamore headquarters, and in the disturbance three police are injured.

22 MAR
A large fire on Nelson Street in Belfast causes thousands of pounds in damage and leaves four women missing and 12 hospitalised.

1916

24 MAR
Sinn Féin organiser Ernest Blythe is arrested for violating the DORA. Liam Mellows, organiser of the Irish Volunteers, is arrested in Co. Galway.

24 MAR
As Aintree has been requisitioned by the military, the Grand National cannot be run there. Instead, a substitute race, known as the Racecourse Association Steeple Chase, is held at Gatwick racecourse. Vermouth, ridden by Jack Reardon, was the winner, with a starting price of 100/8.

28 MAR
Ernest Blythe and Liam Mellows are ordered to be deported to England. Thirteen Sinn Féin volunteers are remanded for shooting at officials 'with intent to kill' at the incident in Tullamore on 20 March.

30 MAR
A protest is held, led by Irish Volunteers' Chief of Staff Eoin MacNeill, against the deportation of Volunteers from Ireland.

1 APR
Linfield win soccer's Irish Cup, beating Glentoran in a replay at Grosvenor Park in Belfast.

After a Week, the Rebellion Ends

Dublin, 1 May – Much of central Dublin lies in ruins after a week when gun- and shell-fire rang out over the city, and a violent inferno destroyed many of the buildings in and around Sackville Street.

The rising against British rule in Ireland led to a swift response from British authorities. The army was moved into the city swiftly on Monday from Dublin barracks and then by rail from the Curragh. On Tuesday martial law was applied to the Dublin city and county area, and later across the whole country. By Wednesday morning troops began arriving at Kingstown by ship.

They city is now once again under the control of the British authorities.

What is known of the events of the week is still, in many ways, unclear. Due to the rebellion no newspapers, except for *The Irish Times*, have been printed all week, and military censorship has meant that many details have been omitted from the reporting.

It is known that the rebellion, though fiercest and most sustained in the capital, was not limited to Dublin. Reports are emerging of skirmishes between Crown and rebel forces in east Galway and Ashbourne in County Meath. Large parts of the town of Enniscorthy in Co. Wexford were also taken by the rebel forces. The rebels in Galway and Ashbourne are now said to have dispersed, and those in Enniscorthy are preparing to surrender.

The carnage wreaked on the city centre is clearly visible in this image of soldiers and pedestrians standing amidst the rubble, with Sackville Street and Nelson's Pillar in the background.

116   REVOLUTIONARY TIMES 1913–23

1916

The main body of rebels in Dublin, headquartered at the GPO until Friday evening, surrendered to General Lowe on Saturday afternoon. Since then, the surrender notice has been ferried to each of the rebel positions, and most men and women involved have been marched under guard to the Rotunda. The process of arrest and surrender continued into Sunday, with those who had held Boland's Mills the last to be taken into custody.

There are now hundreds of rebels in military captivity. It is expected that further arrests will take place in the coming days as the authorities target those involved in the conspiracy.

As a result of the rebellion, many parts of Dublin will have to be rebuilt, which will likely take years to complete. More immediately, the dreadful human cost will have to be dealt with. It is known that many of the casualties were military, with a high number of soldiers being killed on Wednesday on Mount Street. In addition to military losses, several policemen are known to have been killed. The rebels also suffered losses at locations across the city.

By far the largest number of casualties, however, are civilians who were not directly involved in the fighting but were caught in the crossfire, with many children among them. It is also reported that several civilians were killed when they encountered the military, particularly as houses were cleared by force in North King Street.

Civilians pause at the quay wall on Bachelors Walk to watch a group of Volunteers being marched under armed military escort to a detention centre.

2 APR
W.B. Yeats' play *At the Hawk's Well* is first performed, privately in London.

20–21 APR △
The German-controlled cargo steamer SS *Libau*, masquerading as **SS *Aud***, is intercepted by the Royal Navy and scuttled following an unsuccessful attempt to land arms for the Irish Volunteers in Tralee Bay.

21 APR
Roger Casement and two others are arrested after coming ashore at Banna Strand, Co. Kerry.

22 APR
Following the loss of the German arms and the arrest of Casement, Eoin MacNeill, Chief of Staff of the Irish Volunteers, places a notice in the *Sunday Independent* cancelling all Volunteer manoeuvres for Easter Sunday.

REVOLUTIONARY TIMES 1913–23

1916

23 APR
Easter Sunday: The IRB's Military Council meets and decides to begin the insurrection on Easter Monday.

24 APR
The Easter Rising begins in Dublin. Major buildings across the city are occupied, with the headquarters located inside the General Post Office (GPO). At noon Patrick Pearse reads the Proclamation of the Irish Republic outside the GPO.

△ **24 APR**
Ernest Shackleton begins his voyage aboard the small boat *James Caird*. The journey from Elephant Island in the South Shetland Islands to South Georgia in the southern Atlantic Ocean is a rescue attempt to save the men of the Imperial Trans-Antarctic Expedition after the loss of their ship *Endurance*.

25 APR
Martial law is declared in Dublin by the British, initially for a period of a month.

Commission of Inquiry into Rising Established by Asquith

London, 12 May – The British Prime Minister, Herbert Asquith, has announced the establishment of a Commission of Inquiry into the Dublin disturbances.

Mr Asquith stated that the commission would 'inquire into the causes of the recent outbreak of rebellion in Ireland and the conduct and degree of responsibility of the military and civil executive in Ireland in connection therewith'.

Asquith travelled to Dublin this morning to see for himself the state of the city in the aftermath of the rebellion. He was brought to see the devastation around the Sackville Street area, and he held lengthy meetings with the military authorities and government officials in Dublin.

There is intense speculation as to the ultimate meaning of the Prime Minister's arrival, which coincides with the execution of two rebel leaders today, James Connolly and Seán Mac Diarmada, who were shot by firing squad at Kilmainham Gaol this morning.

Prime Minister Asquith arriving off the boat at Kingstown flanked by Maurice Bonham-Carter, his private secretary (and son-in-law), and a staff officer of the Irish Command, who was there to meet them.

A cartoon that appeared in the 13 May edition of Issue and Events *a weekly New York-based magazine.*

John Dillon Savages British Government Response to Rising

Westminster, 12 May – An emotional, dramatic speech from John Dillon MP, a member of the Irish Parliamentary Party, dominated proceedings in the House of Commons in London yesterday.

Mr Dillon savaged the policy of the British government in Ireland, condemning the executions of rebels, the holding of secret military trials, the continuation of martial law, and the wholesale searches and arrests being carried out across the country.

Mr Dillon's contribution to the debate played out before a noisy and hostile House of Commons.

'It is the first rebellion that ever took place in Ireland where you had a majority on your side. It is the fruit of our life work [sic]. We have risked our lives a hundred times to bring about this result. We are held up to odium as traitors by those men who made this rebellion, and our lives have been in danger a hundred times during the last thirty years because we have endeavoured to reconcile the two things, and now you are washing out our whole life work in a sea of blood.'

While critical of the actions of the rebels, Mr Dillon expressed admiration and pride in the way they had conducted themselves and he lambasted the British authorities for the callousness and stupidity with which they had handled them.

'[The rebels'] conduct was beyond reproach as fighting men. I admit they were wrong; I know they were wrong; but they fought a clean fight, and they fought with superb bravery and skill, and no act of savagery or act against the usual customs of war that I know of has been brought home to any leader or any organised body of insurgents.'

Regarding the ongoing executions, Mr Dillon urged the Prime Minister to intervene and stop them immediately.

1916

26 APR ▽
Francis Sheehy Skeffington, Thomas Dickson and Patrick McIntyre are executed at Portobello Barracks, following their arrest the previous day.

26 APR ▽
The **HMS** *Helga* shells Liberty Hall from the River Liffey.

26 APR
The Battle of Mount Street Bridge sees fierce fighting, which leaves four British officers and 216 other ranks of the Sherwood Foresters killed or wounded, and four Volunteers dead.

REVOLUTIONARY TIMES 1913–23

1916

27 APR
Major General Sir John Maxwell arrives in Dublin to take command of the 12,000 British Army troops stationed in Dublin.

27 APR
A newspaper strike begins in Dublin.

27 APR
A gas attack by Germans on the front at Hulluch is concentrated on those trenches held by the 16th Irish Division.

▽ **28 APR**
In the Battle of Ashbourne, Volunteers under the command of **Thomas Ashe**, attack members of the RIC, leaving eight policemen and two Volunteers dead.

28 APR
The body of the first casualty of the Easter Rising, Constable James O'Brien, who was shot outside Dublin Castle on Easter Monday, is exhumed and removed to Mount Argus church. His was one of 13 bodies that had been buried in the Castle's recreational grounds during the week.

14 Men Executed in Kilmainham Gaol

Dublin, 13 May – Fourteen men have been executed in Kilmainham Gaol for their involvement in the recent Dublin rebellion. The executions were carried out by firing squad at dawn.

The men had earlier been tried in secrecy at Richmond Barracks in Dublin at a series of field general courts martial where they were permitted no defence counsel.

The Weekly Irish Times *normally appeared every Saturday, but publication was suspended because of the disruption caused by the Rising. The 13 May edition had a comprehensive account of the rebellion and its aftermath.*

The executions began on the morning of 3 May, with Patrick Pearse, Thomas Clarke and Thomas MacDonagh being shot by firing squad at the Stonebreaker's Yard in Kilmainham. The following morning Joseph Plunkett, Edward Daly, Michael O'Hanrahan and William Pearse were shot, followed by John MacBride the morning after.

Éamonn Ceannt, Michael Mallin, Seán Heuston and Con Colbert were shot on 8 May, followed by Seán Mac Diarmada and James Connolly on 12 May. There are reports that Mr Connolly was already grievously ill and unable to stand in front of the firing squad that shot him.

A further execution in Co. Cork took place on 9 May, where Thomas Kent was shot after his arrest seven days earlier. Mr Kent had been heavily linked with land agitation in Cork, but it is not clear that he had any involvement in the Rising.

Also executed were leaders of various garrisons of volunteers who took over key buildings around Dublin. The decisions to single out William

Pearse and John MacBride for execution appear unrelated to any rank they held, however.

Other rebel leaders – including Éamon de Valera and Constance Markievicz – remain in custody and it is not clear what their fate will be.

In London, Roger Casement awaits trial for treason and is being held in the Tower of London, following his arrest in Co. Kerry on Good Friday. It appears that Casement was attempting to facilitate a shipment of arms from Germany for use in the rebellion.

Meanwhile, the arrests of hundreds of people associated, or deemed by the authorities to be associated, with the Rising continues. Those arrested are being interned, with some being sent across the Irish Sea to Britain.

Martial Law Extended in Ireland

Dublin, 29 May – A proclamation extending martial law in Ireland was issued this weekend by Dublin Castle.

The order has been extended until further notice due to the prevailing 'disaffection and unrest' around the country, which is the cause of anxiety and alarm.

General Sir John Maxwell, the Commander-in-Chief in Ireland, has informed the press that the proclamation had been issued at his request. He reminded the public that civil government was still suspended and that the present state of the country involved certain risks.

He also said that all the arms in the country had yet to be given up and that the courts martial would continue.

Maxwell defended the policy that led to the initial arrests and executions, promising these methods would continue to be used 'in the case of nine or ten fugitives who are said to be deeply implicated in the actual Rising who are still at large'.

General Sir John Maxwell defended his robust response to the Rising.

General Maxwell denied that excessive force had been used in suppressing the Rising: 'I cannot go over it all again now, but I think it ought to be made clear that in the beginning the rebels and those who controlled them were responsible for many acts which, even if one were to admit a state of war, which of course one cannot do in dealing with civil commotion, were quite outside the rules of warfare.

'They were murders in cold blood, and any impartial judge and jury would have been bound to find it so.'

1916

29 APR ▽
The Easter Rising ends as those who had been in the GPO surrender.

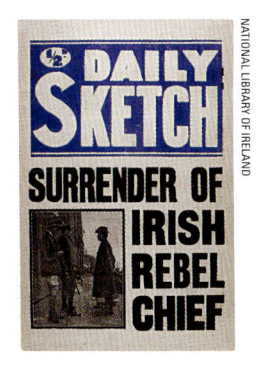

1 MAY
Sir John Maxwell announces that the rebellion in Dublin and elsewhere has ended and that all involved have surrendered. The Chief Secretary of Ireland, Augustine Birrell, has his resignation accepted by Prime Minister Herbert Asquith. Birrell stated that he 'couldn't go on'.

3 MAY
Following their courts martial, Patrick Pearse, Thomas MacDonagh and Thomas J. Clarke are executed at Kilmainham Gaol.

4 MAY
Joseph Plunkett, Michael O'Hanrahan, Edward Daly and Willie Pearse are executed.

5 MAY
John MacBride is executed.

1916

8 MAY
Éamonn Ceannt, Con Colbert, Michael Mallin and Seán Heuston are executed.

▽ **9 MAY**
Thomas Kent is executed and his body buried in a shallow grave in Cork Military Detention Barracks. Kent's arrest followed an altercation with RIC officers at his family home in Castlelyons, during which shots were fired and a police head constable killed.

10 MAY
In the House of Commons Prime Minister Asquith states that the Dublin pacifist Francis Sheehy Skeffington was shot without order.

11 MAY
John Dillon calls on the British government to end the executions of the Easter Rising leaders.

Disturbances in Dublin after Requiem Mass for Rebel Leader

Dublin, 19 June – Three policemen were injured and seven people arrested following a Requiem Mass held in Dublin in honour of the executed rebel leader Thomas Clarke.

At 2 p.m. a procession of 400 people, which was joined by a crowd of 2,000 more, passed through the streets of Dublin from the Franciscan Church on Merchant's Quay.

The procession included men carrying tricolours and green flags with harps in the middle. They passed along Dame Street and College Green into Westmoreland Street, singing songs associated with the Irish Volunteers.

As they passed Dublin Castle, they hissed at the sentries who stood on duty, and hurled abuse at police and soldiers they passed en route.

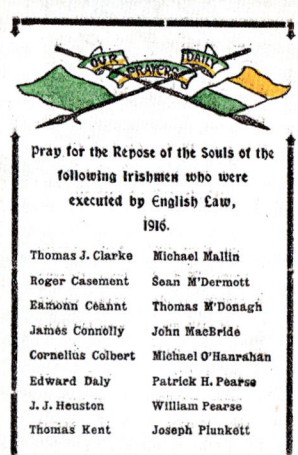

At Westmoreland Street, a large body of police attempted to intervene to seize the flags and disperse the crowd. In the fight that ensued, three policemen received minor injuries and seven processionists – four men and three women – were arrested and brought to Great Brunswick Street Police Station.

After the procession broke up, the crowd headed to the General Post Office on Sackville Street and stood there cheering for a long time.

Souvenir memorial cards began to appear as the popular mood fell in line with the aims of the executed leaders.

Major Offensive Begins Along the Somme

France, 5 July – A major British and French offensive has begun on the Western Front.

The combined attack commenced beneath cloudless skies at 7.30 a.m. on Friday 1 July, along a 25-mile stretch bordering the River Somme in France. It comes in the wake of a major bombardment of German lines that has been less protracted but much more focused than previous efforts.

So far, the main theatres of fighting cover an area approximately 20 miles north of the Somme and 5 miles south of it, and while the full details of the fighting have yet to emerge, initial reports from official and unofficial channels indicate that significant progress has been made. The Anglo-French forces, which include thousands of Irish soldiers, have advanced their position, seized enemy ground and equipment, and have taken large numbers of German prisoners.

A soldier stands beside a German locomotive damaged by French shells in the Somme.

From Paris, reports point to the success of French forces south of the Somme in capturing the village of Feuillères, as well as Buscourt and Flaucourt.

To the north, meanwhile, along what General Haig has said is a 16-mile stretch of the British front, the fighting has been intense, especially in the vicinity of La Boisselle and south of Thiepval, where German counter-attacks have enjoyed some success in recapturing certain positions earlier seized by British troops.

And yet, for all the ferocity of the German resistance, by the end of the weekend's fighting, upwards of 13,000 German soldiers had been taken prisoner, 8,000 of them by the French, the remaining 5,000 by the British.

Somme Slaughter Dampens Twelfth Celebrations

Belfast, 13 July – This year's Twelfth of July celebrations were like none experienced in living memory. There were no drums beating and no Orange sashes worn on the streets of Belfast, and the city fell silent for five minutes as a mark of respect for the men of 36th Ulster Division who lost their lives in France last week.

Belfast was bustling with business as usual throughout the morning, but on the stroke of noon, the noise and clamour came to an abrupt stop as the Lord Mayor of Belfast, Sir Crawford McCullagh, accompanied by the Lady Mayoress and the City Chamberlain, appeared on the steps of City Hall. A death-like hush descended; traffic ground to a halt and every

1916

12 MAY
Seán Mac Diarmada and James Connolly are executed. Prime Minister Asquith arrives in Dublin for a week-long visit and announces a commission of inquiry into the Dublin disturbances.

15 MAY ▽
Roger Casement's initial hearing begins in London. He is charged with high treason for his part in the planning of the Easter Rising and his engagement with the German government.

21 MAY
Daylight saving time begins for the first time throughout the United Kingdom as people put their clocks forward one hour. The purpose is to reduce the number of evening hours to save fuel.

1916

24 MAY
It was announced in the House of Commons that the Prime Minister had appointed the Minister for Munitions, David Lloyd George, to find a solution to the question of Home Rule.

△ **JUN**
Count George Plunkett is dismissed as the curator of the National Museum of Ireland and deported to Oxfordshire as a result of his son's role in the Easter Rising.

2 JUN
Eoin MacNeill is sentenced to life imprisonment for his role in the Irish Volunteers. He will serve his sentence in Dartmoor Prison.

5 JUN
Lord Kitchener, British Secretary of State for War, is drowned when HMS *Hampshire*, the cruiser on which he is travelling en route to Russia, strikes a mine off the Orkney Islands. In all, 737 people perish in the incident.

---

business and most private residences lowered their blinds. Similarly, while Orange flags were everywhere being flown, most were at half-mast. It was, the Belfast correspondent for *The Irish Times* has reported, 'the most impressive spectacle Belfast has witnessed for many a day and showed how deeply all hearts have been touched by the gallantry of the regiments of the Ulster Division'.

The day was dominated by the memory of Ulster's recently fallen sons. A special memorial service was held in the Protestant cathedral, and in a message sent to the Belfast City Mayor, Sir Edward and Lady Carson noted that their 'prayers and solemn thoughts' would, at midday, be with all the people of Belfast 'in memory of our illustrious dead, who have won glory for the empire and undying fame for Ulster. May God bless and help their sorrowing families.'

The solemn scenes in Belfast were replicated in Derry and across Ulster, where traditional Twelfth demonstrations were cancelled at the request of the Orange Order's Grand Lodge of Ireland.

Roger Casement Executed in London

London, 3 August – Sir Roger Casement was executed this morning in Pentonville Prison in London.

At 9 a.m. the hangman placed him in position on a scaffold in the jail and, as soon as the governor of the prison and other officials had taken their place in front, released the lever which opened a trapdoor.

As a bell tolled, about 30 Irish people, mostly members of the Gaelic League, recited prayers on the road outside the jail. When the bells stopped tolling, one among them exclaimed, 'He has gone!'

It is said that shortly before the execution, Casement said, 'I am

Roger Casement arriving at Bow Street Magistrates Court in May to face charges of high treason, for which he was executed at Pentonville Prison.

reconciled. I die for my country.' There were also reports that in his last days he converted to Catholicism and that in his final hours he was ministered to by a Catholic priest.

Shackleton's Men Survive Icy Wasteland Before Rescue

Buenos Aires, 11 September – Sir Ernest Shackleton and Frank Wild have spoken of the survival and rescue of 22 men from Elephant Island after their ship *Endurance* was encased by ice in the Weddell Sea.

The ship eventually sank and the 28 men on board used lifeboats to reach Elephant Island.

The island had precipitous 2,000-foot cliffs, which were shrouded in fog and buffeted by brutal seas. Sir Ernest and five others left to seek help, while those who remained made an ice-hole for themselves and developed a shelter using two small, upturned boats.

They had rations for just six weeks but managed to catch penguins, which they fried in blubber. When the ice began to melt, they collected limpets and seaweed. On one occasion they found undigested fish in the stomach of a seal. They drank water and Bovril.

Life on the island was a monotonous round of storms and fogs, and many of the men suffered from frostbite. They sought to busy themselves with organised exercise in the afternoons and they made pipes from birds' bones and wood. The men read aloud from the few books they had, and every Saturday evening held a concert, which featured the only instrument they had with them – a banjo.

From the moment Endurance *was lost to the ice, Shackleton and his crew had to call on superhuman reserves of strength and fortitude to survive. Tom Crean (left) was one of Shackleton's Irish crew.*

1916

7 JUN
Captain J.C. Bowen-Colthurst, who ordered the killing of Sheehy Skeffington, McIntyre and Dickson without trial, is found guilty but insane by a court martial at Richmond Barracks and committed to Broadmoor Criminal Lunatic Asylum.

12 JUN
The UUC accepts a British proposal for immediate implementation of Home Rule with the proviso that six Ulster counties be excluded.

1 JUL
The Battle of the Somme begins. The 36th Ulster Division, which contains many members of the UVF, suffers huge casualties, with 5,500 men killed, wounded or missing in the first 48 hours.

17 JUL △
Prime Minister Asquith announces that there will be no public investigation into the killings of civilians on North King Street by members of British forces during Easter Week.

REVOLUTIONARY TIMES 1913–23

1916

30 JUL
A new branch – one of several across the north – of an Anti-Partition League is established at a meeting in Killyclogher, near Omagh in Co. Tyrone. P.J. O'Callaghan, presiding, says that while he had been a consistent supporter of John Redmond, he would never consent to partition.

3 AUG
Roger Casement is hanged at Pentonville Prison and buried within the prison grounds.

7 AUG
The first Irish-made film is screened at the Bohemian Theatre in Dublin. *O'Neill of the Glen* had been made by the Film Company of Ireland.

17 AUG
The Dublin Reconstruction Bill, to allow for the rebuilding of Dublin city after the destruction of Easter Week, is given its second reading in Westminster.

19 AUG
The Irish Times announces that its *Sinn Féin Rebellion Handbook*, which runs to 248 pages and details the events of the Easter Rising, is now on sale for sixpence.

Meanwhile, Shackleton's party, which included the Irishmen Tom Crean and Timothy McCarthy, made an 800-mile trip in the tiny *James Caird* across the sea to South Georgia. Shackleton eventually managed to return to bring Wild and his men to safety. The first question Wild asked was, 'Is the war over?'

The party are currently passing through South America on their way back to England.

Tom Kettle: The Death of an Irish Nationalist and British Soldier

Dublin, 24 September – Lieutenant Thomas Kettle has been killed in France, while serving with the 9th Battalion, Royal Dublin Fusiliers. News of the death of the former MP and university professor on 9 September was only confirmed by the War Office on 18 September in a short message, which read, 'Lieutenant T.M. Kettle, of the Royal Dublin Fusiliers, was killed in action on September 9th.'

Dublin-born and educated, Lt Kettle – described in a *Freeman's Journal* editorial as 'one of the most brilliant minds of his generation in Ireland' – was a man of varied interests and overlapping careers.

A qualified barrister and a prolific writer, he was elected an Irish Parliamentary Party MP for East Tyrone in a July 1906 by-election, retaining his seat in the first election of 1910. Appointed as Professor of National Economics at University College Dublin in October 1909, he decided against contesting the second election of 1910.

A supporter of Dublin's locked-out workers during their bitter strike in 1913, he joined the Irish Volunteers before, on the outbreak of war, rallying to the call to defend Belgium against German invasion. Kettle's nationalism was undimmed by the events of recent years, and he spoke frequently on Irish recruiting platforms of his belief that participation in the war was in Ireland's interest.

Although critical of the recent rebellion in Dublin, which saw the death of his brother-in-law Francis Sheehy Skeffington, Kettle attended the court martial and gave evidence in support of Professor Eoin MacNeill. As *The Freeman's Journal* has put it, the 'tragedies of this dark time include none more poignant than this'.

Lt Kettle only left Ireland for France in

Thomas Kettle, 'one of the most brilliant minds of his generation in Ireland'.

July and was involved in the heavy fighting that has been taking place in the Guillemont–Ginchy region. He was killed while leading his men in an attack on enemy positions in Ginchy.

Irish Dentists Advised to Use Cocaine

London, 3 October – Irish dentists will be permitted to use cocaine to assist them in their work.

Registered practitioners are advised to place their orders at once, so that manufacturers of the drug in Great Britain should be able to deliver the required quantity.

The Home Secretary has given notice that unregistered persons who wish to use cocaine to practice dentistry can only do so until 31 October, after which date it will become illegal. The use of cocaine in dentistry is related to its value as a local anaesthetic.

John Redmond Condemns Government's 'Panicky Violence' in Ireland

Westminster, 18 October – The leader of the Irish Parliamentary Party, John Redmond, has condemned the manner in which the British government handled the Easter Rising in Dublin.

In a speech delivered to the House of Commons, Mr Redmond claimed that the actions of the British government had helped transform popular attitudes to the Rising in Ireland. 'At first, the Rising was resented universally by all classes of the people in Ireland,' Redmond remarked. 'It seemed so reckless, so causeless, so wicked ... unfortunately, it was dealt with by panicky violence ... By that proceeding, terror and indignation were spread throughout the country, and popular sympathy, which was against the Rising ... rapidly and completely turned around. All this was a terrible and fatal blunder [by the government].'

Mr Redmond further denounced the conduct of the government, whom he said had given very little credit to the Irish for the numbers in which they had joined the British Army.

As he continued his speech, Mr Redmond launched a bitter attack on the current Irish policy of the British government, claiming that they had re-established Dublin Castle and put into it a Unionist government. 'Is it seriously proposed to maintain the present system to perpetuate martial law, to keep a Unionist executive in office, and to keep hundreds of unaccused and untried prisoners in prison?'

Mr Redmond urged the British government to withdraw martial law, to

1916

9 SEP
Thomas Kettle, poet, journalist and former Home Ruler, is killed serving with the Royal Dublin Fusiliers. He dies near Ginchy during the Somme offensive.

25 SEP
Private publication of W.B. Yeats' poem 'Easter 1916' in London.

1 OCT △
Dublin Mean Time, which was 25 minutes behind Greenwich Mean Time, is abandoned and the time made the same as British time under terms of the **Time (Ireland) Act**, 1916.

6 OCT
In his first major speech in Ireland since the Easter Rising, John Redmond addresses a crowd in his home constituency of Waterford. He tells them that 'Home Rule is safe if Ireland is sane.'

1916

29 OCT
Speaking in Sligo, Redmond urges the British government to change its Irish policy. 'Fighting for the independence of small nationalities on the Continent of Europe, and maintaining martial law in Ireland – the position is intolerable, ridiculous, and shameful.'

3 NOV
The railway steamer SS *Connemara* and the coal ship SS *Retriever* collide in Carlingford Lough. The vessels sink with the loss of 94 lives.

▽ **5 NOV**
Honan Chapel in Cork is consecrated. The chapel is regarded as an exemplar of the Irish Arts and Crafts style.

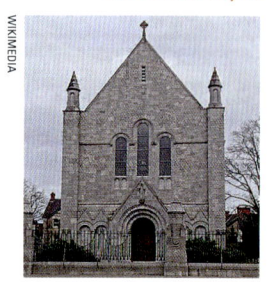

6 NOV
The War Office announces that Lt Gen. Sir John Maxwell will be replaced as Commander-in-Chief of Forces in Ireland by Lt Gen. Sir Bryan Mahon. Born in Galway, Mahon joined the army in 1883 and led the 10th (Irish) Division in the Gallipoli campaign.

MR. REDMOND INVITES THE BRITISH LION TO PERFORM AN OLD TRICK.

Punch reacts to Redmond's speech in their 25 October issue.

permit penal servitude prisoners to be treated as political offenders, and, above all, to 'trust the Irish people … by putting the Home Rule Act into operation.'

He finished to cheers from nationalist MPs.

Irish Prisoners in Frongoch Overrun by Rats

Westminster, 20 October – The House of Commons has heard that 'vigorous measures' have been taken to try to exterminate the rats that are overrunning Frongoch internment camp, where hundreds of Irish prisoners have been held since June.

The Home Secretary, Herbert Samuel, told the House of Commons that the allegation that a prisoner had suffered blood poisoning having been bitten by a rat was untrue.

Mr Samuel also said that the prisoners are provided with additional clothing when the doctor considers it necessary and are allowed to receive approved educational books, including texts in Irish, from the outside.

He added that the US Embassy had inspected the camp and reported most favourably on it.

Gravediggers on Strike at Glasnevin

Dublin, 10 November – The strike at Glasnevin Cemetery has worsened in recent days amid no signs of a resolution.

Of 48 cemetery workers in Glasnevin, 32 are on strike, while the remainder continue to work. Among the strikers are long-serving employees, some of whom have worked up to 26 years in the graveyard.

By the end of last week, it was claimed there were some 150 bodies left unburied in the cemetery, although other sources put the figure at around 30.

The gravediggers are demanding an increase of wages, including a bonus for Sunday work and hazard pay for exhuming corpses that have been buried for a long time. They also ask that when a grave must be sunk six feet or deeper, another man be put upon the bank for protection. Finally, they request that none of the strikers be victimised.

The gravediggers insist that they are not being paid a proper wage even though the cemetery makes a lot of money.

Dillon Condemns British Government as Being 'Deadly for Ireland'

London, 13 November – 'Ireland has been rebutted and treated as a nation hostile to England. The coalition government is deadly for Ireland,' John Dillon, the veteran Irish Parliamentary Party MP, has claimed.

Mr Dillon made the remarks during a lengthy speech he gave near Tottenham Court Road in London about Ireland and the Great War. He lamented the lack of tolerance for debate and dissension in England: 'I think it is the great misfortune that Englishmen should not be more willing than they are at present to bear with differences of opinion.'

Mr Dillon said that it was 'wholly and most disastrously wrong' to follow a policy that treated Ireland and Great Britain as one and the same when it came to the war. He pointed out the seeming contradiction of British claims that they were fighting for freedom and liberty in this war while having a long tradition of oppression and misgovernment in Ireland.

He said that the last 15 or 20 years had begun to redress this and that a great reconciliation was taking place, even if it was not yet complete.

Mr Dillon proceeded to give a brief overview of the missteps of governance undertaken since the outbreak of the war in respect of Ireland, and since the rebellion at Easter: 'Recruitment in Ireland was put in the hands of the ascendancy party – the worst enemies of the people – and the officials in charge of recruiting were to a large extent gentlemen who had been associated in the past with the anti-National fight – persons who used to go about the country abusing the people and telling them that they were slackers and cowards.'

Mr Dillon further stressed how disastrous it would be to bring conscription to Ireland and, to loud applause, asked whether it could seriously be argued that it had 'brought equality of sacrifice to England'. He concluded by saying that if conscription were to be applied to Ireland, then it should also be extended across Canada, South Africa and Australia.

1916

5 DEC
Prime Minister Asquith is forced to resign and refuses to serve under the leadership of Andrew Bonar Law. As a result, David Lloyd George is asked to form a government and become prime minister, which he does on 7 December.

6 DEC
John Redmond states that his IPP will have no role in the new government at Westminster.

9 DEC
A coroner's inquiry hears that 'a baker named John Mulligan died after falling into a kneading machine at the Downes & Co. bakery in Mullingar where he was employed'. A verdict of accidental death was returned.

11 DEC
Lloyd George establishes a War Cabinet. Lord Derby succeeds him as War Minister, Lord Curzon is the Leader of the House of Lords, and Andrew Bonar Law is Chancellor of the Exchequer and Leader of the House of Commons.

13 DEC
Lennox Robinson's play *The Whiteheaded Boy* is premiered at the Abbey Theatre, Dublin.

1916

17 DEC
Wexford are crowned All-Ireland football champions after beating Mayo 3–4 to 1–2. Mayo was the first Connacht team to make it to the final, but the effect of ongoing martial law in the country meant that only 3,000 were in attendance at Croke Park.

18 DEC
Dublin-born Henry Jones, who had won a Victoria Cross during the siege of Sebastopol in the Crimean War in June 1855, dies.

18 DEC
The Battle of the Somme ends after 141 days, stopped by foul weather. It has resulted in thousands of Irish casualties.

19 DEC
It is reported that three patients at the Peamount Sanatorium near Lucan have died.

21 DEC
It is officially announced that all 1916 Irish internees are to be released. The Chief Secretary of Ireland, Henry Duke, explains that the advantages of releasing the men far outweigh the risk. Over the following days, hundreds of released prisoners return to Ireland to a big welcome.

David Lloyd George Becomes New British Prime Minister

London, 8 December – David Lloyd George has accepted His Majesty George V's offer of the post of prime minister and he will form a new government in succession to Herbert Asquith, who resigned.

The formation of the new government comes after a conference at Buckingham Palace attended by the King, A.J. Balfour, Herbert Asquith, Andrew Bonar Law, Arthur Henderson and David Lloyd George.

Initially it appeared that Mr Bonar Law, the leader of the Conservative Party, was poised to become the new prime minister, but during the conference he announced that he would be unable to form a government and agreed to support an administration led by Mr Lloyd George.

Neither the Labour Party nor the Irish Parliamentary Party could have offered support to an administration led by Mr Bonar Law. Labour, however, voted by a slim majority to take part in the new government – a result which came as something of a surprise. They are expected to take two major and several minor positions in the new Cabinet.

This 'National Government' will not include the Irish Parliamentary Party, who have declined formal involvement.

David Lloyd George – Britain's first Welsh Prime Minister.

Republican Prisoners Released from British Jails

Dublin, 26 December – The latest group of Irish prisoners released from English jails and internment camps since the Rising at Easter arrived home on Christmas morning.

The last boat to land was filled with men who had been interned without trial in Reading Jail. They included Arthur Griffith, Sean T. O'Kelly, Terence MacSwiney and Thomas MacCurtain. Almost all the men were members of the Irish Volunteers or the Irish Citizen Army.

Several of the men looked sick and wan. One claimed that they had been fed only porridge for four months and that their survival was due only to the arrival of food parcels from Ireland. In particular, the freezing conditions in their cells was considered to have caused widespread influenza. By contrast, the prisoners who arrived home from the internment camp at Frongoch were 'quite cheerful' and considered themselves to have been well-treated.

1916

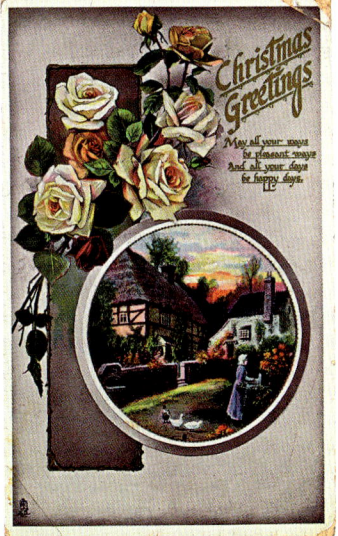

A postcard showing Frongoch Camp and (right) a Christmas card internee Patrick O'Keefe sent from there shortly before the release of the prisoners.

The men passed from the North Wall Quay to train stations and on to the counties from which they hailed.

Recent weeks have seen some 600 prisoners arrive back to Ireland. They have been greeted by exhilarated crowds who wave tricolours and shout, 'Up the Republic'.

Grim Christmas in Ireland

Cork, 28 December – The cheer of the Christmas season has proved in limited supply this December. Despite the return of many rebel prisoners, an atmosphere of mourning and sadness is hanging over the Yuletide festival.

This atmosphere is the result of high prices and bereaved homes. The harsh weather has further dampened the festive spirit.

Despite the hardship of the season, Christmas morning saw large congregations throng churches throughout the country.

There was cheer in some houses, notably those of the released internees from prisons in Britain. Also home, to the joy of their families, were many munitions workers who had returned for the holiday period from various parts of England.

There is no doubt, however, that the enduring war – stretching now into a third year – has destroyed much of the traditional goodwill of Christmas. The death, the drudgery, the pervasive sense of dread has left no family in Ireland untouched, and the fact that no end appears to be in sight makes matters worse.

22 DEC
James O'Kelly, the IPP MP for Roscommon North, dies of pneumonia in London. He had been the constituency's MP since 1895 and had been returned unopposed in the 1910 election.

25 DEC
The last group of released Irishmen who had been interned in Frongoch or in British prisons arrive in Dublin. Among them are Seán T. O'Kelly and Arthur Griffith.

29 DEC
James Joyce's semi-autobiographical novel, *A Portrait of the Artist as a Young Man,* is first published in full book form in New York.

REVOLUTIONARY TIMES 1913–23

Remembering 1916
a hundred years on

The largest public event of the Decade of Centenaries takes place in central Dublin to mark the centenary of the 1916 Easter Rising. Hundreds of thousands gathered to watch a parade of 3,700 members of the Defence Forces, including a UN peace-keeping element, as well as representatives of An Garda Síochána and other State Emergency Services, across a 4.5km route that began at St Stephen's Green and made its way across the city before progressing up O'Connell Street and past the main review stand. The day's ceremonies commenced with a reading of the 1916 Proclamation under the GPO portico and the laying of a wreath by President Michael D. Higgins on behalf of the people of Ireland, followed by the raising of the national flag on top of the GPO, the playing of the national anthem and an Air Corps flypast. The parade was followed by a concert, *A Nation's Voice*, which took place at Collins Barracks and featured thirty-one choirs from across the country.

27 March 2016

ÓGLAIGH NA hÉIREANN

REVOLUTIONARY TIMES 1913–23

133

The Easter Rising, 1916
– 'the starting point for all subsequent Irish history'

FRANK O'CONNOR WAS thirteen years old in 1916, but decades later, as a then celebrated short-story writer, he would recall the impression that newspaper coverage of that year's Irish insurrection would have on his teenage self. It was, he remembered, as if the wreckage of the European war had been brought home. In *An Only Child*, his memoir published in 1958, O'Connor told of how 'the daily papers showed Dublin as they showed Belgian cities destroyed by the Germans, as smoking ruins inhabited by men with rifles and machine guns. At first my only reaction was horror that Irishmen should commit such a crime against England.'

O'Connor's reaction was not uncommon. The insurrection had been unpopular when it occurred: the near consensus across the diversity of Irish newspaper titles was that the rebellion was wrong-headed, irresponsible, unrepresentative and dangerous. Yet there was equally recognition, as *The Cork Examiner* quite quickly concluded, that 'a policy of clemency … is also a policy of wisdom'.

'At first my only reaction was horror that Irishmen should commit such a crime against England.'

The British authorities chose otherwise. Brutal repression was preferred over a policy of leniency. The Easter Rising was a rebellion against British rule that lasted less than a week – from Monday 24 to Sunday 29 April – and ended in predictable military failure given the imbalance of forces: 1,500 insurrectionists were confronted with 20,000 British troops, many of whom shared their Irish origin. But it also ended with the execution of sixteen rebels, including the seven signatories of the Proclamation of the Irish Republic read out by Patrick Pearse in front of the General Post Office (GPO) in Dublin, and the arrest of over 3,000 more, many of whom had no connection to the Rising and yet were still sent to be interned in Britain.

THE EASTER RISING, 1916

If the ferocity of the British response to the Rising was dictated by the wider context of the First World War, then the backdrop of that war is equally vital to an understanding of its planning and prosecution. Indeed, within weeks of Britain declaring war on Germany and John Redmond's subsequent call for Irishmen to join the ranks of the British Army and 'go wherever the firing line extended', a meeting attended by all seven future signatories of the Proclamation was held at the Gaelic League's offices in Dublin, at which it was agreed to hold an insurrection at some point before the conclusion of the war. In doing so, the conspirators were merely reviving an established Fenian creed that 'England's difficulty was Ireland's opportunity'.

So, who were these conspirators and to what organisations did they belong? While the principal organisers of the rebellion were the seven Proclamation signatories, the rank-and-file insurgents were drawn from the several separate organisations: the Irish Volunteers, the ICA, and the separatist, secretive IRB, also known as the Fenians, whose roots lay in the mid-nineteenth century and whose previous effort at uprising, in 1867, had ended in dismal failure. These organisations did not act alone, but with the important assistance of a network of smaller organisations such as Na Fianna Éireann, the republican youth movement, and Cumann na mBan, the women's auxiliary to the Volunteers.

In strictly numerical terms, the Volunteers were the most significant contributors to the Rising. Although the Volunteer movement had split following the outbreak of the First World War and the pledging of John Redmond's support for the British armed effort, what was left was very much a committed core, men who, in the words of one of those who remained, might be relied upon to 'participate in an insurrection when the right moment was revealed'. Led by Professor Eoin MacNeill of University College Dublin and encompassing key members of the IRB (Patrick Pearse, Tom Clarke, Thomas MacDonagh, Joseph Plunkett, Éamonn Ceannt and Seán Mac Diarmada), approximately 1,300 Irish Volunteers participated in the events of Easter Week, with the ICA contributing a few hundred more.

'The birth of the Irish Republic, 1916' – a lithographic print published in Dublin shortly after the Easter Rising reimagines the military failure as a heroic sacrifice.

THE EASTER RISING, 1916

The signatories of the Proclamation – Patrick Pearse along with (TOP) Tom Clarke, James Connolly, Thomas MacDonagh, (BOTTOM) Seán Mac Diarmada, Joseph Plunkett and Éamonn Ceannt – were court-martialled and executed within two weeks of their surrender.

The real orchestrators of the Rising, however, were from the IRB – or at least the inner circle of that organisation. Within this group, Thomas Clarke was undoubtedly the key operator. A committed Fenian, Clarke had spent fifteen years in British jails in the 1880s and 1890s for possession of explosives before emigrating to the United States. There he found work with the *Gaelic American*, the newspaper of the Clan na Gael leader John Devoy. He returned to Ireland in 1907, opening up a tobacconist shop on Dublin's Parnell Street, from where he led the revitalisation of an organisation that had, for decades, been weakened by internal dissension and inactivity. It was at the veteran Clarke's instigation that the meeting had been held in the Gaelic League's library on 9 September 1914 at which it was decided to stage a rising, and it was Clarke, aided by the youthful Seán Mac Diarmada, who subsequently drove the planning and preparations for it.

Of course, had the First World War ended as early as many expected, the opportunity to act might never have arisen. The IRB's plans – and, indeed, its reputation – were saved by the prolongation of the war, which afforded it the time required to organise and arm. Its Military Council, set up to co-ordinate the insurrection, was only formed in May 1915, and the date that was finally chosen was Easter Sunday 1916. On this day, on Patrick Pearse's orders, in his capacity

THE EASTER RISING, 1916

of Director of Organisation of the Irish Volunteers, it was envisaged that all Irish Volunteers would gather at assembly points throughout the country for three days of 'field manoeuvres'. The decision on timing was a straightforward one: as similar large-scale mobilisations had occurred at Easter 1915 and again on St Patrick's Day 1916, it was felt that a further mobilisation, particularly one so publicly advertised, would do nothing to arouse the suspicions of either the authorities or the republicans' less revolutionary-minded comrades. Secrecy was therefore crucial, and right up until to the final days neither Eoin MacNeill, head of the Irish Volunteers, nor Denis McCullough, head of the Supreme Council of the IRB, was aware that the scheduled manoeuvres for Easter were designed as a cover for staging an armed insurrection.

Uniformed members of the ICA in their distinctive slouch hats drilling at Croydon House, their training headquarters in Croydon Park, Clontarf. The unit is shouldering Mauser Model 1871 rifles from the cache that was smuggled into Howth in 1914.

As it happened, of course, the insurrection that took place in Ireland in April 1916 was not the one originally planned. That is because, as historian Joe Lee put it some decades ago, the Rising 'went off half-cock'. The unravelling of the insurgents' plans occurred as the countdown to the insurrection entered its final days. On the Thursday of Easter Week, Bulmer Hobson caught wind of the impending insurrection and informed MacNeill, who, in turn, confronted Pearse. On being told that the plans were set and irreversible, MacNeill was convinced to stand back and not obstruct the Rising; his position was further swayed by a forged 'Castle document', which purported to detail plans by the authorities to suppress the Volunteers and arrest nationalist leaders. But having been swayed one way, MacNeill soon swung back again.

His reversal was a response to the news of Roger Casement's arrest in Kerry and the British interception off the Kerry coast of the *Aud*, a German ship carrying 20,000 rifles bound for the insurgents – it was enough to convince MacNeill that the planned enterprise would be an act of 'madness' and doomed to failure. He articulated his opposition at a highly charged meeting on Easter Saturday night, and the following morning his countermanding order cancelling the scheduled Easter Sunday manoeuvres was published in the *Sunday Independent*. This threw the insurgency plans into chaos. In the confusion of conflicting orders, and in the knowledge of Casement's arrest and the *Aud*'s interception, the conspirators met at Liberty Hall and decided to salvage something from the wreckage of their scuttled strategy. The Rising would go ahead – but on the following day.

However, the insurrection of Easter Monday was not the same Rising deferred by a day. It was different in scale and geography, and its likely outcome was more predetermined. For a start, it was largely confined to Dublin, where key buildings were occupied as garrisons by members of the Irish Volunteers, the ICA and Cumann na mBan, albeit with some strategically or symbolically significant structures, such as Dublin Castle and Trinity College, remaining untouched. Although minor uprisings also occurred in rural Galway, in Enniscorthy, Co. Wexford, and in Ashbourne, Co. Meath, there would be no mass mobilisation – the seizure of the *Aud*'s cargo of arms was the obvious factor in scuppering that prospect.

In the aftermath of the violence the administration in Dublin Castle felt it necessary to issue this public health notice.

The results of the Rising in Dublin were nevertheless devastating. Large swathes of the city centre were destroyed, with Dublin's 'finest street … reduced', in the words of *The Freeman's Journal*, 'to a smoking reproduction of the ruin wrought in Ypres'. While the city could at least be rebuilt (and the British government would later pay out vast sums in compensation for the actions of its own military), the Rising also left 500 dead in its wake, the majority of them civilians, including thirty-eight children. The youngest fatality, twenty-two-month-old Christina Caffrey, was shot in the back while in her mother's arms in the 'precincts' of their inner-city home.

While Caffrey was an innocent caught up in crossfire, the major political aftershocks of the Rising were caused by the deaths of others, notably the drawn-out executions of the rebel leaders that were sanctioned by the British authorities. In defying the growing clamour for clemency, the severity of this British response, reinforced by the large-scale and nationwide flurry of post-Rising arrests, swung the tide of popular public opinion behind what had been, at its commencement, an unpopular insurrection. With remarkable alacrity, critics of the rebellion turned converts to the rebel cause.

The intense British artillery fire resulted in the destruction of the capital's streetscapes, reducing once fine buildings, such as Clery's department store, to rubble.

Complex and controversial as its legacy would prove, the 1916 Rising catalysed a radicalisation of Irish politics that would sweep aside the IPP as the standard-bearers of Irish nationalist aspirations. The events of that April and May would reverberate across the rest of the revolutionary decade – and well beyond, too. A 'Republic' had been proclaimed by the rebels at Easter 1916, and the responses the Rising provoked, both instantly and over time, would ensure, as historian Diarmaid Ferriter has observed, that it would come to be seen as 'the starting point for all subsequent Irish history'.

Prisoners, Politics and Political Change

IN THE DAYS after the surrender of Irish forces on 29 April 1916, the British authorities not only arrested those who had taken part in the Easter Rising but threw their net more widely and arrested many they believed had nationalist sympathies. In all, 3,430 men and seventy-seven women were arrested in the immediate aftermath of Easter Week. The British response to the Rising was brisk and ferocious, and it resulted in execution and mass imprisonment. As the IPP leader John Dillon stated in the House of Commons, 'there has been no rebellion or insurrection put down with so much blood and so much savagery'.

Initially, most prisoners were taken to Richmond Barracks in Dublin, where they were processed by army officers and members of the DMP's G Division. The intelligence held by the British was relatively poor, and they spent days trying to establish who they had arrested and what role, if any, those individuals had played in the Rising. The legal framework for the arrests and processing of prisoners was the DORA, which had been introduced at the start of the First World War, as well as an additional layer of regulations that had been introduced on 25 April when the Lord Lieutenant, Lord Wimborne, had placed Dublin under martial law. What this meant, in effect, was that the prisoners of 1916 were not tried in the normal way of the civil courts; rather they were charged and judged swiftly by military authorities. One hundred and seventy of the rebels, mainly those identified as key figures by the British authorities, were tried by field general courts martial. Conducted *in camera* and in the absence of defence counsel or a right of appeal, these three-judge military courts resulted in ninety of the rebels receiving death sentences, the

> ... 'there has been no rebellion or insurrection put down with so much blood and so much savagery'.

vast majority of which were ultimately commuted. For the executions that did take place, however, it was a protracted exercise, beginning at Kilmainham Gaol on 3 May and continuing for nine days. In all, fourteen men were executed by firing squad and their bodies removed to Arbour Hill for burial.

Following the mass arrests, the British authorities released many prisoners, but the vast majority, 2,486, were deported to Britain. Most of these were sent as internees, as they had not been tried or convicted for any offence, while a minority (140 men and one woman) who had been sent before the courts martial and convicted, were sent as criminals. Those arrested were mainly from the Dublin area, but men and women were detained across the country, particularly in Wexford and east Galway, where risings had also taken place. The prisoners fell into the categories of male internees, male convicts and female internees/convicts (because they were so few, their official status was largely a little unclear).

'Sinn Féin' prisoners being visited by friends at Richmond Barracks in Dublin, where they were interned prior to deportation to prisons in England and Wales.

Once in Britain, the interned men were distributed across prisons such as Knutsford, Wakefield, Wandsworth, Woking, Lewes, Barlinnie, Perth and Stafford. The regimes under which they were held were strict at first: not only were the internees denied visitors, they were not even allowed to send or receive post. Worse still, they were held in conditions of strict silence, food was basic and they were given little opportunity to exercise. Such conditions were relaxed in late May, when internees were allowed to communicate with each other and receive letters, parcels and visitors.

In June, the decision was made to move the vast majority of the male internees to an internment camp at Frongoch in North Wales, the numbers there peaking at 1,800 by mid-July. A small number – considered likely leaders and therefore potentially disruptive – were held separately at Reading. In the summer of 1916, the authorities began releasing those they considered less dangerous, and by September the number held had reduced to 540. A small number accepted parole in the months that followed, and in December the government, under pressure from the IPP, decided to release all the internees. This they did, and Frongoch closed in the days before Christmas 1916. During December, over 600 men arrived home in Ireland, from Frongoch and prisons such as Reading, to be met, in stark contrast to the atmosphere that attended their send-off, by cheering, flag-waving crowds. Newspapers reported on the difference in appearance between those who had been held at Frongoch and seemed well-treated and cheerful, and those who had been held in prisons, who looked sick and wan.

At Frongoch, the men organised regular athletic and football contests, including the playing of an unofficial Wolfe Tone Tournament final in July 1916. That involved representative teams from Kerry and Louth, counties that had both qualified for the semi-finals before the Rising, with the former fielding as many as twelve inter-county players, among them the legendary All-Ireland-winning captain Dick Fitzgerald, who had previously authored the first instructional manual for Gaelic football.

There was, for the most part, a pattern to life in Frongoch. Days passed to a familiar rhythm. Liam Grogan, an assistant curator at the National Museum who had been arrested in the aftermath of the Rising and subsequently sent to Frongoch, offered an account of the daily regime in an interview given to *The Freeman's Journal* on his release in late 1916. Internees rose at 5.30 a.m., took Mass at 7 a.m. and followed it with breakfast at 8 a.m., a simple and nutritionally poor meal consisting of the staples of tea, bread and margarine. Rooms and communal areas were then cleaned until inspected at 10.30 a.m. Dinner followed at noon, a few ounces of meat to which some potatoes and soup were added. The internees then had the rest of the day to themselves. There was the occasional céilí and some painting and reading. However, at 6 p.m. the doors of their dormitories, where rats would scuttle across the floor and infest the shelves where clothes and food were stored, were locked until 5.30 a.m. the next morning, when the routine would be repeated. It was little wonder, then, that Grogan reflected on the monotony of the experience.

PRISONERS, POLITICS AND POLITICAL CHANGE

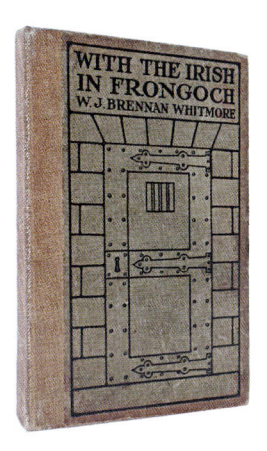

With The Irish In Frongoch, written by one of the inmates, W.J. Brennan Whitmore, gives a classic account of life in the Welsh internment camp. First published in 1917, the narrative is accompanied by a series of handsome drawings depicting life in the 'University of Revolution'. Illustration titles include: (1) Recreation inside the Huts; (2) Methods of the Secret Post; (3) Entrance Gate; (4) The Huts, North Camp; (5) Kitchen and Wash-house, North Camp.

Yet for many, particularly those who lived amongst a militarist cohort in Frongoch, the camp experience was not so much uneventful and boring as personally and politically transformative. Those arrested in the wake of a Rising in which they had taken no part were often young men who had been members of the Volunteers. Their sense of grievance at being held as internees, coupled with their exposure to the ideas and training offered by Michael Collins and others, undoubtedly had a radicalising effect. Indeed, the key part the men held in Frongoch would subsequently exert on mapping a new direction for Irish politics from 1917 onwards led to the camp being dubbed 'the University of the Revolution'.

Those tried by court martial had a different experience. For a start, they remained in prison. To begin with they were held in Dartmoor, Portland and Wormwood Scrubs, and were subject to the full discipline of prison life. By the end of 1916, however, again following pressure from the IPP, the authorities gathered them together under a more forgiving regime in Lewes Prison. Once together, the prisoners became more organised and resistant to prison authority, and a campaign of disobedience aimed at securing political prisoner status culminated in a riot in late May 1917. Due to their actions, the prisoners were broken up and once again dispersed to different prisons until their final release under a general amnesty in June 1917. On arrival home in Ireland, the released prisoners were met by jubilant crowds at Westland Row train station, scenes that were repeated – exceeded even – when they completed their onward journeys to their own home towns. On returning to their native Kerry, for instance, Austin Stack, Thomas Ashe and Timothy Brosnan were met in Killarney by large crowds, bonfires and performing bands. From a hotel window, Ashe declared to the supportive gathering below that English prisons had done nothing to dampen the ardour of the newly freed men's political beliefs. '[T]oday,' he added, 'we stand more firmly for Ireland's independence, an Ireland whole and indivisible, than we ever stood.'

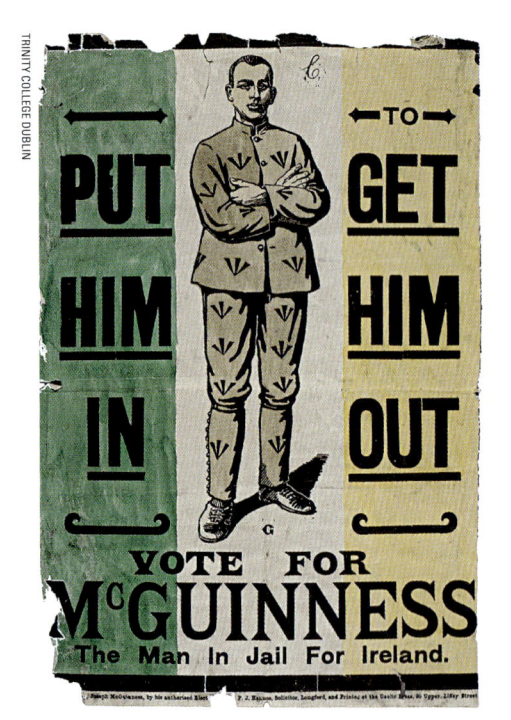

Sinn Féin's memorable slogan 'put him in to get him out', made its first appearance in the successful 1917 South Longford by-election campaign, masterminded by Michael Collins, which resulted in Joseph McGuinness's election to Westminster.

The prisons, of course, were not only used to incarcerate men. Seventy-seven women were also arrested after Easter Week, some initially held in Ship Street Barracks before being moved to join others in Richmond Barracks. Just over half of these were then released, with the remainder moved to Kilmainham Gaol. By 8 May 1916 all women prisoners had been released, with the exception of twelve whom the British authorities considered the most radical. In June, having been initially held in Mountjoy, five of these women were sent to Britain; six others were released. Marie Perolz, Helena Molony, Nell Ryan, Winifred Carney and Brigid Foley were held initially in Lewes Prison before being transferred a number of times; they were all were released between July and December 1916. Constance Markievicz was the only one definitively held as a convict in Mountjoy for some time before she too was transferred to Britain. In contrast to her colleagues, she was held not with other rebels but with ordinary convicts at Aylesbury Prison. While her prison letters are full of her thoughts and details of how she filled her days, one captured the isolation and utter fruitlessness of the prison experience: 'Again, another day! And I don't know why I have delayed so long over this [letter]. Laziness and dullness, I suppose, but really, if you come to think of it, I have nothing to talk about, only vague nonsense.' After serving fourteen months, Markievicz was released under the general amnesty and returned to Ireland in June 1917, although further prison spells would follow, including eleven months in London's Holloway Prison in 1918 and 1919, during which time she would become the first female to be elected to Westminster.

The fate of the prisoners who had been arrested in the wake of the Easter Rising was a critical factor in changing public perception of the Rising. While jeered and booed when they were marched through Dublin to Richmond Barracks, the prisoners' return home was entirely different. Their months of incarceration during the summer of 1916 were increasingly seen as unfair and unjust, and the Sinn Féin publicity machine not only illustrated the poor conditions in which the prisoners were kept but also how their freedom was linked to the future direction of the country. This was especially true around a series of by-elections in 1917, particularly that of South Longford in May, where the Sinn Féin candidate, Joe McGuinness, was still a Lewes Prison inmate. On the day that voters went to the polls, motor cars traversed the constituency emblazoned with such slogans as 'Put McGuinness in to get him out' and 'Free Joe McGuinness and Ireland'. The messaging worked and McGuinness narrowly defeated his IPP opponent.

… **'the more men there are in the country who have been through the mill in the jails, the harder will England find it to govern this country hereafter'.**

The imprisonment of such large numbers of Irish men and women had the twin effect of radicalising the prisoners and engendering a broad public sympathy. In 1918, when languishing in Belfast Gaol, Kevin O'Higgins, a future government minister, wrote that 'nothing has helped so much the unity and solidarity of Sinn Féin as the association of large bodies of men from all parts of the country in the jails and in the internment camps in England in 1916. Besides all these men got out somewhat tougher, somewhat more determined, better equipped for the struggles that lie ahead … in my opinion the more men there are in the country who have been through the mill in the jails, the harder will England find it to govern this country hereafter … Therefore out with the warrants, set on the G men, roll up the Black Maria, fill up the jails.' More succinctly than O'Higgins, the historian of Irish prisoners of the period, William Murphy, concluded that those jailed after the Rising 'became breathing representations of the government's alleged high-handedness. They were grievance embodied.'

WAKE UP, AMERICA!
JAMES MONTGOMERY FLAGG
CIVILIZATION CALLS
EVERY MAN WOMAN AND CHILD!
MAYOR'S COMMITTEE 50 EAST 42ND ST
THE HEGEMAN PRINT N.Y.

1917

'... I advise that the Congress declare the recent course of the Imperial German Government to be in fact nothing less than war against the government and people of the United States ... to exert all its power and employ all its resources to bring the Government of the German Empire to terms and end the war.'

US President Woodrow Wilson in his address to a special joint session of Congress
2 APRIL

1917

18 JAN
The funeral takes place in New York of Esther Redmond Power, daughter of IPP leader John Redmond. Among the attendance at the church are several hundred members of the Municipal Council of the United Irish League (UIL) of America, of which Redmond is president.

▽ **31 JAN**
Hundreds of Irish-Canadian soldiers on their way to the Western Front parade through the streets of Dublin. The **Irish Canadian Rangers Regiment** are all of Irish birth or extraction. They arrived by steamer from Holyhead and spent eight days taking in Dublin, Belfast, Armagh, Limerick and Cork.

Controversial New Science Curriculum for Irish Schools

12 January – The Intermediate Education Board is set to reintroduce the system of uniform examination of science for pass students in Secondary Schools.

This move is being seen by many teachers and headmasters as a retrograde action, removing the elasticity in teaching methods that has reaped educational success in the last decade.

According to some teachers, the introduction of a uniform science examination system could stymie the 'spirit of investigation' visible in this photo taken in 1900 of pupils at work in a laboratory in Waterpark College, Co. Waterford.

The Board has rejected any compromise despite the almost unanimous opposition of teachers and teaching authorities. One headmaster says that the introduction of the new system would mean that the spirit of investigation and research that is central to the scientific method would be replaced by a focus on simply passing the exam. Another says that students would be in danger of cramming instead of pursuing a sound and rounded education. One commentator summed up the views of many concerned parties in saying that examinations were 'destructive of the happiness of boyhood' and were counterproductive.

Chief Secretary Sets Out Future of a United Ireland

15 January – Unionist Ulster's concerns must be addressed before she can be won.

The Chief Secretary of Ireland, Henry Duke, made the remark during a speech after the Corinthian Club dinner at the Gresham Hotel this week. He noted that this was a vital fact that the Irish Parliamentary Party 'still fails utterly to appreciate'.

After some remarks on Ireland's propensity for 'mercurial ... temperamental ... boisterous demonstrations', Mr Duke said that he had come to the country intent on bringing to all events a 'dominant note of dullness'.

He expressed his hopes for a united Ireland and for a just and fair settlement of the Irish question, but restated his view that unity is the task of Irishmen.

The unionist *Irish Times* lauded Duke's speech and concurred with its sentiments: 'If Ireland wants a satisfactory settlement of her eternal question, she must not only reach agreement within her own borders: she must secure the good will of Great Britain and the whole Empire.'

Chief Secretary Henry Duke hoped that the settlement of the Irish question would include a united Ireland and not the scenario illustrated in a Puck Magazine *cartoon.*

Ireland Faced with Worst Food Shortage Since Famine

30 January – Since the early months of the war, the passing of every week has brought deepening concerns over food shortages in Ireland.

The cause of the problem is twofold: firstly, the way German submarine activity has been targeting merchant shipping; secondly the nature of farming practices in Ireland.

Attention was drawn to the former earlier this week by Reverend T. Joyce, VF, at a meeting in Ballinasloe. Reverend Joyce claimed that if the activity of the German U-boats continued at its current rate, Ireland would be confronted with its worst food scarcity since the Famine.

The latter relates to the decades-long drift from tillage to cattle-farming, which has created an agricultural economy that is entirely skewed.

1917

1 FEB
Germany resumes its campaign of unrestricted submarine warfare. The US responds within days by severing diplomatic ties with Germany.

3 FEB
The North Roscommon by-election is decisively won by Count Plunkett, father of executed 1916 leader Joseph Mary Plunkett.

6 FEB
The Dublin Tram Company reports record receipts for the previous year. Chairman William Martin Murphy says the company had staged a 'wonderful recovery' after suffering a 'heavy loss' in traffic as a result of the destruction caused by the rebellion.

REVOLUTIONARY TIMES 1913–23

1917

24 FEB
A temperance meeting in Dublin highlights the increase in convictions for drunkenness amongst women. The increase is partly explained by women's increased income from the wartime separation allowance.

26 FEB
Details of a message sent by British Foreign Secretary Arthur Balfour to the American Committee for Syrian and Armenian Relief are published. It claims that of the 1.8m Armenians in the Ottoman Empire two years previously, 1.2m had been either massacred or deported.

▽ **26 FEB**
The Freeman's Journal reports that a Mayo man had been arrested and charged at Ballinlough Petty Sessions for singing rebel songs. John McNally, a native of Claremorris, climbed onto a stage at the end of a concert at Ballinlough and sang **'Easter Week'**.

A leaflet distributed in January 1917 with the Irish Homestead *outlining instructions to farmers on how to increase their food supply.*

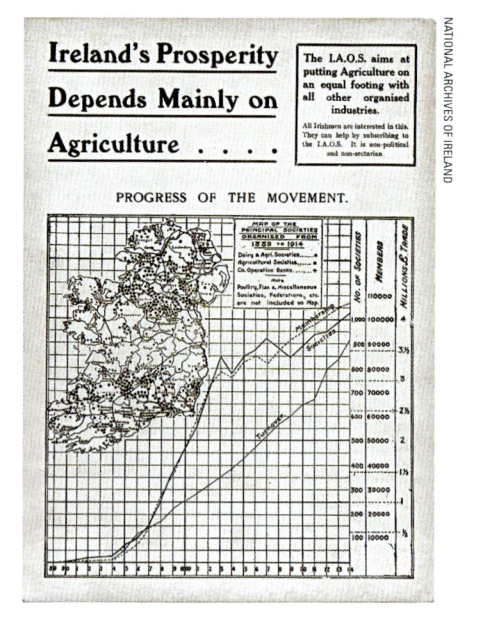

The decline of tillage has left Ireland entirely vulnerable to the shift in the patterns of food distribution brought about by war. The simple fact is that the country does not produce enough crops, and this is now a matter of urgency that must be altered.

The failure to make the shift so far has particularly affected the poor of the country, who are now paying outrageous prices for the most basic of products.

Count Plunkett Victorious in North Roscommon By-election

8 February – The Irish Parliamentary Party has been dealt a huge blow as Count George Noble Plunkett has swept to victory in the North Roscommon by-election.

Count Plunkett ran against Jasper Tully (Independent) and T.J. Devine (IPP). He received 3,022 of the 5,403 votes cast, more than the other two candidates combined.

News of the victory has been met with scenes of jubilation. Across North Roscommon there were torchlight processions and church bells tolled. Everywhere the tricolour was waved, bands played and speeches were made, ending in cheering and shouting. In Ballaghaderreen, tar barrels were lit in celebration.

In a speech in Cortober, Arthur Griffith claimed that the blow struck by Roscommon would reverberate throughout America and the world. It is recognised by all sides that Count Plunkett's victory rests entirely on the fact that he is the father of the late executed 1916 leader Joseph Mary Plunkett.

In response to his victory, Sligo Corporation has passed a resolution in support of Count Plunkett and conferred upon him the Freedom of the Borough.

All across the midlands of Ireland, local newspapers have described the result as 'a knockout blow' for the Irish Parliamentary Party. Indeed, the *Midland Reporter* claimed: 'The result puts the whole Redmond Party in the melting pot. In the west and midlands now, the Party could not get a safe resting spot for one of their nominations.'

Echoes of the Rising as Irish Firebrands Arrested and Deported

23 February – Midnight raids by police across Ireland have led to the arrest and imprisonment of 26 men under the Defence of the Realm Act.

The men were brought to Arbour Hill in Dublin by detectives and were then handed over to the military authorities, who informed several of them that they were to be deported to England, where they were to remain in custody. As of this evening, 19 of the men are reported to have been deported.

Among the men arrested were the prominent writers J.J. O'Kelly and Darrell Figgis; men who had fought in the Rising, such as William Pedlar and Herbert Mellows; and Cork activists Terence MacSwiney and Tomás MacCurtain. Many of the men were active in the Gaelic League and had previously been in prison or in internment camps before being released just before Christmas.

The arrest and imprisonment of the 26 men without any charge was condemned in the House of Commons by John Dillon, MP of the Irish Parliamentary Party, as 'provocative'. Explaining the decision, the British authorities said that those deported were now 'prohibited from residing in Ireland and have been given their choice of place in England, where they may reside'.

Vanity Fair *caricature of a patrician-looking John Dillon MP.*

1917

1 MAR
The American press publishes news of a coded telegram from the German Foreign Minister, Arthur Zimmermann, to the German ambassador in Mexico, which British cryptographers deciphered and which proposed, in the event of US entry into the war, an alliance with Mexico and support for the transfer to them of US territory.

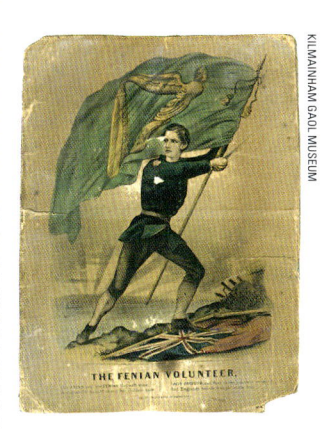

5 MAR △
The Freeman's Journal dedicates an editorial to the 50th anniversary of the 1867 **Fenian Rising**, comparing and contrasting its leaders to those of the Easter Rising. 'It is impossible', the editorial argues, 'to conceive of the men of '67 making war upon a peace … that commended itself to the majority of the Irish people. They were a constructive force not a destructive.'

REVOLUTIONARY TIMES 1913–23

151

1917

▽ **7 MAR**
After extensive alterations, the **Tara Street public baths** in Dublin reopen. From its original opening in 1886 up to 1917, the facility has been visited by more than 3.5m people.

8 MAR
Tens of thousands of women take to the streets of Petrograd (previously and subsequently known as St Petersburg) on International Women's Day to protest against food and bread shortages.

▽ **15 MAR**
Amid growing disturbances over the poor management of the war and the economy, **Tsar Nicholas II** abdicates from the Russian throne. This brings to an end the 300-year rule of the Romanov dynasty over Russia.

Irish Party Stage Dramatic Walkout of Parliament

8 March – The Irish Parliamentary Party today walked out of the House of Commons in London during a debate on Home Rule and Ireland.

The move was criticised inside the house by Tim Healy as 'play-acting' and in the English press as a 'pre-arranged piece of melodrama'.

Preceding the John Redmond-led walkout, T.P. O'Connor MP had made an impassioned speech about Ireland's Home Rule journey, putting forward the following motion: 'That with a view to strengthening the hands of the Allies in achieving the recognition of the equal rights of small nations and the principles of nationality against the opposite German principle of military domination and government without the assent of the governed, it is essential, without further delay, to confer upon Ireland the free institutions long promised to her.'

The British Prime Minister, David Lloyd George, said that any proposal acceptable to the Irish people would be considered, but that he was not prepared to enact Home Rule when there were people in Ireland unwilling to accept it.

Mr Lloyd George said that he was prepared to introduce Home Rule now across those parts of Ireland where it would be welcomed and that he 'believed Ulster would come in at no distant date'.

John Redmond, in reply, said that the only straightforward course of action open to the government was to put the Home Rule Act at once into operation. He said that Mr Lloyd George had had months to consider the matter of Home Rule, but when they asked him for action, he gave them professions.

At this point, Mr Redmond called on his MPs to let the House of Commons do what it wished in terms of the motion in respect of Home Rule and to withdraw from the chamber with him. The entire Irish Parliamentary Party then left the debating chamber amid 'great commotion'.

T.P. O'Connor's impassioned speech preceded the IPP's departure from the house.

Thousands To Be Employed in New Ford Plant in Cork

8 March – More than 2,000 people will be employed in the new Ford tractor plant in Cork. The workers will be paid a minimum rate of one shilling per day. There has been widespread Irish support for the new development, not least because it promises to give Ireland a 'big share' in what is still a 'new industry'. The plant will initially specialise in the creation of motor tractors.

British motor manufacturers oppose the proposals. E. Manville, the president of the Association of British Motor and Allied Manufacturers, has called on the government to delay the building of the factory. Mr Manville said that the building of such a factory by 'any foreign concern' was simply wrong and that if tractors were needed for the duration of the war they could be imported fully constructed.

The Fordson was the first lightweight, mass-produced tractor on the market. Henry Ford's design cleverly combined a small, lightweight and manoeuvrable frame with an affordable price tag that made it cheaper to maintain than horses.

Since 1903, the Ford factory in America has been hugely successful in producing motor cars. The fact that the founder of the factory, Henry Ford, has roots in the Cork area clearly influenced his choice of site.

Ford's family emigrated to America from Bandon in Co. Cork, and his motor assembly business is now referred to as 'one of the wonders of the world'.

America Enters the War

6 April – America has proclaimed a state of war with Germany.

After months of speculation, President Woodrow Wilson formally signed the resolution earlier today.

The declaration of war comes after Congress voted overwhelmingly to support the war. In the House of Representatives the vote was 373 to 50.

Americans believe their entry will bring a swift end to the war. It is thought new legislation will be brought in along

1917

6 APR
The US abandons its neutrality and enters the First World War, declaring war on the German Empire.

6 APR
In advance of the first anniversary of the Easter Rising, Lt Gen. Sir Bryan Mahon, Commander-in-Chief of British forces in Ireland, issues a proclamation – effective until 15 April – prohibiting public assemblies in Dublin, such as 'will give rise to grave disorder, and will thereby cause undue demands to be made upon the Police or Military forces'.

9 APR
Republican colours are hoisted at half-mast on the site of the ruined GPO, while a tricolour is waved from atop Nelson's Pillar to mark the first Easter since the events of the Rising in 1916. On the arrival of police, the flag-waving stopped and the colours at the GPO were removed.

The Evening Star leads with the dramatic news.

REVOLUTIONARY TIMES 1913–23

153

1917

16 APR
Vladimir Ilyich Lenin returns to Petrograd from exile in Switzerland with the aim of overthrowing Russia's Provisional Government.

▽ **17 APR**
Henry Ford, son of a famine-era Irish emigrant and founder of the **Ford Motor Company**, opens an office in Cork. The company plans to build a factory from which it will produce 50,000 Fordson tractors each year and generate thousands of local jobs.

8 MAY
John Dillon MP, speaking in Longford in advance of the pending by-election, warns that there would be conscription introduced in Ireland within a month without IPP efforts at Westminster. He also sets out all that Ireland would lose by the removal of Irish representation in Parliament.

The design of America's most memorable First World War poster, painted by noted New York illustrator James Montgomery Flagg, was inspired by the 1914 'Kitchener Wants You' poster published in Britain. Using himself as a model, Flagg's depiction of Uncle Sam in a persuasive pose to be such an effective recruitment tool that four million copies were printed between 1917 and 1918.

with the declaration, including compulsory military service and budget increases for the military. To this end, the Senate has voted an emergency war fund of $100 million to be used by President Wilson at his discretion.

The seizure of German ships started almost immediately, with merchant vessels taken at New York, Boston and Baltimore. There are also widespread rumours that the US is preparing to send army forces to Europe.

It is immediately apparent that America's entry into the war opens a new chapter in US history, with the continent no longer standing isolated from Europe.

The move has been greeted with delight in London, with David Lloyd George and Herbert Asquith sending congratulatory messages to Washington.

1917

Easter Rising Anniversary Marked Around the Country

6 April – The head of the British Army in Ireland, Lieutenant General Sir Bryan Mahon, has taken steps to discourage groups of republicans from organising any events to mark the anniversary of the Easter Rising.

General Mahon issued a proclamation prohibiting, until 15 April, the holding of any public meeting or procession within the police district of Dublin, in the belief that such assemblages will 'give rise to grave disorder and will thereby cause undue demands to be made upon the police or military forces'.

Republican flags have been seen flying in various parts of Dublin and the sale of republican paraphernalia and memorabilia is drawing a large crowd. Wreath-laying at republican graves is continuing across the weekend.

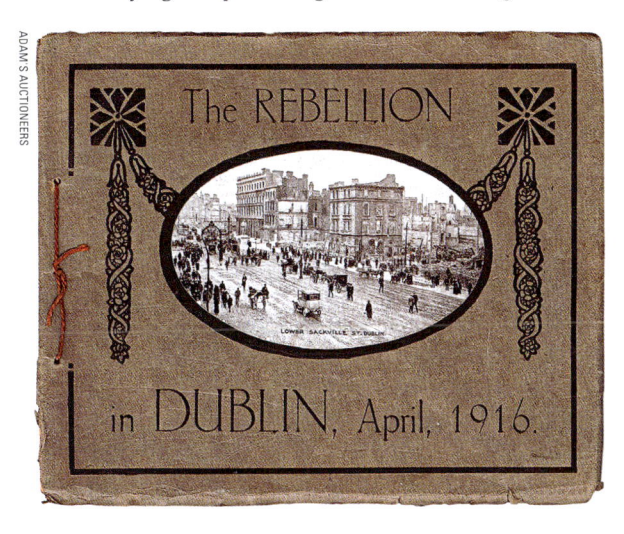

One of the many souvenir booklets produced in the aftermath of the Rising. Publishers were quick to respond to the public demand for photographs and information on the key people and locations at the centre of the action during the momentous week.

Earlier in the week, three soldiers – Privates J. Healy, J. O'Brien and M. Noonan – were court-martialled for assaulting police officers who had confronted them for singing 'Who fears to speak of Easter Week?' All the men denied singing the song, claiming instead they were singing about the 18th Royal Irish Regiment in which they had previously served. They further claimed that the one of the constables in question had followed them, calling them dogs and threatening to break their necks.

The verdict was delivered in private.

In Cork, Bishop Cohalan asked that no street demonstrations accompany the Memorial Masses in the city's churches. Despite this, a crowd of about 600 marched and sang in Irish, several of them wearing republican badges and rosettes. A police baton charge discharged the crowd amid a hail of stones.

9 MAY △
By a margin of just 37 votes, Sinn Féin's **Joseph McGuinness**, interned in an English jail, defeats the IPP's Patrick McKenna to win the South Longford by-election.

18 MAY
A British government decision to stop horseracing elicits a sharp response in Ireland. 'If the Government have the slightest regard for the public opinion and the material welfare of Ireland they will promptly reverse their decision,' *The Freeman's Journal* editorialises.

18 MAY
A strike by Dublin dockers over pay comes to an end following an intervention by the Lord Mayor of Dublin and an agreement between the Shipping Association and the ITGWU. The three-week strike has disrupted the flow of food supplies into the city.

REVOLUTIONARY TIMES 1913–23

1917

THESE WOMEN ARE DOING THEIR BIT

LEARN TO MAKE MUNITIONS

△ **26 MAY**
300 'girls' involved in munitions work gather to discuss pay rates in Dublin's Mansion House. They hear from a representative of the National Federation of Women Workers that the wages of girls in Cork, Dublin, Waterford and Galway had risen to the level of those similarly engaged in England, Wales and Scotland.

31 MAY
A Dublin court dismisses a complaint of animal cruelty against Fred C. Gardner, who had used two dogs in a performance of his show, 'Gardner's Maniacs', at the Theatre Royal. It had been alleged that Gardner had swung one of the dogs around his head several times during the performance.

Irish Convention to Decide Country's Fate

18 May – Prime Minister David Lloyd George has proposed the establishment of a convention of all Irishmen to produce a constitution for the future government of Ireland.

The suggestion comes as Mr Lloyd George forwards a new set of proposals to the nationalist and unionist parties that suggest drafting a bill for the immediate implementation of Home Rule, excluding the six Ulster counties for a period of five years.

After those five years have passed, the position will be reconsidered, assuming partition has not been terminated prior to that date. The bill will provide for a representative Council of Ireland to sit during this time to arrive at a compromise acceptable to the majority.

In making the proposals, the Prime Minister said that the government had been considering for some time what further actions it might take to bring about a settlement of the Irish question. He professed to having a 'deep desire' to 'put an end to a state of affairs which is productive of immense evil, not only to Ireland, but to Great Britain and the Empire'.

There is no optimism that the proposals will succeed, however. Both the Ulster Unionists and the Irish Parliamentary Party have rejected the partition proposals. And while nationalists are broadly in agreement with the idea of the convention, unionists are more negative and see little prospect of success.

EIRN TAKES A TURN AT HER OWN HARP.

PESSIMIST'S DESIGN FOR COSTUME OF CHAIRMAN OF IRISH CONVENTION.

Punch hedges its bets on the likely success of the Irish Convention.

Music hall shows featuring novelty acts were a staple of the popular Hawkins Street venue.

Cruelty Complaint After Dogs Swung at Theatre Royal

Dublin, 1 June – A Dublin man was yesterday charged with cruelty to dogs following a complaint made by a woman attending a performance in the Theatre Royal in the city.

Mrs Shewell, of 26 Upper Pembroke Street, made the complaint following a performance on 12 May called 'Gardner's Maniacs'. Fred Gardner was accused of swinging one dog by its legs over his head several times and forcibly pulling the foreleg of another dog.

The two dogs, Duke and Pincher, had performed on various occasions at the theatre, and Mr Gardner denied all charges of cruelty. He was supported in this by the manager of the Theatre Royal, John Henry Hamilton, who said he had seen the performance on ten separate occasions and there was no cruelty in it. Indeed, patrons had routinely praised the act. A further witness said that the dogs were well-fed and clearly content.

The charge was dismissed.

United They Stand: Irishmen from North and South Join Forces in Messines

Flanders, 8 June – In the capture of Messines Ridge on the Western Front, one of the most striking features of the Allied advance was the sight of northern and southern Irishmen, from opposing political factions at home, fighting alongside each other.

Such was their camaraderie that a group of southern Irishmen presented a cup for a competition between various companies of northerners to see who might get to the top of Messines Ridge first. A commentator from the Front remarked that he did not yet know which company had won.

1917

7 JUN
Members of the 16th Irish and 36th Ulster Divisions fight alongside each other at the Battle of Messines. Together, they help capture the village of Wytschaete.

7 JUN ▽
Major Willie Redmond, MP and brother of the leader of the IPP, is killed on the morning of the first day of the Battle of Messines.

13 JUN
A squadron of 14 Gothas, the Luftstreitkräfte's new heavy bomber, attack London. Over 160 people, including 18 children, are killed in the daylight raid. Air defences developed to combat large, slow Zeppelin bombers prove ineffective against the faster and higher flying biplanes, all of which escape unscathed.

1917

A British officer finds an abandoned German map in the aftermath of the Battle of Messines.

1 JUL
A crowd estimated at between 30,000 and 50,000 attends an anti-partition rally in the Phoenix Park's nine acres. Twenty-four speakers from all four provinces speak from four separate platforms.

9 JUL
Muriel MacDonagh, widow of executed 1916 leader Thomas MacDonagh, drowns while sea swimming. She had been holidaying with other 1916 widows at a house in Skerries, Co. Dublin, rented by the Irish National Aid Association and Volunteers' Dependents' Fund.

The raids began at daybreak, when there was a thunderous crash of noise from a series of mine explosions, some of which were dug a year before, along the German positions. Certain Irish troops in the fighting were involved in five raids in 40 hours.

Well over a million pounds of high explosives were used along a ten-mile front, which followed a weeklong 'preliminary bombardment'.

According to a Press Association report, reproduced in *The Irish Times*, the 'villages of Messines and Wytschaete have totally vanished ... The whole geography of the district has been churned and blown and furrowed out of recognition.'

Extraordinary Celebrations as Final Rebellion Prisoners Released

19 June – There were scenes of jubilation at Westland Row train station yesterday, where thousands gathered to greet the released republican prisoners arriving home from prisons throughout England.

The crowd had been gathering at the station for hours to meet the 117 prisoners who had been arrested in the aftermath of the Easter Rising. Recognisable in the crowd were mothers, sisters and widows of the executed rebel leaders.

Among those released were Countess Markievicz and Count Plunkett, the latter of whom had only been arrested and jailed earlier this month. Countess Markievicz was accompanied by Kathleen Lynn, Helena Molony and Marie Perolz, who had all travelled to Britain to escort her home.

Other senior figures released included Eoin MacNeill, Éamon de Valera, Thomas Ashe and Cathal Brugha.

The prisoners were brought from Parkhurst, Maidstone, Portland and Lewes prisons to Pentonville in London, before being put on a special train leaving Euston Station.

While in Pentonville Prison, some of the prisoners located the grave of Sir Roger Casement and knelt and prayed there for some time. Some took away with them pieces of the sod that covered the remains as mementos.

The returnees arrived in Holyhead at 1.30 a.m., and as they disembarked from the train at the port, they sang 'The Soldier's Song' and were arranged in military order by Mr de Valera before setting sail for home.

The British government minister Andrew Bonar Law, speaking in the House of Commons, remarked that the release was intended to facilitate an 'atmosphere of harmony and goodwill' ahead of the convention of Irishmen to decide how the country is to be administered into the future.

Mr Bonar Law stated that, in releasing the prisoners, the government had satisfied itself 'in the first place, that the public security will not be endangered by such an act of grace; and, secondly, that in none of the cases concerned is there evidence that participation in the rebellion was accompanied by individual acts which would render such a display of clemency impossible'.

This amnesty, which follows an earlier release on Christmas Eve last year, means that all of those arrested due to their involvement in the Rising have now been freed.

1917

10 JUL
Éamon de Valera wins the East Clare by-election caused by the death of Willie Redmond. He declares a victory for the 'independence of Ireland and for an Irish Republic'.

25 JUL
The Irish Convention holds its first meeting at Trinity College Dublin, under the chairmanship of Sir Horace Plunkett. Summoned by Lloyd George to examine the future of Irish self-government, the convention commences with 92 members. Sinn Féin declines to attend owing to its terms of reference, as does William O'Brien's All-for-Ireland party.

31 JUL
Meath poet Francis Ledwidge is killed by a stray shell during the third Battle of Ypres, also known as the Battle of Passchendaele.

Crowds throng Westland Row (Pearse Street) station and surrounds to greet the released prisoners who travelled overnight on the mailboat from Holyhead.

1917

△ 1 AUG
Pope Benedict XV issues a plea for peace in the form of a Papal 'Note to the Heads of Belligerent Peoples'.

△ 10 AUG
W.T. Cosgrave, recently released from prison, wins the Kilkenny City by-election for Sinn Féin. Cosgrave outpolled his IPP opponent, John Magennis, by 772 votes to 392.

18 AUG
Thomas Ashe, who had been sentenced to death for his role in the 1916 Rising and who had only recently been released from prison as part of a general amnesty, is rearrested and charged with sedition for a speech delivered in Co. Longford the previous month.

'England has her answer!': Landslide Win for de Valera

Ennis, 12 July – Éamon de Valera has won the East Clare by-election for Sinn Féin.

The victory margin was an extremely comfortable one – de Valera secured 5,010 votes against the 2,035 won by his Irish Parliamentary Party opponent Patrick Lynch.

Republicans marched through towns across Ireland waving flags and shouting 'Up de Valera' and 'Up the Republic.'

The general view is that local Catholic priests played a prominent role in the victory. They are said to have canvassed doubters and contributed to bringing voters to the polling booths.

After his victory was made clear, Mr de Valera emerged from the courthouse in Ennis and was greeted by cheering crowds who were waving republican flags. A voice from the crowd shouted:

Pamphlet quoting the Catholic Bishop of Limerick's support for Sinn Féin.

Fresh from his by-election triumph and surrounded by well-wishers, Éamon de Valera addresses a crowd from the steps of Ennis Court House.

'England has her answer!' De Valera first spoke a few words in Irish and then said, 'What shall I say to you? I shall simply say to you that you are men of Clare, that you are worthy descendants of Claremen who fought for Brian Boru, with the same spirit in your hearts today that your forefathers had a thousand years ago.'

Mr de Valera was wearing the uniform of an Irish Volunteer officer when he spoke.

The by-election in Clare was to fill the seat left vacant following the death of Major William Redmond, who died at the recent Battle of Messines. His brother, John Redmond, the leader of the Irish Parliamentary Party, is widely rumoured to be considering his future in politics.

Mr Redmond has suffered a brutally difficult year, losing his brother and his daughter. He has also suffered from watching the political sentiment in the country shift away from his party towards Sinn Féin and republicanism, as evidenced by the victories of Count Plunkett and Joseph McGuinness in by-elections elsewhere.

Poet Francis Ledwidge Killed Fighting in Flanders

Passchendaele, 9 August – Tributes have been paid to the 'Meath peasant poet', Lance Corporal Francis Ledwidge, who was killed in action while serving with the Royal Inniskilling Fusiliers in Flanders. He was 29 years old.

Captain Lord Dunsany, who introduced Ledwidge's work to the public, remarked that 'this rare poet' had been born of peasant stock, lived nearly all his life in Slane and, had he lived, 'this lover of all seasons in which the blackbird sings would have surpassed even Burns'. Dunsany remarked that he received the last – and, he considered, 'the best' – of Ledwidge's poems on the very day of his death – 31 July.

Francis Ledwidge's first book was entitled *Songs of the Fields*, and throughout the war – whether in Salonika, Gallipoli, Egypt, France or Belgium – he continued to write whenever he found the time. Some of these poems have been collected in the book *Songs of Peace*.

Ledwidge is the not the first Irish poet to be killed in the war. Tom Kettle, the nationalist MP, university lecturer and poet, was previously lost in battle.

1917

19 AUG
Bishop of Limerick, Dr Edward O'Dwyer, dies after a short illness. A staunch nationalist, Dr O'Dwyer is described by recently elected MP Éamon de Valera as a 'model Irish bishop'.

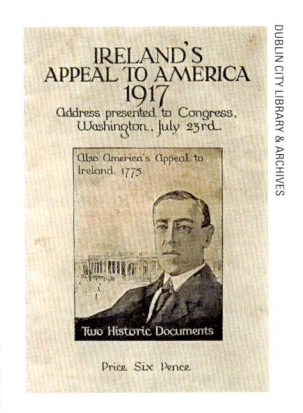

4 SEP △
An '**Irish manifesto**' is smuggled into the US and signed by 26 released Sinn Féin prisoners. Presented to the president and Senate, it takes its inspiration from President Wilson's dictum that 'no people must be forced under a sovereignty under which it does not want to live', and urges that Ireland's case be considered in that light.

6 SEP
Cavan-man Thomas Conaty from Ballinagh is charged at a district court martial in Belfast with carrying a hurley stick in contravention of the DORA.

1917

12 SEP
A Cork labourer is killed during disturbances at Queenstown. Fred Plummer dies when he hits his head on the flagged footpath of the beach after being struck by an America sailor.

12 SEP
In a letter addressed to the secretary of a new Irish college to be established in Drogheda, the Archbishop of Armagh and Primate of All Ireland, Cardinal Logue, claims that the Gaelic League had been turned into a 'political machine' with the effect, he feared, that 'it will prove barren so far as promoting the revival of Irish is concerned'.

21 SEP
An explosion at the Kynoch factory in Arklow, Co. Wicklow, leaves up to 28 workers dead and six seriously injured. An inquest into the explosion records a verdict of accidental death.

22 SEP
The Freeman's Journal reports on a conference held in the Gresham Hotel on the laundry industry in Ireland. The conference hears that nearly 2,000 women work in laundries in Dublin, but questions whether wages in the commercial sector were impacted by the laundry operations of charitable institutions.

Tea Shortage Causes Panic in Dublin

Dublin, 23 August – A scarcity of tea supplies has resulted in extraordinary scenes in the streets of Dublin in recent days.

Crowds besieged shops in almost every thoroughfare of Dublin on Saturday in search of tea supplies. Queues four lines deep blocked pathways outside grocers' shops, and police were called in to regulate the crowds. Hundreds of spectators congregated on the streets, attracted by the unusual scenes of men, women and children struggling and pushing to gain access to the shops.

On South Great George's Street, people became so unruly that Messrs Becker were forced to pull down the shutters of their shop.

Elsewhere in the city, tea was sold in smaller amounts than usual to cater to the greatest number of customers possible. Special dispensation was made to people known to have large families.

Interviewed yesterday, Sir Thomas Lipton has stated that there was plenty of tea waiting to be shipped from India, but it has been held up by freightage difficulties. Across the UK, there is at present a six-week supply of tea remaining. An editorial in *The Irish Times* has highlighted the current shortages as being of 'serious importance to Ireland, where tea constitutes a considerable factor in the food of the people'.

The tea rush is expected to ease once new supplies reach the country.

Grocers such as A.J. Mortimer, Bridge Street, Waterford, were keen to advertise the current cost of stocking the household tea caddy. In 1916 he was selling a 'special blend' of tea at 2s 6d per pound and a 'splendid quality' variety for tuppence less.

Thomas Ashe Dies on Hunger Strike in Mountjoy Prison

26 September – Thomas Ashe has died.

The 1916 rebel leader, who was serving a one-year prison sentence in Mountjoy Prison, died at 10.30 p.m. yesterday in the Mater Misericordiae Hospital, where he had been admitted five hours earlier in a very weak condition. Diminished by hunger strike, the damage to his system was exacerbated by forcible feeding by the prison authorities.

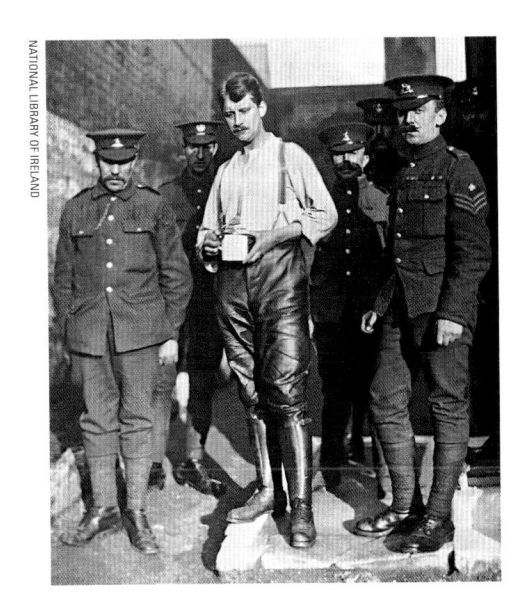

A photograph of Thomas Ashe taken in Kilmainham Gaol where he was held after the Rising. A motorcycle enthusiast, he is pictured wearing his biker gear. Ashe was the proud owner of a 2½ horsepower New Hudson machine, which he used to good effect in the run-up to and during the action around Ashbourne.

The deceased was taken by cab to the hospital at 3 p.m. yesterday and attended to by the hospital staff, alongside the Sisters of Mercy and the hospital chaplain, Reverend T.J. Murray, who administered the last rites to Ashe before his death.

Ashe's death is certain to further inflame an already volatile political atmosphere. An *Irish Independent* editorial is adamant that should 'more ill-feeling' arise because of the shock death, 'the authorities … will, to a great extent, be responsible'.

The 'forcible method' by which Mr Ashe had been fed was 'revolting', the editorial claimed: 'It is obvious that long before his removal to hospital he was in a critical condition. By their negligence in not removing him sooner to a place where he would have been humanely treated the authorities have incurred a grave responsibility.'

After spending time as a prisoner in Dartmoor, Lewes and Portland, Thomas Ashe was released in the general amnesty on 17 June. He was

1917

25 SEP
Thomas Ashe dies after being force-fed while on hunger strike in Mountjoy Prison.

13 OCT
The Theatre Royal in Dublin hosts a performance of *Ghosts,* a play written by the late Henrik Ibsen 36 years previously and banned for almost a quarter of a century as a 'work unfit for presentation in a public theatre'.

15 OCT ▽
Margaretha Geertruida MacLeod, better known by the stage name **Mata Hari**, is executed by firing squad in France. The Dutch exotic dancer was convicted of spying for the Germans.

17 OCT
John Redmond introduces a motion to the House of Commons deploring the policy that is being pursued by the Irish Executive and the military authorities.

1917

▽ **18 OCT**
1,600 collectors take to the streets of Dublin to raise funds for the **Red Cross**. Since the start of the war, Ireland has subscribed £133,000 to the Red Cross Fund.

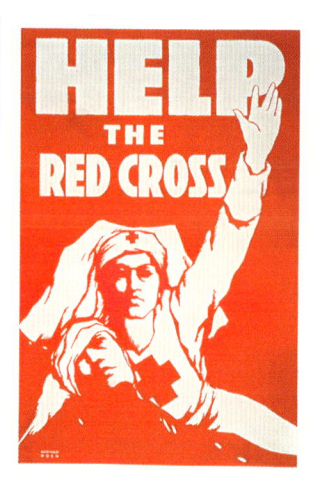

25 OCT
It is reported that Liam Mellows and Patrick McCartan have been arrested in the US, the former in possession of the passport of an American seaman.

25 OCT
Sinn Féin holds its convention in Dublin at which Éamon de Valera is elected party president.

27 OCT
De Valera is elected president of the Irish Volunteers. Michael Collins is elected to its national executive.

rearrested in August for delivering a seditious speech at Ballinalee, Co. Longford, on 25 July, and at his subsequent court martial on 4 September he declined to recognise the authority of the court. The police gave evidence to the effect that he encouraged his friends at a Sinn Féin meeting to 'train, arm and equip themselves'.

Despite contesting the evidence, Mr Ashe was taken to Mountjoy, where he began a hunger strike.

Twenty-eight Dead in Irish Factory Explosion

22 September – An explosion at the Kynoch cordite factory in Arklow has claimed the lives of 28 people and injured many more.

The single blast occurred at one of the most dangerous sections of the facility, which was isolated from the main building.

The majority of those who lost their lives in the factory – which has been operating since the 1890s – were killed instantly. Ten workers were found alive at the site and taken to the local hospital, but two subsequently died there. One of these men was the only locally born employee among the victims; the rest came from various parts of Ireland.

One of the first to visit the scene was the local Roman Catholic curate; he found bodies around the factory, many of them charred and several without limbs.

The force of the blast was felt far beyond the site itself: two nearby houses were destroyed and four or five were seriously damaged. The local coroner heard the explosion from his home two miles outside the town; he told reporters that one of his bedroom windows was thrown open and the whole house was 'lit up brilliantly by the great flashes of light'.

Once notified of the incident, fire brigade and ambulance services were immediately dispatched from Dublin, offering support to the military who had already arrived on the scene.

An inquiry is to be held into the causes of the blast.

The Kynoch munitions factory situated on Arklow's north beach.

1917

Following solemn Requiem Mass in the Pro-Cathedral, the body of Thomas Ashe was taken to Glasnevin Cemetery as a Volunteer guard of honour, with rifles reversed, marched on either side of the hearse. Following prayers and the graveside oration, the Last Post was sounded and a colour party fired a gun salute in a final tribute to their dead comrade.

Huge Crowds Attend Funeral of Thomas Ashe

Dublin, 30 September – Up to 40,000 people attended the funeral today of the republican Thomas Ashe, who died on 25 September at the Mater Misericordiae Hospital, five hours after being admitted from Mountjoy Prison, where he had been on hunger strike.

Newspapers are reporting that the funeral was, in terms of its size, greater than anything that has been seen in more than a generation and was unmatched in terms of the public outpouring of grief. The enormous crowd would have been still greater had more special trains been permitted to enable mourners to travel from various parts of the country.

The funeral procession ran from City Hall to Glasnevin Cemetery and along the route the streets were thronged with mourners.

There were uniformed members of the Volunteers and Cumann na mBan, members of GAA clubs wielding hurleys, members of Gaelic League branches, national schoolteachers, postmen and more. Many of these wore colourful costumes and uniforms and sported Sinn Féin colours.

Around the grave where Ashe's remains were laid there were scenes of unrestrained grief. Tears flowed freely, most notably among the relatives of the deceased, which included his father. Hundreds of floral tributes and

27 OCT
Baseball comes to Lansdowne Road, the home of Irish rugby, when teams from Canada and the US play an international exhibition match in aid of the Dublin Castle Red Cross Hospital. 6,000 spectators attend.

28 OCT
Dublin defeats Tipperary on a scoreline of 5–4 to 4–2 to win the All-Ireland hurling title at Croke Park.

1917

1 NOV
Count Georg von Hertling becomes Chancellor of the German Reich and Prime Minister of Prussia. The 75-year-old Hertling is a former Professor of Philosophy in Munich.

6 NOV
John Hylan, whose father emigrated from Co. Cavan, is elected as Mayor of New York City. A Democrat backed by Tammany Hall, Hylan defeats incumbent John Purroy Mitchel, a grandson of Irish nationalist leader John Mitchel.

7 NOV
Bolshevik revolutionaries, led by Lenin, seize control of government buildings in Petrograd, overthrowing the Provisional Government, which had replaced the Romanov regime. He moves to establish a Bolshevik-dominated Soviet government.

10 NOV
The Third Battle of Ypres, which began with a British offensive in early July, ends at a great cost to human life and with little military progress made.

15 NOV
The release of hunger-striking prisoners begins in Dundalk Jail. Over the following days about 60 prisoners in Dundalk and Mountjoy are released.

---

wreaths were sent from around the country and placed at the graveside.

In keeping with the military-style arrangements, the Last Post was sounded and a volley of shots was fired by a party of eight Volunteers under the direction of Captain Liam Clarke.

Vice-Commandant Michael Collins, standing at the edge of the grave, spoke. 'Nothing additional remains to be said,' he remarked. 'That volley which we have just heard is the only speech which it is proper to make above the grave of a dead Fenian.'

Russia in Revolt Again

Petrograd, 20 November – There has been another revolt in Russia.

Following the abdication of Tsar Nicholas II in March this year and the replacement of his Romanov dynasty by the Provisional Government, earlier this month – on 8 November – Russian Maximalists (often described as the Bolsheviks) succeeded in bringing off a successful coup d'état by ousting from power the government of Alexander Kerensky.

Some ministers in the now deposed Provisional Government are reported to have been arrested, with Kerensky said to have fled the capital.

On Wednesday 7 November, at approximately 5 p.m., the Military Revolutionary Committee of the Soviet published a statement declaring Petrograd to be in their control, acknowledging the assistance of the garrison in enabling the coup to be brought about. The proclamation set out the main objectives of the new government:

1. Propose an immediate and just peace.
2. Hand the land to the peasants.
3. Summon the Constituent Assembly on 8 November.

The coup d'état makes headlines around the world.

Subsequently, the Petrograd Council of Workmen's and Soldiers' Delegates announced that the Provisional Government was no more and that the Provisional Parliament had been dissolved.

The delegates gave sustained and warm applause to Vladimir Ilyich Lenin, who is believed to have led this latest coup.

George Bernard Shaw Calls Irish Extremists 'idiots'

28 November – With the Irish Convention deliberating on the future government of Ireland, and Sinn Féin awaiting a post-war peace conference to make their claims for an Irish Republic, the writer George Bernard Shaw has pitched in with his own views on how to settle the Irish question.

His thoughts, detailed and set out with typical artistic style and argumentative punch, come in a lengthy article that has been reprinted by the *Irish Independent* newspaper.

Mr Shaw launched his series of articles by denouncing Sinn Féin and what he termed the 'Ulster Impossibilists', characterising both as 'idiots'.

The very use of the term Sinn Féin – 'We Ourselves' – was criticised by the writer for being 'a disgraceful and obsolete sentiment, horribly anti-Catholic, and acutely ridiculous in the presence of a crisis which has shown that not even the richest and most powerful countries … have been able to stand by themselves'.

But it was more than the name that was the problem. Mr Shaw accused Sinn Féin of feeding their supporters on 'dreams and Irish air', of being hopelessly ignorant of the size of the military forces the British Empire could muster against them, and of being ridiculously naive in thinking that Ireland would matter a jot to anyone at a future peace conference: 'Sinn Féin really does think that the world consists of Ireland and a few subordinate continents.'

The folly of Sinn Féin, he argues, was matched by that of many Ulster unionists, whose opposition to an Irish parliament was rooted in exaggerated fears and was perhaps not as united as it liked to present itself.

George Bernard Shaw by cartoonist Edmund S. Valtman.

1917

21 NOV
Fifty-three republican prisoners are reported to be still on hunger strike in Irish jails: 37 in Cork, 15 in Dundalk, one in Belfast.

24 NOV
The Provost of Trinity College accuses the British government of 'killing' the Irish Convention and contributing to Ireland's political volatility by its 'feebleness and blindness'. Dr John Pentland Mahaffy levels the charges in a lengthy letter to *The Times* in London.

30 NOV
Five fishermen are lost at sea when their boat capsizes in rough seas at Ballinacarrig Bay, just south of Wicklow town.

6 DEC ▽
Finland declares its independence from the Russian Empire.

1917

6 DEC
A collision between two ships, one carrying explosives, in the busy Canadian port of Halifax, Nova Scotia, destroys large parts of the city and results in nearly 2,000 deaths.

7 DEC
The US declares war on Austria-Hungary.

9 DEC
Wexford defeat Clare in the All-Ireland football decider at Croke Park to secure a third All-Ireland title in a row. The game was played before an attendance of 7,000 spectators.

△ **11 DEC**
General Edmund Allenby enters Jerusalem on foot in respect for the Holy City following its capture from the Turks by the British. He quickly posts guards to protect all the sites held sacred by the Christian, Muslim and Jewish religions.

He suggests the 'Ulster variety of Sinn Féin, like the southern one, has not a leg to stand on'. Mr Shaw suggests that no separation is likely between Ireland and England and there is likely to be 'more union than ever'. Just what that means, he intends to set out in a further article.

Wexford Footballers Complete All-Ireland 3-in-a-row

10 December – Wexford are the All-Ireland football champions again.

For a third year in a row, the Slaneysiders won Gaelic football's most coveted prize when they defeated Clare in front of 7,000 spectators at Croke Park yesterday.

After a night of sharp frost, All-Ireland final morning broke to fine, if bitterly cold, weather, and the Croke Park surface was in splendid condition when, at midday, the ball was finally thrown in.

What followed, however, was a disappointment. If the result went as many had expected, the way it was achieved was less than brilliant. The quality of football was below that to which we've become accustomed in recent years, the flow of the play interrupted by an excessive free count for both sides. Clare, the lighter of the two teams, played against a slight breeze in the first half and did well to trail by only two points at half-time.

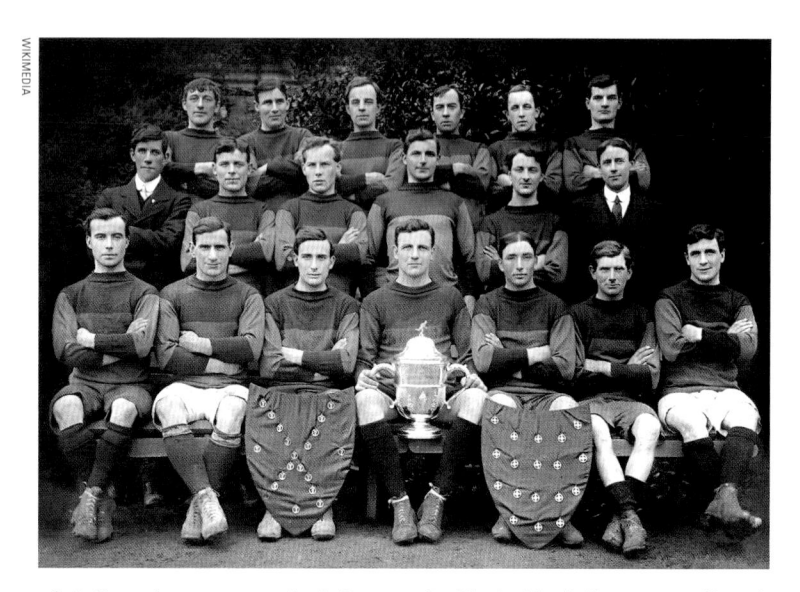

Seán Kennedy (CENTRE), captain of all conquering Wexford football team, was allowed to keep the All-Ireland trophy, the Great Southern and Western Railway Cup.

The margin between the two teams never narrowed, however. Immediately at the resumption of play in the second half, Wexford swept forward, their captain, John O'Kennedy, fisting a point to extend their lead to three points. By the conclusion of the game the margin would be extended to four.

The final score read Wexford 0–9, Clare 0–5.

Boom-time for Irish Christmas Turkey Sales

19 December – With Christmas approaching, turkeys are currently reaching prices of £3 a pair at the Leinster markets, with one vendor in Enniscorthy reporting a high of £3 10s.

The reason for the high prices is the number being exported: 8,000 turkeys were shipped to Britain last week from farms in north Wexford alone, with a good deal of common fowl – as well as geese and ducks – also finding a market there. Scarcity of grain and other foods, together with the seasonal Christmas demand, are factors fuelling the growth in turkey exports.

This growth in exports is set against the backdrop of increasing shortages of butter, milk and flour around the country due to the ongoing war. The extent of the crisis has led one Claremorris merchant to state that 'England is prepared to starve Ireland'.

Carts full of turkeys queueing on the quays in Waterford city at the foot of Conduit Lane and likely destined for Flynn's Poultry Stores.

1917

20 DEC △
For the second time in as many years, Australia holds a **referendum on conscription**. In a blow to Australian Prime Minister Billy Hughes, voters decide again – and by a bigger margin – to oppose compulsory military service. The result is 1,015,159 votes in favour and 1,181,747 against.

23 DEC
The Lord Lieutenant of Ireland opens an Air Service exhibition at Earlsfort Garage on Dublin's Hatch Street. Included in the exhibition are examples of Allied and enemy fighting aircraft and portions of destroyed Zeppelins.

25 DEC
Pope Benedict XV delivers his traditional Christmas message, expressing both his disappointment at the failure of his efforts at international reconciliation and his continued commitment to a mission of peace.

Remembering 1917
a hundred years on

Organised by Kerry County Council and Tralee Irish Volunteers, a parade is held in Tralee to mark the centenary of the death of Thomas Ashe. A member of the Irish Volunteers since its foundation in 1913 and a participant in the Easter Rising as commander of the Fingal Battalion, which saw action at Ashbourne, Ashe had died from force-feeding while on hunger strike at the Mater Hospital in Dublin. He was arrested for sedition in August 1917 and began his hunger strike on 20 September 1917. He died only five days after his hunger strike began from heart failure and congestion of the lungs due to force-feeding. He was remembered by a torchlight parade through Tralee a century after his death as he had been born close by, at Lispole, County Kerry.

25 September 2017

REVOLUTIONARY TIMES 1913–23

'... guilty of the gravest sins'?
– Religion and the Irish Revolution

ON 1 JUNE 1916, a few weeks after the Easter Rising had ended, General John Maxwell, then acting as the temporary military governor of Ireland, wrote to British Prime Minister Herbert Asquith. Maxwell informed the Prime Minister that he was receiving reports from the RIC that priests were 'offering Mass for the repose of the souls of those who have died, or been executed, martyrs to their country's cause etc.' Fearing that the Catholic clergy could become a seditious force in Ireland, Maxwell wondered if Pope Benedict XV could be induced to advise the Irish hierarchy to 'prevent Priests from mixing themselves up with matters, political, seditious or unconnected with the spiritual position'. Separation of the sort that Maxwell desired would prove impossible, and the main Churches on the island would emerge as key players in the identity politics that underscored the revolutionary period.

> ...'prevent Priests from mixing themselves up with matters, political, seditious or unconnected with the spiritual position'.

The 1911 census showed that there were 3.3 million Catholics on the island, 0.5 million members of the Church of Ireland and 0.4 million Presbyterians. Catholics made up 74% of the population and were, numerically at least, the dominant population. By the time the next census was undertaken in 1926, and in the context of partition, it was estimated that the Protestant population of the twenty-six southern counties had dropped by 100,000. The deaths of southern Protestants in the First World War, the departure of those connected with the British administration after 1922, and the decision of others to leave during and after the War of Independence and the Civil War all combined to create two jurisdictions - the Irish Free State

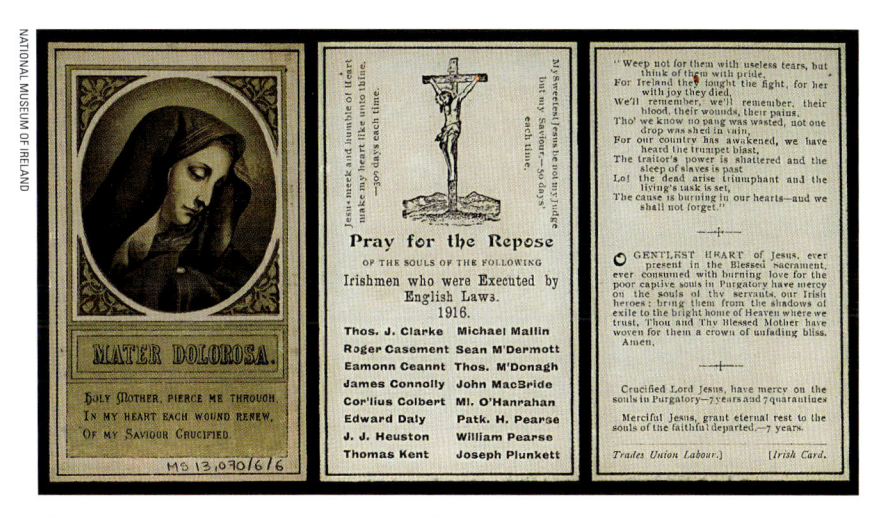

Memorial card for the executed 1916 leaders. The tradition of producing cards requesting prayers for the souls of the departed started at the end of the nineteenth century and it became common practice among Catholics to keep them in prayer missals.

and Northern Ireland – that were closely tied to the religious identities of their majority populations.

Ireland had undergone a devotional revolution in the decades after the Great Famine, and the institutional Catholic Church entered the twentieth century as a powerful force in society. The Church was broadly supportive of the campaign for Home Rule and opposed both the radical republicanism of the IRB and the socialism of Jim Larkin's trade unionism. Leading figures in the Church, such as Cardinal Michael Logue and Archbishop of Dublin William Walsh, were sceptical of the leadership of the Home Rule movement, but, as historian Daithí Ó Corráin has noted, 'a large episcopal middle ground – determined not to interfere in politics, supportive of the national cause and reliable subscribers to the parliamentary fund – separated the sceptics from the party loyalists'. Unionist propaganda was able to cast this Catholic backing for the Home Rule movement as an ominous signifier of what a nationalist-determined future would hold for the Protestant people of Ireland, most notably in the north-east of the country. It was encapsulated in the 'Home rule equals Rome rule' equation that ran as a catchy – and popular – slogan from the 1870s onwards.

Fear of an all-pervasive Catholicism in any future Home Rule Ireland was heightened by the 1908 *Ne Temere* papal decree, which required that all children of mixed marriages be brought up Catholic. The alarm was heightened by the McCann case of 1910. That year the marriage of Alexander McCann, a Catholic, and Agnes McCann, a Presbyterian, broke down. The former subsequently attempted to have their twenty-month-old son baptised in a Catholic church, but the service was disrupted by objections from Agnes.

The break-up of the McCanns' relationship stemmed from the visit of a Catholic priest to the couple, who informed them that their marriage was null and void and that they should remarry in a Catholic church. What was essentially a private matter became intertwined with the very public, political battle over Home Rule, with the *Northern Whig* warning that 'to steal the children of a lawfully married Presbyterian mother, and to turn them into Roman Catholics against her will – to tell her that she is a harlot and her children bastards – all that will come quite naturally after Home Rule'. Unionist politicians and the Protestant Churches started framing the potential fall-out from any enactment of Home Rule as detrimental to non-Catholics because Catholic theology would inform state laws. For unionists, opposition to Home Rule was, therefore, not simply rooted in ties to Britain but was also critically defined as safeguarding their Protestantism against the dangers of an all-pervasive Catholicism.

> **What was essentially a private matter became intertwined with the very public, political battle over Home Rule.**

While the outbreak of the First World War led to the suspension of Home Rule, the events of Easter 1916 blindsided the Catholic Church. And even though the rebel forces encompassed members of the socialist and more secularly minded ICA, they also included many devout Catholic men and women, most obvious among them Patrick Pearse, whose piety was platformed in the religious imagery that ran through many of his pre-Rising writings. In his 1915 play *The Singer,* for example, Pearse's main character remarks: 'One man can free a people as one Man redeemed the world. I will take no pike, I will go into the battle with bare hands. I will stand up before the Gall as Christ hung naked before men on the tree.'

Although there were clerics, such as Edward O'Dwyer of Limerick, who were supportive of Pearse and his fellow rebels, the casualties of Easter Week created issues for many senior churchmen because, as Oliver Rafferty has stated, 'from the viewpoint of Catholic moral teaching the 1916 Rising cannot be regarded as just'. It was a measure of the conflicting sentiments aroused by the Rising that when, in June 1916, the Catholic hierarchy formed a committee to frame its official response, the bishops involved disagreed to such an extent that no statement was ever issued. However, given the hierarchy's failure to condemn the extremes of the British government's response to the Rising, in particular the executions, mass arrests and martial law that had radicalised Irish public opinion, there was a broad sense that the Catholic Church was essentially opposed to the rebels. In the vacuum of its response to the Rising, the Church had momentarily risked its place as a major force in Irish life. The lessons of 1916 were nevertheless learned, so that by 1918, as Rafferty observed, the bishops had come around to joining 'the party of revolution'.

Duty, sacrifice and faith are intertwined in these propaganda images of Volunteers produced between 1917 and 1920.

The British government also looked to apply new thinking. Against the backdrop of the transformed Irish political landscape, it attempted again to resolve the Home Rule conundrum – legislation had been passed, but postponed for the duration of the war, with provisions for Ulster's exclusion still undefined – by convening an Irish Convention in July 1917. It ran until April the following year and, although it ultimately failed to resolve the Home Rule crisis, the Convention stands out as the last all-Ireland gathering to attempt to reach an agreed outcome before the island was politically partitioned. It was significant too that the Convention brought together a wide variety of interests from inside and outside politics, including religious leaders, whose presence underlined their commitment to the idea of a peaceful and inclusive solution to the question of Ireland's future.

For the Catholic Church, however, it was less its association with the Convention than its active role in the campaign to oppose conscription that identified it with the shifting national mood. When the Military Service (No. 2) Act, which would enable the extension of conscription to Ireland, was passed by the House of Commons in April 1918, Archbishop Walsh noted that 'the people collectively and individually need a definite lead as to what to do if conscription is enforced'. In response, and having liaised with leading figures in Sinn Féin, the Catholic bishops of Ireland released a statement that declared their opposition to conscription and warned the British government against 'entering on a policy so disastrous to the public interest, and to all order, public and private'.

But the hierarchy did not simply indulge in empty, hand-wringing gestures: it also acted as a mobilising force for resistance to conscription. Not only did it instruct that the Irish people had a 'right to resist [conscription] by every means that are consonant with the law of God', but it also organised for the Catholics of Ireland to take an anti-conscription pledge at the door of their church as they entered for Mass on 21 April 1918. This had the desired effect: the broad-based campaign of resistance to conscription that materialised in the spring and summer of 1918 succeeded in thwarting its application to Ireland. A further effect of the anti-conscription campaign was to yoke the Catholic Church and Sinn Féin together in a working relationship that, in the aftermath of the 1918 Westminster election, saw the hierarchy accepting the ascendancy of Sinn Féin and recognising its republican ideology as the expressed will of the majority of the people.

It remained a relationship that was subject to occasional strains, however. Just as the 1916 Rising had given rise to theological and moral complexities, so too did the Anglo-Irish war of 1919-21. Throughout, the Catholic Church, in the form of priests and bishops reacting to events in their locality, was constantly critical of killings and condemned political violence from both sides. In December 1920, for instance, the Bishop of Cork, Daniel Cohalan, sparked

A FATEFUL SESSION.
SITTING HEN. "GO AWAY! DON'T HURRY ME!"

Punch *expressed impatience with the Irish Convention as early as August 1917.*

controversy when he issued a pastoral decree stating that anyone taking part in an ambush that involved killing would be excommunicated.

With the signing and ratification of the Anglo-Irish Treaty, the Catholic Church threw its weight behind the new state, and when the Civil War erupted, the hierarchy was unambiguous as to where its allegiances stood. Perhaps its most notable intervention came in October 1922, when a pastoral letter, issued by Cardinal Logue and the archbishops and bishops of Ireland, was read at services across the country outlining how republicans 'carry on what they call a war, but which, in the absence of any legitimate authority to justify it, is morally only a system of murder and assassination of the National forces'. The letter, which met with a swift and sharp anti-rebuttal from one anti-Treatyite priest, made clear that anyone guilty of attacks on the state was 'guilty of the gravest sins, and may not be absolved in Confession, nor admitted to Holy Communion'.

> 'Every devilish thing we did against the British … boomeranged and smote us tenfold … waves of loot and materialism were the result …'

But it wasn't only the ecclesiastical elite who saw in the Civil War the seeds of a spiritual degradation. Writing in 1924, P.S. O'Hegarty, then secretary of the Department of Posts and Telegraphs in a new Irish Free State, remarked on how the revolutionary decade had left behind a corroded public morality. 'Every devilish thing we did against the British … boomeranged and smote us tenfold … the irregulars drove patriotism and honesty and morality out of Ireland … we have degenerated morally and spiritually … waves of loot and materialism were the result … a grave increase in sexual immorality … Jazz dancing … has swept Ireland like a prairie fire.'

The Ireland in which O'Hegarty wrote was nevertheless one where the 'old old restraints', as the poet Padraic Colum put it, were rapidly re-established. It was also an Ireland divided by partition, where the cross-religious approach taken at the 1917 Irish Convention appeared a relic of another era. The new Irish Free State aligned itself intimately with the Catholic Church and contentedly ceded responsibility for education and the welfare of society's most vulnerable to clergy and religious orders, which would, in turn, create a damaging and long-lasting legacy. Northern Ireland, meanwhile, wedded itself to Protestantism, and the discriminating ways in which the Belfast administration dealt with its two principal communities served to copper-fasten community and sectarian divisions that later fuelled civil rights demands, resistance to which in the late 1960s would lead them to spiral into the violence of the so-called 'Troubles'.

Between Armed Rebellion and Democratic Revolution
–The Rise of Sinn Féin

THE HOUSE OF COMMONS filled with noise and animosity. It was 10 May 1916 and John Dillon, the veteran IPP MP, was skilfully skewering the British government's response to the events in Dublin over the previous two weeks: the ongoing executions of the rebel leaders of the Easter Rising, the holding of secret military trials, and the widespread harassment, arrest and deportation of those who were not even involved in the uprising.

Arthur Griffith, journalist and principal founder of the Sinn Féin movement.

The Irish MP, who had witnessed the rebellion close-up, saw, in the prosecution of this punitive policy, the unravelling of decades of constitutional nationalist progress, which had been expected to soon deliver the prize of an Irish Home Rule Parliament. This was, an emotional Dillon put it, the 'fruit of our life [sic] work' and it was being washed away in a 'sea of blood'.

His words would prove prophetic. Just over two years later, compounded by further missteps by the British government, a generation of Home Rule Irish MPs would be swept away and the political order in Ireland turned upside down.

The political beneficiaries of the IPP's demise would be Sinn Féin. Founded in 1905 by Arthur Griffith, and a peripheral political force for the following decade, the party would become popularly, if mistakenly, identified with the events of Easter 1916 and would gather support even before it was clear to many what it actually stood for. As historian Fearghal McGarry has observed, the post-Rising appeal of Sinn Féin was above all else grounded in 'a rejection of the old (Redmondite) order'.

That old order was hardly helped by the bungled British effort to find a quick resolution to the divisive Home Rule issue in the aftermath of the Rising. David Lloyd George, Minister for Munitions in the wartime coalition government, had been entrusted with the task, and he eschewed the approach adopted in July 1914 when nationalist and unionist leaders had been brought together for face-to-face discussions with the British government at Buckingham Palace. Rather than reprise the round table, Lloyd George opted to meet separately with both sets of negotiators and found agreement for a solution on the basis that the Home Rule Act of 1914 would come into force as soon as possible, with certain conditions: that it would not apply to the six northeastern counties; that Irish representation at Westminster would be reduced; and that, at the conclusion of the war, an Imperial Conference would be convened to find a permanent settlement for Ireland.

The Sinn Féin abú crest first appeared on postcards in 1916.

For unionist and nationalist negotiators, the compromise offered sufficient crumbs of comfort to earn their support, but questions remained about the exact nature of the proposed partition and how long it would last. Here, in what historian Éamon Phoenix described as an act of 'premediated duplicity', Lloyd George offered assurances to the two parties that were not only incompatible, but inimical. The result was that what Edward Carson considered to be a permanent exclusion of six Ulster counties, John Redmond understood to be temporary. It was on the basis of these divergent understandings that the nationalist and unionist leaders won the support of their respective organisations, but when it was discussed in Cabinet on 19 July that the exclusion could indeed be permanent, the Lloyd George proposals were effectively sunk.

The failure of the May–July 1916 negotiations was devastating for the IPP. Its position within Irish nationalism, already weakened by a protracted war and the severity of the British response to the Rising, was further eroded. 'We have done with Mr. Redmond,' declared the *Ulster Herald*, while the *Irish Independent* pointed a similarly accusatory finger at the IPP leadership, which it claimed had been 'hoodwinked' and 'tricked' during its negotiations with Lloyd George.

By the end of the year, amidst concern at the British administration of the war effort, Lloyd George had replaced Herbert Asquith as prime minister in a more unionist-leaning coalition that saw Carson pitched into the role of First Lord of the Admiralty. The change signalled a reordering of the priorities of British policymakers to a point where the attitude to Ireland became, as Ronan Fanning observed, one of 'almost utter indifference'. Between January 1917 and March 1918, a time when 'the Cabinet met each weekday, only one substantive discussion of Irish policy' took place.

It wasn't as if there wasn't much to discuss. One of the first acts of the Lloyd George-led government was to release from British jails the remaining Irish prisoners who had been interned in the aftermath of the Rising. The reception they received on their return to Ireland – all 600 of them – suggested that separatist sentiment was gaining ground. Interest in, and support for, the rebels took many forms and found expression in multiple ways: in the routine, sympathetic reportage of the nationalist press; in the public appetite for the 'instant histories', books and souvenir brochures that sprang up in the Rising's wake; in the popularity of songs and lyrics honouring the rebel dead; and in the increased public visibility of republican badges, flags and rosettes.

> **At the very moment that credibility was draining from the IPP, opportunities arose to simultaneously test and parade separatist strength.**

What was missing from all these visible manifestations of separatist sentiment were the major public military drills of the Irish Volunteers, carried out with such frequency prior to the Rising. These were now outlawed, though members still met up under the guise of attendance at social and sporting events, which served as fertile recruiting grounds.

If the growth of separatist politics throughout 1917 owed much to political circumstance, it benefited too from political good fortune. At the very moment that credibility was draining from the IPP, opportunities arose to simultaneously test and parade separatist strength. They presented in the form of a series of by-elections that allowed the Sinn Féin movement – the term had become a shorthand label for the republican movement – to beat the IPP at its own constitutional game. This, Sinn Féin

Illustrated postcards in support of Sinn Féin published between 1917–1920.

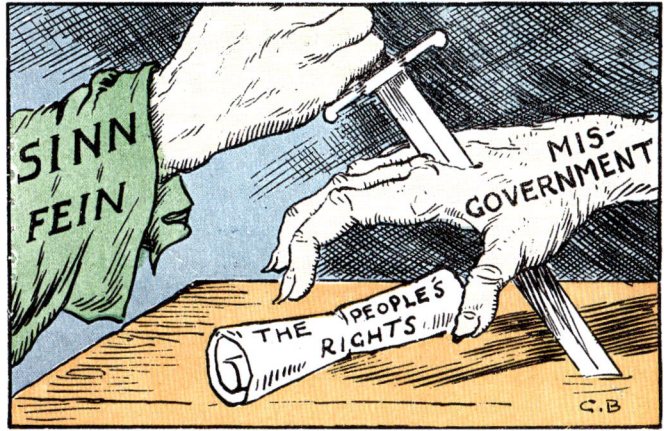

repeatedly did throughout 1917: in North Roscommon in February with Count Plunkett, the father of the executed rebel leader Joseph, standing as a Sinn Féin candidate in spirit if not in name; in South Longford in May with Joseph McGuinness, still incarcerated in Lewes Prison; with Éamon de Valera, a recently released prisoner, who, in July, seized the East Clare seat left vacant by the death in the war of Willie Redmond; and with William T. Cosgrave, another ex-internee, who, in August, claimed a vacant seat in Kilkenny City, the smallest constituency in the country, which hadn't seen an election in twenty-two years.

All of these by-election triumphs were notable for the profile of the victorious candidates – each had a direct link to the Rising – and for the remarkable vigour with which their campaigns were prosecuted. In East Clare, the campaign of de Valera was notable for the involvement of young priests and for its army of canvassers who, using motor cars, collected farm workers from the fields and brought them to and from the polling stations.

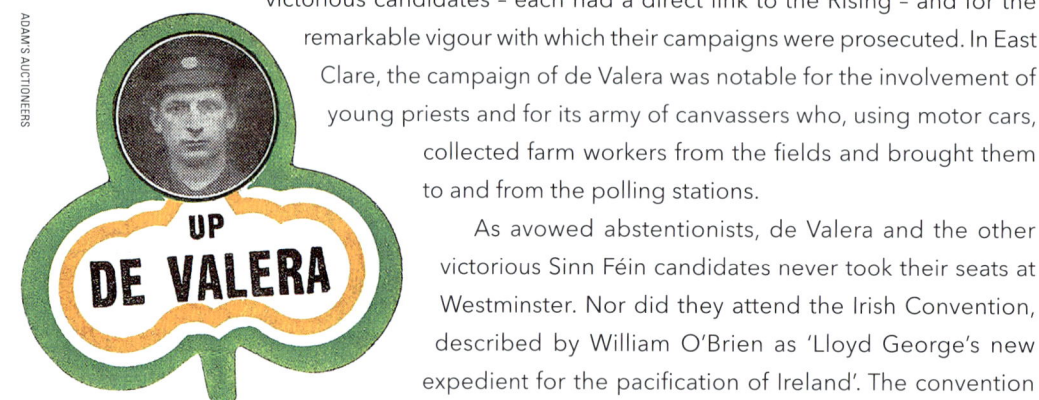

Badge produced for the de Valera 1917 East Clare by-election campaign.

As avowed abstentionists, de Valera and the other victorious Sinn Féin candidates never took their seats at Westminster. Nor did they attend the Irish Convention, described by William O'Brien as 'Lloyd George's new expedient for the pacification of Ireland'. The convention ran from July 1917 to April 1918 and involved Irish representatives of different political parties and interests, whose divisions it served only to underline rather than address.

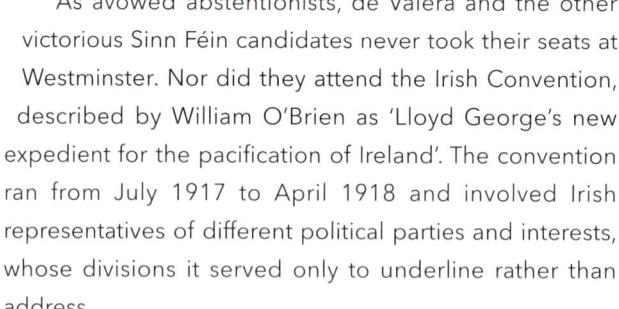

Throughout this period, as the IPP was absorbed in the workings of the Convention, Sinn Féin continued to gather momentum. If the series of by-election triumphs was one measure of this, so too was the party's ballooning membership and its creation of an impressive network of local branches. By the time Sinn Féin held its own historic convention in Dublin's Mansion House in October 1917 – only its tenth ever, and just weeks after the death on hunger strike of another Rising veteran, Thomas Ashe – it attracted over 1,700 delegates from about 1,009 Sinn Féin clubs. A further 200 delegates were refused entry because their clubs had not been affiliated by the prescribed time. The weight of such impressive numbers led the *Irish Independent* to editorialise that Sinn Féin was now representative of 'by far the largest body of Irish Nationalists'.

This did not mean that Irish nationalists had suddenly forsaken constitutional politics for a physical-force tradition. Certainly, there were those who saw themselves as part of that tradition and would have welcomed the opportunity to strike again at the old Imperial enemy, but these were very much in a minority. The rejection of the IPP in favour of Sinn Féin was less a rejection of constitutionalism than of its established Irish form.

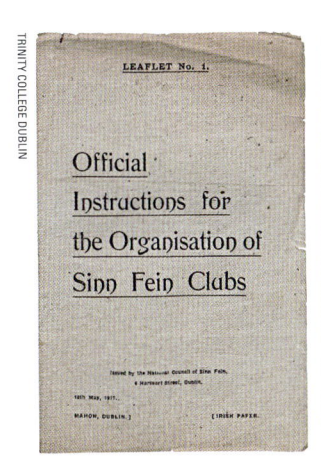

(LEFT) Instruction book published in May 1917 to help party officers deal with the huge influx of members joining Sinn Féin. (RIGHT) Press ticket for the party's convention in the Mansion House at which, for the first time, a republican constitution was adopted.

What, in effect, was being jettisoned was constitutional politics centred on the parliamentary chambers of Westminster. In October 1917 de Valera, addressing the Sinn Féin convention after being unanimously elected the party's new president, spoke to this very issue: 'Some people talk of constitutionalism,' he said. 'Let them show us a constitution that is acknowledged by the Irish people and then tell them I will loyally obey that constitution.'

Sinn Féin emerged from its convention as a stronger organisation with a clear, agreed sense of direction. Unlike the IPP, the modus operandi of which had been to court British political support for Irish nationalist ambitions, Sinn Féin's objective was to ensure that Ireland's case would be considered as part of a much wider reconstruction of the post-war international order. This ambition was set out in its new constitution: 'Sinn Fein aims at securing the international recognition for Ireland as an independent Irish republic.'

Not content to wait until that recognition had been conferred on the country, Sinn Féin more immediately committed to the denial of British authority in Ireland by 'any and every means available'. What this meant in practice would in time become clear.

VICTORY!

1918

'The armistice was signed at five o'clock this morning, and hostilities are to cease on all fronts at 11 a.m. today.'

UK Prime Minister David Lloyd George in an official communiqué
11 NOVEMBER

1918

3 JAN
Readers of the *Irish Independent* learn of the death in action of Capt. William V. Edwards, Irish rugby and water polo international. He was killed during the Jerusalem campaign in late December 1917.

8 JAN
President Woodrow Wilson outlines to the US Congress his 14-point 'programme for the world's peace'.

S.S. Cork Torpedoed.
12 LIVES LOST.
Survivors Landed at Pembrokeshire Port.
Survivors of the s.s. Cork, an Irish vessel which was sunk by an enemy submarine, were landed at a Pembrokeshire port on Saturday morning. All the passengers, numbering seven, and five members of the crew of 35 lost their lives, and the survivors when they landed had lost all their effects and were scantily clad.
BROKE IN TWO AND SANK IN FOUR MINUTES.
Interviewed by a representative, the chief steward said the first intimation he had of anything wrong was when a torpedo struck the

△ **9 JAN**
Twelve lives have been lost at sea after a German torpedo sunk the **SS Cork**, a vessel owned by the Dublin Steam Packet Company.

9 JAN
Sinn Féin congratulates the people of Finland on the 'successful establishment of an independent Republic' and expresses appreciation for the 'enlightened action of the new Government of Russia' in recognising its independence.

No Surrender: Carson's Makes Defiant Speech During Ulster Tour

Covenanter before Cabinet member

Belfast, 8 February – Sir Edward Carson, who recently resigned his seat in the British Cabinet, has said that there will be no settlement in Ireland that involves a sacrifice on the part of Ulster unionists.

'If by settlement people have in their minds surrender, well, then, there will be no settlement.'

Carson delivered his defiant message to a meeting of the Standing Committee of the Ulster Unionist Council in Belfast, which he addressed as part of his ongoing tour of Ulster.

Carson also explained his decision to resign from his position in the British War Cabinet. There was no hidden reason for his departure and there was certainly no disagreement with his colleagues over any special scheme in relation to Ireland. He was motivated by an acknowledgement of the problems that beset the Irish Convention. Should the Convention break down, it would inevitably raise questions as to what steps the government should take, which would create for him a conflict of interest.

He explained, 'Now, I felt that that was a position which put me in a grave difficulty ... If I stayed in the Government I should have to be party to their considerations. So long as you are a member of the Government all your help should be given wholeheartedly to the policy which the Government may think right to adopt. On the other hand, in advising the Government I really was not free, because I had my pledges to observe. I am a Covenanter.'

Edward Carson, who in his speech of 8 February said, 'One of the greatest mistakes that has been made in… the last three years was applying different treatment to Ireland from the rest of the kingdom. What was gained by the exceptional treatment? There came the rebellion in Easter week. I am not going to dwell on it. Heaven knows the more we forget it the better'.

Southern Unionists Issue a Manifesto

Dublin, 5 March – A group of prominent southern unionists have issued a rallying cry in defence of law and order and of the integrity of the United Kingdom.

There are 22 signatories to the lengthy manifesto, the aims of which have been distilled into four key policy areas:

1. The enforcement of the ordinary law with firmness, justice and impartiality.
2. The development of the natural resources of Ireland, and the promotion of commerce, industry and agriculture.
3. The completion of land purchase, as land agitation was the lever upon which the Home Rule movement agitation was based.
4. The obligation and burdens of the war, already imposed on the rest of the United Kingdom, should be shared by Ireland.

The Empire, the signatories claim, is passing through the 'most momentous crisis in its history', one where Ireland was in a 'state of anarchy'.

John Redmond Dies of Heart Failure
Tributes pour in as Irish leader laid to rest

Wexford, 12 March – John Redmond, leader of the Irish Parliamentary Party, died on 6 March.

Mr Redmond, who had been unwell for some time and had been absent from public life, was recovering in hospital from an operation when he suffered heart failure.

His remains were initially taken to Westminster Cathedral, where he was laid on a catafalque before the altar. A Requiem Mass was subsequently held, to which King George sent a representative and at which Mr Lloyd George and Mr Bonar Law, among other leading members of the British government, were present.

On 10 March Mr Redmond's body was taken by the SS *Leinster* to Kingstown, where it was met by a large crowd before being placed on board a black-draped train to Wexford. He was buried among his own people in the family vault of an old churchyard in Wexford town.

Redmond led the IPP for 18 years, making him the longest-serving nationalist leader since Daniel O'Connell.

1918

10 JAN ▽
The House of Lords votes by a majority of 63 to extend suffrage to women, a decision that will allow for the addition of some six million women to the electoral register.

AT LAST!

14 JAN
A Reuters telegram from Petrograd reports that Vladimir Ilyitch Lenin, leader of the Russian Revolution, is unharmed after shots were fired at the car in which he was travelling in the city.

18 JAN
A new volume of verse from William Butler Yeats, *Per Amica Silentia Lunae*, is published in London.

21 JAN
Sir Edward Carson resigns from the British War Cabinet. In a letter to Prime Minister Lloyd George, he refers to pledges 'by which I am bound to my friends in Ulster'.

1918

23 JAN
Major Robert Gregory, the only son of Lady Gregory of Coole Park, Gort, Co. Galway, dies when his Royal Flying Corps aircraft crashes in Italy.

▽ **29 JAN**
A production of *Hanrahan's Oath*, a comedy written by **Lady Gregory**, opens to mixed reviews at the Abbey Theatre, Dublin.

29 JAN
A cablegram is sent to John Redmond from Melbourne, Australia, declaring the 'unabated confidence' of the UIL in the 'Constitutional Home Rule Party'. 3,000 people had attended the UIL's annual demonstration in Melbourne the day before.

1 FEB
Polling day for the South Armagh by-election, where the progress of Sinn Féin is slowed as IPP candidate Patrick Donnelly secures a decisive victory over Dr Patrick McCartan.

If the obsequies at Westminster were, as *The Freeman's Journal* has described them, a 'gathering of the nations', the funeral at Wexford was more 'a coming together of Irishmen of all creeds and classes'.

Tributes for the dead leader have poured in from across Ireland, the UK and further afield.

'He fought the good fight, he kept bright the faith of the Irish patriot,' *The Freeman's Journal* declared on learning of his passing.

In a short message of sympathy, meanwhile, King George remarked that Mr Redmond's death would be 'deeply and widely felt'.

Mr Redmond is survived by his second wife, Ada, his daughter, Johanna, and his son, Captain William Redmond, who is currently MP for East Tyrone.

The coffin of John Redmond in Westminster Cathedral.

Conscription Is Coming to Ireland

Accusations of despotism greet announcement

Westminster, 10 April – Conscription is coming to Ireland.

In a speech delivered to the House of Commons yesterday, Prime Minister Lloyd George put an end to weeks of speculation on the subject. Conscription was introduced in Britain at the beginning of 1916, but Ireland was excluded after extensive lobbying by John Redmond and his Irish Parliamentary Party colleagues.

The so-called 'Man-Power' proposals include:

1. Raising the military age to 50 – and to 55 in certain specified cases.
2. Shortening of the period of call-up from 14 to 7 days.
3. Inclusion of clergymen for non-combat services.
4. Extension of the act to Ireland under the same conditions as in Great Britain.

In the course of his speech, the Prime Minister stated that it was no longer possible to justify Ireland's exclusion. This change of policy comes down to numbers. The government urgently needs more men to help combat German advances on the Western Front.

The speech has inflamed nationalist opinion. Mr Lloyd George was interrupted several times by Irish Party MPs and was denounced by Mr William O'Brien.

Erin grapples with John Bull in this political postcard designed to galvanise support against the move by the government to align Ireland with the rest of the UK with the introduction of conscription.

CONSCRIPTION.
John Bull:— "I am on the Rocks, my dear, but let us DIE TOGETHER!"

In riposte, the Prime Minister referred to previous speeches in the Commons by the former and current leaders of the Irish Party. He said, 'Ireland, through its representatives, assented to the war, voted for the war, supported the war. The Irish representatives, and Ireland, through its representatives, without a dissentient voice, committed the Empire to this war. They are fully as responsible for it as any part of the United Kingdom.'

The *Irish Independent* has editorialised that the Prime Minister has 'committed himself to a policy of despotism, naked and unashamed'.

Divisions Laid Bare in Irish Convention Report

Dublin, 13 April – The report has now been published of the Irish Convention, which concluded its business at Trinity College last week.

It recommends that an Irish scheme of self-government be immediately brought into being.

However, less than half the Convention – 44 members out of 89 – supported this recommendation, while a minority report, signed by 22 nationalists (among them three bishops, Joseph Devlin, William Martin Murphy and the lord mayors of Cork and Dublin), asks for full Dominion Home Rule with full powers over taxation. The number who voted for self-government of one form or another was 66.

1918

6 FEB
Irish newspapers report the release from Broadmoor Asylum of Captain Bowen-Colthurst, who had been found 'guilty but insane' when tried by court martial on charges connected with the shooting of Francis Sheehy Skeffington, Thomas Dickson and Patrick McIntyre at Portobello Barracks during Easter Week, 1916.

11 FEB
Tillage week is launched as an initiative of the Department of Agriculture and Technical Instruction to encourage Irish farmers to increase their food production during 1918.

16 FEB
The Council of Lithuania proclaims the restoration of the independent state of Lithuania.

18 FEB △
It is confirmed that the threatened closure of the **Kynoch** factory in Arklow, Co. Wicklow, has been averted following an intervention by John Redmond and his IPP colleagues. The factory employs 3,500 people and is a mainstay of the town's economy.

1918

23 FEB
It is reported that 33,000 trees have been planted in Co. Roscommon under a scheme adopted by the County Committee.

23 FEB
Three Charleville men (John Hickey, John Cronin and Cornelius McCarthy) who had been on hunger strike at Cork Gaol are released under the terms of the 'Cat and Mouse' Act. The men had been arrested for offences against public order.

24 FEB
Estonia is declared an independent and democratic republic.

26 FEB
Owing to an 'outbreak of lawlessness', Co. Clare is declared a Special Military Area, and an order is issued restricting access in and out of the county.

▽ **27 FEB**
Ireland has been infected by the 'anarchy of **Bolshevism**', *The Irish Times* claims.

The Irish Convention, which sat between July 1917 and March 1918 in Trinity College, discussed how self-government could be enacted, as well as wider questions about the future of Ireland.

According to the chairman of the Convention, Sir Horace Plunkett, the principal bones of contention related to Ulster and customs. Interestingly, the Convention also voted by 54 to 17 that conscription could not be applied to Ireland without the consent and co-operation of an Irish Parliament.

The recommendations of the main report provide, firstly, for the creation of an 'Irish Parliament for an undivided Ireland', with a Senate to comprise 64 members and a Commons of 160 members. Unionists are to be guaranteed 40% of Commons membership, while Ireland is to retain 42 representatives at Westminster.

However, in its conclusions, the Convention exposes the very constitutional fault lines that gave rise to its establishment in the first place. 'Perhaps,' Sir Horace Plunkett observed in a letter to the Prime Minister, 'unanimity was too much to expect. Be that as it may, neither time nor effort was spared in striving for that goal, and there were moments when its attainment seemed possible. There was, however, a portion of Ulster where a majority claimed that if Ireland had the right to separate herself from the rest of the United Kingdom, they had the same right to separation from the rest of Ireland.'

'A declaration of war on the Irish nation':
Rivals Unite in Opposing Conscription

Dublin, 20 April – The disparate strands of Irish nationalism have come together in Dublin to register their opposition to the Military Service Bill. The Bill, which received Royal Assent on 18 April, will introduce conscription to Ireland.

A meeting was held at the Mansion House in Dublin over the last two days at which the Lord Mayor, Mr Laurence O'Neill, presided. Leaders of the Irish Party and Sinn Féin were in attendance, with their attention turned to a unified purpose, despite the parties having clashed in a series of by-elections over the past 18 months. Also in attendance were the representatives of Labour: William O'Brien from Dublin, Thomas Johnson from Belfast, and Michael Egan from Cork.

It was, many observers agreed, 'among the most historic events of Irish history', and it ended with a statement equating the passage of the Conscription Bill by the House of Commons to a 'declaration of war on the Irish nation', one that called upon 'all Irishmen to resist by the most effective means at their disposal'.

The meeting began at 10 a.m. and continued for three hours, when it broke to allow a deputation consisting of John Dillon, Éamon de Valera, Tim Healy, William O'Brien and the Lord Mayor to travel to Maynooth to meet with the Irish Catholic hierarchy.

When the Mansion House proceedings resumed, they did so with a statement of support from the bishops, whose own conference had ended with the issuing of a strong statement. 'An attempt is being made to force conscription upon Ireland against the will of the Irish nation and in defiance of the protests of its leaders,' it began. 'In view especially of the historic relations between the two countries from the very beginning up to the present moment, we consider that conscription forced in this way upon Ireland is an oppressive and inhuman law, which the Irish people have a right to resist by all the means that are consonant with the law of God.'

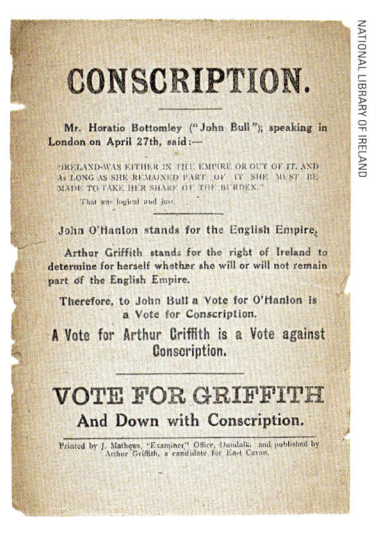

Sinn Féin had been vocal in their assertion that a vote for the IPP was a vote for conscription in the by-elections fought in the early months of 1918. In April the rival parties joined forces to oppose the measure.

1918

28 FEB
An inquiry is held into an application by Dublin Corporation for 301 acres of land to meet the demand for allotments for the provision of food.

6 MAR
John Redmond, leader of the IPP, dies suddenly in London.

13 MAR
John Dillon, MP for East Mayo, is unanimously elected to replace Redmond as leader of the IPP.

21 MAR
The Cork Examiner reports that a special meeting of Queenstown Urban Council has unanimously passed a resolution bemoaning the lowering of moral standards in the town.

21 MAR
A major German offensive begins on the Western Front and succeeds in driving the Allies back to the position they held before the beginning of the Battle of the Somme in 1916.

22 MAR
Captain William Redmond, son of the late John Redmond, defeats his Sinn Féin opponent, Dr Vincent Joseph White, to retain the Waterford City Westminster seat for the IPP.

1918

25 MAR
A meeting is held at Melbourne Town Hall to protest against the display of Sinn Féin flags and 'disloyal' emblems during a recent St Patrick's Day procession. The meeting hears calls for Catholic Archbishop of Melbourne Daniel Mannix to be deported.

26 MAR
Laurence Ginnell MP appears before Dublin Police Court on various charges arising out of alleged incitement of persons to engage in cattle-driving.

△ **26 MAR**
As the German offensive continues on the Western Front, **General Foch** is charged by the British, French and American governments to co-ordinate the action of the Allied armies there and is given the title of Supreme Allied Commander.

Ireland Closes Down Due to General Strike Against Conscription

Dublin, 24 April – Almost all of the country ground to a halt yesterday as workers withdrew their labour in opposition to the proposed extension of conscription to Ireland.

The calling of the general strike followed an Irish labour convention at the Mansion House in Dublin over the weekend. 1,500 delegates attended and a resolution calling for yesterday's strike – 'as a demonstration of fealty to Labour and Ireland' – was passed. William O'Brien remarked that the trade union movement would present an unbroken front and stated they opposed conscription because 'it was sought to be forced upon them by a foreign people, and the workers would equally oppose it even if a native Parliament tried to force it. This was an attempt to exterminate the Irish race.'

Nearly every branch of industry was impacted: shipyards, engineers' shops, factories, railways and tramway cars. No newspapers were published in Dublin or in the south or west of the country.

Shops were closed, as were theatres and picture houses. Many National and Christian Brothers schools joined the stoppage, and in some cases where schools opened, the teachers found they had no pupils to instruct. Government offices remained open as did the Stock Exchange, banks,

Outside churches across the country, people lined up to sign the solemn pledge which had been drafted by the Catholic hierarchy and political leaders in opposition to the threat of conscription.

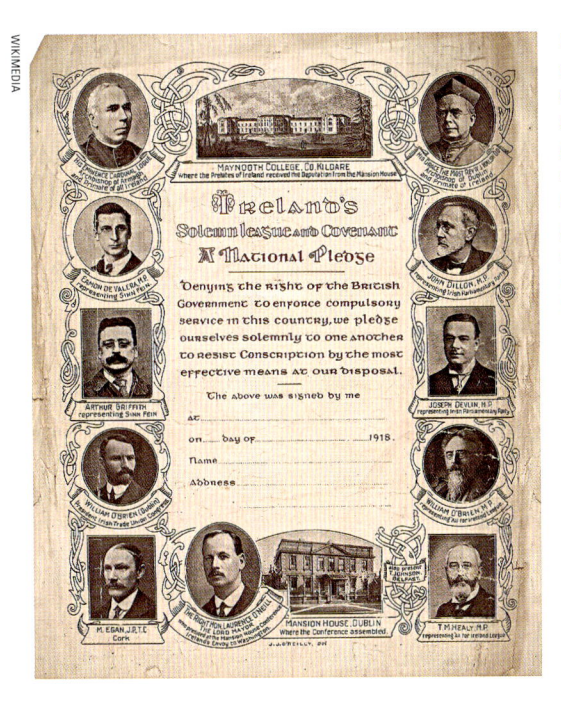

Ireland's Solemn League and Covenant was a national pledge 'denying the right of the British government to enforce compulsory service in this country'. Church and political leaders, such as Cardinal Logue, John Dillon and Éamon de Valera, are depicted.

solicitors' offices and post offices, but this did little to change the impression of a country in shutdown or on holiday.

The general stoppage left many idle, and they spent their time attending Masses, where they availed of the opportunity to sign the solemn pledge drafted by the Catholic hierarchy and national political leaders. An estimated 100,000 signatures were added to the pledge in the capital.

The call-out was not universally observed, however. Work carried on as usual in Belfast and north-east Ulster, with members of the trade unions ignoring the advice of their own leaders. In a number of workplaces, Catholic employees were informed that, should they not turn up for work, their positions would be filled and they would not get them back.

Women's Day of Action Raises Anti-Conscription Temperature

Dublin, 10 June – Heavy rainfall failed to dampen the enthusiasm of thousands of women who turned out in protest against conscription across the country yesterday.

In Dublin city and suburbs alone, an estimated 40,000 women participated in signing a pledge not to fill the workplaces of men let go from their employment for refusing compulsory military service.

1918

27 MAR △
Mayo-born athlete **Martin Sheridan**, winner of five gold medals at three Olympic Games, dies of pneumonia in New York, where he worked as a policeman.

3 APR
The annual congress of the INTO opens in Galway Town Hall. Recent pay battles have seen its membership strengthened by the addition of 'upwards of 1,000 recruits'.

3 APR
The IPP completes a hat-trick of by-election victories when winning the seat for the East Tyrone constituency.

REVOLUTIONARY TIMES 1913–23

1918

15 APR
Addressing an anti-conscription meeting in Limerick, the local bishop, Dr Denis Hallinan, instructs listeners: 'Stand erect, close up your ranks, put your backs to the wall, shout at the top of your voices – and let your voices be in unison – on no account are we Irishmen going to consent to military conscription by the British government in this country.'

16 APR
Sir Thomas Esmonde, MP for Wexford North, presents to the House of Commons a petition signed by 500 residents of Ballindaggin, Co. Wexford, protesting against the imposition of conscription on Ireland.

16 APR
The House of Commons passes the Military Service (No. 2) Act, which provides for conscription to be extended to Ireland. 'The worst day's work done for England since the War began,' declares John Dillon.

16 APR
A baby has been found abandoned in the Cork City suburb of Blackrock, *The Cork Examiner* reports. A note pinned to the child read: 'For God's sake, take him in tonight. Put him in an orphanage or institution tomorrow. He was baptised a Catholic.'

The vestibule of City Hall was the main signing centre for the city itself, and here almost 15,000 signatures were collected, the first three hours being devoted to the members of various women's societies.

There were 700 members of Cumann na mBan and 1,400 Irish tailoresses, but the largest number from any single group to sign the pledge came from the Irish Women Workers' Union (IWWU), who marched from Denmark House to City Hall headed by Louie Bennett.

In all, about 2,400 members of the IWWU signed, including a large number of Protestant labour women.

The impressive scenes in Dublin were replicated in towns and villages throughout Ireland. In Limerick, where the protests were predominantly religious in nature, a shrine was erected in St John's Square. The Dominican Fathers permitted the removal of their Virgin and Child statue from St Saviour's Church so that it could be temporarily placed at the shrine.

In Waterford, 1,500 women were reported to have marched through the city's principal thoroughfares behind a banner inscribed with the message 'The women of Waterford will not have conscription'.

There was also a strong turnout in Strabane, Co. Tyrone, where 2,000 women carrying flowers paraded to the local church; they decorated the statue of the Blessed Virgin in the church grounds. A similar number protested in Cootehill, Co. Cavan.

Reporting on this 'splendidly organised' nationwide day of protest, the *Irish Independent* is convinced that it 'cannot fail to have due effect'.

On 9 June 2,400 members of the IWWU and 700 members of Cumann na mBan signed a pledge against conscription, including Delia Larkin, sister of trade union leader Jim Larkin.

Following the proclamation against Sinn Féin and other nationalist organisations in July 1918, work at the party's headquarters at 6 Harcourt Street continued, but the building was regularly raided by British forces.

Banned: Sinn Féin, Irish Volunteers, Cumann na mBan and the Gaelic League

5 July – Sinn Féin, the Irish Volunteers, Cumann na mBan and the Gaelic League have all been proclaimed as illegal organisations by the Lord Lieutenant, Viscount French.

The proclamation states that the proscribed organisations are dangerous and a 'grave menace' designed to 'terrorise the peaceful and law-abiding subjects of His Majesty in Ireland'.

It goes on to say that these associations 'encourage and aid persons to commit crimes and to promote and incite to acts of violence and intimidation and interfere with the administration of the law and disturb the maintenance of law and order'.

In the immediate aftermath of the proclamation, business continued as usual at the Sinn Féin headquarters at 6 Harcourt Street and at the Gaelic League's head offices at 25 Parnell Square. Both organisations claim that they had not received any direct communication, let alone any visits, from the police or military.

Speaking to a representative of the *Evening Telegraph*, Professor Eoin MacNeill, President of the Gaelic League, struck a defiant note, declaring that the organisation would 'not allow itself to be driven underground' and would continue to 'have the support of the nation and of Irishmen abroad'.

Cumann na mBan has expressed surprise at the actions of the government and has taken it as a sign that 'conscription is now a certainty'

1918

18 APR
Military Service (No. 2) Act receives Royal assent.

18 APR
A conference is convened at the Mansion House by Lord Mayor of Dublin Laurence O'Neill to form an Irish Anti-Conscription Committee. It is composed of all shades of nationalist opinion in Ireland.

20 APR
At a special meeting in Dublin, the IPP decides to withdraw their attendance from the House of Commons to assist the fight against conscription in Ireland.

21 APR
Ireland's Catholic bishops issue an edict at Sunday Masses urging all Irish people to 'resist conscription by the most effective means at our disposal'.

23 APR
A general strike is held across Ireland as a protest against the Conscription Act.

24 APR
It is reported that Eoin MacNeill has been reappointed to the position of Professor of Early and Medieval Irish History at University College Dublin.

1918

28 APR
Gavrilo Princip, the assassin of Archduke Franz Ferdinand in June 1914, dies in prison. *The Irish Times* describes Princip as the 'direct author of the present war'.

4 MAY
The Freeman's Journal reviews a new book which brings together the various strands of writing from the late Thomas Kettle, who died in September 1916 during the Battle of the Somme. The book is entitled *The Day's Burden: Studies, Literary and Political and Miscellaneous Essays*.

△ **9 MAY**
Lt Gen. Sir Bryan Mahon announces he is to leave Ireland and resign his command of the British forces there. He says he will leave 'with the deepest regret'.

WANTED—A ST. PATRICK.
St. Augustine Birrell. "I'M AFRAID. I'M NOT SO SMART AS MY BROTHER-SAINT AT DEALING WITH THIS KIND OF THING. I'M APT TO TAKE REPTILES TOO LIGHTLY."

Two years after the so-called 'Sinn Féin Rebellion', the party is top of the government's threat list in Ireland. It is portrayed in this Punch *cartoon as part barbed-tailed snake and part Pickelhelm-wearing dachshund, a dog breed favoured by the Kaiser. The hapless saint is Augustine Birrell, Chief Secretary for Ireland during the Rising.*

– all of the organisation's recent public work has been geared towards the campaign to oppose conscription.

The Lord Lieutenant made his proclamation under the Criminal Law and Procedure (Ireland) Act of 1887, which gives the authorities the power to outlaw any organisation it believes to be involved in criminal activities.

Gaelic Sunday – Thousands Turn Out for GAA's Day of Protest

5 August – About 1,500 camogie, football and hurling matches were played across Ireland as part of a GAA protest against recent restrictions on the playing of these games without a permit.

Although turnout estimates are difficult to verify, the scale of the protest was such as to lead the nationalist press to claim the participation of around 54,000 so-called Gaels. Games were organised by each of the County Boards and, on the instruction of GAA's Central Council, were scheduled to commence at the same time: 3 p.m.

In Dublin there were approximately 30 fixtures organised in 22 different venues for which no permit was sought. Games were played at the Phoenix Park, as well as at Ringsend and at various venues along the coast stretching from Baldoyle to Sandymount to Bray.

In Cork, 40 fixtures were organised, though heavy rain meant that many of them were abandoned.

Meanwhile, at Duke's Grove, Armagh, about 1,000 spectators turned out to witness a previously banned match between Emmets Club and Hopes in the Mid-Armagh League.

No reports of police interference at any of these games have been received.

The 'Gaelic Sunday' protests are a response to developments in early July when the British government placed restrictions on meetings and public gatherings without a permit. However, last week, in a statement to the House of Commons, the Chief Secretary Edward Shortt stated that it had not been intended 'to interfere with ordinary meetings, games and sports' and that such interference as had occurred had been unfortunate cases where police had misunderstood instructions.

Ambitious Plan for Dublin Housing Announced

27,000 families need proper homes

14 August – A major new housing initiative, which will cost £8,640,000 and deliver at least 16,500 additional dwellings for workers, is to be implemented in the city of Dublin.

The plan, which was devised by P.C. Cowan, Chief Engineering Inspector with the Local Government Board, and submitted to Chief Secretary Edward Shortt, dates from January this year and sets out the following as necessities:

- 14,000 new self-contained houses of sufficient size to enable a separation of sexes, with scullery and WC accommodation for the sole use of each family.
- The improvement and remodelling of 3,803 first- and second-class tenement houses to provide for suitable accommodation, in tenements of one to four rooms, for 13,000 families, with a remaining 5,991 families being catered for in new houses.

In all, Mr Cowan states that there is a need to provide comfortable sanitary houses for 27,000 families; this figure was accepted by a departmental committee almost four years ago. Since then, 936 tenement houses, in which 3,989 families were housed, have been closed by the Corporation. In the same four-year period, only 327 new houses have been built.

1918

12 MAY △
At a low-key ceremony at Dublin Castle, **Viscount French** and **Edward Shortt** are sworn in as lord lieutenant and chief secretary of Ireland respectively.

17 MAY
The British government orders the arrest and imprisonment of leading members of Sinn Féin, alleging that they had been involved in a plan to import arms from Germany. Éamon de Valera, Arthur Griffith, Countess Markievicz and W.T. Cosgrave are among those shipped to English prisons.

23 MAY
The Cork Steam Packet Company's 1,000-ton vessel, the SS *Innisfallen*, is sunk after being torpedoed by a German submarine.

28 MAY
An influenza epidemic continues to spread throughout Spain, Irish newspapers report. The Public Health Committee of Madrid urges members of the public to take steps to help prevent the spread of the disease, including the proper ventilation of rooms.

1918

13 JUN
A fund is launched to benefit Ireland's certified nurses for services throughout the ongoing war.

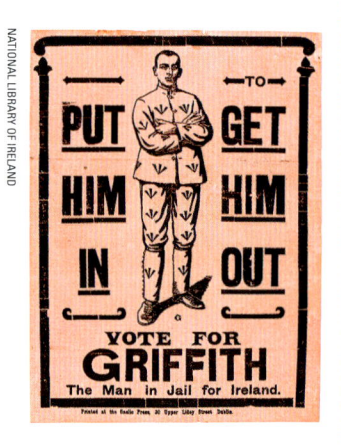

△ **20 JUN**
The imprisoned **Arthur Griffith,** founder of Sinn Féin, is elected to the Westminster seat for East Cavan.

22 JUN
The Irish Times reports on the arrest in the US of former Irish labour leader Jim Larkin, who was posing as the president of the 'New Irish Republic'. Charged with circulating seditious literature, he is subsequently tried and acquitted.

22 JUN
It is reported that order in the Austrian capital city of Vienna cannot be guaranteed as food rations are further reduced.

English Cities No Place for 'Innocent' Irish Girls

Dublin, 7 September – England is no place for Irish girls, a nun based in one of its large cities has claimed. The nun's opinion came to light in a letter to the Reverend Mother of an Irish convent, who had inquired about conditions there on behalf of one of her students.

The message that came back outlined the ways in which the lure of high factory wages and war conditions led to the 'ruin' of Irish girls. In her response to the Reverend Mother, the English-based nun strongly advised against any young Irish girls being sent to England, especially those who were 'inclined to be a bit wild and fond of amusement'.

The nun added, 'We make provision to safeguard these girls, when we find them here, but would never encourage them to come. England, and especially a big city, is no place for an innocent girl. The factories and big wages and war conditions are their ruin. In spite of all the efforts we and others make to save them, the greater number go with the tide, and are lost.

'I am sorry to say that the Irish girls are in greater danger, and more easily ruined, than the town girls, who are better able to look after themselves. Not three minutes from our own hostel is a disreputable coffee house, where, to my own knowledge, there are five young Irish girls whom I have done my best to save. They even waylay my girls and try to lead them to leave us and go to them, where they can have more liberty, which means sin. So if I were to advise you to send your protégé or any other girl, I should be acting against my conscience. She had far better remain at home poor, where she has a chance to save her soul.'

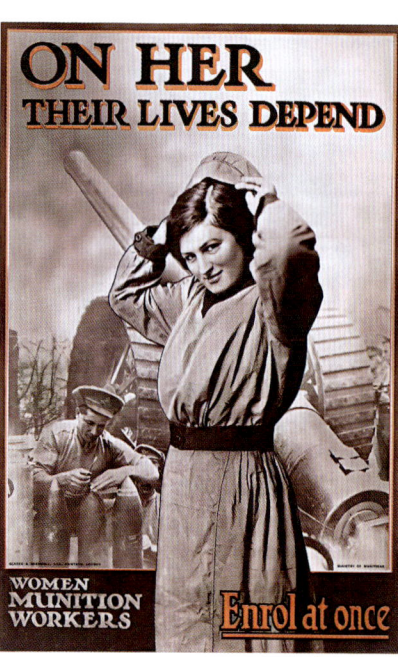

Despite the 'risk to their souls', Irish women, like their British counterparts, enjoyed the lifestyle and financial independence afforded to them by industrial work.

1918

Recruitment Drive Falls Far Short of Target Amid Public Hostility

Ballaghaderreen, 11 September – The British government's plans to voluntarily recruit 50,000 additional Irishmen to the ongoing war effort by 1 October look set to fall far short of that target.

The latest estimates, published in today's *Irish Independent*, indicate that a mere 5,050 have been recruited as part of the drive announced by the Lord Lieutenant in early June. When announcing the voluntary recruitment plan, Viscount French made it clear that if the fixed number wasn't achieved, conscription would be introduced without delay.

THE FIRST IRISH CONSCRIPT.

The numbers joining up continue to grow, but the pace of enlistment is more akin to a trickle than a torrent. Yesterday, an additional 195 names were recruited, 95 from Dublin, 75 from Belfast, 16 from Waterford, with Cork, Limerick and Omagh contributing 16 each. A further ten were enlisted in Mullingar, nine in Armagh, with only five joining up in Galway.

It is clear that the military's efforts are being hampered by hostile crowds at recruitment meetings. In Ballaghaderreen, Co. Roscommon, the setting for a massive anti-conscription rally in early May, there were angry scenes when a motor lorry doubling as a recruiting platform pulled into the town. It was a fair day, so there was a huge crowd in the town and the lorry was quickly surrounded by people who booed and hissed and shouted Sinn Féin slogans. Speakers on the platform, when asking for a fair hearing, were met with cries of 'What about the German plot?' and 'Why don't you give proof of the plot?'

At a recruiting meeting in Strandhill, Co. Sligo, there were similar scenes. Meanwhile, in Dromahair, Co. Leitrim, an anti-recruitment document posted in the village was taken down by the police.

27 JUN △
A Canadian hospital ship, the **Llandovery Castle**, is torpedoed 116 miles west of Fastnet. Of the 258 crew and passengers, only 24 survive.

In this widely distributed anti-conscription postcard, the unwilling 'first Irish conscript' is led away by massive force.

29 JUN
The Freeman's Journal reports that one of the country's best-known surgeons, John Stephen McArdle, has been fined for illegally using petrol to drive his car to a cockfight in Co. Kildare.

11 JUL
The funeral is held of former Mayor of New York City and US army pilot, John Purroy Mitchel, a grandson of the Irish Fenian leader, John Mitchel. He died aged 39 in a fall from his plane while on a training exercise in Louisiana.

REVOLUTIONARY TIMES 1913–23

199

1918

17 JUL
The former Tsar of Russia, Nicholas II, and his family are executed on the orders of the Bolshevik government.

21 JUL
A message from the Bishop of Cork, Dr Daniel Cohalan, is read out at Masses, warning of the 'very grave offence' of mixed marriage. It is inspired by news that an Irish Catholic male had committed the 'very grave offence' of marrying a Protestant woman in a Protestant church in Dublin. The bishop also calls on the man to 'atone for his offence'.

26 JUL
It is reported that Nora Connolly, daughter of executed 1916 leader James Connolly, has been refused re-entry to Ireland.

RMS Leinster *sunk off Irish coast*

Kingstown, 11 October – The mailboat RMS *Leinster* was torpedoed off the east coast of Ireland yesterday while travelling from Kingstown to Holyhead. It is already being described as 'Ireland's *Lusitania*'.

It took to 12 to 15 minutes to sink, with a loss of over 500 lives.

The attack took place in broad daylight and on a vessel that was fully loaded, its passenger list comprising women, men and children.

The first torpedo is believed to have struck the post office quarters and the second, three minutes later, the engine room, giving rise to a deafening explosion. The ship's two prominent funnels were blown high into the air, while the steamer itself, as one crew member described it, 'seemed to crumble into ashes'.

The vessel went under rapidly, its bow submerging first beneath the waterline. Fortunately, between the first and second blasts, the *Leinster* managed to transmit a wireless message to the harbour in Kingstown from where it had earlier departed.

All available vessels were dispatched to the scene, reaching the site within an hour and a half, as crowds assembled back at the harbour and along the Marine Road anxiously awaiting news. For many, the news that came back brought pain, suffering and loss. Of the 22 members of the post office sorting staff, for example, it is known already that only one has survived.

(LEFT) *A postcard advertising the Royal Mail service of the RMS* Leinster *and* (RIGHT) *a dramatic artistic rendering of the sinking of the ship and the attempts of the lifeboats to collect survivors from the water.*

Almost 200 survivors have been found, mostly clinging to upturned boats and floating bits of broken timber. 'All would have been saved,' commented one of the officers who survived, 'but for the second torpedo, which smashed her into matchwood.'

Endgame for the War

Allies advance but US insists on German surrender

Washington, 26 October – The war is approaching its endgame. However, it remains unclear how hostilities will be concluded and on what terms.

The US President, Woodrow Wilson, has indicated that the only way in which the Allies might consider an armistice was if Germany were left in a position that made a renewal of hostilities impossible. He also indicated that if the Allies were to enter into negotiations, they must deal with the democratically elected representatives of the German people. If forced to deal with military authorities, then America must insist on complete surrender.

These intimations from the White House follow the receipt of a diplomatic note in which Germany indicated that it accepted the terms of the peace laid down by the President in his address to Congress on 8 January this year.

While the political machinations are ongoing, the military campaign continues to the Allies' advantage.

The General Foch-led onslaught on German positions is yielding more gains on the Western Front.

Kaiser Wilhelm II depicted in Punch *contemplating the state of German militarism as the final grains run through his sand timer. His abdication was announced on 9 November 1918.*

THE SANDS RUN OUT.

1918

29 JUL
IPP leader John Dillon challenges the British government to put into 'operation without delay' in Ireland the principles laid out by Woodrow Wilson.

17 AUG
Newly released criminal and civil statistics reveal that the vast majority of those killed and injured during the Rising of 1916 were civilians.

18 AUG △
Hanna Sheehy Skeffington returns to Ireland having recently been imprisoned in Holloway Prison, where she had gone on hunger strike. She had initially been denied a permit to allow her passage back to Ireland.

20 AUG
Delegates from more than 65 constituencies attend the annual meeting of the Ard Comhairle of Sinn Féin, held at the Mansion House in Dublin. The Sinn Féin organisation now accounts for 1,666 clubs – up 426 since December 1917.

REVOLUTIONARY TIMES 1913–23

1918

27 AUG
As Labour unrest spreads, the *Irish Independent* reports that the number of workers associated with the building trade on strike has risen to 17,000. This number includes 6,000 aerodrome workers and 500 members of the Coachmakers' Society.

27 AUG
The Irish Times reports that relatives and dependants of the American citizens who perished when a German submarine sank the *Lusitania* in 1915 have had their action against the Cunard Shipping Company dismissed.

30 AUG
Lenin survives another attack on his life. He is shot twice by Fanya Kaplan, a socialist-revolutionary, as he left a meeting of labourers at the Mikhelson Armaments Factory in Moscow, where he had been speaking.

31 AUG
The principle of 'equal pay for equal work' should not be conceded, the *Irish Independent* editorialises.

15 SEP
A note is issued by the Imperial Austro-Hungarian government calling for a peace conference. The offer is rejected by the US.

Flu Epidemic Continues to Rage Throughout the Country

Dublin, 6 November – Churches, theatres and cinemas may all be forced to close in an effort to stop the spread of influenza in Dublin according to the Superintendent Medical Officer for Health in the city, Sir Charles Cameron. Many schools have already been closed.

The number of deaths from influenza in Dublin during the first week of November was 210, up from 123 the week before. Deaths from pneumonia rose from 55 to 72 in the same two-week period. The current Dublin death rate of 72.3 per 1,000 is the highest in Cameron's memory.

Drogheda is reported to be even worse than Dublin, as is the seaside town of Bray.

The epidemic in Limerick shows no sign of abating, the situation not helped by the fact that two medical practitioners are confined to their houses. Furthermore, in one hospital, most of the nurses are incapacitated by the disease. In Waterford, one of the latest victims is the former mayor of the city, Dr J.J. O'Sullivan.

More than 100 prisoners in Belfast Jail are reported to have been impacted, a development that has raised questions about how the authorities dealt with the first sufferers. Reports indicate that the affected men have not been provided with sufficient covering at night, are left to lie on plank beds and are provided with a diet of bread and margarine.

A cartoon by Gordon Brewster that appeared in the Irish Weekly Independent *on 2 November.*

Armistice – War Is Over, Peace at Last!

Paris, 11 November – More than four years after it began, the most devastating war the world has known has come to an end.

Yesterday morning, at 5 a.m. French time, German plenipotentiaries signed an armistice with the Allies, and at 11 a.m. on the 11th day of the 11th month of 1918, hostilities ceased. The war is over and, according to this morning's *Irish Independent* editorial, 'A world from which the black shadow of death is lifted can rejoice its fill today.'

1918

(LEFT) **The Signing of the Armistice** by Harold Hume. (RIGHT) *Paris, where 'Everyone all but went mad. Here is part of the crowd which surged about the great streets around the church of the Madeleine, and extending far down Rue Royale to Place de la Concorde.'*

The terms and conditions of the Armistice impose heavy obligations on the defeated powers. The German Army, for instance, is pledged to surrender weaponry and to evacuate the areas on the left bank of the Rhine.

The King has sent messages of congratulation to the British navy, army and air force. To the army, he noted that the 'soldiers of the British Empire' have won 'the admiration alike of friend and foe': 'Defeat has more than once stared you in the face. Your ranks have been thinned again and again by wounds, sickness, and death, but your faith has never faltered, your courage has never failed, your hearts have never known defeat.'

The Lord Lieutenant of Ireland, Field Marshal Sir John French, has also written messages to the Allied military leaders. To Marshal Foch, he wrote, 'In this hour of victory I cannot find words to express the joy which I feel in congratulating you my old friend and comrade in the field.' He also issued to Foch an invitation to visit Ireland.

On learning of the news, the Archbishop of Armagh and Primate of all Ireland issued a letter to all the clergy in his diocese. The 'glorious news' that had reached them constituted, he wrote, a 'complete victory for the cause of honour and truth' and filled their hearts with gratitude, and he called for a special thanksgiving service in all churches the following Sunday morning.

Ireland and Britain to Go to the Polls on 14 December

Westminster, 20 November – After months of speculation, a date has finally been set for a general election.

Voters in Britain and Ireland will go to the polls on 14 December, although it is not expected that the counting of votes will begin until after Christmas.

24 SEP ▽
Shops, factories and places of public entertainment are set to go dark as a result of a new lighting order issued by the Coal Controller, *The Cork Examiner* reports.

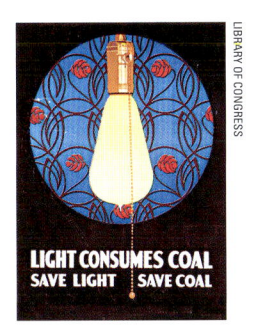

25 SEP
40,000 railwaymen in England and Wales are now on strike. The dispute follows the refusal by a section of railwaymen in South Wales to accept a government award. They have demanded a further increase to be immediately implemented.

REVOLUTIONARY TIMES 1913–23

1918

26 SEP
'A national music is essential for the full development of the idea of a really Irish nation,' *The Freeman's Journal* editorialises.

27 SEP
At a public meeting in Dublin, Cumann na mBan calls for the immediate release of Irish republican prisoners in English jails.

29 SEP
Hundreds of people visit the grave of Thomas Ashe on the first anniversary of his burial.

▽ **1 OCT**
Combined Arab and British forces, including **Major T. E. Lawrence** ('Lawrence of Arabia'), capture Damascus from the Turks.

4 OCT
A 'mammoth' auction in support of the Royal Dublin Fusiliers Prisoners of War fund is held in the Mansion House.

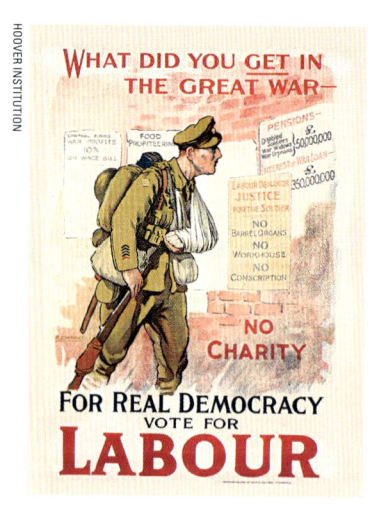

The election of 1918 was the first across Britain and Ireland for eight years.

The announcement of the election was made yesterday in the House of Commons by Andrew Bonar Law: 'The Prime Minister proposes to recommend His Majesty to issue on 25th November a proclamation summoning a new Parliament. When this is done the nomination's day will be December 4th, and the polling day December 14th'.

The announcement has brought to an end the coalition unity that has prevailed in British politics for much of the war. The Labour Party has signalled that the triggering of the election terminated 'the conditions on which they entered the coalition' and they will now fight the election as an independent party.

Under the Reform Act of earlier this year, the number of constituencies up for grabs has been increased from 670 to 707, with Ireland, Scotland and Wales allocated two additional seats each.

However, the redrawing of the electoral map in Ireland means that the representation from the three southern provinces will be reduced by four members, while representation from Ulster will be increased by the same amount, with additional seats being created in Belfast. In the next parliament, Ulster will return 37 members (as opposed to 33 previously) and the rest of Ireland will return 64.

It is believed that changes to the electoral map (which sees an increase of seats in the Down constituencies from four to five and a reduction in Tyrone from four to three) will benefit the Unionist Party. This has drawn accusations of gerrymandering from some nationalist quarters.

The Irish Labour Party has opted to step aside for this election, and a number of Irish Party MPs, including Captain Stephen Gwynn, have announced they will not recontest. More retirements are expected in the coming weeks.

204   REVOLUTIONARY TIMES 1913–23

1918

The majority of the IPP's 84 MPs, seen here in 1914, had, by the time of the 1918 election, died or decided not to seek re-election.

Nearly Half of Irish Party Retire as Parliament Is Dissolved

London, 26 November – The Westminster Parliament has been dissolved and will reconvene on 21 January 1919 after the results of the general election are announced.

In the case of the Irish Parliamentary Party, many of those who served in the outgoing House of Commons will not be returning in the new year.

The disarray in which the party finds itself is becoming clear now that the general election campaign has begun. The large number of resignations and retirements means that many of its outgoing MPs will not be defending their seats.

Despite the obvious implications of these losses of personnel, John Dillon, leader of the party, insists that they will not capitulate but will 'fight Sinn Féin with all the resources at their disposal'. Mr Dillon will himself face off with the Sinn Féin leader, Éamon de Valera, in the constituency of East Mayo.

Election Results In: Irish Voters Favour an Independent Republic

Belfast, 30 December – Ireland has voted – and the result, while not surprising, is sensational.

The Irish Parliamentary Party, the political standard-bearers for Irish nationalism for almost half a century, has been all but destroyed.

The party of Butt, Parnell and Redmond has been reduced to just seven MPs (one of these in Britain) under the leadership of John Dillon, a veteran

8 OCT
Following a week of storms and flooding, the *Belfast News Letter* asserts that the drainage of Lough Neagh is a matter of 'great economic importance'.

14 OCT
The SS *Dundalk*, under the command of Captain Hugh O'Neill and owned by the Dundalk and Newry Steam Packet Company, sinks in three minutes after being hit by a German torpedo. Twenty lives, including O'Neill's, are lost.

30 OCT
The Armistice of Mudros is signed by the Allies and the Ottoman Empire, bringing an end to Turkey's involvement in the war.

1918

of the constitutional movement who himself was unseated in the constituency of East Mayo.

The final breakdown of the 105 Irish seats is as follows:

- Sinn Féin 73
- Irish Party 6
- Unionists 26

The victory of Sinn Féin is no surprise. Pre-election retirements from the Irish Party and a failure to replace them with new candidates meant that 25 of the seats claimed yesterday were unopposed. However, where contests between Sinn Féin and the Irish Party did take place, the swing towards separatist sentiment was undeniable.

Given the general trend, it was the few successes of the Irish Party that stand out. In Belfast Joseph Devlin held off the challenge of Éamon de Valera, who won two of the three constituencies he contested. The only constituency outside Ulster in which the IPP prevailed over a Sinn Féin candidate was Waterford City, where Captain William Redmond, son of the late party leader, defeated Dr Vincent White with just 484 votes to spare.

In a telegram from Belfast, Joseph Devlin told Captain Redmond that the result in Waterford City had been a 'vindication of your father's memory and principles for which he fought and died'.

The other four seats won by the Irish Party were in Ulster constituencies, where a pre-election pact had been brokered by Cardinal Logue to avoid a split national vote where seats might fall to unionism.

Overall, unionists won 26 seats, almost all in the northeast corner of the country.

The election result shows that Ireland is as polarised now as it was on the eve of the war, if not more so. A strengthened unionism and an emboldened Irish republicanism have emerged from this historic election – and the aspirations of the two are antagonistic.

Markievicz Becomes First Female MP

Dublin, 30 December – The results from the Dublin city and county divisions were announced in Green Street Courthouse in Dublin on 28 December.

Outside there were enthusiastic scenes as Sinn Féin supporters celebrated the results, most notably the historic election of Constance Markievicz in the St Patrick's constituency. She is the first woman to be elected to the House of Commons, although she has pledged not to take her seat.

Markievicz was not on hand to savour her moment of triumph, as she is currently imprisoned in Holloway Prison, but Joseph Cleary offered thanks

Sinn Féin Christmas card published during the election campaign correctly predicting 'a cold reception' for John Dillon and his IPP.

9 NOV
The abdication of Kaiser Wilhelm II from the German Imperial throne is announced. Germany is proclaimed a republic.

11 NOV
Poland regains its independence after 123 years of occupation and repeated partitions.

11 NOV
Allied powers agree an armistice with Germany at Compiègne, France, at 5 a.m. – hostilities cease at 11 a.m.

on her behalf, remarking that now that parliamentarianism had been routed in the city, 'the humbug is now over'.

The other female Sinn Féin candidate, Winifred Carney, polled poorly in the constituency of Victoria in Belfast.

Ireland Celebrates Its First War-Free Christmas in Four Years

December – For the first time in four years, the dark shadow of a destructive world war did not hang over Christmas in Ireland.

There was an enthusiasm for the season that had been understandably absent in recent times. Churches were full, the shops were busy, and sports and theatres were well patronised.

In Dublin, city and suburban Catholic churches reported large congregations, as did the churches of the Protestant denominations. At Christ Church, carols were sung on Christmas Eve, and in his Christmas Day sermon, Reverend Dr Bernard made reference to the reestablishment of peace and the promise of a benediction of peace as the ideal of the post-war conference.

More pointedly, and with an eye firmly fixed on the domestic political scene, Dr Bernard remarked, 'Let their Christmas resolve on the one side and the other side be, at any rate, to abstain from bitter words – too frequently on the lips of Irishmen in the past – words which serve no purpose either of righteousness or peace.'

Across the Christmas period, many of the shops reported an excellent trade, and the crowds on the streets of Ireland's towns and cities were augmented by large numbers of soldiers and sailors home on leave.

For the children, of course, it was all about the toys and, for those who can afford them, mechanical toys appear to be growing in appeal at the expense of the simpler toys of previous years.

A Christmas card from the Royal Army Medical Corps that looks forward to many wartime measures, like censorship and the DORA, being thrown in the dustbin.

1918

14 NOV
British Prime Minister Lloyd George announces 14 December as the date of the Westminster general election. It will be the first since 1910.

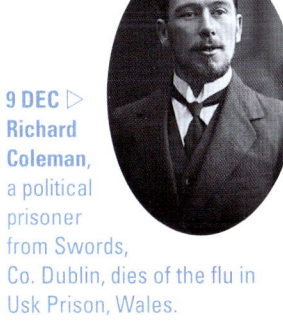

9 DEC ▷
Richard Coleman, a political prisoner from Swords, Co. Dublin, dies of the flu in Usk Prison, Wales.

13 DEC
Woodrow Wilson arrives in Paris for the post-war Peace Conference. He is the first US president to visit Europe while in office.

14 DEC
Election Day. Irish and British voters go to the polls in unprecedented numbers as a result of an extended franchise.

17 DEC
Charles Hurley from Kilbrittain appears before a general court martial at Cork Barracks. He is charged with plotting a 'second rebellion'.

28 DEC
Results of the general election confirm the triumph of Sinn Féin and the demise of the IPP.

Remembering 1918
a hundred years on

On 14 December the 1918 general election took place across Britain and Ireland. The electorate for the election had been utterly transformed by the Representation of the People Act, which had greatly increased the franchise. In Ireland the number of eligible voters rose to two million, including all women over the age of thirty. The campaign for votes for women had dominated the political landscape in the years prior to the First World War, and the changes to the franchise recognised the Suffragette campaign and the role that women had played in the war effort. To mark the centenary of the extension of the franchise to women, the Houses of the Oireachtas organised a series of events, talks and exhibitions, included in which was a display of the original 1908 banner used by the Irish Women's Franchise League, which had been founded by Hanna Sheehy Skeffington and Margaret Cousins.

19 July–14 December 2018

REVOLUTIONARY TIMES 1913–23

'The greatest day in all history'?
– Irish Responses to the Armistice and the End of War

'THE GREATEST DAY in all history' read the title text on the cinema newsreel, and the pictures that followed gave viewers no reason to doubt the veracity of that heady claim. The *Pathé* footage, silent and flickering, relayed joyous scenes from the streets of Paris, London and New York, where thoroughfares and public squares were congested with people welcoming the Armistice and an end to more than four years of a war that had delivered misery on a scale unprecedented in modern history. Here, amidst the on-screen crush of humanity, viewers could observe smiles on faces, and hats and handkerchiefs being waved above heads, as much, one suspects, in relief as celebration.

Despite over 200,000 men enlisting for service in the First World War, and the massive and serial disruptions it had caused, the public mood in Ireland was more muted. In his monthly state of the nation submission to the Dublin Castle authorities, the Inspector General of the RIC remarked at the close of November 1918 that 'news of the armistice' had brought 'a sense of relief to every class of the community but it evokes no universal enthusiasm'.

Which is not to say that the country didn't experience celebrations: it did. In Belfast, where the atmosphere bordered on the jubilant, bonfires were lit, fireworks exploded, and a steady trade was done in the sale of Union Jack flags. In other parts of the country, too, public buildings were garlanded with Union flags and bunting, and Protestant churches sounded their bells.

Irish towns that hosted British Army barracks provided obvious focal points for triumphal displays. Birr was one such town. There, after the holding of a

> … 'news of the armistice' had brought 'a sense of relief to every class of the community but it evokes no universal enthusiasm'.

'THE GREATEST DAY IN ALL HISTORY'?

The end of the war was met by joyful scenes in Britain, France and elsewhere. Those who had served in the war could now be demobilised and return home.

military parade, a woman approached the editor of the *Midland Tribune*, a regional newspaper that had done little to disguise its separatist sympathies, and thrust a Union Jack in his face. 'Make the rebel eat it,' she yelled for the benefit of her pavement audience, before acidly adding, 'Where now is Sinn Féin and German gold?'

This was one incident in one town on one day, but there was nothing exceptional about it.

The ending of the war did nothing to unify Ireland in remembrance of the shared sacrifice of its nationalist and unionist servicemen, about 35,000 of whom were among the Great War dead. What it did was to further expose political divisions that had been deepened by the particular Irish experience of that war.

Just four days after the Armistice, Sir Edward Carson wrote to the *Belfast News Letter* to urge a distinctly Ulster and unionist commemoration of the war. A fund should be opened, he proposed, to support the erection of a monument on the Flanders battlefield to commemorate the 'heroic deeds' of the men of the Ulster Division, with 'any balance' to be channelled into a 'UVF Patriotic Fund'. There was no mention of making common commemorative cause with those servicemen from an Irish nationalist tradition.

The ending of the war did nothing to unify Ireland in remembrance of the shared sacrifice of its nationalist and unionist servicemen, about 35,000 of whom were among the Great War dead.

By the end of the war, the party of John Redmond, now deceased, which had encouraged the Irish Volunteers to serve 'wherever the firing line extends', was in retreat, with the separatist Sinn Féin the new standard-bearer of popular nationalist aspirations. For many soldiers celebrating the Allied victory on the streets of Dublin, this Sinn Féin movement represented a political enemy, and in their moment of triumph, some, not unlike the irate woman in Birr, felt moved to exercise their anger and prejudice. In the early evening of 13 November, for instance, ill-disciplined soldiers and their civilian supporters spent an hour rampaging through Dublin's principal streets armed with sticks. They laid siege to Liberty Hall on the quays, to the Mansion House on Dawson Street and to the Harcourt Street headquarters of Sinn Féin.

This rioting was roundly condemned in the nationalist press and the subsequent decision to confine the soldiers to their barracks was dismissed as being too little, too late. Sinn Féin, meanwhile, issued a statement urging their supporters to 'remain calm, steady and confident'.

Members of the American 5th Infantry Division celebrate the end of the First World War.

They had every reason to do so. Within a matter of days, a general election was called, which would underline the extraordinary and rapid rise of Sinn Féin and reveal the true transformation of Irish political realities. That election, held in December, would be fought in Ireland on the substantive issues of sovereignty and separatism.

Yet for many Irish people, the constitutional dimensions of Ireland's future autonomy were less pressing than the challenges they confronted in their everyday lives. For a start, the Spanish influenza epidemic, which had arrived in Ireland during the summer of 1918, had yet to run its ruinous course. Beyond the massive toll it exacted on human life – it would ultimately account for more than 20,000 Irish deaths – the fear induced by its spread caused serious social commotion, closing down schools and cinemas and, in mid-November, after several prominent members of the Wexford senior hurling team were 'laid up' owing to its effects, forcing a deferral of the All-Ireland final with Limerick.

Another effect of the flu pandemic was that it added to the burden on charitable and religious organisations, such as St Vincent de Paul, which, just days before the Armistice, had mounted a public appeal in Dublin for help to alleviate the suffering and distress of city-dwellers living in poverty. There was no shortage of these, and St Vincent de Paul estimated that their numbers would only increase in the months ahead as troops were demobilised and unemployment rose.

The British government, fearing the same, introduced a temporary scheme of unemployment relief, the 'Out of Work donation', which was introduced immediately after the conclusion of the war to benefit not only discharged soldiers and sailors, but also demobilised members of the women's corps and civilians. The scheme was embraced enthusiastically in Ireland, and by the end of February 1919, 94,000 Irish workers would be in receipt of this emergency donation.

Abuses of this scheme were said by one government official to have amounted to a 'grave public scandal', as large numbers of those availing of the payment were not considered legitimately out of work owing to the cessation of the war. The abuse was widespread (most counties reported problems with fraud) and encompassed men and women from a wide range of occupational backgrounds. According to one official report on the scheme, the claimants were generally 'agricultural labourers, idlers in towns, farmer's sons, and domestic servants', but there were also 'concrete cases of farmers, publicans, second-hand clothes dealers, students' and others who were in receipt of the donation.

The popularity of the scheme and the scale of the alleged abuses reflected a number of wider realities. The first was the willingness of a large number of claimants to play the system and the government dysfunction in the oversight of that system – in many cases, labour exchange officials were said to 'make little or no inquiry'. Second, and perhaps more significant, the willingness of so many of those already in employment to seek out the benefit sheds a light on the problem of poor wages across vast sectors of the economy, where being in a job did not necessarily guarantee an escape from poverty.

The 'out of work donation' scheme was introduced largely as a short-term measure to manage the very real problem of post-war unemployment and the adjustment to a peacetime society. That adjustment was piecemeal and, as subsequent events dictated, protracted in nature.

From mid-November 1918 onwards, with the election campaign in Ireland gathering momentum, certain measures that had been introduced for the purposes of imperial security during wartime were now held to be surplus to requirements. The dismantling of regulations under the DORA was begun and a number of American warships, stationed in Queenstown since the summer of 1917, set sail for home. That not all regulations were repealed – some remained in place in Ireland until 1921 – and that not all the American ships immediately departed, was, nevertheless, a reminder that Armistice did not translate into a seamless return to pre-war ways.

And, of course, for tens of thousands of Irish soldiers who had gone to fight in the war, there would be no return at all. *The Irish Times* had these men in mind when, in anticipation of a revival of sports and pastimes that had been either stopped or disrupted for the war's duration, it remarked on how acutely the absences of those who had died would be felt. 'For many a day the hunting-field, the cricket-ground, and the golf links must recall memories of good friends and gallant soldiers who will ride a horse and drive a ball no more.'

Despite the Armistice with Germany being agreed at 5.10 a.m. and scheduled to come into effect at 11 a.m., fierce fighting continued in many places up to the 'eleventh hour'. US forces in particular were active in two major operations that morning, crossing the River Meuse and taking the town of Stenay. Actions in which they suffered 1,300 casualties. Their death toll included four Irish men: Michael Garvin, Patrick Murray and Michael Walsh, all Mayo-born, and Austin O'Hare, originally from Kilfenora, Co. Clare. Another US soldier with an Irish name to die in the hours before the ceasefire was Hugh McKenna from Illinois, who is buried in Belleau Wood cemetery in France.

Prelude to Partition or a Republic?
–The 1918 Election in Ireland

ELECTION DAY WAS fixed for 14 December 1918, but it took two weeks and a Christmas interval before the votes cast were counted. When they were, on 28 December, the results were at once dramatic and entirely predictable. The near obliteration of the IPP and its replacement by Sinn Féin as the political standard-bearer for Irish nationalist aspirations had been, as one leading official in Britain's Irish administration confided at the time, a 'foregone conclusion'.

That it may have been, yet the scale of the electoral upheaval was no less stunning for it. In the end, Sinn Féin secured seventy-three of the 105 seats available for Ireland; Unionists seized twenty-six; and the nationalists of the IPP, occupiers of seventy-five House of Commons seats at the moment of the previous Parliament's dissolution, were reduced to six, four of which had been retained with the help of a Church-brokered deal that applied across several Ulster constituencies.

> **The IPP would limp on, but it would be hard to quibble ... that it had emerged from the election, in effect, 'as dead as Julius Caesar'.**

The IPP would limp on, but it would be hard to quibble with subsequent assertion of the Cork nationalist MP William O'Brien that it had emerged from the election, in effect, 'as dead as Julius Caesar'.

The Westminster Parliament was dissolved just fourteen days after the Armistice that brought the First World War to a close. Even so, the election it signalled was no snap affair. It had been long anticipated and had been preceded by revisions to constituency boundaries and franchise reform legislation that, taken together, amounted to no less than a transformation in the rules of democratic engagement. After decades of suffrage activism, the

PRELUDE TO PARTITION OR A REPUBLIC?

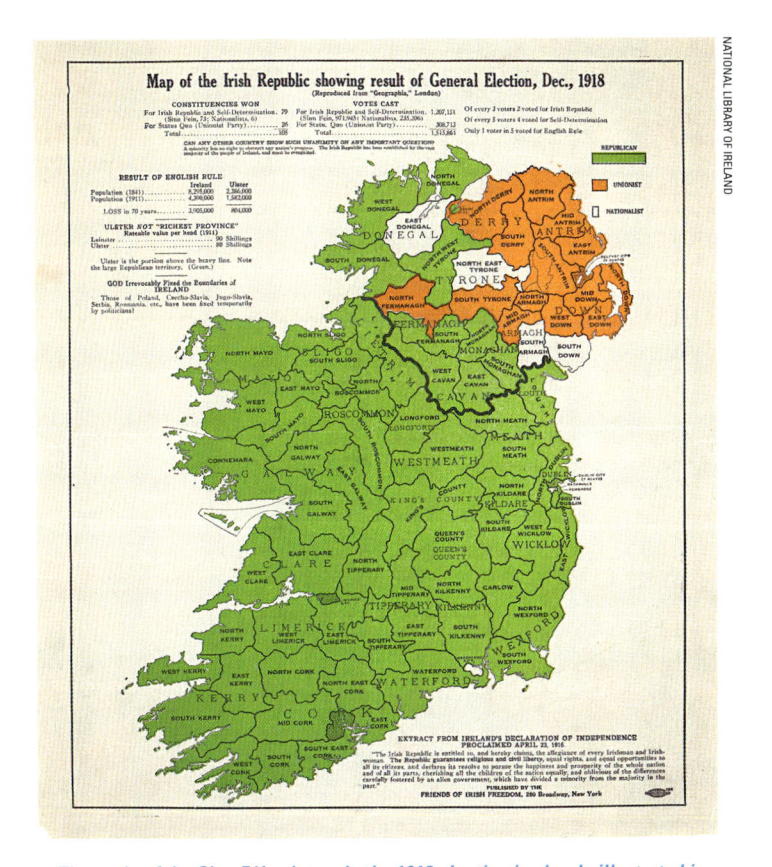

The scale of the Sinn Féin victory in the 1918 election is clearly illustrated in this map, published in the US by the Friends of Irish Freedom (FOIF). Against the green tide of Sinn Féin seats, only the twenty-two Unionist Party seats in Ulster offers any resistance.

right to vote had finally been extended to women, albeit only those over the age of thirty who met a minimum property qualification. The Representation of the People Act, 1918, did not deliver equality of the sexes – far from it – but by extending the franchise to include certain groups of women and virtually all men over the age of twenty-one, it ensured a vastly enlarged electorate. In Ireland alone, the numbers entitled to vote ballooned from just under 700,000 to over 1.9 million. Overall, the Irish electorate now extended to 72.6% of all those aged twenty-one years and over.

During the 1918 election campaign, Sinn Féin positioned itself as the principal and radical alternative to the stale and ineffectual IPP, a choice that was further crystallised by the decision of the Irish Labour Party to stand aside, despite having published its own manifesto in September 1918. Justifying its decision, which its membership endorsed by a margin of 4-1, Labour claimed that they alone were 'prepared to sacrifice party in the interest of the nation in this important crisis'.

Sinn Féin's definition of that national interest was clear-cut. It was the rejection of the Home Rule cause that had been the driving force of Irish nationalism for the previous forty years. In presenting its alternative, Sinn Féin urged voters to escape the 'shadow of a base imperialism' and march out 'into the full sunlight of freedom' by rallying around its call for an Irish Republic.

> Sinn Féin urged voters to escape the 'shadow of a base imperialism' and march out 'into the full sunlight of freedom' by rallying around its call for an Irish Republic.

Significantly, too, the party set out the steps by which it aimed to achieve this Republic: by withdrawing from the Westminster Parliament and establishing a 'constituent assembly' of its own; by 'making use of any and every means available to render impotent the power of England to hold Ireland in subjection by military force or otherwise'; and finally, by appealing for the international recognition of Ireland as an independent nation at the Peace Conference that was set to commence early the following year.

A manifesto that claimed to stand by the Proclamation of Easter 1916 was certainly radical, but was it realistic? Could a Republic really be delivered?

The IPP thought not. Neither did the influential Cardinal Logue, who cautioned his flock against 'ill-considered and utopian methods'. As for the unionists, when addressing a meeting of the UUC in Belfast in the course of the campaign, Sir Edward Carson rejected all talk of Irish self-determination. To cheers from his enthusiastic followers, he declared: 'Self-determination of whom and what? Self-determination by the south and west of Ireland of the destinies of Ulster? Never.'

But if the Sinn Féin message elicited scepticism, it equally aroused excitement.

The party's organisation had been strengthened as a result of the excesses of British policy on conscription and other issues during the spring and summer of 1918, which had the effect of driving new recruits into its ranks. By the end of the year, Sinn Féin could boast a network of 1,666 clubs and a membership that topped 112,000.

This organisational strength was pressed into action during the election campaign, though not always to everyone's satisfaction. In the constituency

A poster issued in 1909 by the Suffrage League demonstrated how women were handicapped in the electoral system. Although the Representation of the People Act of 1918 had massively increased the number of women voters, the vote was still restricted to women over the age of thirty with a qualifying property of rateable value.

of East Mayo, where the outgoing MP and IPP leader, John Dillon, was fighting to fend off the challenge of the imprisoned Sinn Féin president, Éamon de Valera, the former described as 'monstrous' and 'indecent' the prospect that 500 Clare men might travel to the constituency to intimidate the local electorate. De Valera was contesting three constituencies (East Clare, East Mayo and Belfast Falls) and was on the ballot in a fourth (South Down), but it was the decision of the IPP not to contest twenty-five constituencies where they had previously been dominant that freed Sinn Féin supporters to campaign in constituencies other than their own.

Nor was the use of intimidation as a tactic confined to any one political group or to any one constituency. In North Fermanagh, for instance, the Sinn Féin candidate, Kevin O'Shiel, and his election agent found themselves set upon by a crowd of unionist women and youths when leaving the post office in Ballinamallard. Mud was thrown at them, the Pope was cursed and a woman attempted to strike O'Shiel with a wooden gun. And to the south, in the constituency of Waterford City, where the IPP's Captain William Redmond was facing off against Sinn Féin's Dr Vincent White for the second time in nine months, polling day saw scuffles in the street and damage to property as violence flared between supporters of the rival candidates and between the Irish Volunteers and the police.

While there were unruly scenes and incidents in other villages, towns and constituencies, they don't come close to offering a complete picture of the voting-day experience. For those previously excluded from participating in the electoral process, in particular women, it was an occasion for unalloyed joy and celebration. On Dublin's southside, a procession of women from different political traditions marched through the streets to the polls carrying flowers and flags behind a banner of the IWFL. Among them was ninety-year-old Anna Haslam, a pioneering feminist who had helped found the Dublin Women's Suffrage Association in 1876 and whom one newspaper described as 'the oldest suffragist in Ireland'.

Winifred Carney, the trade unionist champion of a workers' republic, who polled a mere 539 votes and lost her £150 deposit, suffered for being in a unionist constituency (Belfast Victoria) with labour-leaning alternatives, but also from a lack of active support from the party on whose platform she stood. In the Dublin constituency of St Patrick's, by contrast, Constance Markievicz, whose campaign also complained of a lack of party support, easily saw off her nationalist opponents to become the first woman elected to the House of Commons. History-making it may have been, but the unionist *Belfast News Letter* believed Markievicz's victory conferred a 'doubtful distinction' on Dublin as the new MP was more representative of 'Militant Sinn Féin than of the gentler sex'.

Markievicz, then in Holloway Prison, was one of thirty-six Sinn Féin candidates who contested the election from jail. Their incarceration did them and their party no harm and, if anything, added to the lustre of their republican appeal. Sinn Féin routed their IPP opponents in all constituencies where they contested against each other bar two – Waterford City and Belfast Falls. The other four seats retained by the IPP were all in Ulster and all in constituencies Sinn Féin did not contest, the result of a pre-election pact negotiated with the help of the Catholic hierarchy that applied across eight constituencies and aimed at avoiding gifting seats to unionism through a split in the nationalist/republican vote.

Notwithstanding this nationalist strategy, Unionists performed strongly in Ulster, winning twenty-three of the thirty-seven seats available for the nine-county province, a return that simultaneously consolidated unionism's hold on the northeast of the country and underlined the isolation of southern unionists.

Countess Markievicz was one of seventeen women who stood for election in 1918 and was the only successful candidate.

Whatever about the post-election forecasts for unionism, the IPP emerged from the vote devoid of almost any prospects at all. *The Freeman's Journal*, the party's traditional champion in print, declared that it had 'practically ceased to exist as a Parliamentary force'. In truth, it could hardly have hoped for any better. Its decision to abandon twenty-five constituencies to its Sinn Féin rivals amounted to nothing less than a capitulation in advance. These non-contested constituencies would ultimately account for more than a third of all seats won by Sinn Féin, but they would equally serve to depress the party's share of the overall vote. Where the IPP claimed six seats with a 21% vote share, Sinn Féin secured their seventy-three with a 46% vote share. Given that the republican vote reached an average of 65.3% in contested constituencies, it is likely that the party's overall vote share would have been greater if there had been more such contests.

In many ways, the results of the 1918 election were at once emphatic and inconclusive. For certain, they underscored the dramatic shift in popular nationalist sentiment in the period since the Rising. They equally reinforced the position of Ulster unionism and exposed as fanciful the idea, earnestly propagated by the likes of Redmond and Tom Kettle, that the shared experience of sacrifice during the First World War might unite the Irish people in a common political purpose.

Less clear from the 1918 results was where Ireland might be headed next, however. For republicans, who moved swiftly towards the creation of the 'constituency assembly' that had been promised in its manifesto, questions now abounded as to how much self-determination they would be allowed to exercise.

Would the Peace Conference, dominated by the Allied powers, grant the Irish Republic the recognition that Sinn Féin craved? How would the British government – or for that matter, the unionists in Ulster – respond to the creation of a new parliament in Dublin, and what would this mean for either its viability or legitimacy? And exactly what did Sinn Féin mean in their manifesto by such terms as the 'use of any and every means available to render impotent the power of England to hold Ireland in subjection by military force or otherwise'.

There were no easy or obvious answers to any of these questions as 1918 drew to a close. The election had simultaneously delivered new political mandates, pointed Irish nationalism in the direction of independence and entrenched pre-existing divisions between Irish nationalism and unionism. To that extent, it clarified much and resolved little.

YOU CAN

Buy Dail Eireann Bonds To-day

- RECOVER IRELAND FOR THE IRISH.
- RE-PEOPLE THE LAND.
- HARNESS THE RIVERS.
- PUT HER FLAG ON EVERY SEA.
- PLANT THE HILLSIDES AND THE WASTES.
- SET THE LOOMS SPINNING.
- ABOLISH THE SLUMS.
- SEND HER SHIPS T[O] EVERY PORT.
- SET THE HAMMER RI[NG]ING ON THE ANVIL.
- GARNER THE HARV[EST] OF THE SEAS.
- DRAIN THE BOGS.
- SAVE THE BO[YS AND] GIRLS FOR IREL[AND].
- [IRE]LAND'S HEAL[TH]

Hand your Subscription to your Local Member of the [Dáil] or his Representative

1919

'Almost at the same moment I heard a report, and the two constables fell on the road. One of the men got into the cart and drove it away in the direction of the quarry with the gelignite. The others took the policemen's rifles and ammunition ...'

Patrick Flynn on the attack at Soloheadbeg
21 JANUARY

1919

6 JAN
Former US President, Theodore Roosevelt, dies unexpectedly, aged 60. The cause of death is attributed to heart failure caused by a blood clot in the heart.

18 JAN
The Paris Peace Conference begins at Versailles. In all, 27 nations are represented, but there is no place for an Irish delegation.

21 JAN
Dáil Éireann holds its first meeting in Dublin's Mansion House.

21 JAN
In the Soloheadbeg ambush in Co. Tipperary, two members of RIC are killed by members of the Irish Volunteers led by Dan Breen and Seán Treacy. It will come to be regarded as the first engagement of the War of Independence.

'In jail for you, get them out' – Sinn Féin Demonstrations Demand Prisoner Releases

Dublin, 6 January – Irish republican prisoners must be released immediately. That's the message from the Sinn Féin party, which, since its landslide election victory last month, has been highlighting the cause of its members imprisoned in British prisons.

The official Sinn Féin newspaper, *Nationality*, has stated this week: 'The first thing the people of Ireland have to do is to see that their interned leaders are released.'

'Almost half of the elected representatives of the Irish people are in British jails today. British tyranny in Ireland must cease. Definitely and defiantly, we must tell the British Government that it cannot go on doing as it likes in Ireland.'

Following on from that, hundreds of meetings were believed to have been held yesterday throughout the country to demand the release of Irish prisoners. On Dublin's O'Connell Street, the attendance was reported to have run into the thousands, with crowds marching to their meeting place behind a band and huge banner bearing the words: 'In jail for you, get them out.'

Peace Conference Prepares to Meet in Paris

Paris, 14 January – Preparations are underway for the commencement of the Paris peace talks later this month. Today, the prime ministers of Great Britain, Australia, Canada, South Africa and Newfoundland depart London for the French capital, where they will begin preliminary conversations with the leaders of the Allies and associated states.

According to a telegram from Paris, the delegations to the conference will be organised as follows: the United States, Britain, France, Italy and Japan will be entitled to five delegates each; Belgium, Greece, Portugal, Romania, Serbia, China and Brazil will be accorded three delegates each, while the Czecho-Slovak Republic and Poland will be represented by two delegates each.

In addition, those states which broke off relations with the defeated German Empire but took no effective part in the war will be entitled to a single delegate each.

The conference will need to address the issue of the renewal of the armistice with Germany and is also certain to discuss the creation of a League of Nations, which could constitute a practical basis for the maintenance of peace in the coming years.

The league was proposed by US President Woodrow Wilson, and it is understood that the majority of the Allied powers are in favour of its establishment.

Two Policemen Killed in Soloheadbeg Attack

Soloheadbeg, 21 January – Two policemen have been shot dead in an attack by masked men in Soloheadbeg, Co. Tipperary.

The constables, who have been named as James McDonnell and Patrick O'Connell, were escorting a quantity of gelignite over a distance of three miles from Tipperary to Soloheadbeg quarry, where it was intended for use in blasting rock. Constables McDonnell and O'Connell were walking with loaded rifles either side of the cart carrying the gelignite when the attack occurred. Alongside them was a county council employee, Patrick Flynn, and the driver of the cart, James Godfrey, both of whom survived.

It was mid-afternoon, between 12.30 and 1 p.m., when, according to an account offered by Mr Flynn, about a dozen masked men jumped over a roadside fence near Soloheadbeg quarry and shouted, 'Hands up.' 'Almost at the same moment,' he continued, 'I heard a report, and the two constables fell on the road. One of the men got into the cart and drove it away in the direction of the quarry with the gelignite. The others took the policemen's rifles and ammunition and went away in the direction of Coffey's forge.' The whole episode was over within just a minute or two.

The government immediately proclaimed the district a military area and therefore subject to martial law.

The day after the incident, police arrested two men in connection with the killings. One of the men has been named as Patrick Gorman, a labourer from Churchfield, Donohill, Co. Tipperary. The other man, as yet unnamed, was arrested in Dundrum, Co. Tipperary.

The dead policemen have been described as 'very popular', and their deaths have been a source of much local outrage. Constable McDonnell, aged 50 and a native of Belmullet, Co. Mayo, was a widower and the father of five young children. Constable O'Connell, 30, was a native of Coachford, Co. Cork, and it was to there that his remains have been taken for burial.

Dáil Éireann Meets in Mansion House

Dublin, 23 January – Ireland has been declared an independent republic again. A Declaration of Irish Independence was adopted following the opening of Dáil Éireann, the new Irish Parliament, in the Round Room of Dublin's Mansion House two days ago.

1919

23 JAN
Workers at the Monaghan asylum, led by Peadar O'Donnell, begin a strike and occupy the asylum in a quest for better pay and conditions.

24 JAN
A general strike involving 40,000 engineering and shipyard workers in Belfast begins. The strike, in pursuit of demands for a shorter working week and better conditions, lasts a month before collapsing.

26 JAN
Delayed due to the previous year's flu epidemic, the 1918 All-Ireland hurling final is played at Croke Park. Limerick comfortably defeat a Wexford selection on a scoreline of 9–5 to 1–3.

3 FEB
Éamon de Valera escapes from Lincoln Prison with the help of Michael Collins and Harry Boland.

7 FEB
Thomas Johnson and Cathal O'Shannon are admitted as Irish representatives to the International Labour and Socialist Conference – the 'First International' – in Bern, Switzerland.

1919

The 'appeal to the nations' by the Parliament of the Irish Republic at its meeting in Dublin on 21 January 1919.

8 FEB
A Sinn Féin delegation arrives in Paris hoping to lobby the representatives of the major powers and gain international recognition of Irish independence.

16 FEB
Before an attendance of 10,000 spectators, Wexford footballers complete an All-Ireland four-in-a row after defeating Munster champions, Tipperary, by 5 points to 4 at Croke Park.

18 FEB
Kathleen Clarke, widow of executed 1916 leader Thomas, returns to Dublin after being released from Holloway Prison in England.

Twenty-nine recently elected MPs were recorded as attending.

A roll call was read out of all those who had been invited. When the names of Sinn Féin members who were in prison were read out, the answer, given in Irish, was 'In Jail'. The room filled with laughter when the name of Edward Carson was spoken.

The six members of the Irish Parliamentary Party who were invited neither replied nor attended.

The audience in the Round Room rose in acclaim for the members of the Dáil as they walked into the room shortly before 3.30 p.m. Many waved tricolour flags and handkerchiefs.

The Lord Mayor of Dublin was in attendance, as were several colonial soldiers, among them an Australian officer in khaki. Great enthusiasm accompanied the entrance of two American naval officers into building; the men responding by smiling and saluting the crowd.

The proceedings commenced with a prayer delivered by Fr Michael O'Flanagan, acting president of Sinn Féin, following which Cathal Brugha was appointed president and speaker, and four others appointed as clerks.

Much of the main business of the assembly was conducted through the Irish language.

A declaration of Irish independence was read in Irish, English and French, and was subsequently adopted. The declaration made reference to the Rising of Easter 1916 and to the democratic mandate achieved at last month's general election.

J.J. Kelly (Sceilg), MP for Louth, then read a message to the free nations of the world, a French translation of which was read by Count Plunkett. This message declared Ireland to be 'one of the most ancient nations in

A group photograph of the members of the First Dáil Éireann, 22 January 1919. Centre front are Count Plunkett and Cathal Brugha.

REVOLUTIONARY TIMES 1913–23

Europe' and asserted its right to self-determination 'before the new world emerging from the War, because she believes in freedom and justice as the fundamental principles of international law'.

The message concluded by calling on 'every free nation to uphold her national claim to complete independence as an Irish Republic against the arrogant pretensions of England founded in fraud and sustained only by an overwhelming military occupation, and demands to be confronted publicly with England at the Congress of the Nations, in order that the civilised world, having judged between English wrong and Irish right, may guarantee to Ireland its permanent support for the maintenance of her national independence'.

Farmers Protest Sinn Féin Efforts to Stop Hunting

Limerick, 28 January – A Sinn Féin campaign to prevent hunting across the country is being met with mixed reaction.

The purpose of the campaign, *The Irish Times* reports, is to 'punish the professional classes because the government has refused to release certain men from internment'.

The move has seen stoppages to hunting in many parts of the country and has drawn a backlash from farmers, many of them Sinn Féin supporters, as well as from local councils.

In Limerick, a hunt organised by the County Limerick Foxhounds was stopped when a crowd of people, including members of the Clouncagh Sinn Féin club, informed the Master of the Foxhounds and his company that until Irish political prisoners were released, the hunt could not be permitted.

De Valera in Sensational Escape from Lincoln Prison

Lincoln, 6 February – Éamon de Valera, MP, has escaped from Lincoln Prison along with Seán Milroy and Seán McGarry.

The prison authorities, despite issuing detailed descriptions of the escaped men, have no clues as to their current whereabouts. One line of thinking is that the men may have taken a motor car and headed for the coast, the nearest coastal point being Grimsby, a distance of some 30 miles from the prison.

1919

20 FEB
A Sinn Féin protest against hunting leads to the abandonment of the Ward Hunt in Meath.

21 FEB
John O'Connor Power, Home Rule MP for Mayo between 1874 and 1885 and, earlier, a supporter of the Land League, dies at his home in Putney, London.

22 FEB ▽
The **FOIF** organisation begins a two-day Irish Race Convention in Philadelphia.

1919

4 MAR
By a margin of 261 to 41, the US House of Representatives votes for a resolution expressing an 'earnest hope' that the Peace Conference would 'favourably consider the claims of Ireland to self-determination'. The unionist *Belfast News Letter* declares the vote an 'act of impertinence', the effect of which was to favour the 'partition of the British Empire'.

6 MAR
Pierce McCan, elected as Sinn Féin MP for Tipperary East in the 1918 election while in prison, dies in Gloucester Prison having contracted influenza.

15 MAR
After ten months of incarceration in Holloway Prison for her alleged role in the so-called 'German Plot', Countess Markievicz returns to Dublin. She is received by delegates from the ICA, the IWFL, Cumann na mBan and prominent members of Sinn Féin, and delivers a speech to thousands of supporters at Liberty Hall, her first since her election as MP the previous December.

Lincoln Prison is situated in the north of the city and is surrounded by a very high wall, about 20 feet high. Positioned between two main roads, Greetwell and Wrangley roads, the only entrance to the prison is via Greetwell Road and this is well guarded by day and night.

It is believed that the fugitives escaped the prison on Monday 3 February, between the hours of 4 p.m., when they had their tea, and 9 p.m., when their absence was discovered and the alarm raised.

The authorities believe the three men opened a back door, possibly using a master key thrown over the prison wall by accomplices. A motor car with a single occupant was seen slowing down at the point nearest the rear door between 7 and 8 p.m. The road on which the car was spotted is one of the main thoroughfares to Hull and, as such, every coastal town was warned.

The three fugitives are all high-profile Sinn Féin figures. Mr de Valera, party president, together with Mr McGarry, a journalist who edited the O'Donovan Rossa memorial publication, was arrested as part of a general round-up of Sinn Féin activists in May 1918. Mr Milroy served several periods of incarceration before the 1916 Rising and unsuccessfully contested a by-election in East Tyrone last year.

Wexford Footballers Complete GAA's First 4-in-a-row

Dublin, 17 February – The Gaelic footballers of Wexford created a significant piece of Irish sporting history yesterday at Croke Park. In defeating Tipperary by the narrowest of margins – 5 points to 4 – in the delayed 1918 All-Ireland football final, they became the first team to win four titles in succession.

The tightness of the match and quality of the play made this a thrilling contest. On a fine, if bitterly cold day, and before a crowd estimated at between 8,000 and 10,000, the two well-trained teams provided an exhibition of 'scientific' football.

Seán T. O'Kelly Delivers Ireland's Paris Plea for Independence

Paris, 24 February – Seán T. O'Kelly, MP, has delivered a letter to the Secretary of the Peace Conference in Paris at the Quai d'Orsay, which claims the right of recognition of the Irish Republic and the admission of Ireland as a member of the League of Nations.

Registered copies of the same letter, which were accompanied by the Declaration of Independence ratified at the first meeting of Dáil Éireann

1919

English text of the Message to the Free Nations of the World drafted by the First Dáil, asking countries to recognise Ireland as a separate nation.

and the message that Parliament issued to the nations of the world, were also sent to each member of the conference asking that Irish delegates be received as soon as possible for the purpose of establishing 'formally and definitely before the Peace Conference and League of Nations Commission Ireland's indisputable right to the international recognition of her independence, and the propriety of her claim to enter the League of Nations as one of its constituent members'.

Dublin Struggles to Cope with Volume of Flu Deaths

Dublin, 6 March – Undertakers at Glasnevin cemetery are struggling to cope with the numbers of interments resulting from influenza-induced deaths.

Over the course of the last three days, they have had 200 burials. This abnormally high number has resulted in delays of a day or so in organising interments.

In one particularly tragic case, an entire family living on Dublin's Corporation Street succumbed to the disease. The alarm was raised when neighbours noticed that members of the Phelan family had not been seen for some time. When the rooms they occupied at Corporation Buildings

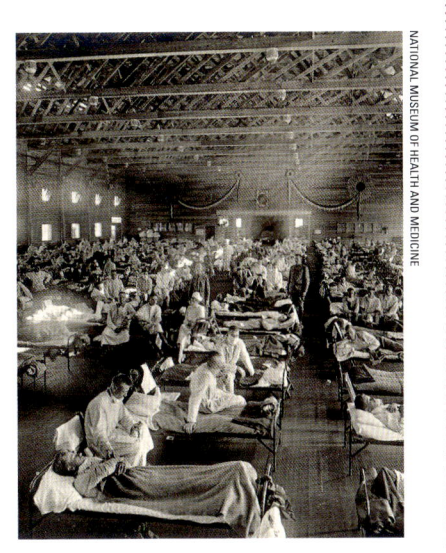

An emergency influenza hospital in Kansas, USA, in 1918.

17 MAR
'To save the national language is the special duty of this generation,' de Valera declares in a St Patrick's Day message to the Irish people.

19 MAR △
Two Marconi engineers, W.T. Ditcham and H.J. Round, based at the **Marconi radio station facility in Ballybunion**, send the first ever voice transmission across the Atlantic from east to west. Their transmission is received at a station in Nova Scotia and opens with the words, 'Hello Canada, hello Canada'.

21 MAR
The *Irish Independent* reports that two warrants have been issued for the arrest of Michael Collins on the charge of inciting raids for arms.

29 MAR
Twenty Sinn Féin prisoners escape from Mountjoy Prison in broad daylight.

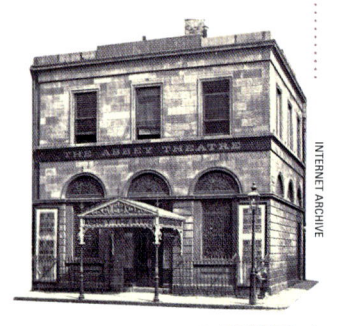

1919

△ **30 MAR**
The **Abbey Theatre** hosts a meeting at which W.B. Yeats and Lennox Robinson discuss its past and future. 'We must horrify Mr. Yeats by telling him', *The Irish Times* later editorialises, 'that the paramount object of all theatre audiences – even Abbey audiences – is "an evening's entertainment".'

31 MAR
Trained nurses work for anything from 60 to 70 hours per week for an average income of £50 to £60 per year, a meeting of the Irish Nurses' Association in Dublin is told.

1 APR
De Valera is elected President at the second meeting of Dáil Éireann, which is attended by 52 elected members.

2 APR
Constance Markievicz is appointed the Minister of Labour in the new Irish government. She is the first female government minister in western Europe.

---

were forcibly entered, Frances Phelan, aged 27, was found dead in bed. Her husband and baby were lying beside her, with Mr Phelan's sister stretched across the foot of the bed; all three were still alive. They were brought to South Dublin Union Hospital, where they later died.

Sir Charles Cameron, Chief Medical Officer for Dublin Corporation, indicated that this week marks a high point for flu deaths. More optimistically, however, he predicts that the epidemic will have run its course within three weeks.

Irish Nurses Demand More Pay and Better Working Conditions

Dublin, 1 April – The pay and working conditions for Irish nurses needs improvement.

That was the message from the president of the Irish Nurses' Association, Alice Reeves, at a meeting in the Royal College of Surgeons in Dublin last night.

Reeves drew particular attention to the question of the hours that nurses, both qualified and in training, are required to work. She also highlighted the inadequate conditions and salaries. According to Reeves, trained nurses worked 60 to 70 hours per week for an average income of £50 to £60 per year.

She urged the abolition of an entrance fee to nursing courses and further advised that a certificate be granted to qualified nurses.

A motion was passed that women engaged in hospital work will elect a committee to represent the whole nursing profession in considering the position of Irish nurses.

Dáil Elects De Valera as President

Dublin, 7 April – Dáil Éireann met earlier this week, on 1–4 April, for the first time since its initial meetings in January.

In the official report of these proceedings, published in both English and Irish, it is confirmed that an executive was elected, with Éamon de Valera installed as President. Other members of the executive include Constance Markievicz, Eoin MacNeill, William Cosgrave, Michael Collins, Arthur Griffith, Cathal Brugha and Count Plunkett. In addition, Laurence Ginnell, Robert Barton and Ernest Blythe were made departmental directors.

It has been confirmed that the next meeting of Dáil Éireann will be held in public session.

Éamon de Valera, Michael Collins and Harry Boland attend the second session of the First Dáil Éireann at Dublin's Mansion House, 1 April 1919.

Dublin's Hotels and Restaurants Closed by Strikes

Dublin, 23 April – The Dublin hotel dispute continues after talks between hotel owners' representatives, the Hotel and Tourist Association of Ireland, and the Hotel Workers' Branch of the Irish Transport and General Workers' Union ended without resolution.

The talks took place at the Ministry of Labour on Lord Edward Street yesterday afternoon.

The dispute has impacted 28 hotels and four restaurants in Dublin, which have been forced to close their doors: among them are the Central Hotel, the Gresham Hotel, the Wicklow Hotel, the Shelbourne Hotel, the Hibernian Hotel, Buswells, the Bray Head and the Royal Hotel, Bray, the Spa Hotel in Lucan, the Royal Hotel in Howth and Jammet's restaurant.

The employees of these and other establishments have demanded a 50-hour week, extra pay on Sundays and recognition of their union, the employment bureau and shop stewards.

1919

5 APR
An urgent public appeal for funds is launched to raise money to assist people living in Connemara, whose difficulties have been compounded by the ravages of the influenza outbreak.

7 APR
Linfield beat Glentoran 2–1 to win the Irish Cup. The game is played at the Solitude ground and is a second replay after the final and first replay end in draws.

9 APR
Many areas of the country are put under additional police control due to growing state of disturbance. These include Cork city, Cork county (east and west), Roscommon, Tipperary (north and south), Limerick city, Limerick county, Kerry and the Westport urban district, which encompasses the adjoining districts of Westport Rural and Kilmeena.

13 APR
At least 379 civilians, assembled for a peaceful demonstration, are killed when the British Indian Army opens fire on protesters at Amritsar in the Punjab. The massacre is ordered by Irish-educated Colonel Reginald Dyer and supported by the Tipperary-born Lieutenant Governor of the Punjab, Sir Michael O'Dwyer.

1919

15 APR
A 'Limerick Soviet' is created as a general strike is organised by the labour movement in the city to protest against the imposition of martial law. The strike committee takes on responsibility for maintaining supplies and public order in the city. It runs until 27 April.

16 APR
The Boyne Cinema in Drogheda is raided by the police, who enter the cinema and remove two reels of a film, the *Sinn Féin Review*, due to be shown that evening. The film has been deemed by authorities in Dublin as 'Sinn Féin propaganda pure and simple'.

23 APR
Many Dublin hotels are closed due to the ongoing strike by the Hotel Workers Branch of the ITGWU.

28 APR
The Covenant of the League of Nations is published in Paris.

◁ **30 APR Sir John Pentland Mahaffy**, Provost of Trinity College, Dublin, dies.

Alcock and Brown Fly into Clifden – and Aviation History

Dublin, 16 June – Captain John Alcock and Lieutenant Arthur Whitten Brown have been feted as heroes in Dublin after becoming the first people in history to fly across the Atlantic Ocean.

It took them and their double engine Vickers-Vimy biplane almost 16 hours to complete the 1,900-mile journey, which began in St John's in Newfoundland, Canada, on the afternoon of 14 June.

Before departing, Lieutenant Brown, the navigator, declared that his intention was to head for a landing at Galway Bay, but he added that he would be satisfied with any point along the Irish west coast.

As it turned out, the landing point was not too far from the original destination. Despite unfavourable weather, the men set their plane down in Derrigimlagh Bog, behind the Marconi station near the small town of Clifden, shortly before 9 a.m. on 15 June. The plane circled the town a number of times before crash-landing near the aerials of the station.

The historic crossing secures the *Daily Mail*'s £10,000 prize for the two pilots and comes just weeks after the well-publicised failed attempt of another pair, Hawker and Grieve.

Flying through the dark in inclement weather at an average speed of 120 miles per hour, sustaining themselves with sandwiches, chocolate and coffee, there were occasions when Alcock and Brown came perilously close to losing their way. At one point it seemed like they had come within a few feet of the water; on another, they felt like they were flying upside down. Because of the poor visibility, the adventurers only caught sight of water about six times during the crossing.

1919

'We have had a terrible journey,' Captain Alcock recounted for the *Daily Mail*. 'The wonder is we are here at all. We scarcely saw the sun or the moon or the stars ... For hours the machine was covered in a sheet of ice, carried by frozen sleet, at another time the fog was so dense that my speed indicator did not work, and for a few seconds it was very alarming. We looped the loop, I do believe, and did a very steep spiral.'

Alcock and Brown had intended to fly onwards to London, but the damage caused to their machine on its landing in Clifden meant that they had to travel by other means.

1 MAY
A new tax on beer and spirits alarms the Irish distilling industry.

3 MAY
Delegates from the US-based FOIF arrive in Ireland.

20,000 Troops March in Victory Day Parade in Dublin

Dublin, 19 July – Victory Day, or Peace Day, has been celebrated across the British Empire, including in many of Ireland's principal cities and towns.

One of the largest parades took place in Dublin, where 15,000 regular soldiers with artillery, armoured cars and light and heavy tanks paraded alongside 5,000 demobilised troops.

A victory parade celebrating the end of the First World War, in Dublin in 1919. In the foreground people sit on the roof of Trinity College Dublin to look down on the parade. A Union Jack flag is flying on the roof.

1919

13 MAY
Two RIC men are killed in an IRA attack on a train. The attack was planned to free Seán Hogan, who had played a key role in the Soloheadbeg attacks in January. He is on board, en route to Cork under police escort. The attack takes place when the train stops at Knocklong Station in Limerick, and, despite Dan Breen and Seán Treacy suffering injuries, Hogan is freed.

17 MAY
The first republican court is established in Ballinrobe, Co. Mayo.

▽ 19 MAY
An attempt by Harry Hawker to complete the first transatlantic flight fails when his **Sopwith** aircraft crashes in the ocean. He is rescued days later, 750 miles off the Irish coast.

21 MAY
An ongoing strike by Cork bakers creates food shortages across the city.

The Dublin parade commenced at 11.30 a.m. and followed a route along Dame Street, College Green, Great Brunswick Street, Westland Row, Lincoln Place, Leinster Street, Kildare Street and then on to St Stephen's Green.

Viscount French, the Lord Lieutenant, took the salute of the parading troops at the Bank of Ireland on College Green, where a large platform was erected to accommodate his staff and a number of government officials. Inside the gates of Trinity College more stands were erected to facilitate viewing by wounded soldiers.

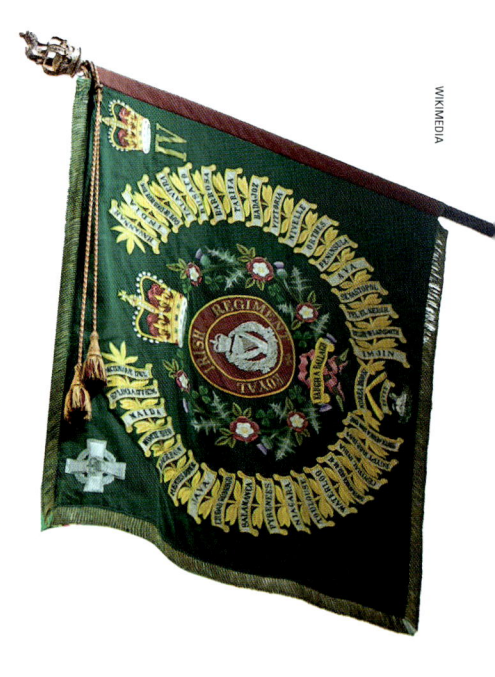

The first body of marchers to pass the reviewing stand was a mounted detachment of RIC men; they were followed by demobilised sailors and soldiers, some in uniform and some in civilian clothes. Perhaps the most impressive group was the detachment of Irish Guards that came from London for the occasion and was headed by a pipe band.

Men from the Royal Irish Regiment, Royal Inniskilling Fusiliers, the Royal Irish Fusiliers, the Connaught Rangers, the Royal Munster Fusiliers, the Royal Dublin Fusiliers and the Leinster Regiment also marched. The tail end of the procession was made up of men from English, Welsh and Scottish regiments.

In advance of the parade, a great effort was taken to brighten and decorate the city with flags and bunting in praise of Britain and the Allied nations. This was especially apparent along the streets through which the parade proceeded, in particular the thoroughfares of Dame Street, Westmoreland Street and Nassau Street. Grafton Street was also a blaze of colour.

The acclaim was far from universal, however. While there were no great disturbances during the day, the atmosphere in the city changed later in the evening. At about 9.30 p.m., on Ormond Quay, two soldiers were attacked, and when Sergeant Roche from the Dublin Metropolitan Police intervened, he received a gunshot wound. Around midnight, police wielded batons, which left 16 people requiring treatment at Jervis Street Hospital for scalp injuries. At Beresford Place, a large body of police charged a crowd of approximately 200–300 people, where an ex-soldier was delivering a short address.

15-year-old Fianna Scout Shot Dead in Clare

Ennistymon, 15 August – The funeral has taken place of 15-year-old Francis Murphy, who was shot dead at his home near Ennistymon in Co. Clare on the night of 13 August.

No motive for the attack can be discerned, but the blame has been directed towards the military, which is likely be the focus of the forthcoming inquest.

Murphy arrived home before 9 p.m. on the night he was shot, his father, John, told reporters, and joined with the family in reciting the Rosary at about 10.30 p.m. Afterwards he sat down in the kitchen to read. Shots were fired at the house between midnight and 1 a.m.; a subsequent inspection found eight to nine bullet marks on the house. Three bullets appear to have passed through the window, with one hitting the young man. Murphy was found on the kitchen floor, lying in a pool of blood.

Francis Murphy was a popular child from a well-known and large local family. He worked as a hardware assistant and was a member of Fianna Éireann, the republican scouting organisation. His father is a prominent Gaelic Leaguer.

Murphy's funeral took place earlier today. A procession a mile long – comprising motor cars, pedestrians, men on horseback and boys wearing mourning badges – formed to accompany his body to the family burial ground at Ennistymon.

Fianna Scouts engaged in field medical training, c.1914.

1919

1 JUN
De Valera leaves Ireland to embark on an 18-month publicity and fundraising tour of the US.

1 JUN △
A Dublin City Council architect claims the rebuilt **O'Connell Street** will be better than the original.

2 JUN
Kathleen Lynn addresses fundraising for St Ultan's Children's Hospital and says that Dublin's infant mortality rate of 164 out of every 1,000 born is too high.

3 JUN
The Local Government (Ireland) Act comes into force.

14 JUN
Questions are asked about the future of Dublin Zoo, given high running costs and low attendances during the war years. The books are balanced by the sale of a number of the zoo's lions.

1919

15 JUN
John Alcock and Arthur Brown complete the first non-stop transatlantic flight, crash-landing in a bog near Clifden in Co. Galway.

17 JUN
The process to establish the First Dáil Arbitration Courts is announced by Arthur Griffith in the Dáil.

23 JUN
RIC District Inspector Michael Hunt is shot and killed in Thurles.

△ **25 JUN**
Loch Lomond, ridden by Martin Quirke and trained by James Parkinson, wins the Irish Derby at **the Curragh**.

26 JUN
Lord French, Lord Lieutenant of Ireland, calls for the construction of an Irish national war memorial to honour those who died in the First World War.

Soldiers Rampage through Fermoy in Retaliation for Church-door Attack

Fermoy, 10 September – Members of the British military rampaged through the town of Fermoy in Co. Cork on 8 September, destroying several properties.

Estimates as to the cost of the damage vary greatly, from hundreds of pounds up to £10,000. At a public meeting held subsequently in the Urban Council chamber, Rev. John O'Donoghue said that the people had in no way provoked the military to wreck the town and if civilians had been present 'lives would certainly have been lost'.

In response, military authorities committed to keeping their troops confined to barracks last night.

The military rampage in Fermoy has been seen by some as retaliation for an attack the previous day, which left one soldier dead and three others seriously wounded. A group of approximately 25 men attacked 15 rifle-carrying soldiers of the Shropshire Light Infantry as they were about to enter the door of the Methodist church in Fermoy.

The attacking party arrived in two motor cars and opened fire with revolvers at close range, felling the four soldiers, including Private Jones, who was killed instantly when a bullet entered his heart.

The attackers then overpowered the remainder of the soldiers and relieved them of their rifles, before escaping in their motor cars, heading in the direction of Waterford. When the police followed them, they found the route out of town blocked with trees.

None of those involved in this attack have so far been apprehended.

Arrests and Raids Follow Proclamation against Dáil Éireann

Dublin, 13 September – Dáil Éireann, the Parliament established by Sinn Féin MPs in Dublin in January 1919, has been prohibited by the British authorities.

The suppression of Dáil Éireann was announced by Lord Lieutenant Sir John French and came into effect on 11 September. Lord French declared that the 'Association known by the name of The Dáil Éireann' has been deemed to be 'dangerous' and has been added to a list of organisations – Sinn Féin, the Irish Volunteers, Cumann na mBan and the Gaelic League – that were banned in July 1918.

This proclamation applies to every county in Ireland as well as the county boroughs of Dublin, Belfast, Cork, Limerick, Derry and Waterford.

At almost the same time as the banning of the Dáil, a series of raids and searches were carried out on the houses of Sinn Féin members, including Count Plunkett, Alderman Thomas Kelly, Michael Staines, Joseph McGuinness, Joseph McGrath and William Cosgrave.

A two-hour search was also conducted of the party's headquarters at 6 Harcourt Street in Dublin. Ernest Blythe and Patrick O'Keefe were on the premises at the time and were arrested and taken to Mountjoy Prison. Mr Blythe is Sinn Féin's director of industry and trades, MP for North Monaghan and editor of *The Southern Star* newspaper in Skibbereen, while Mr O'Keefe is general secretary of the party and MP for North Cork.

Similar raids occurred in Belfast, where literature was discovered and removed, but no arms were found. Seán McEntee, MP for South Monaghan, told the *Belfast Telegraph* that 12 policemen visited his home, searching it from top to bottom and pulling up floorboards.

In Derry, a raid on a Sinn Féin hall is reported as having unearthed rifles, hand grenades, gelignite and ammunition.

A printing company in Omagh, which publishes a number of weekly newspapers, including the *Ulster Herald*, was searched and literature was seized. In Ballycastle, the houses of Ada McNeill and Gertrude Parry, cousins of Ronald McNeill and the late Roger Casement respectively, were also targeted for searches.

The hard-line approach being adopted by the Dublin Castle authorities has been welcomed in the British press. 'The Government in Ireland is taking a firm hand with Sinn Féin at last,' observed the *London Express*. 'Everyone who has at heart the welfare of Ireland will rejoice to see it.'

Closure of Women's Toilet in Dublin Condemned

Dublin, 19 September – The closure of the only women's public bathroom in Dublin has been described as an act of 'malignant stupidity and malign mismanagement'.

The lavatory, located on Burgh Quay near O'Connell Bridge, was shut by the Cleansing Committee of Dublin Corporation a month ago, and they have since refused to reopen it.

The Cleansing Department has defended its decision on the basis that

1919

26 JUN
William Martin Murphy, the businessman and newspaper proprietor, best known for his role in the 1913 lockout, dies at the age of 74. He is buried in Glasnevin three days later.

28 JUN
The signing of the Versailles Treaty officially ends the war between Germany and the Allied powers.

3 JUL
The first Fordson tractor rolls off the production line of the Ford Motor Plant in Cork.

4 JUL
Sinn Féin, the Irish Volunteers, Cumann na mBan and the Gaelic League are suppressed in Co. Tipperary.

8 JUL
The Freeman's Journal editorial claims that Sinn Féin has failed to deliver on its electoral promises.

12 JUL
At the first major post-war 12 July celebrations in Belfast, attended by 300,000 people, Edward Carson tells the crowd he would not hesitate to 'call out the Ulster Volunteers' if Sinn Féin threatened Ulster.

1919

14 JUL
De Valera addresses a crowd of 25,000 in Chicago and states that 'only independence will satisfy Ireland'.

△ **19 JUL**
The temporary wood and plaster **cenotaph** designed by Edward Lutyens is unveiled in London. It remembers all those who died in service during the First World War.

19 JUL
A First World War victory parade is held in Dublin featuring 15,000 soldiers and 5,000 disabled ex-servicemen on parade.

25 JUL
The Earl of Mayo tells the House of Lords that the Dublin slums and the condition of the people living there are a disgrace to the United Kingdom.

30 JUL
Detective Sergeant Pat Smyth of the RIC's G Division is shot in Dublin in an apparent assassination. He dies of his wounds in hospital on 8 September.

Public bathrooms on Westmoreland Street, Dublin.

no provision had been made in the estimates for its maintenance and that it was hardly used in any case.

Writing to the editor in today's *Irish Independent*, J.C. McWalter has criticised the closure of the lavatory as a public insult to the 200,000 women of Dublin. The letter concludes with a call to action: 'Let every woman who thinks her sex wronged or inconvenienced express her opinions to the municipal representatives of her ward, and it is proper that the corporation will make an order to reopen the lavatory at its next meeting.'

Partition Looms as Committee Established to Find Irish Solution

London, 13 October – The British government has appointed a Cabinet committee to draft a new Home Rule Bill for Ireland.

Walter Long has been chosen to chair this committee, and its members include Lord Chancellor F.E. Smith, Edward Shortt, Herbert Fisher, Sir Worthington-Evans and Sir Auckland Geddes, as well as Chief Secretary Ian Macpherson and Lord Lieutenant of Ireland John French.

The fact that many of the members of the new committee have unionist leanings has been met with a sceptical response in the nationalist press. One newspaper suggested that if Sir Edward Carson himself had been responsible for nominating personnel to the committee it would hardly have looked any different.

The expectation is that the Cabinet committee will act speedily in order to submit a plan to Parliament during the autumn session.

It is becoming increasingly apparent that the cabinet committee will not consider all options available to them on the Irish question. Before they even begin their work, it is being reported that no coercion of Ulster unionists will be attempted; assurances have already been given that the 'integral union of Ulster with the British parliament' will not be touched. The idea of recognition for a republic in Ireland is also off the table.

It is also being reported that the most likely safeguard to be offered to Ulster is the exclusion of six counties, giving each county the right to vote itself back into line with the rest of the country if it wants. The six counties would also have to include Fermanagh and Tyrone, both of which have a majority Catholic population: 56.18% and 55.39% respectively.

Any scheme based on the partition of the island is, the *Irish Independent* remarked, 'doomed to failure. Ireland will not submit to mutilation or dismemberment.'

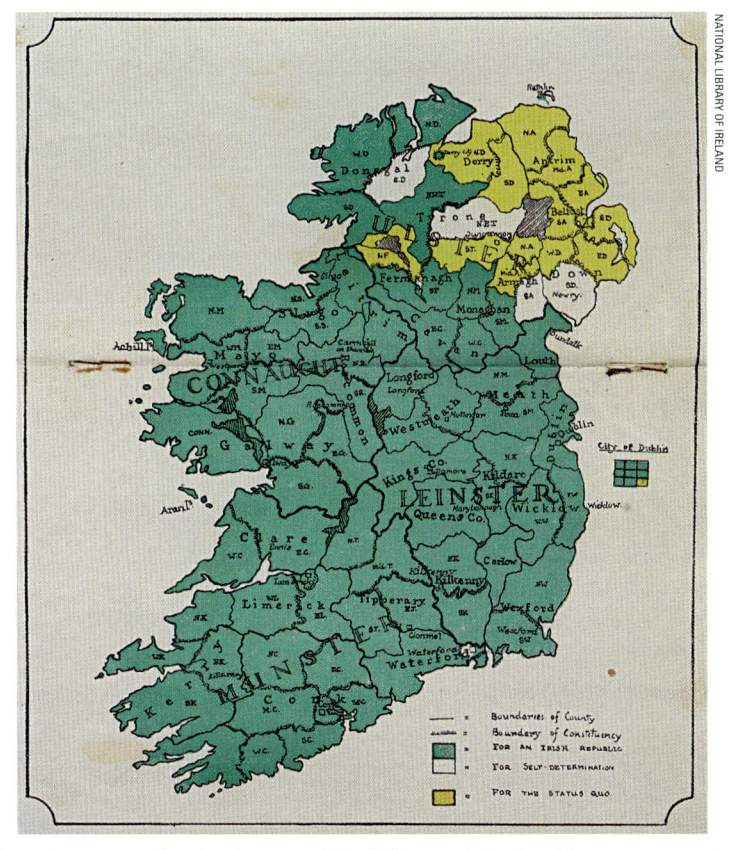

Constituency map showing the result of the 1918 general election. The green represents Sinn Féin, the white represents the IPP and the Orange represents unionist. The most recent Home Rule Bill suggests excluding six counties in the northeast.

1919

3 AUG
Sinn Féin calls for increased resistance to the militarisation of Ireland and for members of the police force to be ostracised.

7 AUG
Lloyd George promises a new scheme for the future government of Ireland and states that the rule of force cannot be the last word.

13 AUG
Glasnevin gravediggers go on strike and demand a pay increase.

15 AUG
The funeral is held of 15-year-old Na Fianna member Francis Murphy, who was shot dead, it is believed by the military, in his home at Ennistymon, Co. Clare.

19 AUG
There are riots in Derry after nationalists are banned from marching on the city walls.

20 AUG
It is proposed that Irish Volunteers swear allegiance to Dáil Éireann.

22 AUG
The Dáil announces ambitious new plans for the country including the raising of funds through the Second Dáil Loan.

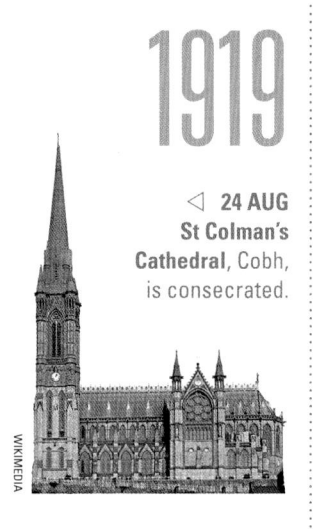

1919

◁ **24 AUG**
St Colman's Cathedral, Cobh, is consecrated.

26 AUG
The Horse Show returns to the RDS after a six-year hiatus due to the First World War.

3 SEP
Edward Carson tells the UUC that the future of Ireland is a straightforward choice between the Union and the ruinous policies of Sinn Féin.

8 SEP
Members of the British military rampage through Fermoy in response to the killing of one of their number the day before. They attack buildings in the town centre and cause £10,000 worth of damage.

8 SEP
The Archbishop of Cashel states that Ireland does not need to follow the US down the road to prohibition.

10 SEP
Sinn Féin and a range of other nationalist organisations are banned in Co. Cork.

Support for Irish Freedom on Display around the World

Melbourne, 5 November – An Irish Race Convention opened in Melbourne, Australia, on 3 November for the purpose of increasing pressure on the British government to grant self-determination to Ireland.

The convention is being attended by 1,000 delegates, among them a great number of the Australian Catholic hierarchy, including Archbishop Daniel Mannix, a native of Cork. Addressing the crowd, he read out an exchange of messages between himself and Arthur Griffith.

Archbishop Mannix, quoting from his message to Mr Griffith, declared that the Irish race in Australia pledged its 'moral and financial support to Ireland's complete self-determination, as that claim was voiced by the recent General Election'. In his reply, Mr Griffith stated that 'the people of Ireland salute their kinsmen of Australia' and expressed confidence that Irish freedom would be attained.

Alongside the convention, a large open-air demonstration was held in Melbourne at which an estimated 50,000 were in attendance. A feature of the speeches was the absence of support for the Irish Party and repeated favourable references to the Sinn Féin movement; resolutions were passed pledging support for Mr de Valera and his campaign.

That campaign has taken the Sinn Féin leader to the United States, where, in the last month alone, his tour has seen him travel to Pittsburgh,

Éamon de Valera (centre) with the New York State Federation of Labour Committee in Syracuse, 28 August 1919.

1919

William T. Cosgrave and Éamon de Valera meeting Irish-Americans (c.1919).

Cleveland, Columbus, Tonystown and Akron (both Ohio). Everywhere he went, pledges of money have been made to an Irish Victory Fund. Speaking to a crowd in Cleveland, Mr de Valera referred to the Ulster question, emphasising the territorial integrity of the island. 'There is only one Irish nation which inhabits as its home, since long, long before Rome was founded, the island known as Ireland. That nation will never dismember itself or partition its home.'

Among the endorsements received by Mr de Valera was his induction as a chief of the Chippewa tribe at a ceremony in Wisconsin. The ceremony took place in front of an audience of 3,000, the highlight coming when Mr de Valera accepted the traditional headdress of the Chippewa chief. He addressed the gathering first in Irish and then in English, his words being translated into Chippewa by an interpreter.

Heavy Snowfall in Dublin but Climate Change Denied

Dublin, 17 November – After a period of severely cold weather in recent days – the coldest experienced in November since 1878 – the streets of Dublin have been transformed into a vision from a Christmas card.

The snowfall was heavy, drifting in places, and grew to a depth of several inches on many streets. These conditions created difficulties for transport across the city.

11 SEP
Dáil Éireann is declared illegal by the British authorities.

12–13 SEP
Raids are undertaken across the country by the British Army on the houses of leaders and known members of Sinn Féin.

19 SEP
The cancellation of the Limerick races, called off after the crowd had been admitted to the racecourse, leads to a riot.

21 SEP ▽
Cork defeat Dublin in the Senior Hurling final at Croke Park, which is attended by a crowd of 14,300.

28 SEP
Kildare defeat Galway in the Senior Football final at Croke Park in front of 32,000 spectators. It is Galway's first ever appearance in an All-Ireland final.

29 SEP
The lord lieutenant announces that the wartime censorship of the press in Ireland is to end.

1919

3 OCT
A railwaymen's strike in Britain spreads to Ireland and begins affecting travel, as well as curtailing the supply of goods into and out of Dublin Port.

13 OCT
The British Cabinet appoints a committee to draft a new Home Rule Bill for Ireland.

18 OCT
Twenty-one Sinn Féin prisoners held in Mountjoy are released due to their failing health. The prisoners were on hunger strike to protest their incarceration.

24 OCT
Two men working on rebuilding the GPO on O'Connell Street are killed when a wall they are working on collapses.

25 OCT
The Home Nations Football Championship begins for the first time since 1914. In the first match at Windsor Park, Ireland draw 1–1 with England.

25 OCT
Six Sinn Féin prisoners held in Strangeways Prison, Manchester, including MPs Piaras Béaslaí and Austin Stack, escape after scaling a 35-foot-high wall.

Delays of up to an hour were experienced across the networks, and where the trams did run, the experience of passengers was often an unpleasant one, disturbed by youngsters throwing snowballs. In Drumcondra, one tram was delayed for some time owing to a snowman having been built on the line.

Around St Stephen's Green, pedestrians had a difficult time as about 150 students from the National University hurled snowballs at anyone who passed, smashing the window of one passing tram.

A steamer sailing from North Wall to Heysham was cancelled and work on the docks was seriously hampered.

In Co. Wicklow, all roads leading to the coastal town of Bray were practically impassable, and an elderly man in the town sustained cuts to his forehead and cheek when struck with a snowball.

A snow scene from around Dublin.

The early arrival of snow has fuelled claims that the climate is undergoing some form of profound change, yet *The Irish Times* has rejected the idea, claiming that there is 'no evidence to support this view'. Instead, the paper argues that 'weather runs in cycles of about 30 years, some 10 of which are likely to be wetter and colder than the average, 10 drier and warmer, while the remaining 10 are transitional and indeterminate'.

Ireland to Get Two Home Rule Parliaments
A 'freakish constitution ... which nobody wants'

London, 11 December – After a Home Rule campaign that has been running since the 1870s, it appears that Ireland is to get not one, but two parliaments of its own – one for Ulster and one for the rest of the island.

This is according to the proposals currently being discussed by a special Cabinet committee. They are yet to be presented to the House of Commons, but much of the detail is already known and has been circulating widely in the press.

A Supreme Council, presided over by the lord lieutenant or the chief secretary, will be established comprising members from the two parliaments. The control of the police will be vested in the council, which may also have control over customs, though it is believed that this has not been settled upon. Naval and military affairs will meanwhile remain the responsibility of the Westminster Parliament.

It is understood that the measures provided will secure the approval of Ulster unionists. Sinn Féin will, in contrast, likely refuse to accept the measure and may advise the Irish people not to take part in any elections held under it.

The *Irish Independent* has today described the proposals as a 'freakish constitution suitable only for exhibition in the museums of the world'. The paper continued that a 'little island of less than four and a half millions of a population is to be given two parliaments – an arrangement which nobody wants'.

Cartoon showing Lloyd George and Edward Carson singing from the same sheet, regarding the partition of Ireland.

Shocking Revelations at Amritsar Inquiry

London, 17 December – As many as 500 civilians were killed and 1,500 were injured in just ten minutes when British troops opened fire on a crowd of unarmed protesters at Jalianwala Bagh, near Amritsar, India, in April 1919, according to evidence given at the Disorders Inquiry Committee. The committee is being chaired by Lord Hunter and has been investigating the incident over the last few months.

The man who gave the order that day to open fire on the crowd of 5,000 people, protesters against the 'Rowlatt' Act, was General Reginald Dyer. In his evidence to the committee, he defended his behaviour, saying that he 'had to do something strong' and had 'arrived at the logical conclusion that he had to disperse the crowd who had defied the arm of the law. There was no medium course. The one thing was force.' He went so far as to call the act 'a merciful thing'.

Reaction to General Dyer's evidence and the detail emerging from the inquiry has been damning. 'There is a smack of Cromwell … in this form of mercifulness,' the *Irish Independent* has observed.

The *Daily Herald,* meanwhile, has remarked that 'No blacker or fouler story has ever been told … Of the various stories of imperial oppression and the revolt against it by the subject races of the British Empire … the most amazing and stupefying in its naked horror is that of the massacre of Amritsar.'

1919

31 OCT
Ernest Blythe, Sinn Féin MP for North Monaghan, is sentenced to a year in prison for distributing seditious literature. He immediately begins a hunger strike in protest.

3 NOV
Britain commits itself to creating two Home Rule parliaments, one each in Belfast and Dublin. The plan is based on the report of the Long Committee, headed by Walter Long. The committee had initially suggested the creation of a 9-county Northern Ireland and a 23-county Southern Ireland, but this was modified to a 6/26-county split.

8 NOV △
Irish Labour leader **James Larkin** is arrested and charged with Bolshevism in New York.

9 NOV
A crowd of 50,000 attends a rally in Melbourne, Australia, addressed by Archbishop Mannix, who calls for the immediate delivery of a free Ireland.

1919

11 NOV
The first issue of the Dáil's new propaganda organ, *The Irish Bulletin*, is published.

11 NOV
The first post-war Armistice Day is observed with a two-minute silence in major towns and cities.

24 NOV
Arthur Griffith declares that no Sinn Féin prisoner will accept criminal status and that they will campaign for political status through the use of the hunger strike.

1 DEC
Irish delivery drivers who are members of the Irish Automobile Driver's Union go on strike to oppose the introduction of a new driver's permit. Delivery lorries and vans are absent from the country's roads.

3 DEC
A funeral is held for Detective Sergeant John Barton, who was shot and killed outside Trinity College in Dublin.

18 DEC
John Alcock, who successfully flew the Atlantic earlier in the year, dies in a plane crash in Rouen, France.

19 DEC
The IRA attempts to assassinate the Viceroy, Lord French of Ypres, near Dublin's Phoenix Park.

The Golden Temple at Amritsar (c.1905).

However, responses to the delayed news from India have not been uniformly critical. *The Morning Post* has described the action of the British troops and the loss of life as 'a mere trifle compared with the loss of life which must certainly have occurred if these heroic men had not done as they did – and as, we hope, Englishmen will continue to do in similar situations'.

In the House of Commons, British Secretary of State for India Edwin Montagu was questioned as to how an atrocity that had cost so many lives had taken eight months to come to public awareness. Responding to Sir Donald Maclean, Mr Montagu said that he knew no detailed circumstances until he read recent reports in the newspapers and that what he had published at the time was information about riots in India that had been sent to him.

Lord Hunter is expected to publish his report in due course.

Lord French Survives Assassination Attempt near Phoenix Park

Dublin, 20 December – The Lord Lieutenant of Ireland, Sir John French, yesterday survived an attempt on his life that has sparked outrage on both sides of the Irish Sea.

1919

The viceroy and his party were travelling in an armoured vehicle as part of a convoy, having just alighted from a train at Ashtown. They were making the short journey to the viceroy's residence at the Phoenix Park when they were fired upon and grenades were hurled at them from either side of the road by a group of five to ten men. His military escort returned fire, and when the assailants fled the scene, they were pursued across fields by soldiers and police.

The attackers are thought to have been thwarted by the fact that the train carrying Lord French arrived a few minutes ahead of schedule. A cart that appears to have been intended as a barricade was not in position when the vehicle approached.

While the intended target of the attack emerged unharmed, one of the assailants – Martin Savage – was shot dead in an exchange of gunfire. Mr Savage is understood to have been employed in a grocery store owned by Mr Kirke at the North Strand in Dublin.

Two members of the Dublin Metropolitan Police, Detective Sergeant Halley and Constable O'Loughlin, were wounded in the incident.

Sir John French.

A soldier points to a bullet hole that was left in Lord French's car after the assassination attempt.

21 DEC
Fifty members of Sinn Féin, armed with revolvers and iron implements, attack the offices of the *Irish Independent* and destroy machinery.

22 DEC
Lloyd George formally announces his plan to give domestic self-governance to Ireland, with Home Rule parliaments in Belfast and Dublin. His plan is criticised by both nationalists and unionists.

23 DEC
The Irish Land Provision for Soldiers and Sailors Act allows the Irish Land Commission to provide housing to any man who served in the British forces.

31 DEC ▷
Con Lehane, who had been a key member of the Irish Socialist Republican Party, dies in New York. Lehane left Ireland in 1902 when he was denounced by the clergy for his atheism, and moved to Britain, where he was a founding member of the Socialist Party of Great Britain. In 1913 he moved to New York and was imprisoned in 1917 for his opposition to the war in Europe.

REVOLUTIONARY TIMES 1913–23

Remembering 1919
a hundred years on

To mark the centenary of the sitting of the First Dáil Éireann on 21 January 1919 a joint sitting of the Dáil and Seanad is held in the Round Room of Dublin's Mansion House. The sitting was addressed by President Michael D. Higgins, as well as the leaders of each of the main political parties. Although not recognised by the British state or unionists in the north, the First Dáil was critical in proclaiming an independent Ireland to the world in enunciating its Democratic Programme. In 2019 the then Taoiseach, Leo Varadkar, told the gathering in the Round Room that the 'meeting of the First Dáil was a bold exercise in democracy, an assertion that the struggle for Irish independence had the support of the Irish people, and derived its legitimacy from them'.

21 January 2019

HOUSES OF THE OIREACHTAS

REVOLUTIONARY TIMES 1913–23

247

Establishing Dáil Éireann and the Counter-State

THE NEW YORK-based *Irish World* was in no doubt as to what Sinn Féin should do next. The December 1918 Westminster election, in which the party had brushed aside the IPP and won seventy-three seats, had shown that Ireland had 'revolutionised herself mentally', so the next step for Sinn Féin, the newspaper asserted, was to deliver on its manifesto pledge and 'summon the first parliament of the Irish Republic'.

This it promptly did. Shortly before 3.30 p.m. on 21 January 1919, before an attendance that included a large body of priests, women and foreign journalists, as well as, incongruously, two uniformed US naval officers and several 'Colonial soldiers', twenty-eight of the newly elected Sinn Féin representatives walked into the Round Room of the Mansion House in Dublin amidst waving flags and handkerchiefs for what became the first session of the First Dáil Éireann. Countess Markievicz, the first woman elected as a Westminster MP, was not among them, nor was Éamon de Valera, the President of Sinn Féin. Both were incarcerated in English jails, as were many of their elected colleagues. Michael Collins and Harry Boland were not in prison, but they were busy in England plotting a daring – and soon to be effected – jailbreak for de Valera. Unsurprisingly absent were the unionists, and missing, too, were the six elected representatives of the IPP, who would stay away from this and all subsequent meetings of the Dáil. It didn't matter. Present or not, republican or not, every candidate returned for an Irish constituency at the recent general election was namechecked in a roll call of deputies that acted as prelude to the main business of the day.

The first meeting of Dáil Éireann was, in its setting and substance, a spectacular exercise in republican political theatre. It was aimed at an audience

> **The first meeting of Dáil Éireann was, in its setting and substance, a spectacular exercise in republican political theatre.**

Assembly of the First Dáil Éireann on 21 January 1919.

that was as much international as domestic, and it was built around a series of set pieces. There were the formalities, of course: the appointment of a ceann comhairle (speaker), an opening prayer, the roll call and the adoption of a provisional constitution, which provided for a five-person ministry, including a president. But there was also the enunciation of three principal texts, each of them, in different ways, calculated to resonate with global audiences at a time when a new international order was in the process of a post-First World War reconstruction.

First up, and most significant, was a Declaration of Independence, which was delivered in Irish, English and French and demanded 'the recognition and support of every free nation in the world'. Echoing in its themes and symbolism the foundational creed of America's revolutionaries of 1776, the Irish Declaration referenced centuries of occupation and resistance, the Easter Rising and the democratic mandate achieved at the previous month's general election. In doing so, it reflected, historian Mary Daly has written, 'the Dáil's hybrid origins in revolution and in parliamentary democracy'.

Following the Declaration was a 'Message to the Free Nations of the World', which emphasised Irish antiquity and distinctiveness, and asserted Ireland's right to self-determination 'before the new world emerging from the War'. This was the crucial context in which the Irish claim to independent statehood was being advanced: the First World War had ended with the collapsing of empires and the forging of new states, and Irish republicans could cite as inspiration the examples of, among others, newly independent Poland, Finland and Ukraine, while trumpeting the doctrine of US President Woodrow Wilson, whose fourteen principles for a new world order, delivered to the US Congress in January 1918, had included acknowledgement of the right to political independence and territorial integrity for 'great *and small nations* alike'.

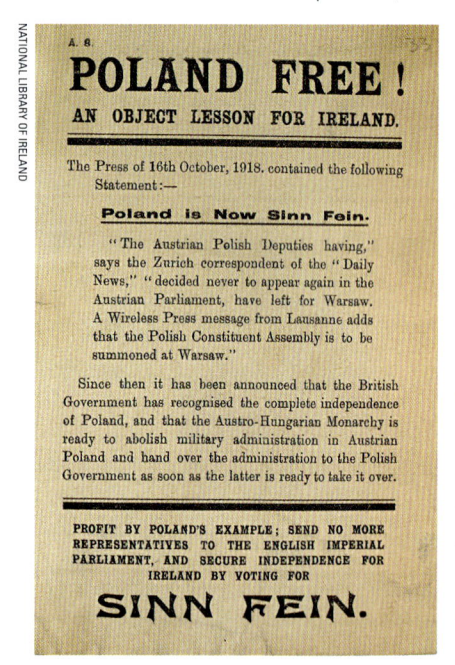

A Sinn Féin poster using the example of Poland to promote Irish independence.

Going global with Ireland's independence claims was, therefore, vital for two essential reasons: it insinuated Ireland into a wider post-war discourse around self-determination, and was considered a necessary step towards international recognition of the Republic that had been proclaimed in 1916 and ratified on the first day of the Dáil. It was a recognition that was not forthcoming. Ireland failed to gain entry to the Paris Peace Conference, which had begun three days before the Dáil first met, and diplomatic support for Irish separatism was in short supply, given Britain's victorious emergence from the war and its centrality to the Paris negotiations. Even the US, buffeted though it was by the vigorous agitation of Irish-American campaigners, declined to press the case for Irish representation at Paris, with President Wilson unwilling to intervene in what he characterised as an internal British matter.

The third, and final, document presented to the first session of the Dáil was no less international in its outlook and influences. Drafted by Labour leader Thomas Johnson and rewritten by Sinn Féin's Seán T. O'Kelly, it was inspired, in part, by Patrick Pearse's last major pamphlet, 'The Sovereign People'. Indeed, the Democratic Programme echoed some of the social democratic elements of the 1916 Rising and asserted that the 'first duty' of a republican government would be 'to make provision for the physical, mental and spiritual well-being of the children, to secure that no child shall suffer hunger or cold from lack of food, clothing, or shelter'. Significantly, the programme contained no firm commitments and, notwithstanding the berating of subsequent Irish governments for reneging on its egalitarian and redistributive promise, it was unlikely to have been written with a view to its actual implementation. Its purpose, as historian Emmet O'Connor has argued, was otherwise and more immediate – 'to advance the Irish cause at the International Socialist Conference at Berne in February 1919', which undoubtedly it did.

If the first day of the Dáil was concerned with projecting Ireland's democratic and separatist claims to a watching world, day two, held in private, was a more low-key and local affair. Procedurally focused and business-like, its centrepiece was the appointment of four ministers and Cathal Brugha as President. More than two months passed until the Dáil met again: its third meeting did not occur until 1 April and, coming in the wake of the March release of the Sinn Féin men and women who had been interned on trumped-up 'German plot' charges in May 1918, it would prove to be better attended than any. Fifty-two deputies were present, amongst them de Valera, who was duly elected as President to replace Brugha, and Countess Markievicz, who was appointed as Minister for Labour in a revamped and enlarged Cabinet.

> **The Dáil avoided this fate by challenging the executive authority of the British authorities in Ireland and by creating, in effect, a counter-state.**

In all, the First Dáil met fourteen times throughout 1919 and only twenty-one times in total between January 1919 and its final meeting on 10 May 1921. But what did it do? In the aftermath of the proceedings of 21 January 1919, *The Freeman's Journal* observed that unless steps were taken to give practical effect to what had occurred, then the Irish people would be made to 'cut a ridiculous figure in the eyes of the world'. The Dáil avoided this fate by challenging the executive authority of the British authorities in Ireland and by creating, in effect, a counter-state. It did this in numerous ways: by establishing portfolios of ministerial responsibility, which acted with varying degrees of effectiveness in such areas as home affairs, local government, labour, industries, defence and foreign affairs; by denying the legitimacy of local policing and calling on the social boycotting of members of the RIC; and by establishing a rival system of justice through a network of county-based arbitration courts that evolved into a fully-fledged system of what became known variously as Dáil or Republican Courts. 'The whole development was maddening to the Castle people,' Kevin O'Shiel said of the British administration's reaction to these courts. In a statement to the Bureau of Military History some decades later, the barrister cum judicial commissioner to the Dáil's land court recalled, 'They could not compel litigants to come into their Courts, and accept their adjudications; nor could they prevent them from submitting their cause to the Arbitration Courts of the Dail.' The success of the Dáil Courts, reliant upon public support, occurred in tandem with a steady increase in localised attacks on RIC barracks by IRA volunteers, which, over time, would lead to their widespread abandonment and the retreat of the widely boycotted police force to the towns and cities. The result was that by mid-1920 vast swathes of the countryside had been essentially ceded to republican control.

Funding an underground government and parallel state was nevertheless a costly matter. In September 1919 Michael Collins, as Minister for Finance, launched a domestic Dáil Loan scheme, which acted as a forerunner to a series of external bond drives. These not only provided a vital source of financing for the Dáil (principally from America and often in small denominations), but, according to historian Robin Adams, 'added weight to the Dáil's pretensions to statehood'. If the size of that state was still strikingly small – it has been estimated that the number of full-time employees of the Dáil reached 300 during 1920, supported by the voluntary labour of about 2,000 others – it increasingly came to be seen as a de facto government. On 16 July 1920, indeed, an *Irish Times* editorial suggested that an 'Irish Republic is very nearly in being. Today the Republican organisation controls three-quarters of the local bodies in Ireland, makes and administers its own laws, rejects or accepts taxation at its own will. The Sinn Féin flag flies already over the whole province of Munster, and soon will fly over the whole of Leinster and Connaught and over a large part of Ulster.'

The British policy response to the myriad attacks on its authority would shift over time. A brutal military coercion was decided upon in 1920, but before that, in November 1919, a decision was taken to impose a ban across the

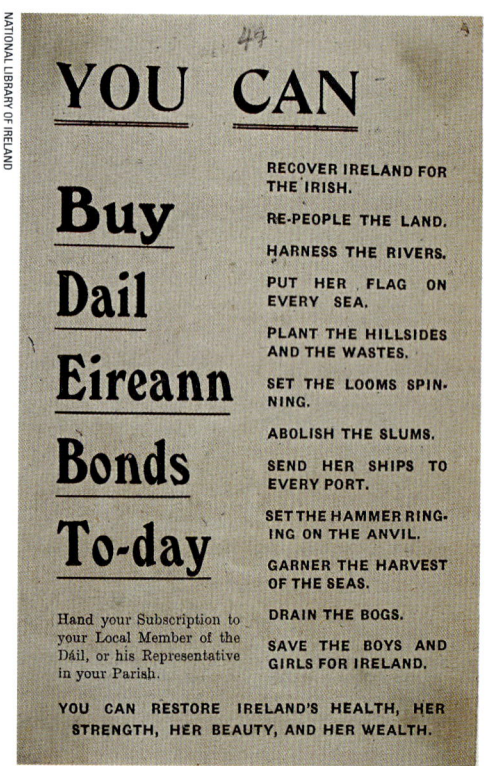

Leaflets and posters promoting the Dáil Éireann bonds scheme were distributed widely across Ireland so that Sinn Féin could generate the necessary funds for the process of attempting to build an independent state.

country on Sinn Féin, the Gaelic League, the Irish Volunteers and Cumann na mBan. And before that again, on 11 September, Dáil Éireann was banned. This made it difficult and dangerous for members to attend meetings and ensured that ministers were often on the run and working from makeshift offices when attempting to tend to their briefs. Still, suppression proved a propagandist gift to Irish republicans abroad, among them de Valera, who had departed Ireland for the US in June 1919 to spearhead the Dáil's fundraising drive and bolster American support for Irish independence.

The democratic legitimacy of that separatist ambition would be reinforced by the results of the local elections of January and June 1920.

The democratic legitimacy of that separatist ambition would be reinforced by the results of the local elections of January and June 1920. Significant for their pioneering use of proportional representation, intended to act as a curb on the republican vote, these elections only served to further highlight the extent to which Sinn Féin had become the dominant political force across Ireland. They also led to many local authorities issuing pledges of allegiance to Dáil Éireann alongside rejections of the British Local Government Board. With Sinn Féin local control came a slew of proposals aimed at a symbolic remaking of towns and cities through the changing of the names of streets and bridges to rid them of their colonial associations. In Enniscorthy, Co. Wexford, for instance, a 1916 veteran and recently elected member of the urban district council, Thomas D. Sinnott, declared his support for proposed changes to two street names on the grounds that it would 'help to destroy the remnants of the mental conquest'.

International opinion took note of these dramatic political drifts. In March 1920 *An t-Óglach*, the magazine of the Irish Volunteers, remarked on how one French newspaper had, some weeks earlier, likened the situation in Ireland to 'two governments waging war on one another'. This was not the international legitimacy that Sinn Féin and Dáil Éireann had so determinedly sought; it was, however, a measure of the moral and political authority it had rapidly attained.

Dáil Éireann's publicity machine produced stamps which could be affixed to letters to promote the loan scheme. Such stamps prominently featured the tricolour.

Guerrilla Days
– *Fighting a War of Independence*

ON 21 JANUARY 1919 shots were fired at Soloheadbeg, Co. Tipperary, and two RIC constables guarding a transport of gelignite were killed. This was on the same day that the first meeting of Dáil Éireann was being held amidst a blaze of publicity in Dublin's Mansion House. While the self-declared Irish Parliament in Dublin would give voice to the aspirations of an independent nation, the skirmish at Soloheadbeg – denounced from the pulpit by the Catholic Archbishop of Cashel as an 'outrage … against Christian morals' – would come to signal the beginning of a war of independence that would run until the summer of 1921. It was not a conventional war, of course, but a guerrilla campaign that pitted the forces of the Irish Republican Army (IRA) (as the Irish Volunteers gradually became known) against those of Britain, which appeared in the various guises of the British Army, the RIC and, from mid-1920 onwards, the notorious 'Black and Tans' and the paramilitary-styled and operationally autonomous Auxiliary Division, a temporary division of the RIC composed of ex-army officers.

The ambush at Soloheadbeg was not the first attack on the police, nor did it immediately trigger their widespread targeting.

The ambush at Soloheadbeg was not the first attack on the police, nor did it immediately trigger their widespread targeting. The war – and its early phase barely warranted the term – was initially limited to localised and occasional armed actions. And, notwithstanding the enthusiasm of Dan Breen, one of the Soloheadbeg ambushers, for the gun – his principal regret was that they didn't kill more 'Peelers' – the reality remained that most policemen were less at risk of being shot than shunned. That is because, in April 1919, the Dáil approved a policy aimed at socially ostracising members of the RIC, who were branded by Eoin MacNeill as a force of spies, traitors and perjurers. The policy meant no fraternisation of any sort. Explaining how it applied in practice, an IRA commandant in Co. Mayo later recalled how traders were 'cautioned … not to serve them [the RIC] with goods and the people were warned not to associate or speak to them. Posters were put up in the town and surrounding districts to this effect.' More colourful was the account provided by Tom Barry in his best-selling memoir, *Guerilla Days in Ireland*, first published in 1949. He wrote: 'Except for a very few, no one would speak to them, old men spat as they passed, old women looked through them with contemptuous stares, children jeered at them, no girl, except the unfortunates, would meet them, and some publicans and shopkeepers refused to serve them.'

Coupled with an onset of attacks on isolated, rural barracks – outposts considered concrete symbols of British rule – the policy worked. It deepened the divide between the people and police, and forced a retreat of the latter into the major towns and cities. Moreover, it precipitated a rash of resignations: some 1,600 members abandoned the force in 1920 alone.

An RIC wanted poster for Dan Breen, who was one of those involved in the Soloheadbeg attack.

The police boycott fitted neatly into a pattern of civil resistance that had been used to great effect to thwart the introduction of conscription to Ireland during the First World War. In the new context of the War of Independence, such acts of resistance were deployed to deliver a different suite of objectives. When Catholic workers were expelled from their workplaces in Belfast shipyards, and sectarian violence spiralled in the north in the summer of 1920, Dáil Éireann imposed a boycott – lasting until January 1922 – on goods and services originating from Belfast and other northern towns, and withdrew funds from Belfast-based banks.

The trade union movement in Ireland lent support to the republican campaign by refusing to move military materiel through the Dublin docks or British troops on the Irish railways. The 'Munitions Strike' ran from May to December 1920 and, notwithstanding the occasional resort to intimidation tactics against those disposed to break the embargo, it demonstrated the depth

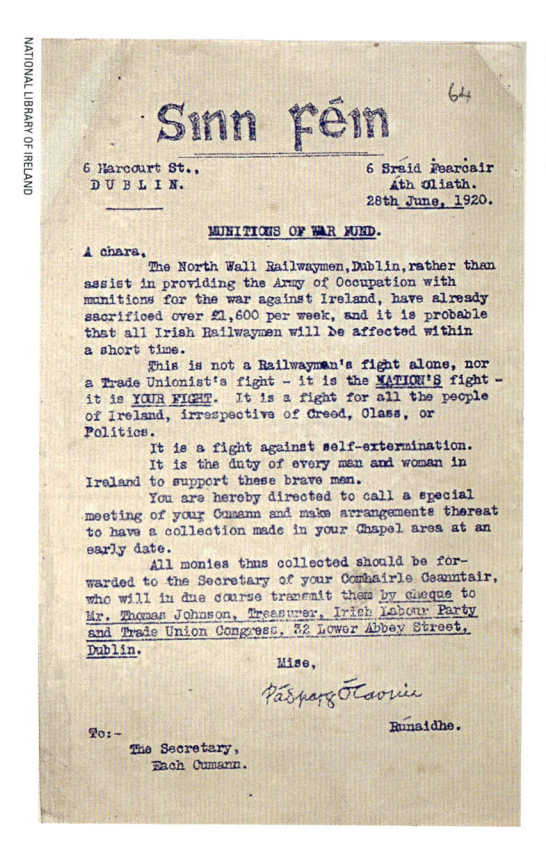

A Sinn Féin letter signed by Secretary Padraig Ó Caoimh praising the North Wall Railwaymen, Dublin, for their stance against moving munitions for the British Army.

of popular support for a strategy aimed at rendering Ireland ungovernable. On occasion, even the British authorities conceded its effectiveness. As General Nevil Macready, who only assumed command of the British forces in Ireland in spring 1920, acknowledged during the strike, 'no amount of Martial Law or any other form of repression will make the men drive the trains, and if we put them all in prison, I fancy there will be more than the prisons over here can hold'.

If the ability to sustain strike action for so long – and Irish trade unionists were not, in this instance, supported financially by their British counterparts – offered one measure of the steadfastness of public support for the separatist campaign (if not necessarily for its associated violence), it was not the only one. This was evidenced too in Sinn Féin's political performances, which were tested in the local elections of January and June 1920. While the results were not as emphatic as the Westminster election of 1918 – on this occasion the Labour Party did not step aside, and a system of proportional representation was used – they still showed Sinn Féin to be the dominant political force within Irish nationalism. And despite not being the most ideologically or socially cohesive,

Sinn Féin was not as raggedly diverse as suggested by Constance Markievicz's characterisation that they were 'just a jumble of people of all classes, creeds and opinions, who are all ready to suffer and die for Ireland'.

The 1920 election results allowed Sinn Féin to cast itself as the government of a legitimate state, which it sought to make real through the organisation of local republican police forces to administer justice and the setting up of arbitration or special land courts across the country to rule on local disputes. The local elections also introduced a cohort of new Sinn Féin representatives, among them Tomás MacCurtain, who was duly elected as Sinn Féin's first lord mayor of Cork city. His tenure, however, was mercilessly brief: in March that same year, in reprisal for the killing of an off-duty policeman, MacCurtain was shot dead in his own bedroom during an early morning raid on his home in Blackpool by RIC officers in disguise. *The Freeman's Journal* editorialised that MacCurtain had been murdered because of who he was and what he represented, and that

> **The 1920 election results allowed Sinn Féin to cast itself as the government of a legitimate state.**

Sir John French reviewing British troops in Dublin Castle, c.1921.

he was the victim of a 'conspiracy of vengeance, formed by the enemies of the Sinn Féin movement and supporters of British rule in Ireland'.

The circumstances of MacCurtain's killing and the imprisonment of his republican successor, Terence MacSwiney, underscored both the spiralling of violence throughout 1920 and the increasingly repressive methods adopted by the British authorities in their efforts to wrest back their loosened control. Those methods took various forms, including legislative. In early August 1920, the passing of the Restoration of Order in Ireland Act endowed the authorities with sweeping powers that bypassed normal judicial procedures, permitting the internment and court martial of civilians. These repressive instruments were promptly targeted by British authorities against republican suspects, with the conviction rate rising to fifty cases per week. But the incarceration of large numbers of republicans – as many as 6,129 would be imprisoned by June 1921 – had the effect of turning the prisons into an active front of republican struggle, dramatically so when hunger strikes spread through the system resulting in the deaths of Michael Fitzgerald and Joseph Murphy in Cork, as well as, to the wonderment of the world's press, Cork's Lord Mayor Terence MacSwiney, who had been transferred from Cork to Brixton Prison.

> **The change in the way the war was fought was also influenced by the decision to bolster the RIC with recruits from Britain in the form of the Black and Tans and Auxiliaries.**

The British response to what they saw as lawlessness across Ireland, and particularly in Munster, influenced the way the war was fought. Confronted by a more punitive justice system and increased rates of imprisonment, the IRA pivoted towards a campaign of insurgency based around flying columns, agile groups of full-time Volunteers led or trained by the likes of Tom Barry, Liam Lynch and Ernie O'Malley, who would be available to act alone or in support of local IRA units. In turn, they could call upon the women of Cumann na mBan for all manner of operational needs – from carrying dispatches and arms to catering, first aid, intelligence-gathering and propaganda.

The change in the way the war was fought was also influenced by the decision to bolster the RIC with recruits from Britain in the form of the Black and Tans and Auxiliaries. These forces promptly earned a reputation for brutality, and they engaged in reprisal attacks on individuals, creameries, businesses and property. They engaged in what Marie Coleman has called 'physical, gendered and psychological' violence against women, as well as rare acts of sexual assault, and they were guilty of extrajudicial killings. A pattern developed where

IRA attacks on Crown forces were met with collective punishments of civilian populations, increasing in frequency in the later months of 1920 and into 1921. A policy of reprisals was widely pursued, impacting on such locations as Fermoy (Sept. 1919), Tuam (July 1920), Balbriggan and Trim (both Sept. 1920). It was, however, in Munster that the majority of reprisals took place, most spectacularly in Cork city on the night of 11-12 December 1920, when soldiers ran riot after an ambush of a party of Auxiliaries by members of the IRA's 1st Cork Brigade at Dillon's Cross, just a few hundred yards from Victoria Barracks and just a few weeks after sixteen Auxiliaries had been killed in another IRA ambush (the largest of the War of Independence) at Kilmichael, near Macroom. When the 'orgy of destruction and ruin' – as local TD Liam de Róiste, described it – in the city abated, 2,000 people were out of work owing to damage to buildings and businesses, the cost of which was estimated at £3 million.

The ambush site at Kilmichael.

While the reprisal strategy of Crown forces was economically and physically ruinous to targeted areas, it was also reputationally damaging to the British government. Moreover, it undermined its claims to legitimacy in Ireland. So concerned was Britain's Labour Party that it established a commission to investigate the question of violence on the part of Crown forces, which it considered degrading to the British people. At a broader level, British government policy at this time was striking for its absence of coherence or clear political design. For all its heavyweight political personalities and thinkers, the British Cabinet, historian Joe Lee has observed, 'could not make up its mind on either a war policy or a peace policy'.

This dithering served only to prolong the conflict, the final phase of which – starting in late 1920 – was by far its most violent and bloody. In a signal of the British authorities' continued preference for coercion over conciliation – and a further tacit admission of its loss of authority – the number of counties placed under martial law was doubled from four to eight, most of them in Munster, where the war was fought with its greatest intensity. For its part, the IRA continued with its campaign of ambushes and assassinations, largely localised and uncoordinated, and only brought under the official direction of the Dáil as the war entered its final months. An exception to this strategy was the disastrous assault on the Custom House in Dublin on 21 May 1921, which resulted in the deaths of five members of the Dublin Brigade of the IRA and the capture of eighty others. This chaotic retreat to the methods of 1916 was a reminder of the unsuitability of the IRA for conventional warfare in an urban setting.

The IRA was, unquestionably, an effective insurgency force, but its violence was not exclusively directed at the British enemy. Suspected spies and informers were targeted and killed, their bodies often labelled and dumped in public places as a warning to others; the burning of the big houses of loyalist sympathisers was begun; and women suspected of 'keeping company' with police or military men were subjected to physical violence, forcible hair-cropping (also a practice of the Black and Tans) and, in the most extreme cases, sexual assault. Historiographical rows have also raged over whether a sectarian or ethnic motive inspired the killings of, for instance, thirteen Protestants in Dunmanway in West Cork in April 1922 and six Protestants in the Co. Armagh townland of Altnaveigh the following June, or whether these attacks were motivated by genuine suspicions that those targeted were informers or abettors of the Crown forces.

From April to October 1919, Austin Stack was imprisoned in Strangeways prison. Throughout this time he corresponded with leading Sinn Féin figures, including Michael Collins, who wrote this letter to Stack on 20 July.

The controversial killings in Cork and Armagh came after the endpoint of the War of Independence, which, perhaps unsurprisingly given the character of guerrilla campaigns, resulted in neither the outright victory nor defeat of the IRA. It concluded instead with a Truce on 11 July 1921 and the beginning of moves towards political settlement, which, in the creation of an Irish Free State and the partition of the island, delivered far more autonomy than the British government had theretofore been willing to concede and far less than Irish republican separatists had determinedly sought. The cost in human life to arrive at that endpoint was the deaths of 2,346 people between 1917 and 1921. The killings of these years were not evenly distributed but heavily concentrated in the counties of Munster, as well as the urban centres of Dublin and Belfast. In contrast, counties such as Laois, Wicklow, Carlow and Cavan experienced relatively few fatalities, as did most of the counties of what would become Northern Ireland, with exception of Belfast and Derry, where communal divisions were such that the violence carried a distinct sectarian flavour. Nor were all those killed combatants. On the contrary, as Daithí Ó Corráin and Eunan O'Halpin set out in their brilliant chronicle of violence and loss during the revolutionary era, *The Dead of the Irish Revolution*, as many as 919 of those killed could be classified as civilians.

> ... the restraints on behaviour that prevented the war from being bloodier than it was, nor does it capture the trauma of those who witnessed, perpetrated or suffered the violence of these years ...

Yet a crude calculus of death is an inadequate measure, O'Halpin acknowledged, of the impact of the violence on society and on the lived experience of the Irish people. It doesn't explain the restraints on behaviour that prevented the war from being bloodier than it was, nor does it capture the trauma of those who witnessed, perpetrated or suffered the violence of these years and were left to carry it through their often-troubled lives. Neither does a recitation of the statistics of killing reflect the diversity of Irish revolutionary experiences (for many, it involved little of what might be termed serious 'action'), nor does it come close to measuring what it meant to contribute to Ireland's push for self-determination or to gauging the acute personal hurt felt when the state founded upon these efforts deemed many of these contributions unworthy of modest financial recognition. Of these there were many: it was notable that of approximately 82,000 applications submitted under Military Service Pensions Acts of 1924 and 1932, only 15,700 were successful. The vast majority, including applicants who detailed lives of material deprivation and physical distress, and those who sought nothing more than an acknowledgement of patriotic services rendered, received no recompense at all. The slight stung some more than others, but the residue of resentment was undeniable. Speaking in the Dáil in 1945, a former Fianna Fáil TD turned Independent, B.J. Maguire, observed that while there had been broad public approval for the principle of paying a pension to the 'Old IRA' – they were already considered 'old' by then – the decisions taken by the Pensions Board Assessors had caused 'disquiet, distrust, anxiety and vexation'. There was, Maguire added, a 'great call for redress' to be made – 'justice demands it'.

GREAT CHALLENGE MATCH
(FOOTBALL)
Tipperary v. Dublin
AT CROKE PARK
ON SUNDAY, NOVEMBER 21, 1920
MATCH AT 2.45 P.M.

ADMISSION 1/-

1920

'... men who work in the transport industries have laid it down emphatically that they will not be parties to the attempted reconquest of Ireland by British military forces. Railwaymen, dock workers, and carters are quite fixed in their resolve and they will be supported by the organised workers in every other industry.'

Labour Party Statement
9 JUNE

1920

▽ **10 JAN**
The peace treaty with Germany, which draws a line under the war that has raged in Europe since the summer of 1914, is formally ratified at the **Quai d'Orsay** in Paris.

12 JAN
The head of the RIC, Brigadier General Sir Joseph Byrne, is removed from his post.

12 JAN
The River Shannon and its tributaries burst their banks in Limerick, leaving some low-lying areas completely submerged by water and the roads in and out of certain localities impassable.

▽ **24 JAN**
The entertainer and composer of many of Ireland's favourite ballads, Percy French, dies of pneumonia, aged 66. 'He found fame with songs such as *The Mountains of Mourne, Come Back, Paddy Reilly* and *Ballyjamesduff*.

Dublin's Homeless Crisis Becoming More Acute

Dublin, 15 January – The problem of homelessness in Dublin is becoming more acute.

Figures released by the St Vincent de Paul free night shelter on Back Lane in the city centre indicate that there were a total of 16,785 admissions last year, a 5,180 increase on the previous year. In addition, the number of free meals supplied has increased by 9,401 to reach a new total of 26,801.

Also included in the shelter's latest report is a sobering reminder that not all the people using the shelter were elderly or infirm. They also include labourers, skilled artisans and clerks, who may have endured a bad run of luck or a period of severe illness. The report highlighted the fact that for a large section of society it is utterly impossible during times of good health and regular employment to save sufficient funds to tide themselves over if they endure a slump in trade or have to convalesce for a long time after an illness.

'One cannot be surprised to find among them cases not of depravity, but simply of neglect,' the report stated. 'For them a visit – a stay of a few nights in the shelter – is a great grace.' Their time there 'revives memories of early instructions' and activates in them 'an energising love for God which is so easily awakened in our Irish working class'.

The report also noted some of the difficulties the charity was facing: 'The cost of food, fuel, lighting, and all incidental charges has gone up alarmingly, and the committee are forced to make an urgent appeal for help in this Christlike work.'

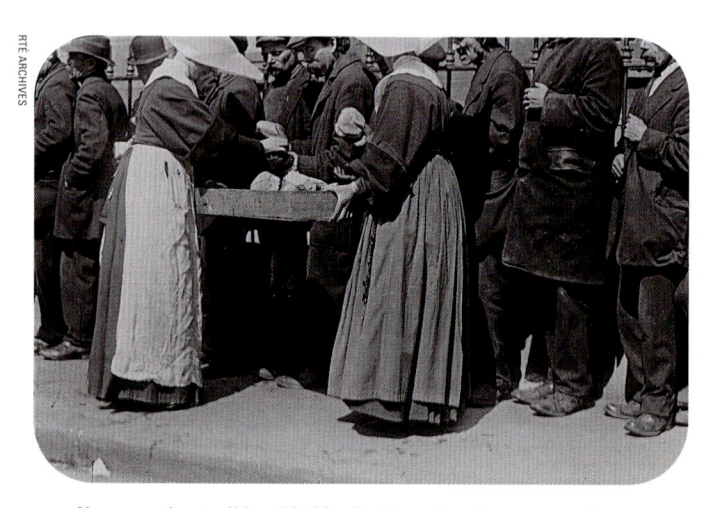

Nuns wearing traditional habits distribute bread to men queuing on the street, c.1920.

Municipal Elections – Sinn Féin and Labour Perform Strongly as Unionists Falter

Dublin, 19 January – Just over a year after the party surged to a remarkable victory in the general election, Sinn Féin has again emerged as the country's dominant political force in the municipal elections.

However, the picture that has emerged is more fragmented than that revealed in the wake of the December 1918 vote. This is largely attributable to the system of proportional representation that has been used and the increased level of political competition in many areas, particularly from Labour. Absent from the general election in 1918, Labour candidates secured a total of 329 seats in the municipal elections, taking from the Sinn Féin and Unionist vote in different parts of the country.

The breakdown of parties and votes in Dublin is as follows:

- Sinn Féin – 28,133 votes, 42 seats
- Labour – 9,648 votes, 14 seats
- Nationalists (including IPP) – 7,924 votes, 13 seats
- Municipal Reformers – 8,530 votes, 10 seats
- A single Unionist was also returned.

A Sinn Féin election poster that instructs people on how the new proportional representation system worked.

For the municipal elections in January 1920, all the parties, including Labour, appealed to voters through their posters.

1920

26 JAN
Fire destroys the beautiful Catholic **Church of Our Lady of Refuge** in Rathmines.

30 JAN
Alderman Tomás MacCurtain is elected as lord mayor of Cork and Alderman Hugh O'Doherty, a nationalist, is elected mayor of Derry.

10 FEB
Opening the new session of the Westminster Parliament, King George V declares that the 'condition of Ireland causes me grave concern'.

14 FEB
In their first international rugby contest since the end of the war, Ireland loses to England at Lansdowne Road on a 14–11 scoreline. The match is played before an attendance of almost 20,000.

23 FEB
A curfew order comes into effect across the DMP district. It requires those without a permit to remain indoors between the hours of midnight and 5 a.m.

1920

27 FEB
The British government publishes its long-anticipated **partition** plan for the future government of Ireland. It provides for a 52-seat assembly for Northern Ireland and a 128-seat assembly for Southern Ireland.

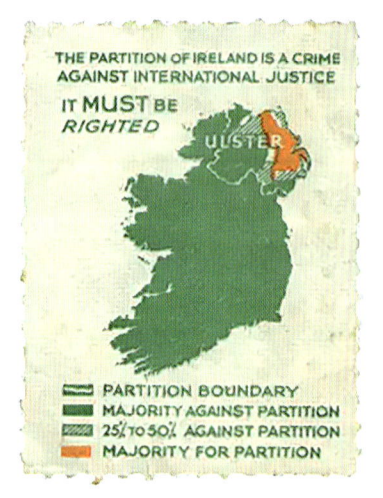

10 MAR
The UUC endorses the proposal to create a six-county Northern Parliament, despite opposition from unionists in Cavan, Monaghan and Donegal. 'Ulster is safe,' Sir Edward Carson declares.

17 MAR
Éamon de Valera delivers a St Patrick's Day message to the Irish in America: 'Never before have the scattered sons of Erin had such an opportunity for noble service. Today you can serve not only Ireland, but the world.'

Five women, all Sinn Féiners, were returned in Dublin city, including Kathleen Clarke and Nell Humphreys (née Rahilly) in Pembroke. Women fared even better in the townships of Dublin, with 12 women returned, six of them in Rathmines alone.

The strongest Unionist showing was in the northeast of the country, yet there was some surprise that unionism didn't enjoy as strong a performance as might have been expected. Where official Unionists held 52 seats on the old Belfast City Council, they will now occupy 35 (alongside two 'Independent' Unionists) in the new chamber.

Sinn Féin and the Nationalists have each returned five members to the council – the Nationalists held eight seats on the old council. But, while nationalism has made slight gains in Belfast, the principal reason for the fall in Unionist seats is the rise of Labour, which claimed 13 seats.

With 56 seats up for grabs in Cork, over 50 of the candidates were drawn from two political groupings: Sinn Féin and Labour. *The Cork Examiner* has reacted positively to the results and has devoted an editorial to setting out the possibilities for the city and county's commercial and industrial improvement.

British Government Publishes Plan to Partition Ireland

London, 28 February – The British government has published its long-anticipated plan for the future government of Ireland.

The plan is closely modelled on that outlined by Prime Minister Lloyd George on 22 December 1919. It is to divide the island of Ireland into two jurisdictions, each with its own Home Rule parliament.

The Northern Parliament area will be made up of the counties of Antrim, Armagh, Down, Fermanagh, Derry and Tyrone, with a separate Parliament representing the rest of the island. It is proposed that the Northern Parliament will comprise 52 members, with 128 sitting in the southern chamber, while the two parliaments will be linked by a 40-member Council of Ireland. Both parliaments will return representatives to Westminster, 12 from the North and 30 from the South.

The new bill, if passed, will repeal the 1914 Government of Ireland Act.

The unionist *Belfast News Letter* has cited its adherence to the Union in registering its opposition to the plan. 'We object to partition because we object to being divorced from full parliamentary representation in the Imperial Parliament, not for ourselves in the North alone, but for our country.'

The nationalist press is equally aghast at the proposals. *The Freeman's Journal* has called it a 'poisonous plan' and 'the worst proposal ever made for the settlement of the secular quarrel between Great Britain and Ireland … The partition, too, is to be a sectarian cut.'

In addition to the partition plan, the *Irish Independent* has denounced the financial provisions of the Bill as 'simply a swindle upon Ireland'. Ireland, North and South, would contribute £18m for what are called 'imperial services', and neither Irish parliament would have control over customs and excise nor income tax, etc. What the Irish parliaments would have the power to do is impose surcharges or 'any new taxes that ingenuity can devise'.

Gunfire and Rioting at Irish Cup Semi-Final in Belfast

Belfast, 19 March – Serious riots and revolver fire led to the abandonment of the Irish Cup semi-final clash between Belfast Celtic and Glentoran at the Cliftonville ground in Belfast on 17 March.

The match, a replay, attracted about 10,000 spectators, and the political undertones to the fixture were apparent from early in the game when a crowd of young men in the unreserved stand started singing 'The Soldier's Song' and waving Sinn Féin flags, though they did not interfere with the conduct of the game.

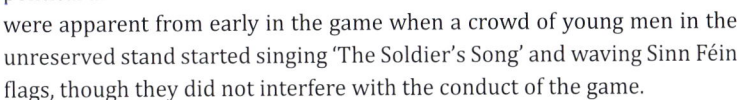

The disruption came when the referee ordered a Celtic player off the field for a bad tackle. This led to annoyed Celtic supporters invading the pitch with the intention, it seemed, of attacking the referee.

In an attempt to move out of danger, the official and the players went towards the pavilion. The situation escalated when supporters from another section of the stands began to throw stones at the pitch invaders. Revolver shots were then fired from the pitch at the crowd throwing stones, causing a stampede towards the exit, with some people tearing down palings in their rush to escape.

Police raced onto the pitch and arrested the youth believed to be responsible for firing the revolver. He was kept under guard in the centre of the field, while other members of the police baton-charged the crowd in an attempt to clear the ground. Ten people were reported to have been injured in the affray, four with bullet wounds.

1920

19 MAR
The House of Commons is informed that General Nevil Macready is to replace Lieutenant General Sir Frederick Shaw as General Officer Commanding the British forces in Ireland.

20 MAR
Lord Mayor of Cork Tomás MacCurtain is shot dead by members of the RIC at his home in the early hours of the morning.

2 APR ▷
Sir Hamar Greenwood replaces Ian Macpherson as Chief Secretary of Ireland.

3 APR ▽
Ireland end the rugby Five Nations with the wooden spoon after losing an international match to France for the first time. *The Irish Times* says it will be remembered in the annals of rugby football as a 'black day for Ireland'.

REVOLUTIONARY TIMES 1913–23

1920

▽ 5 APR
Republican prisoners begin a hunger strike in Mountjoy Prison. Within days over 65 men are refusing food in a demand for political status.

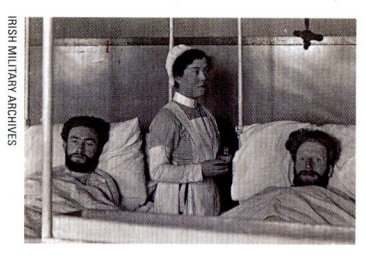

30 APR
Three brothers from Tuam forcibly cut the hair of Bridget Keegan of Cloondarona for allegedly 'going with Tommies'. The men are subsequently sentenced to six months in prison with hard labour.

3 MAY
Following his recent conviction in New York on a charge of criminal anarchy, it is reported that former Irish labour leader James Larkin has been sentenced to between five and ten years in prison with hard labour.

9 MAY
Twenty-five-year-old Francis Gleeson dies in the Mater Hospital shortly after he had been on hunger strike in Mountjoy. A coroner's jury finds that his death had been 'accelerated by his hunger strike in defence of his principles'.

Cork Lord Mayor, Tomás MacCurtain, Murdered at Home

Cork, 20 March – The Lord Mayor of Cork, Alderman Tomás MacCurtain, was shot dead this morning in his home at 40 Thomas Davis Street in the Blackpool area of the city, where he also ran a shop.

The Lord Mayor was in bed in the early hours of the morning when a loud knocking was heard at the door. When his wife, Eilís MacCurtain (née Walsh), opened it, she was brushed aside by two men carrying revolvers who wore caps and had blackened their faces.

More men followed them with rifles, while others entered through the shop door. Two of them took control of the entrance to the house and prevented Mrs MacCurtain from going upstairs or leaving.

The raiders, who were described as tall and young, knocked on the bedroom door. When MacCurtain protested that he was getting dressed, they demanded that he 'come out here'. When he eventually appeared, wearing his pants and nightshirt, he was shot twice with a revolver. He fell backwards on the landing with blood flowing copiously from his chest.

A group of Sinn Féin politicians, Dublin 1919. Seated middle front is Tomás MacCurtain. Terence MacSwiney stands second from the right.

It is understood that four days prior to his killing, the Lord Mayor had received a threatening letter, which he had not treated seriously. It read: 'Thos. McCurtain [sic], prepare for death. You are doomed.'

The Roman Catholic Bishop of Cork, Dr Daniel Cohalan, has denounced the attack as a murder and a crime but has asked that no thought be given to 'retaliation or reprisals', which, apart from being unlawful, might be directed in error against individuals or classes of men unconnected with the murder.

Tomás MacCurtain, a fluent Irish speaker, had been a commandant in the Irish Volunteers since 1914 and was interned in the aftermath of the rebellion of Easter week in 1916. He was elected Lord Mayor of Cork on 31 January 1920, the first republican to hold the office.

Irish Administration Gets Major Overhaul

Dublin, 5 April – The British government has undertaken a major overhaul of its Irish administration.

It has been confirmed that Ian Macpherson has left the role of chief secretary of Ireland to move to the Ministry of Pensions. He has been replaced by Canadian-born Lieutenant Colonel Sir Hamar Greenwood, who has been Under-secretary of State for Home Affairs since January 1919. Prior to that he was a captain in the King Edward's Horse Regiment and commanded the 10th South Wales Borderers from 1914 to 1916 at the Western Front.

With an eye on international public opinion, Greenwood has said that his appointment will serve as a sign to every American that the government was committed to bringing order and prosperity to Ireland along the lines of its Home Rule proposals, which he was confident would be applied logically and willingly.

Ian Macpherson (1880–1937), Chief Secretary for Ireland and 1st Baron Strathcarron.

The departure of Mr Macpherson is not a surprise. He has been in poor health, and it is understood the change of post will relieve him of what has been a tremendous burden of responsibility as conditions in Ireland become ever more volatile.

Macpherson is not the only senior administrator to be vacating his position in Ireland. General Sir Frederick Shaw, Commander of the British Army in Ireland since May 1918, is also to step down. He will be replaced by General Sir Nevil Macready, who, Prime Minister Lloyd George says, will bring experience from both his police and distinguished military careers, as well as 'remarkable powers of organisation' and 'exceptional judgment and tact' that will help 'strengthen the administration of the law in Ireland'.

Macready's appointment is seen as evidence that the government believes it needs a firmer hand in control of the military in Ireland.

Bishop Tells of Attack on Widow's Home as 'Land Greed' Grows in West of Ireland

Loughrea, 3 May – Referring to the growing number of incidents of land agitation in the west of Ireland, the Roman Catholic Bishop of Clonfert, Dr Thomas O'Doherty, has said that, despite the fact that land reform is an important national issue, 'no matter how good or noble your purpose … unjust means must not be used in the effort to attain it'.

1920

3 JUN
The *Irish Bulletin*, newspaper of Dáil Éireann, publishes a list of cases settled by republican courts over the previous year. It indicates that 19 Irish counties 'administer their own law' in defiance of the British administration.

19 JUN
It is reported that two young women have had their hair shorn by a gang of young men in an attack at their home in Castletownroche, Co. Cork. It is alleged that the women were attacked for entertaining two military officers.

26 JUN
Lady Dudley, philanthropist and wife of a former Irish viceroy, drowns while swimming near her Screebe Lodge residence in Connemara.

28 JUN ▷
Soldiers in the 1st Battalion of the **Connaught Rangers** based in India mutiny over the oppression of their friends in Ireland. Sixty-one are arrested and 14 sentenced to death, though only one is executed.

1920

Dr O'Doherty, preaching last month in the cathedral in Loughrea, stated that there were many examples he could cite of these 'unjust means' being used, but he provided details of just one case – this involved the house of a widow being fired into in the dead of night because she refused to give up land that she was entitled to hold.

If the woman had been killed, the bishop continued, those responsible would have been guilty of murder in the eyes of God and man.

The bishop added that, as a principle, a person could not justly be forced to give up what they lawfully possessed without fair and adequate compensation. It was not right or proper to threaten an owner and simply say, 'We must have your land and at our own price.'

Irish Labour Pledges Support for Anti-Munition Strikers

Dublin, 16 June – The Irish Labour Party and Trades Union Congress has pledged its support for workers in Dublin who are refusing to handle war munitions.

A statement issued by the party on 9 June – signed by leaders Thomas Farren, J.C. O'Connor, William O'Brien and Thomas Johnson – claims that the 'men who work in the transport industries have laid it down emphatically that they will not be parties to the attempted reconquest of Ireland by British military forces. Railwaymen, dock workers, and carters are quite fixed in their resolve and they will be supported by the organised workers in every other industry.'

Irish Labour Party leader Thomas Johnson c.1920.

The statement adds that it is the 'imperative duty of every man and woman in Ireland to rally to the support' of the more than 400 men who have been 'locked-out of their work for nearly three weeks' owing to their refusal to handle war materiel. It also calls on trades councils throughout Ireland to create local committees to organise collections in support of the workers and their families.

The munitions strike has exposed divisions between trade unionists in Ireland and their counterparts in Britain. It is notable that the British labour leaders, including executives of the National Union of Railwaymen, have been unwilling to support the strike to date, with the *Belfast News Letter* speculating that to do so would risk splitting the labour movement in Britain 'from top to bottom'.

△ **6 JUL**
Sinn Féin Councillor Seán Ó hUadhaigh proposes – after a period of just over 98 years – that the name of Kingstown UDC be changed to **Dún Laoghaire**. The new name takes effect on 5 August.

12 JUL
In a militant 'Twelfth' address to Belfast Orangemen at Finaghy, Sir Edward Carson threatens that the UVF would 'take matters into their own hands' if the British government failed to protect 'Ulster' from Sinn Féin.

19 JUL
Major General Strickland issues an order of a curfew for Cork city between the hours of 10 p.m. and 3 a.m. The following month it is extended across Munster.

Panic on the Streets of Derry as Rioting Leaves at Least 17 Dead

Derry, 25 June – Derry city is recovering after a week of intense sectarian fighting.

A clear picture of events has been difficult to piece together, but from the fragments of information that have emerged, the scale and seriousness of the violence is clear. According to reports, the city was in a state of panic over prolonged exchanges of gunfire between republicans, unionists and the authorities in such places as Long Tower Street and Upper Fountain Street, as well as in the neighbourhood of Upper Fahan Street and Bishop Street, and in the Waterside district.

One exchange company telegram reported dead and wounded men lying in the streets, their bodies unable to be removed because of snipers concealed on rooftops on a number of streets.

The sectarian nature of the fighting was underlined by the killing of William O'Kane, a Catholic railway worker. According to a report by *The Cork Examiner*'s Derry correspondent, Mr O'Kane was held up by an Orangeman and asked his religion. When he responded 'Catholic', he was immediately shot. In his dying declaration he gave the name of his assailant to the police.

Alongside the gunfire, there have been forced evictions in different quarters of the city. There have also been reports of large-scale looting, mainly focused on food, which is in short supply.

A large contingent of the Norfolk Regiment was dispatched to the city and two military destroyers aimed searchlights on a number of the troubled areas. Sinn Féin volunteers also took to patrolling different parts of the city, claiming that their purpose was to protect the interests of the city as a whole.

1920

19 JUL
The town of Tuam is sacked as a reprisal for the ambush and killing of two Dunmore-based RIC officers, Constables James Burke and Patrick Carey. Homes and business are destroyed, and the town hall is burned to the ground.

21 JUL
Sectarian violence erupts in Belfast as thousands of Catholic workers are forcibly expelled from their jobs in the shipyards. The attacks spread to areas of Catholic housing as well as to other industries and other towns.

27 JUL
The first recruits to the Auxiliary Division of the RIC – 'the Auxies' – arrive in Ireland.

In scenes from Derry, soldiers are photographed standing by an armoured car fitted with a Lewis gun, and, on the right, posted behind sandbags to tackle any further riots.

1920

10 AUG
British Prime Minister David Lloyd George declares the 'independence of Poland' to be an 'essential part of the structure of European peace' and that its 're-partition … would not merely be a crime, it would be a peril'.

11 AUG
Sixty-five republican prisoners in Cork Gaol, all awaiting trial, commence a hunger strike.

△ **12 AUG**
British forces surround Cork City Hall and arrest, amongst others, Lord Mayor **Terence MacSwiney**. MacSwiney goes on hunger strike and is subsequently court-martialled for sedition and transferred from Cork to Brixton Prison.

A drawing depicts the sectarian attacks on Catholic-owned businesses in Belfast.

The city of Derry has been in a state of turmoil for the last couple of months; official reports indicate that this most recent period of rioting has left at least 17 dead and 29 injured.

Writing in the *Irish Bulletin*, Arthur Griffith, Sinn Féin TD, claimed that the rioting in Derry had no accidental origin. Rather, he states, it was planned and directed by unionist leaders in collusion with eminent individuals in England and with agents of the British government in Ireland.

Catholic Workers Forced from Belfast Shipyards as Violence Erupts in the City

Belfast, 27 July – Sectarian violence has erupted in Belfast with attacks on Catholic workers in the city's shipyards and on Catholic areas such as Ballymacarrett and the Falls Road.

The disturbances, which began in the Harland & Wolff shipyard, followed informal meetings of workers on the afternoon of 21 July during which resolutions were passed condemning Sinn Féin and its operations in Ireland. The sentiment that was stirred up in these meetings overflowed, resulting in a series of forced expulsions of Catholic workers. Trouble ensued when a number of the men told to leave took issue with the instruction: blows were struck and iron bolts were thrown. At least a dozen were injured and taken to the Royal Victoria Hospital.

A number of men who were attacked were able to escape by jumping into the Musgrave Channel and swimming across to the Sydenham shore.

1920

Throughout the afternoon, search parties, some carrying Union Jacks, sought out Sinn Féiners in the shipyards and elsewhere. Houses were looted in the Ballymacarrett district, while the military was drafted into the Falls Road area, where they opened fire, killing one man and wounding 11 others.

In the aftermath of these initial disturbances, the unionist *Belfast News Letter* did not deny the use of violence against Catholics. But the newspaper said that it shares the view of Sir Edward Carson that, however terrible the provocation from Sinn Féin, disorder and bloodshed in Ulster, particularly in Belfast, can do nothing but damage the unionist cause.

The rioting has extended to other northern towns, such as Lisburn, where 22 shops were destroyed, and Bangor, where six shops were wrecked and an attempt was made to burn down the Catholic Girls' Hostel.

The Sack of Balbriggan – Night of Violence Leaves Town Destroyed and Three Dead

Balbriggan, 22 September – The north County Dublin town of Balbriggan was subjected to a night of burnings and brutality as police and military went on a rampage following the killing of RIC District Inspector Peter Burke on 20 September.

On the day in question, Burke travelled to Balbriggan with his brother and some friends. At about 9 p.m., while in a public house in the town, they got involved in an altercation and were forced to leave the premises. As they were making their way towards their motor car, shots rang out; Burke was killed and his brother was injured.

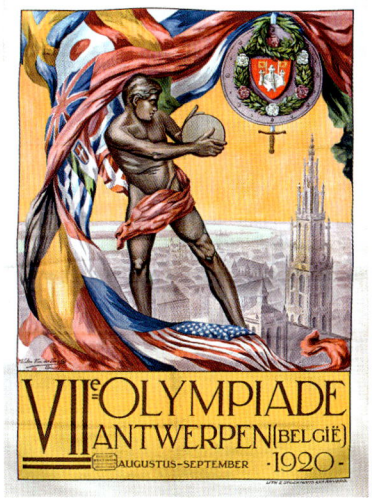

18 AUG
Representing the US, Limerick native Paddy Ryan wins gold in the hammer throw at the **Olympic Games** in Antwerp, Belgium.

22 AUG
Oswald Swanzy, widely blamed for the assassination of Tomás MacCurtain, is shot dead in Lisburn. Sectarian rioting and attacks on the Catholic population of the town ensue.

16 SEP
More than 30 people are killed and hundreds injured after a bomb is exploded at the heart of New York's financial district on Wall Street.

Roofless cottages in Clonard Street, Balbriggan, in the wake of the sack of that village by the Black and Tans on the night of 20–21 September 1920.

REVOLUTIONARY TIMES 1913–23

1920

18 SEP
In a letter to *The Irish Times*, Dean Innocent Ryan, parish priest in Cashel, dismisses alleged sightings of bleeding statues and other religious objects in Templemore and Cashel.

△ **20–21 SEP**
The north county Dublin town of Balbriggan is subject to a night of burnings and brutality by the **Black and Tans** in a reprisal for the killing of RIC District Inspector Peter Burke. In the course of the reprisal, two suspected republicans, James Lawless and John Gibbons, are bayoneted to death. Subsequently the British Labour Party states that the Crown forces were 'utterly out of hand and took the law into their own hands to inflict punishment on the people of the town'.

Burke was a native of Oughterard and had 16 years' service in the RIC.

The reprisal was swift and savage. Just over an hour later, a party of Black and Tans arrived in the town from the Gormanston direction aboard several motor lorries, pulling up outside the local barracks before embarking on a ruinous rampage through the town. Windows were smashed and houses set on fire, with reports suggesting that 20 or 30 were completely destroyed.

The rampage left two men – James Lawless and John Gibbons – dead.

A sister of Gibbons claims that at about 1 a.m. a party of about 50 uniformed men attacked their family's house, in which her mother, brother, two sisters, a servant boy and two women visiting from Bray were asleep. John Gibbons was reportedly removed to the local barracks, where he was questioned about his involvement in the Volunteers; he told them that he served as a secretary. It is alleged that he was then beaten, placed against a wall and had shots fired all around him. Later, both Gibbons and Lawless were taken to a corner of Quay Street, where they were bayoneted and shot. Two large pools of blood are still visible on the spot.

Lloyd George Criticised Over 'Hellish Policy' for Ireland

Prime Minister condones reprisals and says partition bill to proceed

Carnarvon, 10 October – In a speech that has angered his critics in Ireland and Britain, Prime Minister Lloyd George condoned the reprisals in Ireland, promised further stern measures and confirmed that his government will proceed with its partition scheme.

Amongst the most controversial aspects of the speech, delivered yesterday in Carnarvon, Wales, was the Prime Minister's defence of the acts of reprisal carried out by the Crown forces in Ireland. 'Policemen and soldiers did not go burning houses and shooting men down wantonly without provocation,' he said. 'Therefore, you must, if you are to examine reprisals, find out how they arose. I think during the last year 283 policemen have been shot in Ireland – 109 shot dead. Something like 100 soldiers, I think, have been shot, and many more have been fired at. I think about 67 courthouses … have been burnt, and there have been attacks on police barracks. The police endured this state of things in a way that is the highest testimony to their discipline and self-restraint for two or three years. There is no doubt that at last their patience has given way and there has been some severe hitting back.'

The Prime Minister explained that if it was a war the British government was involved in, then it must be a war on both sides: 'We cannot have a one-sided war. In a war you don't have on one side men standing up to be shot at and never firing back. In war men were in uniform, but in Ireland a harmless-looking citizen might pass a policeman in the street, and there was nothing to indicate that he had murderous weapons or to arouse suspicion. When he had passed the policeman, he would pull out a revolver and shoot him in the back. Scores of policemen had been killed in that way. That was not war, but murder. If it was war, give the soldier and the policeman a fair chance, and they would give a good account of themselves. Were the policemen to stand to be shot down like dogs in the streets without any attempt to defend themselves?'

As to how order might be restored, Lloyd George signalled that sterner measures might need to be applied. The British government, he asserted, could 'not permit a country to be debased into the condition of complete anarchy, where a number, a small body of assassins, a real murder gang, were dominating the country and terrorising it and making it impossible for reasonable men to come together to consider the best way to govern the country'.

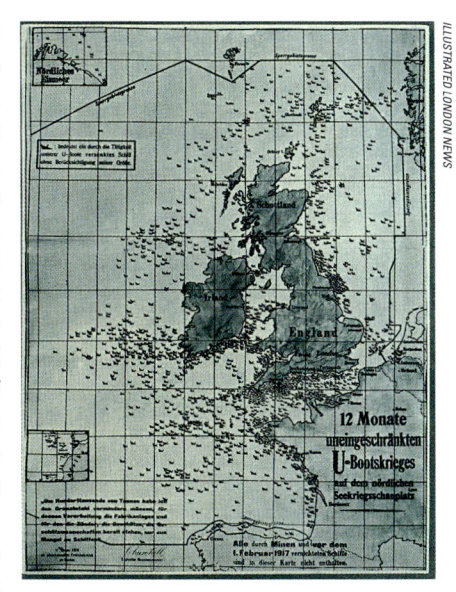

A German map of U-boat sinkings used by Lloyd George in his Carnarvon speech to illustrate the danger of Ireland being used as a base to attack Britain from in future wars.

Terence MacSwiney Dies After 74 Days on Hunger Strike

Brixton, 26 October – Lord Mayor of Cork Terence MacSwiney has died in Brixton Prison after 74 days of hunger strike.

Mr MacSwiney drew his last breath at 5.40 yesterday morning with his brother Seán and his chaplain, Fr Dominic O'Connor, at his bedside.

News of the death has made headlines across the world but has been met with particular sorrow in the city of which MacSwiney was lord mayor. In a message to the Deputy Lord Mayor, Dónal Ó Ceallacháin, Fr Dominic requested that his fellow citizens exhibit the same calm, dignified bearing that they had after the assassination of Tomás MacCurtain earlier this year.

A native of Cork city, Terence MacSwiney attended school at the Christian Brothers, North Monastery. Although he left school at 15, he later gained entry into university, where he obtained an honours Bachelor of Arts degree.

1920

20 SEP
Three British soldiers, members of the Duke of Wellington's Regiment, are killed in an IRA ambush at the junction of Church Street and North King Street in Dublin. A member of the ambush party, 18-year-old UCD medical student Kevin Barry, is arrested at the scene.

21 SEP
Ill health forces French President Paul Deschanel to resign after only seven months in office.

22 SEP
An ambush at Rineen, Co. Clare, results in the killing of five RIC officers and a Black and Tan. Five civilians are killed and property is destroyed in the brutal reprisals that follow.

22 SEP △
Sinn Féin member of Limerick County Council, John Lynch, is killed when British soldiers raid his bedroom at the **Exchange Hotel** in Dublin in the early hours of the morning.

REVOLUTIONARY TIMES 1913–23

1920

The funeral procession of Terence MacSwiney crosses Blackfriars Bridge in London.

26 SEP
A successful IRA attack on Trim Barracks is met with reprisals as a party of Black and Tans and Auxiliaries loot and destroy shops and homes in the town.

28 SEP
After a successful morning raid for arms by the IRA's Cork No. 2 Brigade on Mallow Barracks, in which a soldier is killed, Crown forces go on the rampage in the town, burning houses, the town hall and the local creamery. Two civilians are shot and wounded.

Mr MacSwiney's commitment to the cultural and industrial life of his native country was reflected in his involvement with the Irish Literary Society, the Gaelic League and the Cork Industrial Development Association. He was a fluent Irish speaker, a poet and a dramatist. He became involved with the Volunteer movement and subsequently, in the aftermath of the Easter Week rebellion in 1916, was arrested and interned, spending terms of imprisonment in Richmond Barracks, Wakefield Prison and Frongoch. Elected unopposed for the Mid-Cork constituency in the 1918 general election, he also became a Cork city councillor and was the unanimous choice to fill the vacancy of lord mayor following the murder of his predecessor, Tomás MacCurtain, in March.

The Home Office authorities have granted permission to seven Irish political prisoners in Brixton Prison to bear MacSwiney's remains from the mortuary to the prison gate. The remains will then lie in state in St George's Cathedral in Southwark, from where, following a Requiem Mass, a funeral procession will take place to Euston station. The Lord Mayor's remains will then be returned to Cork for burial.

1920

18-Year-Old Student Kevin Barry Hanged in Mountjoy Prison

Dublin, 2 November – Eighteen-year-old student Kevin Gerald Barry was executed in Mountjoy Prison yesterday morning.

The young man's hanging was confirmed by a typed notice that was posted on the prison door. 'The sentence of the law passed on Kevin Barry, found guilty of murder, was carried into execution at 8 am today. By Order.'

Thousands of Barry's sympathisers gathered to pray outside Mountjoy from early morning, among them a large number of students from University College Dublin, where he studied. Shortly before the moment of his execution, a bell tolled in the prison tower and many of the crowd started to sob. A reporter on the scene described the stillness and sorrow on display as a 'moving, thrilling, historic scene'.

Barry, a medical student, was sentenced to death for his involvement in an ambush on 20 September to capture arms and ammunition from a military patrol on North King Street in Dublin. Three soldiers died in the attack. He was court-martialled on 20 October and his sentence was announced shortly afterwards.

The decision to proceed with the execution was taken despite increasing pleas for mercy and calls for the British government to intervene.

Sinn Féin TD Arthur Griffith described the sentence as an 'outrage upon the law and customs of nations' and contrasted the treatment of Barry with how British armed forces captured by the Volunteers had been treated. 'The English government now proposes to set aside the high standard maintained by the Irish Volunteers, and to execute prisoners of war, previously attempting to brand them before the world as criminals.'

Kevin Barry was taken in procession from his cell to the scaffold, accompanied by his executioners and prison warders. Two clergymen stood beside him as he was restrained on the scaffold; he objected to being pinioned and blindfolded, stating that he was a soldier and was not afraid to die. A white cap was nevertheless lowered over his face and within 30 seconds the hanging was completed.

Barry's willingness to face death has been evident since his sentencing. He told his sister and brother in recent days that he was quite prepared to die and considered it an honour to give his life on the scaffold for Ireland, as Sir Roger Casement had done in 1916.

1 OCT
Londoner and ex-soldier Albert Flint tells *The Freeman's Journal* that he resigned from the Black and Tans because they operated more like a corps of bandits than a police force. It is reported that he is one of 137 Tans to have tendered their resignations.

17 OCT
Michael Fitzgerald, one of 11 hunger strikers in Cork Prison, dies after 67 days without food.

18 OCT ▽
Unemployed ex-servicemen clash with London police as **riots** erupt in Whitehall, near Downing Street.

19 OCT
A meeting of Ireland's Catholic bishops in Maynooth accuses the British government of being the 'architects' of anarchy in Ireland and asks for a tribunal to inquire into recent atrocities by Crown forces.

REVOLUTIONARY TIMES 1913–23

1920

Funeral of a British soldier killed by the IRA on 21 November 1920, Bloody Sunday.

25 OCT
Lord Mayor of Cork Terence MacSwiney, 41, dies in Brixton Prison. On the same day, with his family at his bedside, Joseph Murphy, 24, dies after 76 days on hunger strike.

◁ **28 OCT**
Suffragist **Sylvia Pankhurst**, 36, is sentenced to six months' imprisonment for communist sedition. *The Irish Times* editorialises that she is 'lucky to have escaped so lightly'.

Killings in Dublin

Dublin, 22 November – Twenty-seven people were killed and many more were seriously wounded in Dublin yesterday in a series of atrocities that has shocked the country.

The day began with a number of premeditated and co-ordinated attacks by republicans on select members of the Crown forces in their various lodgings across the city. The attacks took place at 9 a.m. Twelve army officers or ex-officers and two Auxiliaries were killed.

The view in London is that these attacks were motivated by a desire to cripple the machinery of justice in Ireland, as the assailants searched the residences of their victims for papers.

Reprisal at Croke Park

Later that afternoon, a large force of military, RIC and Auxiliaries turned up at Croke Park where a big Gaelic football match between Dublin and Tipperary was being played before a crowd of around 5,000 spectators. The match had not long started when the forces arrived. Shooting began immediately, sparking panic among spectators, who fled in various directions to escape the bullets.

As it stands, it is known that 12 people were killed, 11 more were seriously wounded and 54 others injured. The dead include 14-year-old William Scott, who is alleged to have died from bayonet wounds, and 10-year-old Jeremiah O'Leary. Also among the dead was Tipperary full-back Michael Hogan, a native of Grangemockler, who was shot on the pitch.

Given the seriousness of the injuries suffered by some of those in the sportsground, an increase in the death toll cannot be ruled out.

The official line adopted by Dublin Castle is that a number of gunmen involved in the morning's attacks were in the ground and that 'pickets' placed on the approach roads to Croke Park were designed to raise the alarm on the arrival of the Crown forces. An official report, issued last night, indicates that shots were fired on troops as they arrived, and it was only then that they returned fire. The report further alleges that more than 30 revolvers were retrieved from inside Croke Park, having been dropped on the ground by spectators.

At Least 16 Auxiliaries Killed in Kilmichael Ambush

Kilmichael, 1 December – At least 16 members of the Auxiliary police force were killed in an ambush in west Cork on 28 November 1920.

In addition to the number confirmed dead at the scene, a further member of the force is reported to be dying, while another member is missing.

The ambush is the most daring and lethal yet to be carried out in Ireland.

The incident occurred in Kilmichael at around 10.30 p.m., at a bend on a secluded stretch of road between Macroom and Dunmanway, when two lorryloads of Auxiliary police under District Inspector Craig were attacked by a group of armed men numbering between 70 and 100.

The Auxiliaries were based in Macroom Castle and had been conducting searches along the southern stretch of countryside towards Dunmanway.

The lead lorry is understood to have struck a mine; the occupants were, according to a report from a special correspondent from *The Irish Times*, blown up and killed instantly. The second lorry, travelling some way behind, attempted to pull up, but got stuck in a trench in the road. The occupants of this lorry exchanged fire with the ambush party, but by the time the bullets ceased, almost all of them had been killed.

The dead Auxiliaries are to be removed to London for interment. The missing Auxiliary has been identified as Cadet C.J. Guthrie.

As soon the news of the ambush reached Macroom, all business was suspended, and many families fled the expected reprisals, which, when they came, left very few, if any, houses in the district undamaged, and destroyed some completely.

1920

1 NOV
Recruitment begins for a controversial Special Constabulary for Ulster, which includes provision for an unpaid volunteer force. The *Belfast Telegraph*, in welcoming the new constabulary, confirms its political purpose is to 'assist the military and police in combating the Sinn Féin campaign'.

2 NOV △
Voters go to the polls for a US presidential election that sees Ohio-based **Senator Warren Harding** comfortably defeat his Democrat opponent and Ohio governor, **James M. Cox**.

12 NOV
After 94 days, Arthur Griffith intervenes to bring an end to a hunger strike in Cork Gaol, which has already claimed the lives of two men. The nine surviving men still on strike, reduced to 'mere living skeletons', are nursed back to health.

1920

14 NOV
A young Galway priest, Fr Michael Griffin, is lured from his home by three men. His body is discovered a week later in a bog at Cloch Scoilte, north of the village of Barna. He had been shot through the head.

16 NOV
Details are published in the Irish press of a letter from Michael Collins to the *Gaelic America* newspaper in New York, in which he denies any disunity between moderates and extremists within the Sinn Féin organisation.

▽ **17 NOV**
A plane carrying military dispatches crashes into two houses on Barrack Street, Waterford city, after colliding with a wireless mast. There are no fatalities.

27 NOV
The Cork Examiner reports that barricades eight feet high have been erected around Downing Street and the House of Commons for fear of an attack by Irish republicans.

Firemen extinguish fires among the ruins of Patrick Street in Cork city in December 1920.

Extensive Damage to City Centre as Cork Burns in Night of Terror

Cork, 15 December – Businesses have been ruined and many landmark buildings reduced to smouldering rubble in fires that have ravaged the centre of Cork city.

The outbreak began on the evening of 11 December, when the quiet of the city was disrupted, at around 10 p.m., by intermittent bursts of gunfire that sent pedestrians running for the safety of their homes. Shortly afterwards, a serious conflagration erupted in the premises of Grant and Co. Outfitters on Patrick Street. Within an hour, the building lay in ruins and the blaze had spread to neighbouring buildings, with further fires breaking out elsewhere in the city.

One side of Patrick Street, the principal commercial street, was levelled by the flames. Among the buildings burned to the ground were many of the major businesses on the street, including a number of large drapery establishments, which are big employers in the city. Other thoroughfares in the city were also affected, including Grand Parade and Oliver Plunkett Street. On Winthrop Street, the Lee Cinema was almost completely destroyed, as was Tylers' boot shop. Buildings and businesses were also damaged on Cook Street, Robert Street, Morgan Street, Caroline Street, Maylor Street and Merchant Street. Across the river, the City Hall and the Carnegie Library were gutted by fire.

The city centre continued to smoulder throughout the following day – the local fire brigade received assistance from the Dublin fire brigade, as well as from firemen from Limerick and Waterford, to keep it under control. As the damaged buildings were inspected, it became clear that many had been forcibly entered and looted. These businesses would have been fully stocked in anticipation of the Christmas rush.

No lives were lost in the tragedy, but the material and personal costs are expected to run to about £3m, and the jobs of 2,000 persons are thought to be in jeopardy.

King George V Gives Royal Assent to the Partition of Ireland

Westminster, 27 December – The Government of Ireland Act, which allows for the partition of the island, received royal assent on 23 December.

This is the most recent piece of Home Rule legislation to be enacted and sets up two parliaments in Ireland – one for six counties in Ulster and another for the rest of the country. Delegates from both parliaments will sit on a Council of Ireland, where issues of importance to both jurisdictions will be discussed.

In a speech yesterday proroguing Parliament, King George V expressed profound grief at the current situation in Ireland and deplored the 'campaign of violence and outrage by which a small section of my subjects seek to sever Ireland from the Empire'.

Expressing sympathy with his armed forces and a hope that constitutional methods might yet reassert themselves, the king gave his assent to a bill which, he said, 'provides the means whereby the people of Ireland can of their own accord achieve unity'.

Against the backdrop of the current unrest, the King may have been speaking more in hope than expectation when he said that the Act 'will finally bring about unity and friendship between all the peoples of my kingdom'.

Irish pickets at the White House in 1920 over British policy in Ireland.

1920

28 NOV
First World War veteran Tom Barry leads men from the IRA's 3rd Cork Brigade in an ambush at Kilmichael, Co. Cork, that leaves 16 Auxiliaries dead.

10 DEC
The British government reveals that it has been in contact with 'intermediaries' about a possible Irish peace, but Sinn Féin insists that while Ireland 'desires to live in peace', there have been no talks about a truce or negotiations of any kind.

11 DEC
Éamon de Valera is smuggled aboard the SS *Celtic* in New York harbour. After 18 months in the US, he is returning to Ireland.

11–12 DEC
Following an ambush on a lorry of Auxiliaries at Dillon's Cross, Crown forces burn the commercial centre of Cork city in reprisal.

14 DEC
An end to the munitions strike, ongoing since May, is signalled by the chairman of the Irish Labour Party. 'Changed conditions require a change of tactics, and we have decided to advise the railway and dock workers to alter their position to carry everything that the British military authorities are willing to risk on the trains.'

Remembering 1920
a hundred years on

The day after ceremonies are held at Croke Park to remember those killed by British forces on Bloody Sunday 1920, Tipperary play Cork in the Munster Senior Football Championship final at Páirc Uí Chaoimh. The ceremonies at Croke Park took place during the pandemic, so no crowd was in attendance, but the event marked the killing of fourteen people at Croke Park, and the dead were honoured by wreaths laid by the President and Taoiseach, and the reading of the names of those who died. The Bloody Sunday match of 1920 had involved Dublin and Tipperary in a challenge Gaelic football match, but a century later Tipperary were in competitive action in the Munster Championships. To mark the centenary, the Tipperary players wore replica jerseys from 1920; they defeated Cork by three points and won their first provincial championship since 1935.

22 November 2020

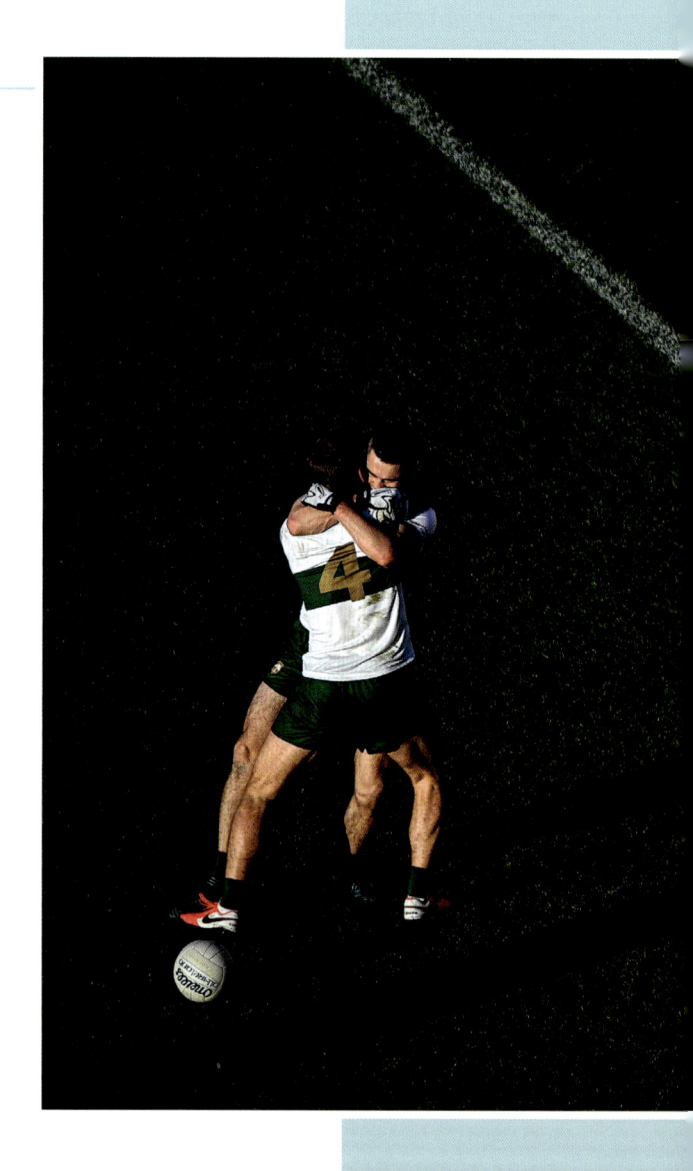

REVOLUTIONARY TIMES 1913–23

Sacrifices Supreme:

Hunger Strikes and the Separatist Struggle in Ireland

IT STARTED WITH the suffragettes – and in Britain.

In the years preceding the outbreak of the First World War, the campaign to extend voting rights to women took a radical turn when imprisoned suffragettes added a new, self-destructive weapon to their political armoury. The first to do so was Scots-born Marion Wallace Dunlop, who, in refusing food in Holloway Prison in 1909, began the modern practice of hunger-striking, her fast lasting ninety-one hours before the authorities relented and allowed her release. As a means of registering political protest and courting public sympathy, use of the tactic spread – including, in time, to Ireland.

Between 1912 and 1914, twenty-two women held in Irish prisons went on hunger strike.

Between 1912 and 1914, twenty-two women held in Irish prisons went on hunger strike. Among their number were three English suffragettes – Gladys Evans, Mary Leigh and Sarah Baines – who, in July 1912 were arrested in Dublin for their dramatic attempts to disrupt a visit to the city by Herbert Asquith, the British Prime Minister. As part of this, the women threw an axe at the carriage of the passing Asquith (hitting the IPP leader, John Redmond) and tried to set fire to the beautiful and grand Theatre Royal. On being committed to Mountjoy Prison, the women, all members of the WSPU, opted to go on hunger strike in pursuit of a demand that they be accorded the status of political prisoners. Imprisoned members of the IWFL were divided on how to respond to the strike, but four of them decided to join the protest: Hannah Sheehy Skeffington, Jane Murphy, Margaret Murphy and Margaret Palmer. All four were freed within a matter of days and the release of Sarah Baines followed soon after.

For Evans and Leigh, however, the experience would be more prolonged and altogether more traumatic. In keeping with a brutal practice already in operation in British jails, they would be subjected to a regime of force-feeding by nasal and stomach tube, the ruinous impact on their bodies and minds documented daily and in detail by the prison medical officer. The women would survive and be released when prison medics became concerned for their health, though not before Evans had spent fifty-eight days on hunger strike.

The suffragette example was such that the hunger strike soon entered the arsenal of Irish male prisoners who considered themselves political, as opposed to criminal, inmates. For instance, in September 1913, after being sentenced to three months' imprisonment, the labour leader James Connolly went on hunger strike in Mountjoy Prison, only to be released a week later when his health deteriorated, and after his wife pleaded his case with the British authorities. Later, in the wake of the mass imprisonments that followed the 1916 Rising, hunger strikes were more extensively used by republicans as a way of protesting against prison punishments. Éamon de Valera undertook a hunger strike in Dartmoor Prison for just this reason, abandoning his protest once the punishment had been revoked. And yet, notwithstanding his own adoption of the tactic, de Valera questioned its effectiveness as a strategy. Writing to fellow republican inmates from his Dartmoor Prison cell in 1917, he cautioned, 'You may be tempted to hunger strike. As a body do not attempt it whilst the war lasts unless you were assured from the outside that the death of two or three of you would help the cause. As soldiers I know you would not shrink from the sacrifice, but remember how precious a human life is.'

In September 1917 the British government inadvertently turned de Valera's message on its head and proved how powerful hunger striking was as a propaganda tool. Thomas Ashe, the Kerry-born 1916 rebel leader and ex-internee, had been arrested for delivering a seditious speech in Co. Longford and sentenced to two years' hard labour in Mountjoy, where he promptly informed the deputy governor that he would not 'work or obey any order relating to criminal prisoners as I do not consider myself a criminal'. Determined to acquire political status, Ashe and his fellow prisoners began a

Mary Leigh.

hunger strike, to which the authorities responded, as they had earlier with the suffragettes, with forcible feeding. For Ashe, the brutal treatment would prove fatal. As fellow hunger-striker Fionán Lynch recounted, force-feeding involved a harrowing ordeal, each of the men being 'strapped, legs and hands, to a high chair, mouth forced open with a wooden spoon and then the stomach pump pushed in by a doctor and the food poured in through it'.

The death of Ashe on 25 September 1917 – five days into his strike – led the authorities to abandon the practice of force-feeding and to concede to the prisoners' demands. More broadly, Ashe's death, and the massive, carefully choreographed funeral that followed, was a propaganda coup for Sinn Féin and the Irish Volunteers. The lesson was not lost on republicans and ensured that, throughout the subsequent War of Independence, hunger-striking became a regular part of the prison experience and a strategic weapon of Irish separatists. In 1919 alone, there were eight separate hunger strikes across the Irish prison system, including at Mountjoy, where, at one point, fifty prisoners were refusing food at the same time. Again, the demand was a straightforward one: the securing of political or prisoner-of-war status and, again, it had the effect of securing their release by authorities fearful of creating further republican martyrs.

Throughout the subsequent War of Independence, hunger-striking became a regular part of the prison experience and a strategic weapon of Irish separatists.

But the outcomes were not always so benign, and the risks associated with hunger-striking were most certainly real. In May 1920, in the course of a hunger strike at Mountjoy, twenty-five-year-old prisoner Francis Gleeson died at the Mater Hospital from 'toxaemia, following nephritis and acute appendicitis'. Significantly, however, the coroner's court ruled that the causes of his death had been 'accelerated by his hunger strike in defence of his principles'. The hunger strike in which Gleeson had been a part had started in April and, led by Peadar Clancy from the Dublin Brigade of the IRA, included over sixty-five prisoners. As momentum for the strike built within the prison – many inmates joined, perceiving the health hazards to be at a low level – support for their demands swelled outside. Large crowds congregated at the gates of Mountjoy and, in an impressive show of solidarity, the Trade Union Congress called a general strike in which an estimated 60,000 workers took part. 'No other government save the British would be conscienceless as to set at defiance such a national protest,' the *Irish Independent* editorialised.

As it transpired, it didn't. Rather than let the hunger strike run or attempt a return to force-feeding, the government relented and released those men who were on remand or in danger of death from their refusal to take food. Much the same happened the following month in England when, after 200 Irish internees at Wormwood Scrubs Prison went on hunger strike in May 1920, they were released within a week to the care of local hospitals to recover. That the British authorities were losing control of the prisons and appeared powerless in the face of the hunger-strike tactic was undeniable. In the wake of the Mountjoy releases, the unionist *Belfast News Letter* accused the government of 'surrender' and raged that it had abandoned 'law-abiding people in Ireland to the horrors of Sinn Féin authority'.

The British approach was soon to change, however. As the government's policy on Ireland hardened over the summer of 1920, so too did the official attitude towards prisoners. What this meant in practice soon became apparent when, on 11 August 1920, sixty-five men interned without trial in Cork Gaol went on hunger strike, demanding recognition of their status as political prisoners. The day after the hunger strike had begun, the Lord Mayor of Cork, Terence MacSwiney, was arrested at City Hall. A court martial was held at which MacSwiney

Terence MacSwiney lying in state in Southwark Cathedral, London, October 1920. Father Dominic (left) and Seán MacSwiney overlook the casket with unidentified men and wreaths surrounding the coffin.

was sentenced to two years' imprisonment and sent to Cork Gaol, where he joined the hunger strike on 22 August. In an attempt to break the strike, the authorities released some of the men, moved others to British prisons and left eleven in Cork. MacSwiney was transferred to Brixton Prison. While the entire protest gained widespread press attention, it was the plight of MacSwiney, a lord mayor elected by popular vote, that garnered global attention.

On 19 September, forty days into his hunger strike, MacSwiney released a statement denouncing the decision of the British authorities not to find a way to end the strike as 'callous and cold-blooded murder' – British Prime Minister Lloyd George had previously let it be known that he would not be taking responsibility for the fate of MacSwiney and that it was, regretfully, his own decision to 'starve himself'. To do otherwise, to intervene and release

MacSwiney would, Lloyd George maintained, be to countenance a 'complete breakdown of the machinery of law and government in Ireland'. The message from MacSwiney, issued on his own behalf and that of his fellow hunger-strikers, was that 'we forgive all those who are compassing our death. This battle is being fought with a clean heart purely for our country. We have made our peace with God, and bear ill will to no man.' MacSwiney's words echoed around the world in newspapers that were drawn to the tragedy of his distressing plight and by a grim fascination with the extent to which the human body could hold out without food to sustain it. Where previously he had been 'unknown outside Ireland', Madrid's *El Sol* newspaper reported that suddenly the 'whole world' had become familiar with MacSwiney's name.

The hunger strikes begun in Cork in April 1920 ended with the deaths of three men. The first to die, on 17 October, his sixty-seventh day without food in Cork Gaol, was thirty-eight-year-old Michael Fitzgerald. Just over a week later, on 25 October and after seventy-six days, Joseph Murphy also died in Cork. Both men were destined to be overshadowed in the historical memory by the death in Brixton Prison, on the same day as Murphy died in Cork, of Terence MacSwiney, his seventy-fourth without food. In a message that would echo down the decades to future generations, Sinn Féin founder Arthur Griffith insisted that MacSwiney's ultimate sacrifice had served to prove the point that he, MacSwiney, had made in his inaugural address as lord mayor some months earlier: that victory in the struggle for Irish freedom would belong not with those who could inflict the most suffering, but those who could endure it. 'The might of this country's enemies,' Griffith remarked of MacSwiney, 'failed to shake his faith or break his will. In death he exemplifies to mankind the truth that the spirit of the Irish nation is indestructible and unconquerable.'

For Irish republicans, MacSwiney's death was not the end. Rather, it signalled the beginning of new phase in its propaganda campaign to summon international sympathy and support to the Irish separatist cause, linking it to struggles against tyrannical forces in other parts of the world through history. As the news from Brixton made headlines around the world and tributes were paid to his heroic sacrifice, the return of MacSwiney's remains to his native Cork for burial was protracted to maximise its propagandist effect. The shrunken body of the deceased Lord Mayor lay in state in London's Southwark Cathedral long enough for 30,000 mourners to file past and pay their respects. On its return to Ireland, the British government redirected the body away from Dublin to prevent an additional republican demonstration there and threatened to intervene if the funeral cortège exceeded 100 people. Instead of suppressing the turnout, the threat had the opposite effect. The funeral was a massive event, and – in spite of the Catholic Church's view of hunger-strike deaths as suicide and their clear disapproval of such actions on other occasions – was attended by three archbishops and a plethora of bishops, while Requiem Masses were held in crowded churches in towns and villages throughout the country.

The final words, however, were left to Griffith. After a volley of shots was fired over MacSwiney's grave at St Finbarr's Cemetery, the acting President of Dáil Éireann declared that his sacrifice had assured his triumph over the enemies of Irish independence. Moreover, it had ensured a lasting legacy: 'He is not dead. He is living forever in the hearts and conscience of mankind.' And yet, it was Griffith who effectively called a halt to the still ongoing hunger strikes in Cork Gaol after he deemed that no further human sacrifice was necessary. Having proved their willingness to die for Ireland, Griffith declared that the prisoners in Cork should 'prepare again to live for her'. The result was the abandonment of the tactic for what was left of the War of Independence (though it would be deployed again by republicans, with further deaths, during the Civil War that followed the Anglo-Irish settlement of December 1921).

But did the ending of the hunger strikes in November 1920 ultimately justify the hard line adopted by the British government? Did it succeed in removing the hunger-strike weapon from the arsenal of republican resistance within the British and Irish prison system? The answer is not straightforward, and the legacies of the 1920 hunger strikes were undoubtedly complex. But if the ending of the hunger strikes is to be presented as a victory for an uncompromising British policy, it was, historian Gabriel Doherty has observed, a pyrrhic one. Not for the first time, and notwithstanding the calamitous cost in human suffering, British policy on Ireland had delivered a propaganda coup to Irish republicans and fuelled a further radicalisation of Irish society.

> **Griffith declared that his sacrifice had assured his triumph over the enemies of Irish independence. Moreover, it had ensured a lasting legacy: 'He is not dead. He is living forever in the hearts and conscience of mankind.'**

Bloody Sunday, 21 November 1920

FOR ITS BRUTALITY and sheer bloody theatre, it was, as historian Anne Dolan has assessed, 'quite unlike any other day in the Irish revolution's calendar'.

On Sunday, 21 November 1920, violent death in Dublin was delivered in three principal instalments. It began with a series of co-ordinated killings by the IRA of fourteen suspected British intelligence officers in their various lodgings, all bar one in a relatively compact network of streets on the southside of the city. This was followed by the indiscriminate shooting of civilians attending a football match at the GAA's Croke Park headquarters, where a further fourteen people were killed. The day ended within the confines of Dublin Castle, headquarters of the British administration in Ireland, where three men arrested the previous evening were brutalised and killed in the custody of their captors.

The day's violence began early. As clocks ticked towards 9 a.m., squads of IRA men fanned out across Dublin with the purpose, as one participant put it, 'to liquidate members of the British Intelligence Service who resided in private houses and hotels throughout the city'. Nineteen suspected intelligence officers would be shot and fourteen killed. 'All slain at fixed hour,' *The New York Times* reported the following morning.

This was as daring an enterprise as yet undertaken by the IRA in a War of Independence that had seen momentum swing against them in the spring and summer of 1920. In order to arrest its loosening grip on the country – large areas had been left unpoliced by large-scale resignations and the retreat of the RIC to towns and cities – the British government had overhauled its Irish administration and begun the job of replenishing its depleted police force with new recruits – these were the 'Black and Tans' (mostly English in origin and former British servicemen) and the Auxiliaries (ex-officers of the British Army recruited as a temporary, paramilitary police force), who arrived in Ireland in March and July 1920 respectively, to join 40,000 soldiers already in situ.

This signalled the start of a British counter-insurgency, with the newly arrived forces quickly earning for themselves a reputation for ill-discipline and ruthlessness on account of their propensity towards the destruction of property and acts of casual brutality against the civilian population. A reprisal strategy was deployed whereby IRA attacks on Crown forces drew disproportionate violence down upon entire communities. In July 1920 the town of Tuam in Co. Galway bore the brunt of these reprisals, and in September, Balbriggan, Mallow and Trim suffered similar fates and worse.

A deputation from the British Labour Party, which travelled to Ireland in late 1920 to investigate reports of reprisals, would discover, contrary to the official propaganda, that an 'atmosphere of terrorism' prevailed in all parts of the country, with people fearing that their houses might be burned or that they might be 'arrested or even dragged from their beds and shot'. And it wasn't just personal property that was targeted by Crown forces. Creameries, factories, shops and other large business premises were also destroyed, often by fire.

An artist imagines the killing of a suspected British intelligence officer on the morning of 21 November 1920.

BLOODY SUNDAY, 21 NOVEMBER 1920

On the night of 20-21 September, following the killing of an RIC inspector, the north Dublin town of Balbriggan was sacked by Crown forces (a mixture of Auxiliaries, Black and Tans and RIC), who, in addition to killing two 'suspected Sinn Féiners', destroyed or damaged seventy-five houses, four pubs, two grocers, a newsagent, a dairy and one of the town's biggest factories. Along a single long street almost every property was either burned or otherwise damaged, the trail of destruction leaving about fifty families homeless and hundreds out of work when an English-built hosiery factory was reduced to little more than a shell.

All this had a calculated effect: it enabled the Crown forces to establish what historian Michael Foy called a 'psychological ascendancy' and to render the IRA increasingly impotent. On 9 November, British Prime Minister David Lloyd George trumpeted that his government had 'murder by the throat' in Ireland.

The killings of Bloody Sunday morning, intimate and personal, made a mockery of that assertion. Many of those killed were still in their pyjamas, and a number were in the company of their wives. Of the killing of Captain Newberry at 92 Lower Baggot Street, an IRA Volunteer recalled, 'The man's wife was standing in a corner of the room and was in a terrified and hysterical condition.' Newberry was one of those killed at eight locations that morning – a fifteenth would die from his wounds in early December. Not all of them, it transpired, were spies. Yet for Michael Collins, the killings had been justified and necessary, and, though not personally involved, he declared his conscience to be clear. 'By their destruction the very air is made sweeter,' he later remarked.

The events of the morning transformed the atmosphere in a city where Dublin and Tipperary Gaelic football teams were scheduled to meet in a challenge

A ticket for the fateful match played at Croke Park on 21 November 1920.

BLOODY SUNDAY, 21 NOVEMBER 1920

Bloody Sunday, November 1920. Friends of the victims and members of the military outside Jervis Street Hospital during the military enquiry into the Bloody Sunday shootings at Croke Park on Sunday, 21 November 1920.

football match at Croke Park that afternoon. Should the game have gone ahead? Not according to three members of the Dublin IRA, who approached Croke Park prior to throw-in to warn the GAA of intelligence about an impending military raid. With spectators already in the ground and conscious of the difficulty of evacuating at such a late stage, the GAA decided to press ahead.

The match had not long started when the anticipated raid began. A mixed force of military, RIC and Auxiliaries arrived in a dozen or more armoured lorries. Suspecting that those involved in the morning's killings had taken refuge amongst the attendance, their plan, it was claimed, was to mount a stop and search operation on all males leaving the ground. What they did was very different. Such searching as was done only occurred after they had fired indiscriminately into the Croke Park crowd, ensuring a stampede to the exits as players and spectators fled. A reporter present described the scene as a 'mass of running and shouting men and shrieking women and children'. The firing was short-lived and concentrated. And it was deadly. One player – Michael Hogan – and thirteen spectators would be killed. The dead included three children. Among their number, too, was Jane Boyle, who was shot clinging to the arm of a fiancé she was due to marry the following week.

Later that night, across the city, Dublin IRA leaders Dick McKee and Peadar Clancy, along with civilian Conor Clune, were shot in the grounds of Dublin Castle, allegedly while trying to make their escape. In reality, the men – who had been arrested the previous night – were tortured and murdered as a further reprisal for the IRA attacks of that morning.

This catalogue of killing made headlines across the world. So dramatic and shocking were the events of the day that the British authorities in Ireland realised they needed to move speedily to control the narrative around what had happened, particularly in relation to the catastrophe at Croke Park, where the casualties were all too obviously civilians. This wasn't just about imposing a singular interpretation upon those events; it was about the dissemination of an account of the afternoon's atrocity that would deflect responsibility away from the Crown forces and onto the spectators. A line was spun, first by the Chief Secretary for Ireland, Sir Hamar Greenwood, and later by a military tribunal, that the soldiers had not initiated the firing; rather they had reacted to it. Put simply, the defence was that they had acted defensively. This flew in the face of eyewitness testimony and was dismissed as 'another base lie' by *The Freeman's Journal*. After the British Labour Party delegation visited Croke Park as part of its reprisal investigations, it also took issue with the official version of events and saw 'no justification' for the actions of the Crown forces, which it deemed to have been guided by a 'spirit of calculated brutality and a lack of self-control'.

There was no pause to either the violence or the repression in the immediate aftermath of Bloody Sunday. An escalation ensued instead. Exactly a week later, on 28 November 1920, men from the West Cork Brigade of the IRA, led by Tom Barry, ambushed and killed sixteen Auxiliaries at Kilmichael, an episode that was every bit as audacious – and, in time, controversial – as that undertaken the previous Sunday morning in Dublin. Meanwhile, in British policy terms, Bloody Sunday led to what historian Charles Townshend has called a 'step-change', which involved a ramping up of its counter-insurgency campaign. In practice

> There was no pause to either the violence or the repression in the immediate aftermath of Bloody Sunday. An escalation ensued instead.

this meant the arrest and incarceration of some 500 republicans, including several TDs; the introduction of martial law across four counties in the south-west of the country; and the continuation of reprisals, the most spectacular of which was the burning of buildings and businesses in Cork city on the night of 11 and 12 December 1920, the 'crowning sequel', *The Manchester Guardian* reported, 'of a long series of incendiary fires by which servants of the Crown sought to terrorise the city and crush its militant Sinn Féin'. What it meant in Dublin was an intensification of raids and arrests – where only sixty-six raids were undertaken in Dublin in the month of October 1920, 274 were carried out between 26 and 31 November, and 859 in the following month. This represented the peak of Crown-force activity in the city and county for the entire period of the Anglo-Irish war.

That war, then, had already moved on as the dead of 'Bloody Sunday' were being laid to rest. Nine of those killed on the Sunday morning were returned to London for burial, where they were afforded all the trappings of a state funeral – Lloyd George attended, as did Greenwood, Field Marshal Sir Henry Wilson and a representative of the King. Before these bodies had been transported from Ireland, gun carriages draped in Union Jacks carried their coffins through the streets of Dublin accompanied by a cortège of more than a thousand troops.

Stricter rules applied to the funerals of the Croke Park victims, though their funeral Masses in Dublin and elsewhere attracted large crowds of local sympathisers. Among those victims, however, it was only Michael Hogan whose name would take hold in the public imagination, helped by the GAA who, in the 1920s, named their main Croke Park stand in his honour and erected a monument to his memory in his native Grangemockler. Of the other Croke Park victims, little was known of their personal stories, and eight would lie in unmarked graves until sportswriter Michael Foley afforded them, in all their innocence and uniqueness, a principal billing in his 2014 book *The Bloodied Field*. Foley's book provided the impetus for a 'Bloody Sunday Graves Project', where the GAA and Glasnevin Trust liaised with relatives of victims to ensure that headstones were erected where necessary and graves were properly tended to where needed.

One of the first gravestones to be unveiled was in honour of James Matthews, a thirty-eight-year-old labourer from North Cumberland Road at the time of his death. Sixty of Matthews' living relatives attended the ceremony in August 2016, among them his daughter, ninety-five-year-old Nancy Dillon, who was born three months after the events of Bloody Sunday. 'I did not know him,' she said of her father, 'I had only seen his picture.'

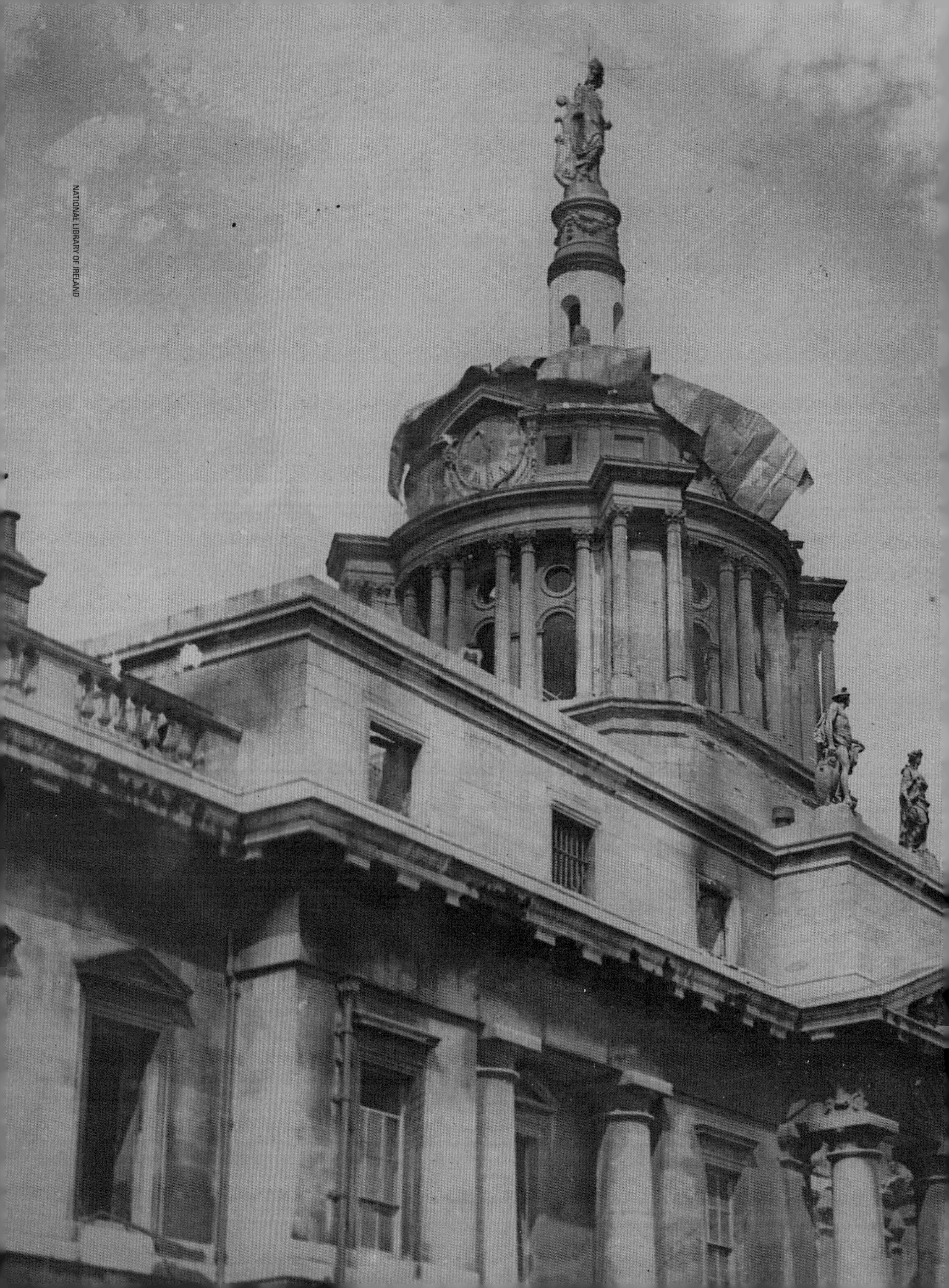

NATIONAL LIBRARY OF IRELAND

1921

'If I am a traitor, let the Irish people decide it or not, and if there are men who act towards me as a traitor I am prepared to meet them anywhere, any time, now as in the past.'

Michael Collins
14 DECEMBER

1921

7 JAN
The propaganda department of Dáil Éireann dismisses reports that Éamon de Valera, President of Sinn Féin, has been invited to talks in London with the British Prime Minister.

8 JAN
The National Executive of the Irish Labour Party and Trades Union Congress (ILP&TUC) issues an open letter to British workers urging their support for Ireland to decide its constitutional future.

11 JAN
For the first time in the long history of the Old Bailey, women are sworn onto juries for the trials of prisoners.

▽ **17 JAN**
A 40-hour military blockade of Dublin's north inner city ends – the area impacted encompassed North King Street, Church Street, Inn's Quay and **Upper Ormond Quay**.

Surrounded by salvaged possessions, a woman stands outside the farmhouse of her widowed mother in Meelin, Co. Cork, destroyed in a reprisal attack, January 1921.

Ambushes and Reprisals Signal the Start of 1921

10 January – Despite speculation about a possible truce, the cycle of violence has continued into the New Year.

Much of the most recent unrest has been reported in areas under martial law.

In County Cork, a large group of republicans ambushed two military lorries near Newmarket on 5 January. The lorries, each carrying five soldiers and one policeman, were driving near Meelin when they were fired at from a steep hill which overlooks the road. According to a correspondent for *The Cork Examiner*, the attackers used a machine gun in the ambush. The soldiers and police jumped out of the vehicles and took shelter before returning fire. Reinforcements soon arrived from Kanturk, and the attackers were chased back up the hill. No member of the Crown forces was injured, but blood at the scene indicated that some of the attacking party were wounded. Reports that 16 Sinn Féiners were killed in the exchange have been denied by the Press Association.

After the attack, the military visited the village of Meelin and six men were arrested and taken to Newmarket. Later, in reprisal for the ambush, four houses in Meelin were destroyed by 'order of the Military Governor'.

In Cork city, Finbarr Darcy, formerly of the Alexian Order, was shot dead when Crown forces raided the Imperial Hotel at 1 a.m. on 5 January. It is understood that when Darcy became aware that the military were on the premises, he tried to flee but was arrested. En route to the Bridewell, it was claimed that Darcy tried to escape and he was shot dead. Darcy, a native of Riverstown, had been a lay brother at Twyford Abbey Nursing Home for Gentlemen near London for two and a half years. He left Twyford for Manchester three years ago and returned to Ireland in 1918.

In Waterford, two members of the IRA were killed on 7 January when a military patrol was ambushed on the outskirts of Tramore. At the time of the attack, the patrol, led by the County Inspector Captain O'Beirne, was en route to help relieve Tramore RIC Barracks, which had been attacked the previous night. Heavy fighting ensued, during which two Sinn Féiners are understood to have been killed. The dead were identified as Michael McGrath, a carpenter of Poleberry, Waterford, and Thomas O'Brien from Ballycraddock. Nine or ten of the ambush party are understood to have been wounded. In the aftermath of the attack on the police station and the ambush, the Sinn Féin hall in Tramore was burned.

Irish White Cross Founded to Assist in Relief and Reconstruction of Country

2 February – A new organisation, the Irish White Cross, was established at a meeting in Dublin's Mansion House yesterday. Its purpose will be to assist with relief and reconstruction in the country.

It is envisaged that the Irish White Cross will act in cooperation with similar relief committees that have been established in America. The meeting, presided over by Lord Mayor of Dublin Laurence O'Neill, heard that the Society of Friends in New York had already contributed $50,000 to help launch the initiative.

Among those to welcome the new organisation has been Sinn Féin President Éamon de Valera, who has promised every support he can offer. Cardinal Michael Logue, Catholic Primate of All Ireland, has also offered his assistance: 'Even if peace were restored, of which there seems little prospect at present, all the help which can be obtained shall be necessary, to restore the country from the wreck to which it has been reduced, and to help those who have been left destitute by the

Cardinal Michael Logue, Catholic Primate of All Ireland.

1921

18 JAN
It is reported that two women have been abducted from outside their homes in Ranelagh.

27 JAN ▷
In an open letter to his Wexford constituents, **Roger Sweetman** announces the resignation of his Dáil seat due to a 'radical disagreement' with fellow Sinn Féin TDs. This follows a Dáil discussion on possible truce negotiations.

29 JAN
It is reported that 50,000 Dubliners, among them 8,000 ex-servicemen, are unemployed. In all, 40,000 war veterans are understood to be without work.

1 FEB
Cornelius Murphy, a farmer and IRA Volunteer from Rathmore, Co. Kerry, is executed at Victoria Barracks, Cork, after being found guilty of possessing a loaded revolver.

1 FEB
The Irish White Cross is founded at a meeting in Dublin with the aim of assisting relief and reconstruction efforts across the country during the Anglo-Irish war.

1921

4 FEB
Sir Edward Carson resigns as leader of the Ulster Unionists in favour of Sir James Craig.

◁ **5 FEB**
Seventy-six-year-old **Katharine Parnell**, widow of the late Irish nationalist leader, Charles Stewart Parnell and better known as Kitty O'Shea, dies in Brighton.

14 FEB
Representatives of the American Committee for Relief in Ireland visit the town of Balbriggan, destroyed by the Black and Tans the previous September.

14 FEB
A man is discovered dead on a street in Cork with a note attached to his body. It reads: 'A convicted spy. Penalty: Death. Let all spies and traitors beware'.

◁ **15 FEB**
Three IRA men and nine civilians are killed after the IRA attempt to ambush a train at Upton, Co. Cork.

murder of those on whom they depended, or ruined by the destruction of their property.'

The Cardinal will become president of the new organisation, the trustees of which include Archbishop of Dublin William Walsh, Sinn Féin TD Arthur Griffith, Molly Childers, Jennie Wyse Power and Tom Johnson. The Executive Committee will include Hanna Sheehy Skeffington, Kathleen Clarke and Mary Kettle.

Carson Steps Down but Urges New Ulster Parliament to Serve the Whole Community

5 February – With a new Parliament in Belfast set to open later this year, the leadership of the Ulster Unionist Party has transferred from Sir Edward Carson to Sir James Craig.

The changeover was confirmed at a meeting of the Ulster Unionist Council yesterday in Belfast, where a large attendance of delegates unanimously endorsed Craig's appointment.

Mr Carson, who presided at the meeting, explained that his decision to step down as leader was due to age and energy and his belief that the man who will be required to build the new Parliament will need to work morning to night. While Mr Carson will continue to serve in Westminster, he said the fact that there would be a Parliament in Belfast would ensure that Ulster would no longer be a pawn in the political game. He urged delegates to show his successor the same loyalty that they had accorded to him in the past.

To the Ulster Unionist Council delegates he said, 'You will be a Parliament for the whole community. We used to say we could not trust an Irish Parliament in Dublin to do justice to the Protestant minority. Let us take care that that reproach can no longer be made against your Parliament, and from the outset let us see that the Catholic minority have nothing to fear from a Protestant majority.'

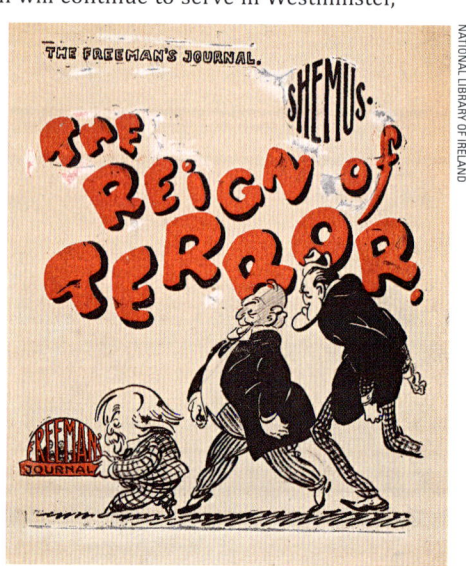

Edward Carson shown in a Shemus cartoon with David Lloyd George and Hamar Greenwood. Lloyd George carries a small cage-like item with miniature prisoners inside.

300   REVOLUTIONARY TIMES 1913–23

Among those paying tribute to Mr Carson is the *Belfast News Letter*, which stated in an editorial today that the people of Ulster owed a deep debt of gratitude to the Dublin-born barrister for 'the courage, wisdom, and single-minded devotion to their interests with which he has led them for so many years'.

As Carson steps away from the leadership, the choice of successor comes as no surprise. Sir James Craig has been his top lieutenant and is a staunch imperialist. He secured election to Westminster in 1906 for the East Down constituency. He increased his majority in the 1910 election, and in December 1918 he returned with a majority of 9,932 votes over his Sinn Féin opponent in mid-Down.

Large crowds turn out for the funerals of Alderman George Clancy and Councillor Michael O'Callaghan, 11 March 1921.

Limerick in Shock After Mayor and Former Mayor Murdered

9 March – The city of Limerick is in a state of shock in the wake of the murder of its mayor, Alderman George Clancy, and former mayor, Councillor Michael O'Callaghan, in the early hours of 7 March.

In an episode that evokes memories of the killing of Cork Lord Mayor Tomás MacCurtain almost a year ago, both men were killed after midnight in their respective homes in the presence of their wives.

The *Limerick Chronicle* has described the murdered men as 'exemplary citizens' and 'young men in the prime of their life'. Both were Sinn Féiners, although the *Chronicle* says that they were 'men of moderate views,

1921

19 FEB
Frank Percy Crozier resigns as commanding officer of the Auxiliary Division in disgust at the behaviour of his men and the British system of administration in Ireland.

20 FEB
Twelve IRA men are killed in Clonmult, east Cork, when the disused farmhouse they were using as a base is attacked by members of the Hampshire Regiment, the RIC and the Auxiliaries.

24 FEB
Muriel MacSwiney attends the first production at the Abbey Theatre of *The Revolutionist*, a play written by her husband, Terence, who died on hunger strike at Brixton Prison the previous October.

26 FEB ▽
Ireland edge Scotland 9–8 in the **Five Nations** rugby championship at Lansdowne Road in Dublin.

28 FEB
Six IRA men are executed in Victoria Barracks in Cork, among them five who were captured a month earlier during an ambush at Dripsey.

1921

△ 6–7 MAR
Dubbed the 'Curfew Murders', Limerick's Mayor **George Clancy** and ex-Mayor **Michael O'Callaghan** are murdered in their respective homes by Auxiliaries, as is Joseph O'Donoghue of the Mid-Limerick Brigade, IRA.

11 MAR
Six IRA men are killed when ambushed by Crown forces at Selton Hill, near Mohill, Co. Leitrim.

▽ 14 MAR
Six men are hanged in Mountjoy Prison: four (Francis Flood, Bernard Ryan, Thomas Bryan and Patrick Doyle) for their involvement in an ambush in Drumcondra on 21 January and two (**Thomas Whelan** (centre) and Patrick Moran) for their involvement in the killings on Bloody Sunday morning, 21 November 1920.

and tolerant towards those who differed from them politically, while as corporators they stood for the efficient administration of civic affairs'.

Today, the city flag is being flown at half-mast and death notices draped in black have been affixed to the entrance door of the Town Hall. They read: 'Alderman George Clancy, Mayor of Limerick, murdered 7th March, 1921, RIP'; 'Councillor Michael O'Callaghan, ex-Mayor of Limerick, murdered 7th March 1921, RIP'.

The raid that resulted in Mr Clancy's death began at 1.30 a.m. The household was woken by a loud knock on the door, and when Mr Clancy asked who was there, a voice responded, 'Military.' When he opened the door, there were three men in front of him. 'Are you Mr Clancy?' one of the men asked, and when he responded, 'Yes', he was ordered to go outside. When he refused, one of the men fired three shots at him, before levelling the revolver and firing three more times. Mrs Clancy was hit on the wrist when she moved to protect her husband.

The circumstances surrounding Mr O'Callaghan's murder are very similar. He and his wife, Kate, were awoken by a loud knocking. When they asked who was there, they were told 'Police and military.' When O'Callaghan asked what they wanted, the response was, 'We want you.' When Mrs O'Callaghan opened the door, a group of men ran into the house. They fired a shot at Mr O'Callaghan, causing him to fall down the stairs, and as he lay on the ground, they shot him several more times.

De Valera: Ireland Desires Peace, but Partition Cannot Be Basis of Settlement

1 April – David Lloyd George can have peace with Ireland tomorrow if he wants it, according to Éamon de Valera.

The Sinn Féin leader, in a statement delivered to press representatives yesterday, stressed that the Irish people desired peace but rejected the idea that England's interests were on a par with Ireland's rights. 'Time after time,' Mr de Valera said, 'we have indicated that if England can show any right with which Ireland's right as a nation would clash we are willing that these be adjusted by negotiation and treaty.'

Mr de Valera said that, notwithstanding the Prime Minister's claims to the contrary, the British government had never shown any appetite for dealing honestly with them – he argued that Lloyd George's only contribution to a settlement has been the 'odious Partition Act', which Mr de Valera did not believe could provide the basis of a lasting peace.

He was speaking in the wake of the Prime Minister's recent announcement that this legislation, officially known as the Government of Ireland Act, which allows for the creation of two new Parliaments in

A peace vigil held in 1921 outside the Mansion House was symbolic of the public's desire for the conflict in Ireland to end.

Ireland, remains the policy of choice. Lloyd George informed the House of Commons that the Act will come into force on 3 May, with arrangements being made to hold elections North and South the following month.

Speaking in the House of Commons on 23 March, Mr Lloyd George insisted that he was prepared to sit down and discuss the situation with responsible, elected Irish leaders, but there had been no response to his invitation. He added that the reluctance to do so suggested that there was no Irish leader with the moral courage to tell the people that 'for the sake of Ireland I am going to abandon this and accept that'.

Craig and De Valera Hold Historic Meeting, but Ulster Will Offer No More Concessions

9 May – Ulster will make no further concessions to find a solution to the Irish question, James Craig has stated during a speech at a Unionist Party meeting.

In accepting the Government of Ireland Act, Ulster has gone as far as it is willing to go and no further discussion will be entered into.

Craig was speaking in Belfast on 6 May in the aftermath of his historic meeting with Éamon de Valera, Sinn Féin President. Mr Craig said that he had left Mr de Valera in no doubt that Ulster would not accept a republic, and he defied any authority, whether it be the British government or Mr de Valera, to take their Parliament from them once it was rooted in the soil.

Craig said the invitation from Mr de Valera had come like a 'thunderbolt' after he had been summoned to Dublin to meet with the new Lord Lieutenant, Edmund Talbot.

1921

14 MAR
Sixty-year-old Protestant woman Maria Lindsay and her chauffeur, James Clarke, are killed by the IRA in Cork on charges of being informers and contributing to the capture by Crown forces of ten men at the ambush in Dripsey, five of whom were subsequently executed.

17 MAR
The IRA ambush a four-man RIC patrol in Clifden, County Galway and two are killed. In response, the RIC attacks buildings in Clifden and burns down 16 houses. A hotel owned by Alexander McDonnell is also burned and his son, John Joe, shot dead.

18 MAR △
Shaun Spadah wins the Aintree Grand National. The horse was bred in Streamstown, Co. Westmeath, by Patrick McKenna.

21 MAR
Austen Chamberlain is elected to succeed Andrew Bonar Law as the new leader of the Tory Party in the House of Commons. Bonar Law had resigned the position due to ill health.

1921

21 MAR
The IRA ambush a train at Headford Junction in Kerry that is carrying British troops. A gun battle ensues and at least 13 (eight British soldiers, two IRA men and three civilians) are killed.

25 MAR
After the killing of an RIC sergeant in County Mayo four days earlier, members of the RIC attack and burn houses in Westport and the surrounding area.

29 MAR
Eleven-year-old Thomas Fitzhugh is killed when the IRA set fire to a telephone exchange in Killiney, Co. Dublin. Fitzhugh lived above the exchange with his mother, who was the resident operator.

▽ **1 APR**
A court martial in Belfast sentences Sligo-based nurse Linda Kearns to ten years' penal servitude. The case against Kearns rested on a Dublin Castle charge that on 20 November 1920 rifles, revolvers and ammunition were discovered in her car when it was intercepted en route from Sligo to Dublin.

He was accompanied by Captain Herbert Dixon to the meeting with the Sinn Féin leader. According to the *Irish Independent*, Dixon described how Craig had 'gone alone and unarmed and had met the Sinn Féin leader in a house far from Dublin. He thought the Ulster loyalists might be proud of a leader who had shown such dauntless courage, for he did not think a pluckier thing was performed even during the war than to venture alone right into the camp of the enemy.'

Dixon explained that Craig used the opportunity to make it clear to Mr de Valera that Ulster 'stood where she stood', that they wished for peace and that they would go to any lengths to help the South of Ireland.

Despite the lack of an immediate agreement, the very fact that the leader of Sinn Féin and the leader of northern unionism had come together, 'if only for half an hour', has been described by *The Irish Times* as 'a political event of the first importance'. 'It is', the newspaper editorialised, 'the most hopeful news that a despondent and almost despairing country has heard for a long time.'

The Ulster Cabinet. L-R: Sir Dawson Bates, the Marquis of Londonderry, Sir James Craig, H.M. Pollock, E.M. Archdale and J.M. Andrews, July 1921.

Iconic Custom House Destroyed During IRA Attack

Dublin, 26 May – One of Dublin's most iconic buildings, the James Gandon-designed Custom House, which has stood on the banks of the River Liffey since the late 18th century, has been destroyed in an arson attack for which Dáil Éireann has claimed responsibility.

An official report issued by the military authorities in Dublin stated that about 100 assailants rushed the building at about 1.10 p.m. on 25 May. The attackers gathered the staff in the central hall before setting on fire the offices and other rooms throughout the building.

According to the statement, Crown forces rushed to the scene and raced into the burning building, where they discovered petrol tins and discarded revolvers. Their arrival was followed by a gunfight with IRA patrols posted in the vicinity. The *Irish Bulletin* states that 'in the fighting, both at the doors of the building and outside it, there were casualties on both sides, the exact number of which it is not yet possible to ascertain'.

1921

According to an *Irish Independent* report, at least seven people were killed and ten wounded as a result of the fighting. Among the dead is Patrick O'Reilly, who is described as an IRA captain. He was employed as a clerk in Arnotts.

The purpose of the attack was to frustrate the work of the Local Government Board and other public departments by destroying official papers and records, including those of the Customs and Inland Revenue departments.

Lamenting the damage done to what it has described as 'one of Dublin's largest and most beautiful buildings', *The Irish Times* has expressed doubt that even its framework can be saved. In a barbed editorial, the newspaper notes, 'This destruction is the work of Irishmen – the latest triumph of the republican arms. The burning of Gandon's Custom House is the costliest and most reckless "operation of war" from which Dublin has suffered since the rebellion of 1916.'

The *Irish Bulletin*, in justifying the attack, said the damage to the building was regrettable but necessary, and it criticised elements of the British press for a double standard in not expressing the same outrage at the destruction being done to cities, town halls, shops and residences throughout the country. 'We, in common with the rest of the nation, regret the destruction of historic buildings. But the lives of 4,000,000 people are a more sacred charge than any architectural masterpiece. The Custom House was one of the seats of an alien tyranny … The destruction was an unavoidable military necessity.'

Dublin's Custom House on fire, 25 May 1921.

The statue of Hope still standing on the top of the Custom House after the fire.

3 APR
Vincent Fovargue is found dead on the Ashford Manor Golf Course in Middlesex. His body has four bullet wounds; nearby lies a piece of paper that states: 'Let spies and traitors beware – IRA'.

6 APR
The Irish Labour Party publishes a 20-point manifesto aimed at tackling what it has termed the 'evil' of unemployment and poverty.

11 APR
The Executive Committee of the Women's National Liberal Federation calls on the government to announce a truce and amnesty in Ireland, and to withdraw all Auxiliary forces with immediate effect.

REVOLUTIONARY TIMES 1913–23

1921

17 APR
Constable William Duncan of the RIC is accidentally shot dead in Dungarvan Police Barracks. Some members of the force were playing in 'a friendly manner' when a revolver went off unexpectedly.

△ **2 MAY**
Lord FitzAlan (or Lord Edmund Talbot as he is also known) arrives into Dún Laoghaire, accompanied by Lady FitzAlan. The new viceroy is the first Roman Catholic to hold the office in recent times and hails from a well-known British aristocratic family.

4 MAY
Members of the RIC in Rathmore, County Kerry, are sent to inspect a bog road on news that a body has been found with a label attached stating: 'Convicted Spy – Spies Beware'. On finding the body, the RIC come under attack by the IRA and eight RIC men are killed or fatally wounded.

Unionists Win 40 Seats in New Ulster Parliament

31 May – Unionists have swept to a convincing victory in the Northern Parliament's first elections, held on 24 May, winning 40 out of the 52 available seats.

The remaining 12 seats have been shared between Sinn Féin and the Nationalist Party, with each securing six seats. Neither Sinn Féin nor the Joseph Devlin-led Nationalists will take their seats in the new chamber. Devlin was elected in two constituencies, and it is expected that he will be replaced by a Unionist when he vacates one of them, which will further increase the pro-partition majority.

The first parliamentary session is set to be held in Belfast City Hall on 7 June, with the formal opening taking place on 22 June.

For those opposed to partition, the results, while disappointing, are not unexpected; they have been attributed to a number of factors including accusations that nationalist voters were intimidated and terrorised, and that the gerrymandering of constituencies made it impossible for anyone other than Unionists to win. The *Irish Independent* has accused the British government and its agents of not just 'winking' at this policy but of having 'deliberately encouraged and assisted it'.

Alongside the gerrymandering, there were many reports of intimidation at polling booths and elsewhere. A Sinn Féin election agent at Drumbo, Co. Down, for instance, alleged that he and a colleague were expelled from a polling station and met outside by a crowd shouting, 'No popery in Drumbo.'

Union Jack-waving shipyard workers in Belfast, May 1921.

REVOLUTIONARY TIMES 1913–23

A train from Belfast was also attacked by a large crowd at Lisburn station. On board the train were expelled Catholic workers returning to cast their vote. The windows of the train were smashed, and it is reported that the passengers had to flee the station.

In a celebration to mark the election of six Unionists in Ballymoney, Co. Antrim, a procession was held, which was headed by a large banner bearing the inscription: 'What we have won at the ballot we will hold with the bayonet'.

Leinster Votes to Break Away from Belfast-based Irish Football Association

2 June – Last night, at the annual meeting of the Leinster Football Association (LFA) in Dublin, an overwhelming majority of committee members voted to break away from the Belfast-based Irish Football Association (IFA), which until now has governed soccer in Ireland.

The meeting of the LFA, held in Molesworth Hall, was chaired by Harry Wigoder, who was re-elected president of the Leinster association.

The following resolution, advocating for a split in Irish soccer administration, which had been sent to all clubs, was put to the meeting: 'That the time has come when a new association should be formed independent of the Irish Football Association Ltd. That the newly elected Council of the Leinster Football Association should constitute themselves for the purpose of establishing a new body and report to a full meeting of the clubs when the draft constitution and rules have been considered.'

Proposing the resolution, Larry Sheridan insisted that ultimately this was a decision for the clubs and was an unprecedented step that would cut Leinster adrift. Mr Sheridan noted that some of the Leinster clubs, including Shelbourne and St James's Gate, had been victimised by the IFA and thought it would be in the interests of Leinster football if they took their courage in their hands and cut the connection to Belfast.

The 1920s IFA badge.

The Leinster-based Shelbourne FC team in 1914.

1921

6 MAY
James Craig, speaking in Belfast in the aftermath of his historic meeting with Sinn Féin president Éamon de Valera, which took place in secret on 5 May, says that in accepting the Government of Ireland Act, Ulster has reached the limit of its concessions and no further discussion will be entered into.

24 MAY
Unionists sweep to a convincing victory in the first elections to the soon to be opened Northern Parliament. They win 40 of the 52 seats amid intimidation and gerrymandering claims.

25 MAY △
Over 120 members of the Dublin Brigade of the IRA storm the iconic **Custom House** building on the banks of the River Liffey in broad daylight. The attack results in the deaths of five IRA men and four civilians, with between 70 to 80 IRA men arrested.

1921

3 JUN
A 21-year-old woman, Kathleen Anderson Wright, is shot dead in the grounds of Trinity College Park while watching a cricket match.

7 JUN
The new Northern Parliament is formally inaugurated at Belfast City Hall. The ceremony is presided over by the Lord Lieutenant of Ireland, Lord FitzAlan, who, in a speech after the short ceremony, makes the extraordinary observation that while nobody seems to want the new Parliament, Northern Ireland has still done the right thing in accepting the Government of Ireland Act.

△ **22 JUN**
There are spectacular scenes of pomp and celebration in Belfast as King George formally opens the new Northern Parliament.

Short Royal Visit Marks Formal Opening of New Northern Parliament in Belfast

23 June – There were spectacular scenes of pomp and celebration in Belfast yesterday as King George V formally opened the new Parliament of Northern Ireland, which was established under the terms of the Government of Ireland Act, 1920.

King George and Queen Mary travelled from London to Holyhead and sailed into Belfast Lough on the royal yacht, escorted by 13 warships, for the event.

The centrepiece of the occasion was the speech delivered by the King, in which he recalled his happy memories of Ireland and expressed confidence in the fairness that he believes the Northern Parliament will extend to every creed and interest. The speech did not set out any legislative programme, but rather emphasised a desire for harmony among Irish people into the future: 'May this historic gathering be the prelude of a day in which the Irish people, north and south, under one Parliament or two, as those Parliaments may themselves decide, shall work together in common love for Ireland upon the sure foundations of mutual justice and respect.'

The speech delivered by the King was prepared on the advice of his ministers in Westminster.

Following the opening of the Parliament, Ulster leader Sir James Craig sent a telegram to Prime Minister David Lloyd George, noting the 'scenes of unexampled enthusiasm' that accompanied the occasion. The King and Queen, Mr Craig wrote, had personally expressed their appreciation of the arrangements for the day and were 'deeply' touched by 'the demonstrations of loyalty and affection'.

For the general public, the procession through two miles of Belfast city streets afforded an opportunity to welcome the royal party, their route taking in Dublin Road, Great Victoria Street and Donegall Place. The streets along the route were festooned with red, white and blue flags and bunting, with the archways in the street bearing such mottoes as 'Down with Sinn Féin', 'Down with traitors', 'Our King, Our Queen, Our Empire' and 'Victory and Peace'. The event drew crowds of people from all over Ulster.

King George and Queen Mary attend the opening of the new Belfast Parliament.

Lloyd George Invites Craig and de Valera to Attend Peace Conference

29 June – British Prime Minister David Lloyd George has extended an offer to James Craig and Éamon de Valera to travel to London for a conference with the purpose of 'exploring to the utmost the possibility of a settlement' of the Irish question.

The move has been described by the *Irish Independent* as an 'event of the greatest importance'. It comes without conditions, and Mr de Valera and any of the colleagues he chooses to bring with him are ensured a safe passage to London.

The invitation, dated 24 June, refers to the recent conciliatory speech by King George V at the opening of the Northern Parliament, where he voiced his keen desire for a 'satisfactory solution of the age-long Irish problems which for generations embarrassed our forefathers as they now weigh heavily upon us'.

After a discussion with his colleagues, Sir James Craig, Prime Minister of Northern Ireland, has accepted the invitation and will travel to London with all members of his Cabinet, with the exception of Sir Dawson Bates, the Home Secretary.

Mr de Valera has responded to the British Prime Minister without giving a definite answer as to whether he would attend or not. 'I am in consultation,' he wrote, 'with such of the principal representatives of our nation as are available. We most earnestly desire to help in bringing about a lasting peace between the peoples of these two islands but see no avenue by which it can be reached if you deny Ireland's essential unity and set aside the principle of national self-determination. Before replying more fully to your letter I am seeking a conference with certain representatives of the political minority in this country.'

Lloyd George tries to entice the Irish into peace talks, with a suspicious Craig watching on.

1921

24 JUN
British Prime Minister David Lloyd George extends an offer to Craig and de Valera to travel to London for a conference with the purpose of 'exploring to the utmost the possibility of a settlement' of the Irish question.

11 JUL
The Anglo-Irish war ends in a truce, which takes effect at noon.

14 JUL △
Éamon de Valera travels to London and meets with **David Lloyd George** at Downing Street for the first time.

20 JUL
Éamon de Valera is appointed Chancellor of the National University of Ireland.

25 JUL
A mysterious figure, who has been riding a horse through the streets of Dublin in full cowboy dress, is identified. A recently returned emigrant from Wyoming in the US, he goes by the name of Liam de Burca and is known as 'Tipp' to his Dublin friends.

REVOLUTIONARY TIMES 1913–23

1921

8 AUG
The growth of the ITGWU continues unabated. Figures disclosed by the Labour Party and Trade Union Congress show that membership has reached approximately 100,000, with 375 branches represented countrywide.

10 AUG
The 33 remaining members of Dáil Éireann held by the British are released from prison. Dublin Castle announces that the release is to facilitate the steps towards peace and allow the men to attend the meeting of the Dáil on 16 August.

◁ **16 AUG**
The **first meeting of Dáil Éireann** since the May elections is held at the Mansion House in Dublin. The elected representatives reaffirm their loyalty to the Dáil, swear an oath of allegiance and pledge themselves to 'support and defend the Irish Republic and the Government of the Irish Republic, which is Dáil Éireann, against all enemies, foreign and domestic'.

Hostilities Cease as Truce Agreed Upon Between Britain and Ireland

12 July – The Truce negotiated between Britain and Ireland came into effect at midday yesterday.

The cessation of hostilities was accompanied by an announcement from British military headquarters that curfew restrictions are to be lifted across the country.

Mr de Valera has urged discipline and compliance with the Truce and said that 'each individual soldier and citizen must regard himself as a custodian of the nation's honour'.

De Valera added that the political representatives would do their 'utmost to secure a just and peaceful termination of this struggle', but he cautioned that history was a warning against 'undue confidence'. Should force be resumed against the Irish nation, Mr de Valera advised that citizens 'must be ready on your part once more to resist'.

Prime Minister David Lloyd George telegrammed the Sinn Féin leader to say that he would be 'happy' to see him and his colleagues at Downing Street this week on a day of de Valera's choosing.

The terms of the Truce were agreed upon at a meeting at the British Military Headquarters on Parkgate Street, which was attended by General Nevil Macready, Colonel John Brind and Assistant Undersecretary for Ireland Alfred Cope acting for the British authorities; and Commandant Robert Barton and Commandant Éamonn Duggan acting on behalf of Dáil Éireann.

The Truce has been widely welcomed and a more relaxed atmosphere is evident in many parts of the country.

Original caricatures of Éamon de Valera and Arthur Griffith by David Low, published in The Star, *14 July 1921.*

310   REVOLUTIONARY TIMES 1913–23

1921

Dáil Éireann meets in the Mansion House, August 1921.

Second Dáil Opens in Dublin's Mansion House

17 August – The opening session of the Second Dáil was held in the Round Room at the Mansion House in Dublin yesterday. This is the first meeting since the May elections, which saw many Sinn Féin candidates elected unopposed.

The elected representatives reaffirmed their loyalty and swore an oath of allegiance, pledging themselves to 'support and defend the Irish Republic and the Government of the Irish Republic, which is Dáil Éireann, against all enemies, foreign and domestic'.

The centrepiece of the occasion was a lengthy speech by Éamon de Valera, who exclaimed, 'We are not Republican doctrinaires.' However, in setting out the position of Sinn Féin in relation to the peace negotiations, Mr de Valera said that the Irish Republic should be recognised by the British government, and that it was only on the basis of such recognition that Sinn Féin would deal with them. Mr de Valera added that there would be no need for negotiations if Britain recognised the right of Ireland to self-determination on the principle enunciated by Prime Minister Lloyd George in respect of Belgium and Poland.

2–3 SEP ▽
Cleeve's Mills and Bakery in Bruree, Co. Limerick, is handed back to its owners after a week, during which time it was occupied and controlled by its workers and a red flag was flown above the premises.

1921

All members, many of them wearing a *fáinne* – indicating fluency in the Irish language – stood to take the oath of allegiance; then they were called separately to sign the roll. As he was representing the constituency of Armagh, Michael Collins was the first up, and the calling of his name was met with loud applause, which the Speaker attempted in vain to silence.

Margaret Pearse, TD for Dublin county and mother of two executed leaders of the 1916 Rising, signed the roll dressed in mourning attire, as did Kate O'Callaghan, TD for Limerick city, whose husband was murdered by Crown forces earlier this year.

△ **11 SEP**
Michael Collins TD, Minister for Finance in the Dáil Éireann administration, throws in the ball to start the Leinster hurling final at Croke Park. In excess of 17,000 spectators turn out in fine weather to see defending champions Dublin withstand the challenge of Kilkenny on a scoreline of 4–4 to 1–5.

17 SEP
The soccer season begins with eight Dublin-based teams competing in the inaugural season to be played under the control of the Football Association of Ireland (FAI), which split from the Belfast-controlled Irish Football Association (IFA) earlier in the year.

30 SEP
The Irish agree to talks with the British government on the future relationship between the two nations.

Anti-partition Protests Gather Momentum as Deputations Meet with De Valera

17 September – Nationalist momentum is building in the Six Counties behind a campaign to resist the imposition of partition on the island of Ireland.

A deputation from Co. Armagh travelled to Dublin's Mansion House yesterday to meet with Sinn Féin President Éamon de Valera to express the firm determination of nationalists in that county to oppose any attempt to coerce them under the new six-county Parliament.

In addition to highlighting Armagh's proud place in Irish history, the delegation pointed out that there was a solid anti-partition bloc in South Armagh and the adjoining constituencies of South and East Down.

Seamus O'Reilly, who chaired the deputation, argued that the partition act went against the principle of self-determination expressed by the great majority of the Irish people, as it was contradictory to the form of government they had voted for and created.

Mr O'Reilly noted that in the recent elections, the combined vote from Armagh, Tyrone and Fermanagh resulted in a 5,000 majority opposed to partition, meaning that the larger part of the area under the control of the Northern Parliament must be considered anti-partitionist. He concluded by pointing out that, while Catholics accounted for 40% of the population of Armagh (32% are Church of Ireland, 15% Presbyterian, 4% Methodist and 2% other), Catholics paid more rates than any other religious grouping, and he urged that a special means of resistance be devised should it be necessary.

The Armagh deputation is the latest in a series of groups from the Six Counties to visit Mr de Valera in recent days. A group of Sinn Féiners from the city of Derry has previously been received in Dublin, as well delegations from south and east Down, Tyrone and Fermanagh.

1921

Historic Anglo-Irish Peace Conference Begins at Downing Street

London, 12 October – A historic conference to determine the constitutional future of Ireland and its relationship with the United Kingdom began yesterday in London.

At 11 a.m. the first session commenced at No. 10 Downing Street, the Irish delegation being welcomed on arrival at Whitehall by thousands of Irish sympathisers who sang Irish songs, hymns and recited the Rosary.

Representing the British at the conference were Prime Minister David Lloyd George, Lord Chancellor F.E. Smith, Winston Churchill, Laming Worthington-Evans, Hamar Greenwood and Gordon Hewart. The Irish were represented by their plenipotentiaries Arthur Griffith, Michael Collins, Robert Barton, Éamonn Duggan and George Gavan Duffy. Absent for the British team was Austen Chamberlain, who was unwell.

9 OCT △
A Dublin-bound passenger steamer, the **SS Rowan**, sinks in the Irish Sea shortly after midnight as it is making its way, in dense fog and darkness, from Glasgow to Dublin. Thirty-six crew and passengers drown.

Arthur Griffith departs for London from Dun Laoghaire en route to conference talks in London.

REVOLUTIONARY TIMES 1913–23

1921

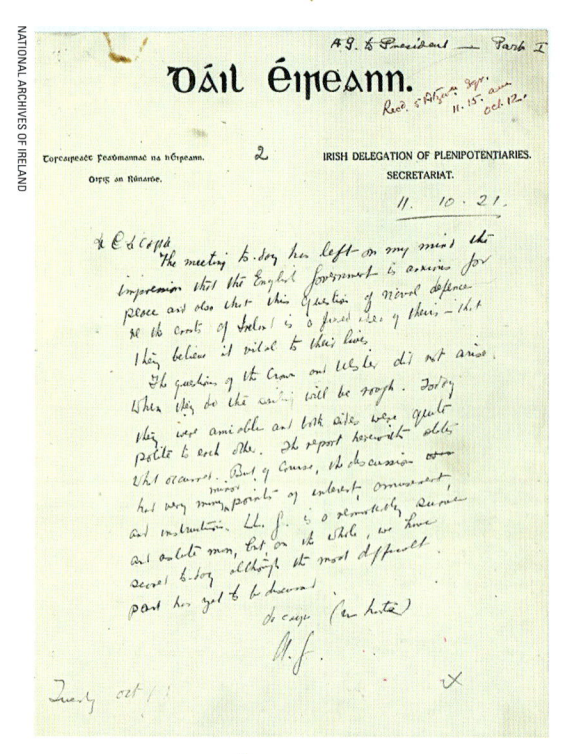

Arthur Griffith writes to Éamon de Valera following the first meeting of the Irish and British delegations, giving his impressions of the day.

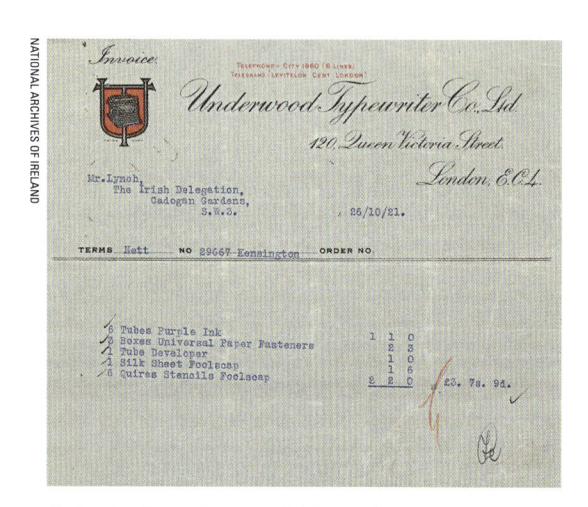

An invoice for stationery and office equipment delivered to the Irish delegation's office at Cadogan Gardens in London.

Also in attendance were Thomas Jones and Lionel Curtis, the British secretaries, and their Irish counterparts, Erskine Childers and John Chartres.

On entering No. 10, it is understood that the Irish delegation and their secretarial staff were shown into a reception room before being taken to the Cabinet room, where Art O'Brien, Dáil Éireann's representative in London, introduced them all individually to the waiting British Prime Minister, who shook hands with each of them. Mr O'Brien then withdrew and the Irish delegates were directed to the chair each was to occupy for the conference, where they stood opposite their British counterparts.

Before taking his own seat, Mr Lloyd George announced the names of the Irish and British parties present, who each bowed and sat down. The British Prime Minister sat directly opposite Mr Griffith.

Ulster Leaders Accused of Blocking Path to a Settlement in Peace Conference

11 November – The Cabinet of Northern Ireland met in London yesterday and reaffirmed its unwillingness to make any more concessions that might compromise the new-found status of the Belfast Parliament.

Sir James Craig, Prime Minister of Northern Ireland, arrived in London last week and attended meetings with David Lloyd George, Austen Chamberlain and Sir Laming Worthington-Evans. Following these meetings, he insisted that he had 'arranged that if and when Ulster's interest are reached in the conference all our representatives will be asked to attend. In the meantime nothing will be settled behind our backs.'

At this point he summoned his Cabinet colleagues. They met at the Savoy Hotel, where Craig briefed them on developments in the ongoing Anglo-Irish peace conference insofar as he had been made aware of them. He also outlined the course that he had pursued in these meetings. After the meeting, the Cabinet issued a statement in which it 'unanimously approved of the firm attitude maintained [by Craig] in the interests of Ulster'.

1921

The most recent proposals, to which the Ulster politicians were responding, are understood to include the establishment of Ulster as a province of an Irish dominion controlled by an all-Ireland Parliament comprising two houses. This is the type of settlement that Mr Craig's Cabinet has essentially ruled out.

The hard-line attitude of the Ulster unionist leader and his Cabinet is nevertheless supported by the great bulk of Conservative members of the coalition government, none more so than Andrew Bonar Law, who, according to friends, feels that he is honour-bound by the pledges he made to protect Ulster. It is Mr Bonar Law's belief that it would be tantamount to coercion if, after the passage of the Government of Ireland Act, 1920, Ulster were to be forced against her will into a role in an all-Ireland dominion scheme similar to that of Québec in Canada.

Ulster Division Memorial at Thiepval Unveiled

21 November – An impressive memorial to the Ulster regiment that fought and died in such large numbers on the first day of the Battle of the Somme, 1 July 1916, has been unveiled in France.

The Ulster War Memorial Tower in Thiepval is the site of the already famous advance of the 36th (Ulster) Division, and it was formally opened by Field Marshal Sir Henry Wilson, Chief of the Imperial General Staff, and dedicated by the Anglican Primate of All Ireland, Charles D'Arcy, on 19 November.

Due to illness, neither Lord Carson nor the Prime Minister of Northern Ireland, Sir James Craig, could attend the ceremony, though a party of approximately 70 did travel from Ireland. The tower at Thiepval is built on the crest of a hill where the German trenches, many of which are still intact, were dug. The Thiepval tower is an exact replica of Helen's Tower in Clandeboye, Co. Down.

In Craig's absence, the honour of unlocking the door of the tower was given to Sir Henry Wilson as 'one of Ulster's most distinguished soldiers'. Addressing the gathering, Wilson stated, 'If somebody only eight years ago had told us that we should be assembled here today on Irish soil to open a memorial to Irish dead, how we should have marvelled, how we would have smiled. You stand this morning on a sacred little bit of Ulster – that far

The Ulster Memorial Tower at Thiepval, a replica of 'Helen's Tower', which overlooks Belfast Lough.

The Duchess of Abercorn unfurling the flag on top of the Thiepval Memorial Tower.

1921

11 OCT
The historic conference to determine the constitutional future of Ireland and its relationship with the United Kingdom begins in London.

28 OCT
Over 1,600 delegates attend the opening of the 13th Sinn Féin Ard-Fheis at the Mansion House in Dublin. Éamon de Valera, who is re-elected as the party's president, describes the gathering as a 'meeting in miniature of the nation'.

4 NOV
The bodies of 26 Irish soldiers who were killed during the Great War while serving in the army of the United States arrive in Ireland for burial.

△ **15 NOV**
Tadhg Barry – journalist, trade union activist and alderman of Cork Corporation – is shot dead at Ballykinlar internment camp, Co. Down, by an 18-year-old sentry.

distant land whose sons came running to help you – and you see a beautiful building, whose foundations we trust will go deep down into the heart of France. I often think that, should clouds of suspicion and misunderstanding ever come between our two nations, a visit here to Thiepval and the sight of this memorial and all it means will quickly dispel them. Therefore, now and always, you are warmly welcomed to our Ulster home.'

Anglo-Irish Treaty Signed in London

7 December – Nearly five months after a truce brought an end to the Anglo-Irish war, and three months since the commencement of peace talks, negotiators representing the British government and Dáil Éireann have reached a historic agreement.

The Anglo-Irish Treaty was signed at 2.15 a.m. yesterday, and 15 minutes later the Exchange Telegraph Company sent the following message: 'An agreement has been reached.'

The terms of the Treaty will now be recommended for acceptance to the Westminster Parliament and to Dáil Éireann. A copy of the agreement has also been sent to Sir James Craig by special messenger.

When asked if he had anything to say when leaving Downing Street at 2.20 a.m., Michael Collins, who was accompanied by Arthur Griffith and Robert Barton, replied, 'Not a word.'

Michael Collins attending meetings in Dublin after his return from London in December 1921.

1921

Michael Collins, one of the Irish signatories of the Treaty, is greeted by supporters on arriving at the Mansion House, December 1921.

19 NOV
The Ulster War Memorial Tower at Thiepval, to commemorate the men of the 36th (Ulster) Division and all those from Ulster who fought and died in such large numbers on the first day of the Battle of the Somme, 1 July 1916, is dedicated in France.

1 DEC
The Anglo-Irish talks in London pause while the Irish consider a draft treaty tabled by the British.

3 DEC
The Irish Cabinet meets to discuss the draft treaty put forward by the British.

6 DEC ▽
The **Anglo-Irish Treaty** is signed in London.

The agreement came at the end of a day of feverish activity, which saw the British Prime Minister visit King George V, and saw the Irish plenipotentiaries visit Downing Street twice.

After the Irish delegates left Downing Street, following an afternoon discussion, an official statement issued by the British government stated that 'proposals with certain alterations and modifications had been given to the three delegates, who had gone to consult with their colleagues at the Irish delegation headquarters'.

According to the text of the Treaty, Ireland is to be afforded Dominion status with a Parliament of its own but will remain within the British Empire, similar to Australia, Canada, New Zealand and South Africa. It will be known as the Irish Free State, and the Crown will be represented by a governor general, similar to the system in Canada.

Furthermore, the agreement provides for an oath of allegiance to be taken by the members of the new Irish Free State Parliament. The Treaty allows for the territory of Northern Ireland, established under the Government of Ireland Act, 1920, to remain outside of the Free State, and should Northern Ireland exercise that option, a boundary commission is to be established to determine the borders between North and South.

REVOLUTIONARY TIMES 1913–23

1921

◁ *Margaret Pearse, the mother of Patrick Pearse, arriving at Earlsfort Terrace for the debate on the Treaty.*

△ *The Council Chamber in Earlsfort Terrace where Treaty ratification discussions were held.*

Treaty Divisions Exposed as Dáil Adjourns Until New Year

Dublin, 23 December – The Dáil Éireann debate on the Anglo-Irish Treaty has adjourned for Christmas and the New Year.

The debate began on the morning of 14 December in the Council Chamber of University College Dublin on Earlsfort Terrace. A large anxious crowd gathered outside the venue, the entrances and surrounds of which were guarded by Volunteers.

The Speaker, Eoin MacNeill, sat in a carved armchair on a dais at one end of the room. In front of him on the left-hand side was Éamon de Valera, with Austin Stack and Cathal Brugha, all opponents of the Treaty. To MacNeill's right was Arthur Griffith, and seated next to him was Michael Collins, both signatories and supporters of the Treaty.

A measure of the gravity of the discussions that followed can be gauged from the fact that approximately 60 journalists were in attendance,

1921

On 16 December 1921 the Anglo-Irish Treaty was ratified by the British Parliament. John Lavery captured the scene in his painting The Ratification of the Irish Treaty in the English House of Lords, 1921.

including representatives from newspapers as far flung as Melbourne, Madrid, France, Sweden, Germany, Rome and Washington.

After a roll call and prayers, Mr de Valera was the first to address the chamber. He began by outlining the powers of the plenipotentiaries, which, he believed, had been exceeded by the signing of the Treaty. According to Mr de Valera, the plenipotentiaries had full plenary powers to negotiate, 'with the understanding, however, that when they reported, the Cabinet would decide its policy, and whatever arrangement they arrived at, it would have to be submitted to the Dáil for ratification'. Both Griffith and Collins rejected the suggestion that they had gone beyond their remit.

At one point, and to cries of 'No, No', Mr Collins mentioned that he was aware that he had been called a traitor, adding, 'If I am a traitor, let the Irish people decide it or not, and if there are men who act towards me as a traitor I am prepared to meet them anywhere, any time, now as in the past.'

When the first public session ended, four days of private sessions followed, during which time it was difficult for the public to gauge the progress of the debates. Nevertheless, journalists congregating outside the venue observed TDs speaking amicably, if sometimes in an animated manner, with each other outside the council chamber.

The Dáil debates adjourned for Christmas on 22 December. By this point, 20 speeches had been delivered in favour of ratification of the Treaty and 18 against, with one TD, Dr Patrick McCartan, declaring that he would vote neither for nor against it.

It has been agreed that there shall be no speeches between the adjournment and 3 January, when the Dáil will reconvene, and there is growing belief that this will work to the benefit of those advocating for acceptance of the Treaty.

12 DEC
The process of releasing the final internees from jails in Ireland and Britain begins following the signing of the Anglo-Irish Treaty in London.

14 DEC
Dáil Éireann begins debating the Treaty.

16 DEC
The Westminster Parliament ratifies the Anglo-Irish Treaty.

REVOLUTIONARY TIMES 1913–23

Remembering 1921
a hundred years on

The National Day of Commemoration is held at Collins Barracks, Dublin. Between March 2020 and February 2022 Ireland was under strict Covid-19 regulations. These changed the course of the events programmed for the Decade of Centenaries, with much of the programme, such as exhibitions and conferences, cancelled or else moved online. The National Day of Commemoration commemorates all those Irishmen and Irishwomen who died in past wars or on service with the UN and is held annually on the Sunday closest to 11 July, the date on which, in 1921, the Anglo-Irish Truce was agreed. The 2021 ceremony, held on the very centenary of that Truce, was illustrative of the impact of Covid-19 restrictions on commemorative activity: the crowd that attended was significantly reduced from that of other years and social distancing was observed.

11 July 2021

REVOLUTIONARY TIMES 1913–23 321

Partition and the Creation of Northern Ireland

THERE WAS A great deal of pomp to announce a Parliament that nobody had wanted. Having agitated and armed against the idea of a devolved Irish Parliament, the unionists of the northeast of the island were now rejoicing at its arrival with a demonstration of loyalty to the Crown that had, the *Belfast News Letter* suggested, 'never been surpassed in any part of the Empire'.

Belfast, parts of it anyway, were *en fête* for the occasion, festooned with Union Jack bunting to greet the arrival of King George V, who sailed in and out on the same day, stopping long enough to deliver a speech at City Hall that urged peace and conciliation among the people of Ireland, while confidently anticipating that the new Northern Parliament would function with 'fairness and due regard to every faith and interest, and with no abatement of that patriotic devotion to the Empire which you proved so gallantly in the Great War'. Yet the speed with which the royal party entered and exited Belfast, and the reinforcements that had been brought in to ensure their security – the cordon of offshore destroyers, the extra detectives from Scotland Yard and northern England – spoke less to the optimism of the monarch's remarks than to prevailing northern divisions.

The source of this discord lay deep in a history of colonial conquest and settlement, and it found fresh expression in the violence that would serve as both a prelude and postscript to the creation of Northern Ireland. The Belfast Parliament, opened by King George V on 22 June 1921, was a product of the work of a committee established by the British government in late 1919 under the chairmanship of the staunchly unionist Walter Long, a Tory MP virulent in his hostility towards Sinn Féin. The job of Long's committee was effectively to replace the version of Home Rule that had been placed on the statute books

PARTITION AND THE CREATION OF NORTHERN IRELAND

The Robinson and Cleaver Department Store in Belfast decorated to welcome the King and Queen for the opening of the first Northern Ireland Parliament, 22 June 1921.

in 1914 but deferred for the duration of the war. This it did without any Irish nationalist representation or input; in contrast, James Craig had a significant influence on the shape of the legislation that emerged.

The Government of Ireland Act, 1920, provided for the creation of not one, but two Home Rule Parliaments on the island: one in Belfast, the other in Dublin, with representatives of both intended to join in a Council of Ireland. Such a partitioning of Ireland had been part of British political thinking since 1912 and was reluctantly accepted – as a temporary expedient – by nationalists from March 1914, when John Redmond conceded that Ulster counties could opt for exclusion for a period of six years, after which they would automatically come under the jurisdiction of the Irish Parliament. The Dublin-born Edward Carson had famously rejected this as a 'stay of execution', and unionist opposition remained fixed on securing a permanent exclusion from Home Rule – if not of the whole island, as was Carson's preference, then at least of the unionist stronghold of Ulster. A six-county exclusion had been discussed in failed negotiations with Lloyd George in the summer of 1916, and though Long's

Committee preferred that the historic nine counties of Ulster be left out of the Dublin Parliament area, Ulster unionist pressure helped whittle this back to six, sacrificing in the process (to understandable anger) their fellow Protestants in Cavan, Monaghan and Donegal.

The most striking feature of Long's proposals, and that which deviated from all previous Home Rule initiatives, was the Belfast Parliament itself – this was the first time a British government had made such a recommendation. The question to be asked of Ulster unionists was why, having committed so much to opposing the principle of Home Rule, did they now accept it for themselves? The answer, political scientist Brendan O'Leary has written, was because it provided 'a bulwark against the untrustworthy intentions of British governments as well as the claims of Irish republicans'. Furthermore, the calculation made in opting for a six-county carve-out over that of the historic nine counties was as simple as it was crude: this was the maximum amount of territory that Ulster unionists could expect to securely, and presumably permanently, dominate.

Yet within the territory of the new Northern Ireland there was still a large Catholic minority; indeed, in Fermanagh and Tyrone Catholics outnumbered Protestants, and there were large Catholic concentrations in Counties Armagh, Derry and Down, as well as in Belfast. Sectarian tensions across these areas were, of course, not historically unknown, but in July 1920, less than a year before the Belfast Parliament opened, these ignited into intercommunal violence of a different magnitude. Over 5,000 Catholic workers and 2,000 leftist Protestants ('Rotten Prods') would be expelled from Belfast's big shipyards, and thousands of families were forced from their homes. The expulsions – and the backlash they sparked – were not confined to the shipbuilding industry or geographically to Belfast. When, for instance, members of the Cork IRA shot dead RIC District Inspector Oswald Swanzy outside Lisburn Cathedral in August 1920 as revenge for his naming in a coroner's jury verdict on the 'wilful murder' of Cork's Lord Mayor Tomás MacCurtain at his home the previous March, angry loyalist mobs turned on the local Catholic community, destroying homes and businesses and leaving behind a scene that resembled war-ruined Ypres or Arras. Generally, loyalists gangs were accused of mounting a 'pogrom' against Catholics (the appropriateness of the term has been questioned by some historians), which, in the late summer of 1920, the Bishop of Down and Connor, Dr Joseph MacRory, maintained would be indicative of the 'intolerable condition' that would face 'more than 36 per cent of the inhabitants of the six counties' in the event of partition taking effect.

After receiving royal assent in December 1920, the Government of Ireland Act did take effect, but it succeeded in settling neither the Irish nor the specifically 'Ulster' question. Northern Ireland acquired its own Parliament and government, and a prime minister in Sir James Craig, but the Anglo-Irish Treaty signed in December 1921 indicated that the territorial integrity of the jurisdiction remained open to challenge and, potentially, to major change. Under the Treaty's terms, an Irish Free State was to be created from which Northern Ireland could opt out, though not without triggering a boundary commission to examine the border 'in accordance with the wishes of the inhabitants, so far as may be compatible with economic and geographic conditions'. The absence of a more serious scrutiny of the northern clauses of the Treaty – accounting for almost one-third of the text – in the subsequent Dáil debates reflected perhaps a naive and certainly mistaken confidence on the part of many Sinn Féiners that the boundary commission would redress the rupture of partition by reducing Northern Ireland to such an extent as to render it economically unviable. Yet a similar reasoning also fuelled unionist dismay at the Treaty, with Ulster Unionist MP Hugh O'Neill accusing Lloyd George of being in 'flagrant violation of his written pledge' and James Craig insistent that his government would have nothing to do with the proposed boundary review.

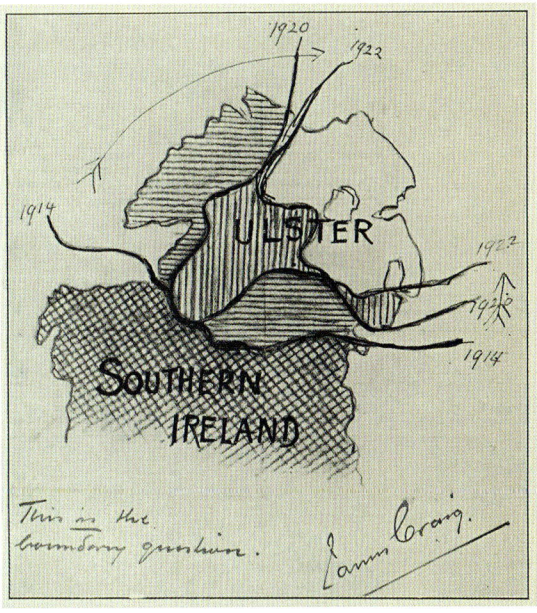

A rough map of the border dispute signed by James Craig.

If the commission proposal stoked unionist feelings of vulnerability, its sense of siege was further fuelled by an ongoing IRA campaign, which the Craig administration confronted by coupling strict coercive measures within the six counties with conciliation efforts with the Provisional Government in the South. Twice, in January and again in March 1922, Craig forged a pact with Michael Collins, the first of which saw Collins agree to an abandonment of the Dáil-sanctioned boycott of Belfast goods (begun in August 1920 in protest at the forced removal of Catholic workers from Belfast shipyards), and Craig agree to the return, where economic conditions allowed, of expelled Catholic workers to their jobs. Equally, both sides endeavoured to find 'a more suitable system than the Council of Ireland [provided for in the Treaty] for dealing with problems affecting all Ireland'.

The second pact between the two leaders was a measure of the failure of the first to either prevent continued IRA activity along the border (instigated, paradoxically, at Collins' command) or effect an improvement in the treatment of the Catholic minority by the Northern authorities. 'Peace is today declared,' Winston Churchill stated after the announcement of the second pact, but it would fare no better than the first, its own dismal failure attributed by one contemporary to a focus on 'certain symptoms of the unrest' rather than to their root causes.

Some of the violence experienced throughout the first half of 1922 was shocking in its detail. On 24 March 1922, for example, the family home of Owen McMahon, one of Belfast's most prosperous Catholic businessmen, was attacked, with McMahon and four of his sons all murdered, along with a barman who was present in the house at the time. A 'slaughter house' was how the *Belfast Telegraph* described the scene: large pools of blood were discovered 'rubbed and disturbed' in places 'as if someone had macerated fresh bullocks' liver and strewn it about'. There was an outraged reaction to the McMahon murders, in which policemen were implicated, as there was in the wake of the harrowing murders the following June of six Protestants at Altnaveigh, near Newry, when several farmhouses were bombed and burned by members of the IRA's 4th Northern Division, who had crossed the new border from Co. Louth to a district that was, one IRA Volunteer later asserted, 'reputed to have connections with a lot of local shootings of Republicans'.

The spiralling violence of 1922 underscored how little impact the Truce of July 1921 had on a northern experience that saw no pause in bloodletting. Between July 1920 and mid-1922, 500 people were killed across the six counties, most in Belfast and mostly civilians. But it was the minority Catholic community that bore the brunt of this violence, and its position within the new Northern Ireland progressively worsened as unionism moved to consolidate its control. Even before local powers (well short of those of a fully-fledged state) had been devolved to Belfast, the character of what was to come was encapsulated in the establishment as an authorised force – in late 1920 – of a Protestant Ulster Special Constabulary (USC) from the ranks of the UVF, which would subsequently stand accused by Nationalist MP Joseph Devlin of being 'worse than the Black and Tans' for its sectarian callousness. The USC would evolve into the 'B' Specials and be retained as a reserve force for the RUC, which was founded in April 1922 as a replacement for the RIC. Significantly, changes to policing were accompanied by a bolstering of their emergency powers, with the controversial Civil Authority (Special Powers) Act (1922) equipping Northern Ireland's Minister for Home Affairs to 'take all such steps and issue all such orders as may be necessary for preserving the peace and maintaining order'. The associated powers were extensive – and extensively used – and they permitted internment without trial and floggings for individuals caught in possession of firearms.

Politically, too, there was a copper-fastening of unionist power as local council constituency boundaries were redrawn, as the swearing of an oath of allegiance was insisted upon, and as proportional representation for local elections (extended later to Westminster elections) was abolished in favour of a first-past-the-post electoral system that worked to disadvantage nationalism and entrench sectarian divisions.

On everything from political participation to educational planning, nationalism chose disengagement. If, perhaps inevitably, such a course exposed nationalists to accusations that their misfortunes were, in part, self-inflicted, subsequent experience did little to suggest that the pursuit of an alternative approach might have resulted in any alleviation of Catholic woes. For the Catholic nationalist population of the six counties, hopes that partition would be short-lived proved dismally unfounded: the onset of civil war in the South (and the killing of leaders like Collins) deflected political focus towards the safeguarding of the new Free State, which, under the leadership of W.T. Cosgrave, would adopt a policy of peaceful, if cool, coexistence with the North. Nor did the Boundary Commission fulfil the promise that nationalists had originally invested in it: collapsing in 1925, it left the 1920 boundary intact, severing many border territories from their natural hinterlands and estranging certain political and religious communities from more obviously sympathetic administrations North and South.

The political arrangements established for Northern Ireland between 1920 and 1922 would not, however, see out the century. Instead, they lasted for only fifty years, when unionism's refusal to reform led, amidst spiralling violence, to the imposition of direct rule from London in 1973. Devolved government based on genuine power-sharing would have to wait until the signing of the Belfast/Good Friday Agreement in 1998, which, like the Treaty of 1921, again opened up the prospect of future changes to the border and a change to the constitutional status of the six counties, conversations around which were given fresh impetus by the UK's vote to leave the European Union in 2016.

Endgame 1921:
Towards Truce and Treaty in Ireland

THE MOMENT WAS marked by a minor act of defiance in a Manchester courtroom. There, a large of group of Irishmen were standing trial on charges of treason and felony, and when the clock struck noon, Patrick O'Donoghue, Officer Commanding the Manchester IRA, uttered an instruction in Irish and the men in the dock, to the surprise of the trial judge and almost everyone else, leapt to their feet to 'salute the Truce'.

Back in Ireland, midday on 11 July 1921 was also being marked. After two and a half years, the onset of a truce in the Anglo-Irish war was widely and warmly welcomed. In the midst of a summer heatwave, news of the event brought bigger crowds onto the streets of Dublin than had been seen in months. 'The very air held a new lightness and was irradiated not only with sunshine but with hope,' *The Irish Times* observed.

A truce was not of course a settlement, and elements within the IRA regarded it as little more than a 'temporary respite', a hiatus in a war that would resume with even greater ferocity when the negotiations following the cessation broke down – as some assumed they inevitably would. At the same time, the achievement of the Truce was the culmination of months of public and private peace talks, political solo runs, kite-flying initiatives and indirect communications across the Irish Sea, which had as their purpose the stopping of violence to allow space for politics and negotiation to take centre stage.

Most of these peace manoeuvres were unsuccessful, and few were even appreciated: in late 1920 and early 1921 the Sinn Féin leadership had deemed a lot of 'Truce talk' to be damaging due to the impression it promoted the idea that republicans were on the cusp of surrender. Pointedly and publicly, Michael Collins warned of the 'grave danger that the country may be stampeded on false promises, and foolish ill-timed actions'.

ENDGAME 1921

Perhaps the most significant of the pre-Truce peace efforts was the one led by the Clare-born Archbishop of Perth, Patrick Clune (his nephew Conor had been killed in custody in Dublin Castle on Bloody Sunday). Throughout December 1920 Clune acted as an intermediary between Dublin and London, and he met with Lloyd George on a number of occasions before a curtain was drawn on their discussions. De Valera, having been briefed by Michael Collins on developments on his return from the US at the start of January 1921, attributed the abandonment of Clune's efforts to 'die-hard' members of the British Cabinet, such as Andrew Bonar Law, who had demanded an 'absolute surrender of all arms'.

This had indeed been the case, and the Clune episode exposed tensions within the British Cabinet as to whether coercion or conciliation was the preferred policy direction towards Ireland. In early 1921 it was clear that those favouring the former held sway. From that point on, until the summer, there was little serious engagement with the idea of peace on the part of the British government. A mistaken belief in the imminence of the IRA's demise (alongside a reluctance to confer recognition upon the same force) undoubtedly guided British calculations. However, the British government's decision-making was also informed by a hierarchy of priorities which, as historian Ronan Fanning

A man lies dead on Beresford Place, Dublin, after the IRA attack on the Custom House in May 1921. Peace efforts would only gather renewed momentum the following month.

has observed, placed the appeasement of Ulster unionist concerns and the 'copper-fastening of partition' above the imperative of peace.

The result was that real momentum towards a truce only came after the May elections had been held and King George V had travelled to Belfast in June for the formal opening of the new Northern Parliament, where his speech, mollifying and forward-looking, accelerated moves towards the achievement of a truce. Within days, and citing the 'spirit' of the King's words, Prime Minister David Lloyd George was sending invitations to James Craig and Éamon de Valera as the representatives of Northern and Southern Ireland to go to London for talks to 'explore to the utmost the possibility of a settlement'. To underline his sincerity, several leading Sinn Féin TDs, including Arthur Griffith, had already been released from prison, and de Valera was promised that should he accept the invitation, he would be allowed to travel to and from the London conference without fetter.

De Valera would travel, though not immediately. First, he convened a conference in Dublin with representatives of the 'political minority', of which Sir James Craig and Lord Midleton were among the invitees. While Craig declined the invite, the Mansion House gathering on 4 July started a flurry of political activity on both sides of the Irish Sea, with Lord Midleton conveying to Lloyd George the necessity of agreeing to an armistice before de Valera would consider travelling to London. South African statesman General Jan Smuts, acting as an unofficial intermediary, met Sinn Féin leaders in Dublin on 5 July, and he too reported back to the British Cabinet on the need for a truce as a precondition to a conference. When Lord Midleton returned to the Mansion House on 8 July, he did so with the British Prime Minister's agreement to an unconditional truce – something to which the British government had been unwilling to accede in the previous December.

Three days after the Truce had come into effect, on 14 July, de Valera met with Lloyd George at 10 Downing Street. Over the course of a week, the two men met on several occasions, and though they parted without reaching agreement, they did commit to the maintenance of the Truce and to keeping open the lines of communication between them. Those July meetings laid the foundations for the negotiations proper that commenced in October, and they also saw the British lay out their own initial proposals for an Irish settlement. Set out in a letter to de Valera on 20 July, the British offered 'Dominion status' within the Empire, whereas the Irish had sought full self-determination outside of it. De Valera swiftly rejected the proposals.

ENDGAME 1921

In July 1921, after the Truce had been declared, de Valera travelled from Dublin to London for initial talks with Lloyd George in Downing Street.

The slow march from talks about peace to the achievement of a truce and the commencement of negotiations proper came at a massive human cost. The numbers killed in the first six months of 1921 were estimated at 999, and that figure rose uncomfortably in the frenzy of violence that immediately preceded the Truce. Indeed, it transpired that the bloodiest day of the Irish War of Independence would be its last. Thirty-four people were killed on 10 July, the day before the Truce, and about ten more on the day of the Truce itself, the youngest a thirteeen-year-old Catholic girl in Belfast, Mary McGowan, who was killed by a gunshot fired by a member of the USC from an armoured car as she crossed the street with her mother. There would be more killing between then and the end of the year, with much of it centred on Belfast and the wider Antrim area.

For much of the country, however, the Truce delivered what it promised and gave licence to ordinary Irish people – combatants included – to go about their daily lives in a peaceful and more politically tranquil atmosphere. Evidence of this calmer normality was easy to discern. It was apparent in the restoration of Dublin street-lighting at night, in the lifting of restrictions on fairs and markets in the martial law areas, and in the granting of permission for previously closed creameries to reopen. And it was apparent too in the experience of sports.

When, on his attendance at the Leinster hurling final at Croke Park in September 1921, Michael Collins was photographed speaking to players and hurling a sliotar back and forth with his friend and fellow Sinn Féin TD Harry Boland, one newspaper observed his relative carefree ease. Collins resembled, one reporter observed, 'no longer a hunted fugitive or a Minister of Finance, but a schoolboy at play'.

> **The Truce delivered what it promised and gave licence to ordinary Irish people to go about their daily lives in a peaceful and more politically tranquil atmosphere.**

If the Truce allowed for a measure of relief and rest for many IRA volunteers, it didn't mean they would spend this period of hiatus in a state of idle distraction. The fighting may have stopped, but drilling, allowed under the terms of the Truce, continued, and Volunteer training camps were set up to maintain discipline and a military preparedness in the event of a resumption of war. There was also a significant influx of new recruits to the IRA, though 'Trucileers' or 'Truce Warriors', as new entrants were often ungenerously labelled, were not always well-regarded. And while the smooth operation of the Truce was entrusted to a system of liaison officers, breaches were not unknown, and claim and counter-claim of Truce transgressions reverberated upon the Anglo-Irish negotiations that commenced in London in mid-October 1921. At one plenary session in Downing Street, on 17 October, the delegation of Irish plenipotentiaries, led not by de Valera but by Arthur Griffith, would cite examples of Truce breaches and acts of bad faith on the part of the British side. Éamonn Duggan, who added to his plenipotentiary responsibilities that of chief liaison officer, complained that the movements of Sinn Féin people were being tracked, a charge supported by Michael Collins, who informed his interlocutors that an English agent had followed him to Mass in London the previous morning.

The Truce nevertheless held. It did what it was intended to do. It created the space and a relatively peaceful backdrop – Belfast and its environs aside

– that enabled the negotiations to progress and a settlement, ultimately, to be reached. That settlement conferred a Dominion status, similar to Canada, upon a new Irish Free State; it made provision for an oath of allegiance to the Irish Free State with an added pledge to be 'faithful' to the King and his successors; it allowed for British use of three ports in the south of the country; and, in the event of Northern Ireland opting out of the Irish Free State (within a month), it provided for the creation of a boundary commission to consider the 'boundaries between Northern Ireland and the rest of Ireland'.

The Anglo-Irish Treaty was signed in London on 6 December 1921, and its terms would become a source of deep division and heated debate when, over a period of nine days, they were presented before public sessions of Dáil Éireann. That the plenipotentiaries had signed the Treaty under a threat of 'war within three days' if they didn't was understood, as was the obvious question that arose on the Irish side as it contemplated this possibility: was the IRA ready or equipped for a return to guerrilla warfare? As the IRA's Chief of Staff, Richard Mulcahy, saw it, the answer was no. He calculated that even a numerically strengthened and efficient IRA would have had difficulty in sustaining a war beyond a short period of time.

Ultimately, the Treaty shattered the unity of the broad post-Rising Sinn Féin movement and exposed schisms in personality and politics that would too easily be caricatured as a straightforward divide between pragmatic nationalists and fundamentalist republicans, or hard-headed realists versus romantic idealists. There was undoubtedly something of this to the split that followed, but as with the distinctions drawn (significant to some, immaterial to others) between de Valera's preferred 'external association' model and the Dominion status secured, considerable nuance was involved in the Dáil's deliberations on the Treaty. The question for the writer, revolutionary and Kerry TD Piaras Béaslaí, was whether it was worth jeopardising the 'lives and happiness of the people' over this nuance – the 'sophistries and legal quibbles' and the 'theoretic dialectics' as he chose to describe it. As Béaslaí saw it, acceptance or rejection of the Treaty ultimately came down to a choice between 'Truce or War'. In the end, Ireland would get both. The Dáil would vote for a permanent truce, yet the country still careered towards a renewed state of war – just not with Britain.

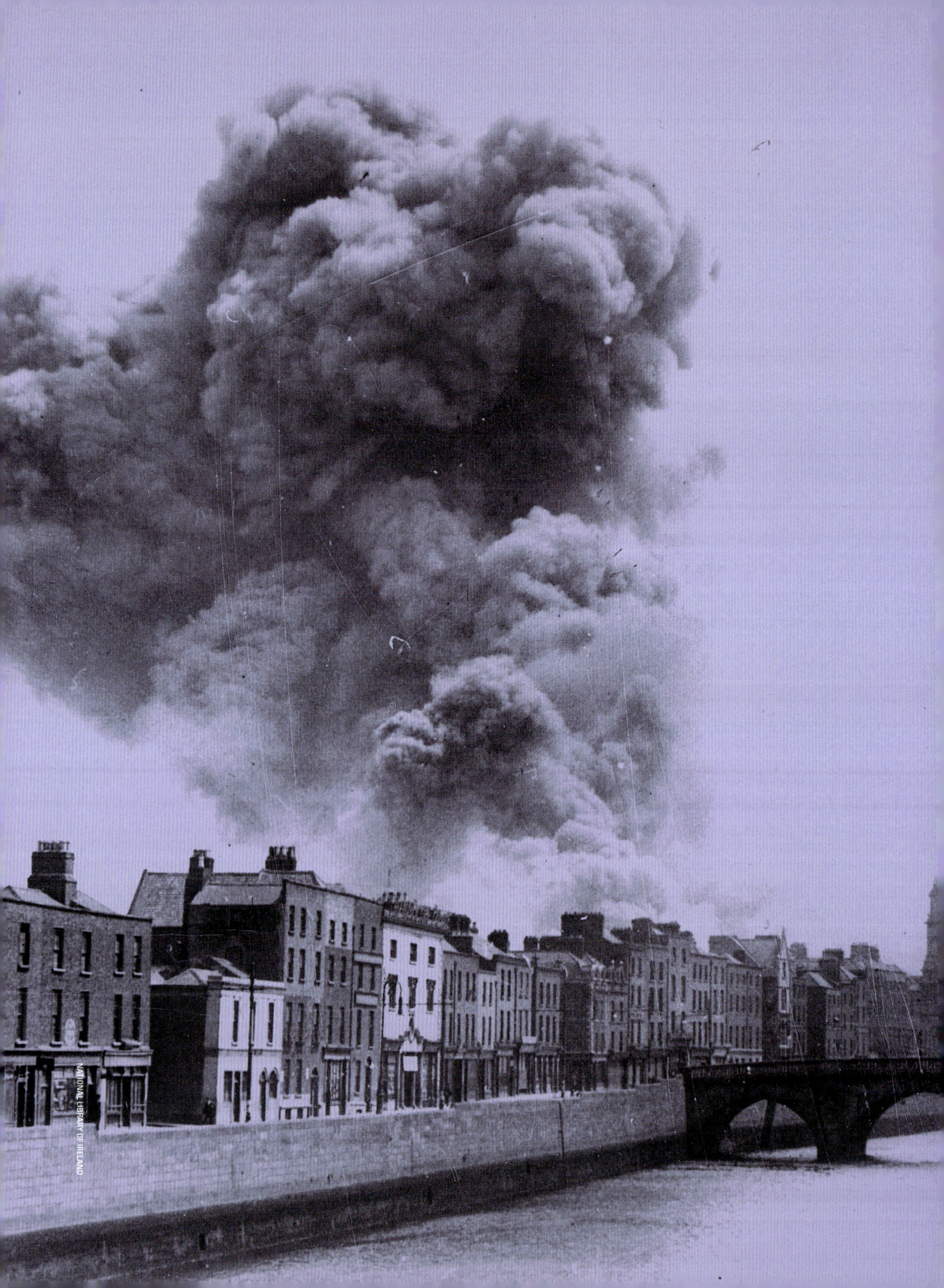

NATIONAL LIBRARY OF IRELAND

1922

'The members of the Provisional Government received the surrender of Dublin Castle at 1.45 p.m. today. It is now in the hands of the Irish nation.'

Official statement from the Provisional Government
16 JANUARY

1922

3 JAN
Dáil Éireann debates on the Anglo-Irish Treaty resume after the Christmas break.

△ 5 JAN
Antarctic explorer **Ernest Shackleton** (right) dies of heart attack at sea on board the vessel *Quest*.

7 JAN
The Dáil votes to approve the Treaty by 64 votes to 57.

9 JAN
Éamon de Valera, leading opponent of the Treaty, resigns as President of Dáil Éireann but stands for re-election.

10 JAN
De Valera is defeated in the vote for the Dáil presidency by 60 votes to 58. He and all anti-Treaty deputies walk out, and Griffith is elected president of Dáil Éireann. The Dáil is adjourned until 11 February.

14 JAN
A Provisional Government is established with Michael Collins as chairman.

Dáil Votes for Historic Treaty by Margin of Just Seven Votes

9 January – Dáil Éireann has ratified the Anglo-Irish Treaty signed in London on 6 December.

The vote took place on 7 January, with the margin of victory a mere seven votes, 64–57. The speaker of the Dáil, Eoin MacNeill, was not called upon to cast a vote, while Frank Drohan, TD for Waterford–Tipperary East, resigned his seat on 5 January because he was anti-Treaty, but his Sinn Féin branch was pro-Treaty and had instructed him to vote in favour.

A group shot of anti-Treaty TDs, which includes Éamon de Valera, Cathal Brugha and Margaret Pearse in the centre of the front row.

The narrow margin was not a surprise, despite the fact that the case for ratification enjoyed overwhelming support in the press and from public bodies around the country. The *Irish Independent* reported that, of the elected and other bodies (local councils, Sinn Féin clubs, labour bodies, boards of guardians, etc.) that had publicly expressed an opinion of the Treaty, 316 were in support, while only 14 opposed it.

In spite of this, on the final day's debate in the Dáil, Cathal Brugha likened acceptance of the Treaty to 'national suicide'.

The final day's debate was begun at 11.20 a.m. by Harry Boland, who spoke of the feeling in America, where the public opinion was in favour of the agreement, but where the people who had contributed money to the Irish cause looked upon it as a betrayal.

This theme of betrayal was picked up by Mary MacSwiney who, after the vote was counted and the decision was taken, described the ratification of the Treaty as 'the grossest act of betrayal that Ireland has ever endured'.

Arthur Griffith, who spoke for about an hour, said that 98% of the Irish people backed ratification, while pointing out that they had been misled when they were told that the plenipotentiaries violated their mandate by coming back with less than a full republic. He asserted that the alternative proposal – the one presented by Mr de Valera and widely referred to during the debates as Document No. 2 or external association – was a claim to Dominion status. Mr Griffith said that unionists north and south would have fair play in the new Free State, and he paid tribute to Michael Collins as the man who fought the Black and Tan terror until England was forced out.

Mr Collins himself was low-key in his reaction to the result of the vote. The passing of the motion to ratify the Treaty should not, he said, be regarded as a triumph of one side over the other, and he paid tribute to those on the opposing side of the argument, especially Mr de Valera, who occupied the same place in his heart now as he had always done. Collins called for unity and a coming together to 'preserve public safety'.

Speaking immediately after the announcement of the result, at about 8.45 p.m., a clearly emotional Mr de Valera declared that the republic still existed and would continue to do so until the Irish people disestablished it.

After the session concluded, advocates and opponents of the Treaty met separately and in private.

Arthur Griffith Elected New President of Dáil Éireann

11 January – Arthur Griffith was elected the new President of Dáil Éireann yesterday.

Mr Griffith succeeds Éamon de Valera, who had resigned his position and then failed to secure re-election by 60 votes to 58.

Mr Griffith, 54, was proposed by Michael Collins, who declared that the nation was currently 'a ship without a captain', adding, to shouts of 'hear, hear', that there was a need to 'form some kind of stable Government to stop the position of anarchy that we are allowing the country to drift into'.

Before the vote could take place, however, Éamon de Valera and his supporters walked out of the Dáil chamber as a 'protest against the election as President of the Irish Republic of the Chairman of the Delegation, who is bound by the Treaty conditions to set up a State which is to subvert the Republic, and who, in the interim period, instead of using the office as it should be used – to support the Republic – will, of necessity, have to be taking action which will tend to its destruction'.

1922

16 JAN
British authorities formally hand over Dublin Castle to the control of the Irish Provisional Government.

21 JAN
The Irish Race Congress opens in Paris with representatives from 19 countries. It establishes 'Fine Ghaedheal', an organisation that aims to represent Irish people throughout the world.

22 JAN
Pope Benedict XV dies in the Apostolic Palace, Vatican City.

31 JAN ▽
Beggars Bush Barracks, headquarters of the Auxiliary Division, is handed over to the **National Army**.

2 FEB
Ulysses, a new novel by James Joyce, is published in Paris on the occasion of the author's 40th birthday. The book had previously been serialised in the Chicago-based journal *Little Review*.

1922

2 FEB
The fight against partition will go on with 'gloves off', the nationalist Mayor of Derry, Hugh O'Doherty, tells an anti-partition demonstration in the Guildhall.

◁ 3 FEB
Irish artist **John Butler Yeats** dies in New York city. The 83-year-old is the father of the writer and poet William Butler Yeats and painter Jack B. Yeats.

5 FEB
Cumann na mBan votes to reject the Anglo-Irish Treaty by 419 votes to 63. A special convention endorses a Mary MacSwiney motion affirming allegiance to the 'Republic of Ireland'.

6 FEB
Ambrogio Damiano Achille Ratti becomes Pope Pius XI and is installed as leader of the Catholic Church.

7 FEB
The Provisional Government appoints two inspectors to investigate and report on famine-like distress in Connemara. The inspectors, dispatched by the Minister for Agriculture, Patrick Hogan, are both Galway TDs: Pádraic Ó Maille and Professor Joseph Whelehan.

The new Provisional Government, photographed with supporters in the background. The new President, Arthur Griffith, is in the front row, fifth from the right.

As he left the chamber, David Kent, TD for Cork East and North-East, shouted, 'Up the Republic!' Michael Collins responded that they were 'Deserters all! ... Deserters all to the Irish nation in her hour of trial. We will stand by her.'

Mr Griffith was then elected as President, and he proceeded to nominate his new Cabinet, all of whom were ratified by the depleted chamber.

The Dáil has now been adjourned until 14 February.

Irish Race Congress in Paris Attracts Delegates from Across the World

22 January – The Irish Race Congress opened in Paris yesterday.

About 200 delegates and visitors attended the event that was held in the *salle des fêtes* of the Continental Hotel.

No fewer than 22 countries will be represented, including the United States, Canada, Australia, South Africa, China, Brazil, Bolivia, Chile, Mexico and Java. The delegates were seated according to the names of their respective countries, and the walls and platforms were decorated in Irish colours and the flags of the various countries represented. The delegates from Ireland included the lord mayors of Dublin and Cork, Éamon de Valera, Mary MacSwiney, Constance Markievicz, Michael Hayes and Diarmuid Coffey, along with many experts in Irish arts and crafts.

The object of the congress, Mr de Valera explained in a conversation with members of the press, was to 'assist in every way Irish culture and expression and the illustration of Irish individuality. At present nine-tenths of the great deeds of Irishmen in the past are attributed to other races and other peoples. We have already organisations in various countries for this purpose. The present congress is intended to provide not another organisation, but as it were a bureau through which all organisations can get into touch with each other.'

Delegates from Ireland at the Irish Race Congress. L–R: Seán T. O'Kelly, child, Mary MacSwiney, Éamon de Valera, unknown, Constance Markievicz and Lord Ashbourne.

Dublin Castle 'Surrendered' by the British into the 'Hands of the Irish Nation'

23 January – Dublin Castle, for several centuries the seat of British rule in Ireland, was passed into the 'hands of the Irish nation' on 16 January.

The atmosphere in the city for the occasion was one of excitement and expectancy. From early morning, crowds began to assemble in the streets around the Castle, their number swelling to the thousands by noon, when the handover was due to take place.

The representatives of the Provisional Government arrived in three taxi-cabs at the gates of Dublin Castle at 1.40 p.m. to cheers from the waiting crowd.

Michael Collins was present, and with him were William Cosgrave, Éamonn Duggan, Patrick Hogan, Fionán Lynch, Joseph McGrath, Eoin MacNeill and Kevin O'Higgins.

A few minutes later Lord Lieutenant Edmund Talbot arrived in a large car from the vice-regal lodge. He proceeded immediately to the Privy

1922

11 FEB △
England defeat Ireland by a scoreline of 12–3 in a Five Nations' rugby international, played at Lansdowne Road before a crowd of almost 20,000 spectators.

19 FEB
About 20 Sinn Féin prisoners, convicted the previous year of shooting with intent to kill, arson and other offences, are released from British prisons. They are honoured at a dinner and dance reception at the Grosvenor Hotel in London, hosted by the Irish Self-Determination League.

22 FEB
The Sinn Féin Ard-Fheis agrees that no elections will take place within three months.

25 FEB
The first issue of the pro-Treaty *An Saorstát: The Free State* newspaper is published. It sells for two pence.

1922

Michael Collins, Kevin O'Higgins and W.T. Cosgrave leaving Dublin Castle after the British ceremonially surrendered it, 16 January 1922.

FEBRUARY–11 MAR
Confrontation in Limerick between pro- and anti-Treaty forces. Mayor of Limerick Stephen O'Mara and prominent leaders from both sides strive to prevent an outbreak of hostilities. Both forces evacuate the city on 11 March.

3 MAR
Max Green, son-in-law of the late John Redmond and chairman of the Irish Prisons Board, is shot dead attempting to stop an armed robbery in St Stephen's Green.

15 MAR
Cumann na Poblachta, the anti-Treaty League of the Republic, is formed by Éamon de Valera.

17 MAR
As part of a series of public speeches, de Valera gives a warning in Thurles to the effect that acceptance of the Treaty by the people would interpose an Irish government and army between the British government and any body of Irishmen that might subsequently desire to seek complete independence by armed force.

Council Chamber, where he received the members of the Provisional Government in private and handed over formal powers. The government members were then introduced to the heads of the various departments. Their stay in Dublin Castle lasted 55 minutes.

On their return to the Mansion House, an official statement was issued, signed by Collins. It began: 'The members of the Provisional Government received the surrender of Dublin Castle at 1.45 p.m. today. It is now in the hands of the Irish nation.' The statement went on to say that 'for the next few days' the functions of the existing departments of Dublin Castle 'will be continued without in any way prejudicing future action'.

Cumann na mBan Convention Votes Against Anglo-Irish Treaty

5 February – A special convention of Cumann na mBan was held at the Mansion House yesterday, at which a large majority of members voted against supporting the Anglo-Irish Treaty.

Present at the convention were 482 delegates from branches all over the country and from overseas. These included notable members, such as Constance Markievicz, Mary MacSwiney and Dr Ada English.

Mary MacSwiney spoke first and, in a rousing speech, put forward the following resolution: 'The executive of Cumann na mBan reaffirms its allegiance to the Republic and therefore cannot

Cumann na mBan banner taken from a first aid certificate presented to Máire Nic Shiubhlaigh.

1922

Kathleen O'Callaghan TD and Mary MacSwiney TD (sister of hunger-striker Terence MacSwiney), arrive at the Treaty debates, Earlsfort Terrace, January 1922.

support the Articles of Agreement signed in London on Dec. 6 1921.'

Jennie Wyse Power, arguing in favour of the Treaty, agreed that the Irish people should 're-affirm our allegiance to the Republic' but said that they also needed to realise that 'the Treaty signed in London will, if accepted by the Irish people, be a big step along the road'.

In the debate that followed, the *Irish Independent* noted how it quickly became obvious that the opponents of the Treaty were in an overwhelming majority. 'Speaker after speaker arose to speak against Mrs Wyse Power's amendment and in favour of Miss MacSwiney's motion.'

On the final count 419 of 482, or 87%, voted in favour of the motion.

Limerick Steps Back from 'Brink of Civil War' After Mayor's Intervention

13 March – A potential crisis has been averted in Limerick after an agreement was reached between pro- and anti-Treaty forces in the city. With tensions escalating, the mayor of the city, Alderman Stephen O'Mara, helped broker a resolution to a stand-off that had threatened to erupt into violence.

The two factions had been drawn to the city by news of the withdrawal of British troops from the local barracks and its handover to local forces.

Acting as a mediator between the two sides, Alderman O'Mara travelled to Dublin with officers of the unofficial forces for negotiations that led to an agreement on 11 March that will see the withdrawal of all outside forces – official and unofficial – from the city. The agreement will also see the military barracks in Limerick occupied by

Michael Brennan, commander of the Free State forces in Limerick, whose stand-off with anti-Treaty fighters under Ernie O'Malley was resolved by an agreement brokered by Stephen O'Mara.

22 MAR
De Valera denies suggestions that his recent statements were an incitement to civil war.

24 MAR
Catholic publican Owen McMahon and four of his sons are slaughtered in an attack on the family's Belfast home. A barman, present in the family home at the time, is also killed.

26 MAR △
Members of the IRA opposed to the Treaty hold an army convention in defiance of a prohibition by the new Dáil Cabinet.

5 APR
It is reported that the six counties of Northern Ireland are to acquire a new police force to be known as the RUC.

9 APR
The anti-Treaty army convention adopts a new constitution, acknowledging no responsibility to Dáil Éireann or to any political authority and elects an executive including Liam Lynch, Liam Mellows and Rory O'Connor.

REVOLUTIONARY TIMES 1913–23

1922

10 APR
A major European Economic Conference opens in Genoa, Italy, with the aim of restarting the European economy after the devastation of war. Delegates from 34 nations are represented.

▽ **13 APRIL–16 MAY**
A Dáil Peace Committee meets a number of times before the final breakdown of talks on 16 May. De Valera and **Cathal Brugha** for the anti-Treaty side and Michael Collins and Arthur Griffith for the pro-Treaty side attend the Mansion House Conference called by the Archbishop of Dublin, Dr Edward J. Byrne, and Lord Mayor Laurence O'Neill.

14 APR
The Four Courts in Dublin is occupied by anti-Treaty forces led by Rory O'Connor.

16 APR
In an Easter message to the young men and women of Ireland, de Valera tells them: 'Ireland is yours for the taking. Take it.'

maintenance units of the mid-Limerick Brigade pending the IRA convention to decide its attitude to the Treaty.

Following the meeting, Alderman O'Mara declared that the crisis in Limerick had now been 'happily averted', though the incident, he suggested, should give Irishmen pause to reflect. 'At many moments during the last two weeks we were on the brink of civil war, for the first shot fired in Limerick would have been the signal for a similar outbreak in every town and village in Ireland.'

Well-known Catholic Family Slaughtered in Attack on Belfast Home

31 March – Five people have been killed following a sectarian attack on the home of a Catholic in Belfast on 24 March.

The victims were named as Owen McMahon and his sons, Francis, Patrick and Thomas. A fourth son, Bernard has life-threatening injuries. Another son, John, was also wounded in the raid on the Kinnaird Terrace property.

The fifth man to be killed, Edward McKinney, worked as a barman in the McMahons' pub.

The entrance to No. 3 Kinnaird Terrace, the home of the MacMahons, after the shooting took place.

Owen McMahon was a well-known businessman in Belfast. He was a former chairman of the Belfast and North of Ireland Licensed Vintners Association and had been part of a number of deputations to the Westminster Parliament to represent licensed businesses over the years. He was also a very recognisable figure at Irish race meetings and took a keen interest in boxing. He was not known to have any political affiliation.

Mr McMahon and his family were in bed at the time the killers arrived. It was shortly after midnight when the front door of the family home was broken down and men with revolvers stormed in. The men of the house were dragged from their beds and ordered downstairs at gunpoint. As the women of the house were gathered in a back room, the men were lined up against a wall and told to say their prayers.

The murderers were no more than ten minutes in the house, and they left behind them a scene of utter horror. As the victims' blood pooled in the room, some of them died instantly, while others writhed in agony until they eventually succumbed.

The attack occurred during curfew hours, and several press correspondents are reporting that the perpetrators wore uniforms. An empty shell from a Webley revolver cartridge was found at the scene.

The *Belfast Evening Telegraph* has described the murders as the 'most dreadful of all the crimes yet perpetrated' in a city that has seen many awful acts in recent years.

New Collins-Craig Pact Promises to Bring Peace to Ireland

5 April – A pact has been agreed in London between the Prime Minister of Northern Ireland, Sir James Craig, and the Chairman of the Provisional Government in Dublin, Michael Collins.

The opening line of the agreement reads, 'Peace is today declared.'

The pact was concluded on 30 March, after two days of prolonged discussions involving Craig, Collins and representatives of the British government led by Winston Churchill.

The principal points of the agreement provide for the following:

- Special police in mixed areas to be composed half of Catholics and half of Protestants.
- A Catholic advisory committee to be set up to select recruits.
- Expelled persons to be allowed to return to their homes.
- Mutual release of prisoners.
- Persons accused of a serious crime to be charged by the Six County Lord Chief Justice and a Lord Justice of Appeal without a jury.
- £500,000 to be provided by the British government for relief work.

A cartoon depicting the different issues around violence in Northern Ireland.

1922

20 APR
The issue of pensions dominates the annual congress of the Irish National Teachers Organisation in Dublin. One delegate accuses the British Treasury of the 'despicable plunder' of Irish pensions.

23 APR
A general strike is held to protest against 'militarism' in Ireland. Work stops across the country except in Ulster. Labour meetings are addressed in Dublin by, amongst others, Thomas Johnson, secretary of the ITGWU and Miss Callanan, president of the Women's Productive Workers' Dublin Branch.

26 APR
The Irish Catholic hierarchy issues an appeal to Irish civilian and military leaders to resolve their differences peacefully, by means of an election free from violence. In a statement from Maynooth, the bishops emphatically condemn the 'unconstitutional policy of certain leaders who think themselves entitled to force their views upon the nation, not by reason, but by firearms'.

1922

2 MAY
Dublin defeat Cork 4–9 to 4–3 in the deferred All-Ireland hurling final for 1920. A crowd of 22,000 attends.

9 MAY
An *Irish Independent* editorial describes the sharp rise in potato prices as 'alarming'. It states that the 'immediate problem for the Irish Government is the conserving of supplies to satisfy home demand, and it may even be found necessary to prohibit the export of potatoes'.

20 MAY
A pact is agreed between Collins and de Valera regarding the outcome of the general election to be held in June.

22 MAY
W.J. Twaddell, member of Belfast Corporation and MP in the Northern Parliament, is shot dead on a Belfast street. His murder is condemned both by Sir James Craig and Arthur Griffith.

The agreement also makes provision for a further meeting to ascertain whether the unity of Ireland can be secured.

Reacting to the pact, an enthusiastic Joseph Devlin, Nationalist Party MP, told the House of Commons in Westminster that it was the best work that had ever been done for Ireland, the Empire and for the world.

Anti-Treaty Forces Seize Four Courts but Deny Coup d'État Allegations

18 April – Anti-Treaty forces have seized control of the iconic Four Courts in Dublin; between 300 and 400 armed men have occupied the building.

The leader of the occupying IRA force, Commandant Rory O'Connor, has denied the takeover is a coup d'état or the beginning of an open revolt.

The move on the Four Courts began at about 12.15 a.m. on 14 April, when the building was surrounded by armed men, some of whom arrived on the scene on foot and others in motors.

According to O'Connor, the purpose of the occupation is to establish a military headquarters, transferring from their former premises on nearby Parnell Square. He also mentioned that a publicity department would be set up in the buildings.

Already Commandant O'Connor's forces have begun to fortify their new surroundings. Windows overlooking the River Liffey have been sandbagged or filled with law books and sacks of paper. Armed sentries have been stationed at all the principal vantage points.

The actions of Commandant O'Connor do not appear to have been sanctioned by a political leader and he does not appear to be subject to any civilian authority.

Since the seizure of the Four Courts, an armoured car, equipped with a machine gun and manned by regular troops from General Headquarters at Beggars Bush, has appeared in the vicinity of the Four Courts. So too have several armoured lorries, also containing pro-Treaty troops.

Rory O'Connor, commander of the anti-Treaty Four Courts garrison, addressing members of the Dublin City Brigade IRA at Smithfield, Dublin, 2 April 1922.

1922

Labour Holds General Strike Against Irish Militarism

24 April – A general strike in protest against 'militarism' was held yesterday in Dublin.

The stoppage, which began at 6 a.m. and lasted 15 hours, was organised by the Irish Labour Party and Trades Union Congress (ILP&TUC) and saw calls from labour leaders for political peace in Ireland.

In advance of the strike, the ILP&TUC signalled its intent, on behalf of the workers of Ireland, to protest against the 'growth of the idea that the military forces may take command of the civil life of the nation without responsibility to the people; that military men may commit acts of violence against civilians and be immune from prosecution or punishment; that possession of arms is the sole title to political authority'.

In Dublin, members of various trade unions gathered at Beresford Place and marched to Sackville Street where three platforms had been erected to allow for speeches to be delivered.

Thomas Johnson, secretary of the ILP&TUC, told the gathering that he hoped some of the young men from Beggars Bush and from the Four Courts would declare publicly that they would not take up arms against their fellow citizens.

The strike itself saw around 75,000 workers abstain from work. Railway and tram services were suspended as were post office deliveries. Cinemas, theatres, public houses and restaurants were closed. Furthermore, no shipping was allowed from Irish ports, and only enough workers remained to allow incoming vessels to dock.

Thomas Johnson (left), secretary of the ILP&TUC; O'Connell Street deserted due to the strike (centre); Ms Callanan making a speech (right).

25 MAY
A new Irish political party, **The Farmers' Party**, is founded to contest the forthcoming election. The party emerges from a meeting of the National Executive of the Irish Farmers' Union (IFU).

29 MAY
Church of Ireland Archbishop of Dublin Dr John Gregg tells a meeting of the Diocesan Synod in Dublin that Southern Irish Protestants require 'fair play' from their 'fellow countrymen'.

31 MAY
Joseph McGuinness, the pro-Treaty Sinn Féin TD for Longford–Westmeath, dies from pneumonia. It was his by-election success in May 1917 that signalled the emergence of Sinn Féin as a powerful political force.

1922

11 JUN
Tipperary are crowned All-Ireland football champions for 1920 after defeating Dublin at Croke Park in front of a crowd of 25,000. The two teams had met at the same venue less than two years earlier, on a day that became known as 'Bloody Sunday'.

▽ **12 JUN**
Six South of Ireland regiments are disbanded and their 'colours' presented to King George V at Windsor Castle.

ILLUSTRATED LONDON NEWS

14 JUN
In a speech in Cork, Collins virtually repudiates the Collins–de Valera pact.

16 JUN
The proposed constitution of the Irish Free State is made public while polling takes place in the general election.

Condemnation Follows Murder of Protestants in West Cork

3 May – The recent murders of ten Protestants in west Cork have been universally condemned. Most of the victims were killed in the Dunmanway and Ballineen districts.

An inquest into the deaths of Francis Fitzmaurice, a well-known local solicitor, James Buttimer, a retired draper, and David Gray, a chemist, concluded that all died from gunshot wounds after being attacked in their own homes in Dunmanway on 27 April.

More attacks occurred the following night. Alexander McKinley, John Chinnery and Robert Howe – all from the Ballineen area – and Robert Nagle from Clonakilty, were murdered in similar fashion.

It is understood that other houses in the district were also visited, but the intended targets managed to escape.

Vengeance and sectarian hatred are the motives given for the murders. A statement issued by the Cabinet of Dáil Éireann claims that 'certain elements in the community are taking advantage of the present transitional period in Ireland to wreak private vengeance in the hope that under the unsettled conditions they may escape justice'. The statement continued that it would be the 'first concern of the Dáil and the Provisional Government to secure their capture and trial. Every good citizen is exhorted to assist in apprehending the murderers of innocent people.'

On the anti-Treaty side, Éamon de Valera has urged Irish republicans not to engage in attacks upon the Protestant minority in the south of the country. Speaking in Longford on 30 April, he stated, 'Let us not tarnish that glorious record that is unequalled by any country in the world by acts against a helpless minority.'

Collins and De Valera Agree Election Pact with Prospect of Future Coalition Government

22 May – Michael Collins and Éamon de Valera, representing the pro- and anti-Treaty factions of Sinn Féin respectively, have reached an agreement on the holding of an election and the make-up of a future Irish government.

The vital elements of their pact are that prior to the election, a panel representing both sides is to be established based on each party's existing strength, and that after the election, a coalition government is to be established.

The agreement, signed by both men on 20 May, has been hailed as 'momentous' by *The Cork Examiner,* whose special reporter also considers it likely to herald an immediate improvement in 'economic and other conditions' as the country returns to a more settled state.

There were cheers in Dáil Éireann when the terms of the unexpected pact were presented to TDs.

'Sons of Liberty'. A handbill poking fun at Michael Collins and Éamon de Valera for overwhelming the electors and seemingly giving them little choice when voting.

Border Battles: IRA Occupations of Pettigo and Belleek Ended by British Army

9 June – Tensions along the border between Northern Ireland and the Free State have escalated in recent days, with serious clashes reported between IRA troops and Crown forces in the villages of Pettigo and Belleek.

The IRA had occupied parts of the mostly Protestant village of Pettigo. The British operation to retake the town took place on land and water, and the ground seized by their troops after an offensive on 4 June includes territory on the Free State side.

A statement issued by IRA GHQ at Beggars Bush on 5 June described the attacks by British troops on Pettigo as 'entirely unprovoked' and dismissed claims that British troops were fired at from Free State territory as 'false and malicious'. It is understood that Michael Collins has written to Winston Churchill in the Colonial Office to request an inquiry into these events.

The unionist *Belfast News Letter* has nevertheless defended the actions of the British troops. The paper claims that Northern Irish territory had been 'violated by Sinn Féin invasion and occupation'.

The Lincolnshire Regiment reoccupied Belleek after it had been in the hands of the IRA.

1922

22 JUN
Field Marshal Sir Henry Wilson, military adviser to the government of Northern Ireland and former chief of staff of the Imperial General Staff, is assassinated in London, leading the British authorities to demand action from the Provisional Government.

24 JUN
The general election results are announced: pro-Treaty Sinn Féin (58 seats), anti-Treaty Sinn Féin (36 seats), Labour (17 seats), Farmers (7 seats) and Independents (7 seats).

27 JUN
General J.J. 'Ginger' O'Connell, deputy chief of staff of the National Army, is kidnapped and detained by the Four Courts anti-Treaty garrison of the IRA.

REVOLUTIONARY TIMES 1913–23

347

1922

The funeral of Sir Henry Wilson.

Sir Henry Wilson Assassinated in London in Alleged IRA Attack

23 June – Field Marshal Sir Henry Wilson, MP and the chief military advisor to the Northern Ireland government, was assassinated yesterday outside his London residence.

The killing of the Irish-born officer took place at 2.30 p.m. as he returned from unveiling a Great Eastern Railway Company war memorial at Liverpool Street Station.

Field Marshal Wilson was stepping out of a car when he was approached by two men with revolvers who began firing. He stooped to avoid the shots and had made it to his front door, where he was attempting to insert his key in the latch when he was shot again. He fell to the ground and died. Some reports state that his last words were defiant, shouting at his attackers, 'You cowardly swine!'

Two men were subsequently arrested after being pursued by police and civilians. It is understood that both men claimed to be soldiers and that at least one is suspected of being a member of the IRA.

Eoin O'Duffy, the Chief of Staff of the Irish Army in Beggars Bush, has rejected the suggestion that the shooting was the work of the IRA. Referring to reports that a copy of an 'official organ of the IRA' was found in the possession of one of the arrested men, O'Duffy said that this was referring to *An t-Óglach*, which had been on sale at public bookstalls for some time.

News of Wilson's assassination has been met with condemnation on both sides of the Irish Sea.

---

28 JUN
The ultimatum given to the Four Courts anti-Treaty garrison to surrender is ignored, resulting in the shelling of the building by pro-Treaty forces using artillery borrowed from the British, starting the Civil War.

30 JUN
The Four Courts garrison surrenders.

◁ **12 JUL**
The 232nd anniversary of the **Battle of the Boyne** is enthusiastically celebrated by Ulster Protestants across Northern Ireland, where on many platforms 'No surrender' is a common cry.

Six Protestants Murdered in Farmhouse Raids Near Newry

23 June – With violence continuing across Northern Ireland, an inquest has opened into the murder of six Protestants – five men and a woman – near Newry.

Early in the morning of 17 June a number of farmhouses owned by unionists in Lisdrumliska and Altnaveigh in south Armagh were attacked with rifles and bombs.

These attacks left the following dead: John Heaslip, a farmer from Lisdrumliska and his 17-year-old son, Robert; Thomas Crozier, a farmer from Altnaveigh, and his wife, Elizabeth; James Lockhart, a single farmer from Lisdrumliska; and Joseph Gray, also from Lisdrumliska, who died later. The victims' houses were also set on fire, with some being burned to the ground and some badly damaged.

James Lockhart, the inquest heard, had been found dead at his mother's feet. The young man had turned around to talk to her after the raiders demanded that he accompany them down the road. One of the raiders went up to him and shot him dead, declaring, 'You disobeyed orders.'

One witness to the inquest was the sister of Joseph Gray, who stated that when her mother asked the raiders why they were being targeted, the response given was, 'It is being done for the Roman Catholics of Belfast.'

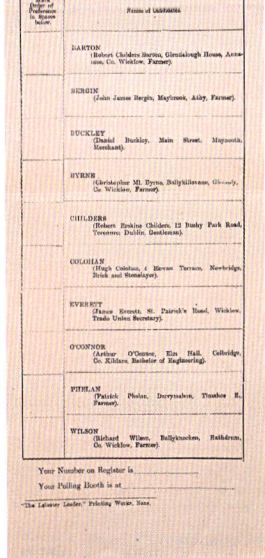

Sample ballot paper for the general election 1922.

Free State Decides – Pro-Treaty TDs Set to Make Up Largest Group in New Dáil

28 June – The people of the Irish Free State have spoken and the membership of the next Dáil has been decided after the country went to the polls on 16 June.

The 128-member chamber will comprise 58 pro-Treaty Sinn Féin, 36 anti-Treaty Sinn Féin, 17 Labour Party, 7 Farmers' Party and 7 Independent TDs. The results, *The Freeman's Journal* states, are an indication of 'the nation's overwhelming verdict for the treaty … and heralded the dramatic rise of our first Parliamentary Labour Party'. They also suggest that the agricultural and farming sector will play a significant role in national policymaking in the future.

1922

13 JUL
Winston Churchill informs the House of Commons that, while a 'rigid passport system' between Britain and Ireland is not currently planned, it might be needed in the future.

21 JUL
It is reported that over 300 internees are being held in steel cages for 18 hours a day aboard a prison ship, *Argenta*, which is anchored in Belfast Lough.

JULY–AUG
De Valera undertakes his 'Southern Tour' of military operations in and around Carrick-on-Shannon and Clonmel.

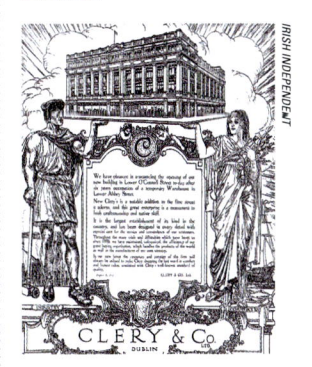

9 AUG △
Almost six years after it was destroyed in the fighting of Easter Week 1916, one of Dublin city's principal department stores, **Clerys**, reopens.

12 AUG
Arthur Griffith, president of Dáil Éireann, dies at the age of 51.

1922

16 AUG
The *Irish Independent* editorialises that the failure of a London conference called to consider German war reparations 'has left European finances in a hopeless tangle'.

▽ **22 AUG**
Michael Collins, Commander-in-Chief of the National Army, is shot dead in an ambush at Béal na mBláth, Co. Cork, in the evening. **Richard Mulcahy** will succeed him as Commander-in-Chief.

24 AUG
It is reported that the cost of living in Ireland has increased for the wage-earning classes by 85.2% since July 1914. This is one of the headline findings of a report submitted by the Department of Economic Affairs to the Provisional Government.

30 AUG
William T. Cosgrave is appointed Chairman of the Provisional Government, succeeding Michael Collins.

The relative strength of the different parties' performances is perhaps best illustrated by looking at how they fared in contested seats – 37 seats were not subject to competition. There were 48 pro-Treaty candidates, of which 41 were returned and 7 were defeated. In contrast, of the 41 anti-Treaty candidates, only 19 were elected.

Labour fielded 18 candidates of which only one failed to secure election. This is a remarkable performance and justifies the party's decision to ignore calls to stand aside as it had done in the previous Dáil elections. The Farmers' Party's 7 seats were won despite only fielding 12 candidates.

The new Dáil session is scheduled to open on 1 July.

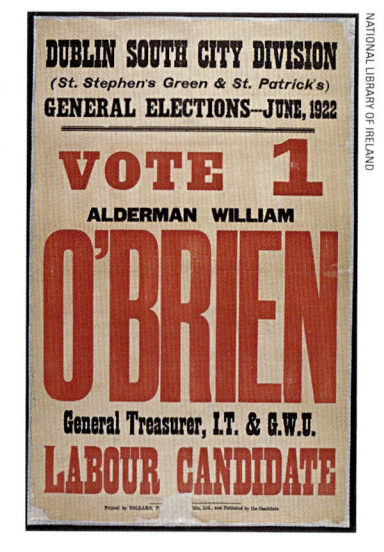

Poster for Labour candidate William O'Brien.

Four Courts Shelled by Free State Troops as Dublin Erupts in Worst Violence Since 1916

29 June – The centre of Dublin city has descended into violence – the fiercest since Easter Week 1916 – after Free State troops launched an attack on positions held by anti-Treaty forces.

▷ *Smoke billowing over Dublin rooftops following an explosion at the Four Courts.*

△ *A drawing lamenting the death of Cathal Brugha during the fighting in Dublin in July 1922.*

The iconic Four Courts has been at the centre of the Free State operation. The building, which has been occupied by anti-Treaty forces led by Rory O'Connor since April, was subjected to a sustained artillery bombardment from dawn yesterday.

Preparation for the assault on the Four Courts began with the suspension of the telephone system across Dublin in the early hours of the morning. Entrenchments with barbed-wire entanglements were established in front and around the Four Courts.

An estimated force of 1,000 Free State troops, accompanied by two armoured cars and a number of armoured lorries, took up positions on the quays on the south side of the Liffey and on principal streets on the north side. Troops also occupied houses at particular vantage points, requiring residents to leave.

At 3 a.m. a message was sent to the officer in charge of the Four Courts ordering them to immediately release Lieutenant General J.J. O'Connell, Assistant Chief of Staff, who had been kidnapped earlier in the week. A further order was issued for the Four Courts to be evacuated and the occupants' arms and ammunition to be surrendered. The anti-Treaty, or 'irregular', forces were given an hour to comply. When they didn't, the bombardment began.

Michael Collins, Chairman of the Irish Provisional Government, has defended the actions of the Free State troops as 'absolutely necessary'.

At the same time as the Dáil forces opened fire on the Four Courts, they did likewise on Fowler Memorial Hall, which was also occupied by anti-Treaty troops.

It is reported that 14 people were killed and about 30 wounded on the opening day of the battle.

National Army troops shell the occupied Four Courts.

1922

10 SEP
In opposition to proposed wage cuts, Irish postal workers begin strike action. This becomes the first nationwide strike since the establishment of the Provisional Government.

16 SEP
World-famous Irish tenor John McCormack returns to Ireland for a brief visit with his family. They stay in the Royal Marine Hotel in Dún Laoghaire.

20 SEP
On four occasions the business of the Dáil is interrupted by shouts from women sitting in the public gallery protesting the mistreatment of untried prisoners. Among the women are Maud Gonne MacBride, Hanna Sheehy Skeffington and Charlotte Despard.

26 SEP
As the Dáil debates the new Irish Constitution, a proposal by George Gavan Duffy to remove a reference to the King is likened to an invitation to proclaim a Republic. Duffy, a signatory of the Anglo-Irish Treaty, says it is not so much an issue of leaving the King out of the Constitution as 'putting him in his proper place'.

28 SEP
The postal strike ends.

REVOLUTIONARY TIMES 1913–23

1922

▽ **OCT**
Italian soprano Madame Luisa Tetrazzini – dubbed the 'Prima donna with the million-dollar voice' – performs before a full Theatre Royal in Dublin.

15 OCT
The Army Emergency Powers Bill becomes effective.

19 OCT
David Lloyd George resigns as British Prime Minister. He is succeeded by Andrew Bonar Law.

▽ **20 OCT**
W.T. Cosgrave dismisses suggestions that armed revolt and 'irregularism' is a consequence of high unemployment.

Hostilities Spread to Provinces as Both Sides Commit to Continuation of Conflict

22 July – Hostilities which began in Dublin with the bombardment of the occupied Four Courts on 28 June have now spread to other parts of the country.

Fighting between national troops and anti-Treaty forces has been reported in Wexford, Waterford, Tipperary, Limerick, Galway, Mayo, Sligo and Donegal. No end to the conflict is in sight, with neither party showing any real interest in reaching a peaceful resolution at this point.

A statement by the Provisional Government in recent days has indicated that peace at any price is not on the cards: 'A peace built upon a compromise with forces that have behaved as the Irregulars have behaved would be a peace too costly for the Irish nation.'

Republican forces are equally committed to a continuation of hostilities. A statement issued to all their volunteers declared: 'The fight is not over … the blood and sacrifices of this fight would not be shed and endured in vain. Let every soldier of the Irish Republican Army prepare for the great days ahead, stand together, encourage one another, be alert always, and be faithful to your solemn pledge to rid the nation of her enemies.'

The enemies that the republicans now face are their former comrades who make up the National Army. Since a call to arms has been issued, there has not been a single day when less than 500 men have enlisted and, on some days, the number has topped 1,000.

Reports from various areas suggest that the National Army has retaken territory from the anti-Treaty forces, including Limerick city.

An anti-Civil War cartoon entitled 'Erin: It's not me you're fighting for. It's my shadow.'

The coffin of Michael Collins being carried from the Pro-Cathedral in Dublin.

A cartoon shows Hibernia full of grief after the killing of Michael Collins. The pillars surrounding her include the names of other dead national leaders.

Michael Collins Slain in West Cork Ambush

26 August – Michael Collins TD, chairman of the Provisional Government and Commander-in-Chief of the National Army, has been killed in an ambush in west Cork. The ambush by anti-Treaty troops occurred on 22 August near Béal na mBláth, on a stretch of road between Macroom and Bandon.

According to a statement issued by the army, the ambush led to an hour-long conflict between Free State and anti-Treaty troops, which ended with the Commander-in-Chief fatally wounded. His body was removed from the scene to Shanakiel Hospital in Cork.

News of the ambush and the fatal shooting was brought to wider public attention by a special early edition of the *Evening Echo*. The official account claims that General Collins 'fought throughout the action' and set a 'splendid example to his men', continuing to fire from the ground 'until his strength failed, and he collapsed'. He died within minutes.

The Cork Examiner is reporting that General Collins's dying words as he lay on the roadside were 'Forgive them.'

The Commander-in-Chief had been visiting various military posts in the south-western command and, at the time of the ambush, had been travelling in an open touring car, which was supported by an armoured car and accompanied by national troops in a tender. The group was sticking to the by-roads of the region owing to reports that some of the main roads had been blocked. The route was wild and rugged and situated amongst hills with poor roads.

It is believed that the fatal shot that killed General Collins came towards the end of the hour-long exchange, when the firing had become less intense and when the anti-Treaty troops were on the point of retreating from their positions.

20 OCT
The Dáil hears allegations of widespread voter fraud in the recent Irish elections. Conduct in the June 1922 general election was in places so bad as to render it, Minister Ernest Blythe declares, 'something in the nature of a farce'.

21 OCT
The Cork Examiner reports that the water supply to the people of Cork city is a danger to public health and that a new system of water purification is required.

22 OCT
A refined version of the pastoral letter of Cardinal Logue and the bishops of Ireland condemning the 'Irregular' campaign and calling for an end to its 'immoral methods' is read at all principal Masses.

1922

25 OCT
At the request of the executive body of the anti-Treaty forces and of the anti-Treaty members of the second Dáil elected in May 1921, de Valera accepts an appointment as 'President of the Republic and Chief Executive of the State' and forms a Council of State of 12 members and an 'emergency' republican government.

25 OCT
The Constitution of the Irish Free State (Saorstát Éireann) Act, 1922, embodying the Constitution, is enacted by Dáil Éireann.

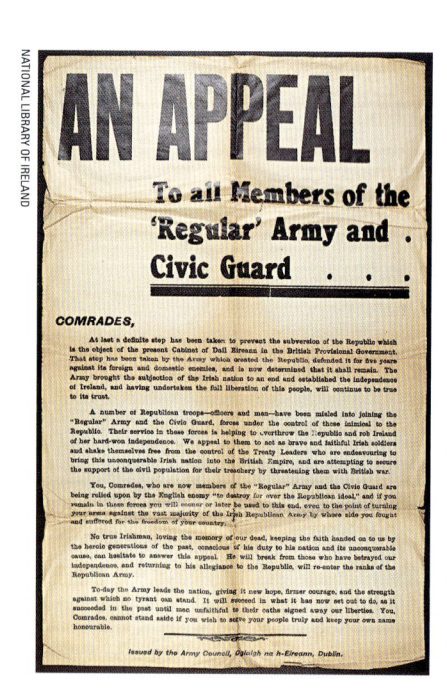

The government has declared that the day of General Collins's funeral, 28 August, will be a day of mourning in Dublin. All work and other essential services will cease. In other parts of the country business is to be suspended between the hours of 11 a.m. and noon, and Masses for the repose of the soul of the late Commander-in-Chief will be celebrated at 11 a.m.

Report on Northern Irish Education System Regrets Absence of Catholic Input

26 August – An interim report on the future of the Northern Irish education system has been prepared by Unionist MP Robert Lynn. The report, commissioned by the Minister for Education, the Marquess of Londonderry, Charles Vane-Tempest-Stewart, runs to 104 pages and is the product of both the Lynn-led committee, which met on 24 occasions, and sub-committees, which held a further 49 meetings.

Critically, the report was prepared in the absence of input from the Catholic–Nationalist minority in the six counties.

'It is greatly to be regretted,' the report notes, 'that on this committee, reflecting as it does almost every other shade of opinion in the six counties, Roman Catholic interests have not been directly represented.'

'We understand, however, that the responsibility for this circumstance rests entirely with the Roman Catholics themselves, as invitations to serve on the committee were issued to representatives of the Roman Catholic Church, and were in every case refused.'

The report adds that Roman Catholic institutions and organisations also refused to give evidence to the committee. 'We hope that, notwithstanding the disadvantage at which we were placed by this action, it will be found that Roman Catholic interests have not suffered.'

Catholic Hierarchy Condemns Anti-Treaty Campaign and Calls for an End to 'Immoral Methods'

11 October – Following a meeting in Maynooth yesterday, the Catholic bishops have published a pastoral letter to the priests and people of Ireland, in which they declare that the anti-Treaty civil war campaign has no moral justification.

Ireland, the bishops allege, has become a byword internationally for a domestic strife that is as 'disgraceful as it is criminal and suicidal'.

An anti-Treaty poster urging members of the Civic Guard and National Army to defect from their current service to the anti-Treaty forces.

The 'Irregular' campaign, they assert, has wrecked Ireland 'from end to end', and they made three appeals: to the leaders to abandon their immoral methods; to the rank and file to return to their homes; and to the country to support the government in every way.

The message from Maynooth is unequivocal and makes clear that the bishops consider the killing of national soldiers to be murder and the seizing of public and private property to be robbery. Similarly, the destruction of roads, bridges and railways is a criminal act, and the invasion of homes and the ill-treatment of citizens is a 'grievous crime'.

People guilty of such crimes cannot, the pastoral letter makes clear, be 'absolved in confession nor admitted to holy communion if they persist in such evil courses'.

Anger at Execution of Erskine Childers and Four Others Raises Concerns of Reprisals

27 November – Erskine Childers was executed by firing squad on 24 November at Beggars Bush Barracks – previously the headquarters of the Auxiliary Division of the RIC.

The execution occurred at 7 a.m. and was communicated to the public via an official announcement stating that he had been found guilty by a military court of being in possession of an automatic pistol without the proper authority. Mr Childers had been apprehended by a party of the national forces at Annamoe House, Co. Wicklow, on 10 November, and seven days later, on 17 November, was tried *in camera* at Portobello Barracks.

Addressing the Dáil on 28 November, George Gavan Duffy described Mr Childers as man whom he 'deeply revered', and prior to the execution, in a doomed attempt to save Childers' life, Éamon de Valera issued an appeal on behalf of the people of Ireland for a man he considered to be a 'faithful servant and a loyal son'.

The execution of Childers, who voted against the Treaty in the Dáil earlier this year, follows that of four others – James Fisher, Peter Cassidy, Richard Twohig and John Gaffney – in Kilmainham Gaol on 17 November after a military court found them guilty of the same offence: possession of a revolver without proper authority.

Speaking of these prior executions, Minister of Defence Richard Mulcahy acknowledged that these were drastic measures but stated that there was no alternative.

Erskine Childers, c. 1920.

4 NOV
Mary MacSwiney is arrested during raids on various houses in Dublin and subsequently goes on hunger strike. In another raid, at 36 Ailesbury Road, Ernie O'Malley is arrested, and Aíne O'Rahilly, who was accidentally shot by O'Malley, is removed to hospital.

17 NOV
The first executions under the Army Emergency Powers Act take place at Kilmainham Gaol, with Peter Cassidy, James Fisher, John Gaffney and Richard Twohig all executed for possession of revolvers.

24 NOV
Erskine Childers is executed at Beggars Bush Barracks for unlawful possession of a revolver.

6 DEC
The Constitution of the Irish Free State (Saorstát Éireann) comes into operation. T.M. Healy becomes the first Governor General and W.T. Cosgrave becomes President of the Executive Council (Cabinet).

1922

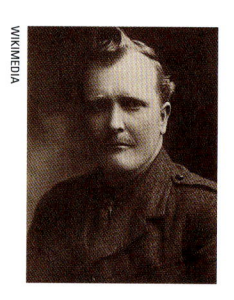

△ **7 DEC**
Seán Hales TD is assassinated in Dublin on his way to the Dáil by anti-Treaty forces. Pádraic Ó Máille TD is injured in the attack.

7 DEC
The Parliament of Northern Ireland withdraws Northern Ireland from the jurisdiction of the Parliament and government of the Irish Free State.

△ **8 DEC**
In reprisal for the killing of Seán Hales, Rory O'Connor, Liam Mellows, **Joe McKelvey** and Richard Barrett are executed by firing squad at Mountjoy Prison. The government states that this is a solemn warning against other assassinations.

No Fanfare or Celebrations as Irish Free State is Born

7 December – A year after the signing of the Anglo-Irish Treaty in London, the Irish Free State has officially come into existence.

The Provisional Government is no more, and when TDs reconvened on 6 December, they did so to choose a Cabinet, which will be known as the Executive Council, and to elect members to the first ever Seanad. Once the Seanad meets for the first time, the Oireachtas will be officially constituted.

The first formal sitting of the Saorstát Parliament was notable for its lack of pomp and ceremony, and the occasion attracted only a small crowd outside Leinster House, where a magnificent new tricolour flag, specially made, flew in the breeze.

An order recently introduced prohibiting admission to the public galleries ensured a low-key atmosphere. And while opponents of the Treaty were understandably absent, a large number of reporters representing newspapers in Ireland, England, Continental Europe and the United States were in attendance.

Once the proceedings began, the ministers in the new Free State government took the controversial oath of allegiance. The speaker, Michael Hayes, then proceeded to administer an oath that had, Labour leader Thomas Johnson pointed out, been imposed upon the Irish people 'by the threat of superior force'.

British troops leaving Dublin in December 1922 on the Arvonia.

REVOLUTIONARY TIMES 1913–23

The centrepiece of the first sitting of the Free State Parliament was the presidential address of William T. Cosgrave, head of the new Executive Council. He described it as a 'notable day when our country has definitely emerged from the bondage under which she has lived through [seven] centuries'.

President Cosgrave devoted much of his speech to the future relationship between the Free State and Northern Ireland.

Four More Prisoners Executed in Mountjoy Prison as Act of 'Reprisal' for Hales Killing

9 December – Four prominent IRA figures – Rory O'Connor, Liam Mellows, Joe McKelvey and Richard Barrett – were executed in Mountjoy Prison yesterday. They had been captured and imprisoned after the fall of the Four Courts to the National Army earlier this year.

In a statement issued by the National Army's General Headquarters, the latest round of executions are explained as a 'reprisal for the assassination … of Brigadier Seán Hales TD, and as a solemn warning to those associated with them who are engaged in a conspiracy of assassination against the representatives of the Irish people'.

The executions took place at 9.20 a.m. The prisoners were marched blindfolded to the rear of the Mountjoy Prison buildings with three clergymen in attendance. They were shot by firing squad and their bodies were subsequently interred within the grounds of the prison.

The Labour Party leader, Mr Thomas Johnson, has called upon the Free State government to end the policy of executions as a method of punishment, likening the processes involved to 'lynch law once removed'.

Twelve men have now been executed by the Free State authorities since the policy was commenced on 17 November.

1922

11 DEC
The Senate of the Free State holds its inaugural meeting.

17 DEC
The last contingent of British soldiers leaves Ireland from Dublin Port.

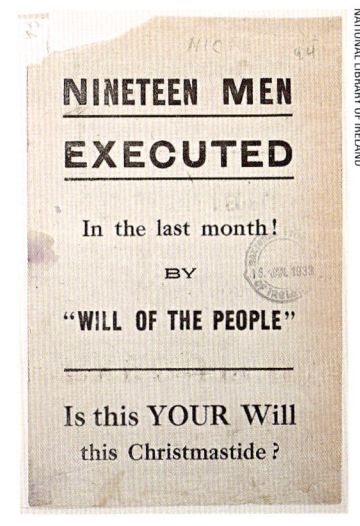

19 DEC △
Seven anti-Treaty prisoners are executed at the Curragh Camp in Kildare.

◁ *Republican prisoners on board a Free State troop ship about to depart Cork for Dublin, saying goodbye to friends.*

△ *A prisoner is depicted by Countess Markievicz waving a handkerchief through the bars of a prison.*

Remembering 1922
a hundred years on

Thousands gather at Béal na Bláth, Co. Cork, to mark the centenary of the killing of Michael Collins at this site during the Civil War. The event there has taken place annually since Collins' death, but, in the context of the Decade of Centenaries, the 2022 ceremony was by far the biggest. It was also the first time that the commemoration had been addressed by a leader of Fianna Fáil, in the form of its leader, Micheál Martin. In acknowledging the success of Irish democracy in the century since Collins had been killed, Martin, a fellow Corkonian whose Fianna Fáil party had been born out of the Civil War divide and from the opponents of the Anglo-Irish Treaty that Collins had negotiated, recognised that 'this commemoration is an important statement of remembrance and gratitude. It is a mark of our respect for one of the great heroes of Irish history, a man who played an irreplaceable role in securing Irish freedom.'

21 August 2022

REVOLUTIONARY TIMES 1913–23

359

'It is now in the hands of the Irish nation':
The British Evacuation of the Irish Free State

ON 18 DECEMBER 1922, the day after the last British troops finally departed Ireland, the *Evening Echo* reported on how 'the evacuation of British troops was completed during the course of the day. It was an event of great historic interest and importance and was not marked by the smallest unpleasant incident'. The *Evening Herald* declared 'that the evacuation of the British in the twenty-six counties is now complete'. The paper also listed Henry Robinson, the Chief Embarkation Officer, and his assistant, Captain Shepherd, as the last two British officers to leave Dublin, and remarked that 'some handover hutments, small flags trampled into the mud, and some floating flotsam and jetsam are the sole remainders of the departed British troops'.

While the evacuation of British troops from the Irish Free State was widely heralded by the Irish press in December 1922, the terms of the Anglo-Irish Treaty meant that British forces remained on the island north of the border and that three deep-water ports in the Free State – at Berehaven, Spike Island and Lough Swilly – were retained by the British.

When the Truce ending the War of Independence came into force in July 1921, there had been 51,000 members of the British forces stationed in Ireland. The process of arranging peace talks in London ran until October, and it took until January 1922 for the Anglo-Irish Treaty to be finally ratified. Given that there were fears that hostilities might restart during the period of negotiations, the size of the British garrison actually grew to 57,000 men in the second half of 1921. The ways and means of getting these soldiers out of Ireland would occupy the minds of at least some of those contributing to the lengthy and impassioned Dáil debates on the fate of the Treaty. On the final, emotion-filled

British troops had to be evacuated from across Ireland in 1922 following the signing and ratification of the Treaty. Here, at the Cork docks, members of the Royal Army Service Corps load vehicles onto a train ferry for their return to Britain.

day of the debates, Arthur Griffith appealed to heart and head when arguing that ratification of the Treaty could do what the War of Independence had failed to do: the British Army, he insisted, could be 'got out of this country tomorrow by the ratification of this Treaty; those who vote against are giving a vote to keep the British Army in Ireland. If you expect that when you reject this treaty you will drive the British Army out, then you are even more credulous than I believed you to be all the time.'

The Dáil did vote for ratification, and, as a result, a Provisional Government in Dublin was established and the British authorities began planning their retreat from the twenty-six counties of the new Free State. The whole process was overseen by General Sir Cecil Frederick Nevil Macready, who had been appointed as General Officer Commanding in Chief, Irish Command, in the spring of 1920. Before the troops could begin to fully leave, however, there was the major matter of the formal handover of the control of government from the representative of the British Crown in Ireland, Lord Lieutenant Lord FitzAlan Howard, to the Provisional Government. FitzAlan had been the first Catholic to hold the office of viceroy, and his appointment, in April 1921, had been a calculated sop to Irish nationalist sentiment that came too late to be of any practical consequence. Put simply, it cut little ice with either the nationalist press or the Catholic prelates. On being questioned about the religious affiliation of the new appointee, an unimpressed Cardinal Michael Logue, leader of the country's Catholic Church, tartly retorted that 'Ireland would as soon have a Catholic hangman'. In so much as FitzAlan would have any input into Irish affairs, it would be as an advocate within the British establishment for an accommodation with Irish nationalists, and, in the wake of the signing of the Anglo-Irish Treaty in December 1921, it ultimately fell to him to perform the symbolic handover of power and bring down the curtain on seven centuries of British rule over most, if not all, of the island of Ireland. And when the moment came at Dublin Castle on 16 January 1922, he congratulated the representatives of the new government, wished them well and 'expressed the earnest hope that under their earnest auspices the ideal of a happy, free, and prosperous Ireland would be attained'.

The historian Martin Maguire has described the transfer of Dublin Castle into Irish control as a 'revolutionary event'. The only precedent where Britain had been brought to such a point across its vast Empire was in 1783, when it lost the thirteen colonies that became the United States following the American Revolution. It was hardly surprising, therefore, that in January 1922 contemporary newspaper coverage dwelled upon the historic weight of the moment. The *Irish Independent* appeared in no doubt that what had occurred was 'certainly the most significant event in Irish history for hundreds of years'. The *Belfast News Letter* interpreted it in much the same way, albeit for different reasons. Viewed through its loyalist lens, it considered the Lord Lieutenant's relinquishing of a 'fortress of British rule' to be 'one of the most humiliating' events in British history, an act of surrender that was in 'every way deplorable'.

And yet, as a piece of political theatre, the Castle handover was underwhelming. Little planning went into it, and there was a marked absence of ceremony or public pomp. Even on the morning of the handover, final arrangements still had to be firmed up, though the fact that it had been reported in the press meant a large crowd congregated on Dame Street at the entrance of the Castle. It was along this street that three cars carrying members of the Provisional Government – coming from the Mansion House, where a Cabinet meeting had been held that morning – were driven before turning into the Lower Yard and then into the Upper Yard of Dublin Castle. There, shortly after 1.30 p.m., they alighted in front of the chief secretary's office. A 'motley assemblage' was how one civil servant described the members of the new government, who were led by Michael Collins. They were followed a few minutes later by Lord FitzAlan, who had made the short journey across the River Liffey from the vice-regal lodge in the Phoenix Park. The meeting that followed, held in the Privy Council chamber, lasted just over an hour, with members of the Provisional Government exiting the Castle buildings at around 2.30 p.m. to cheers from the crowds assembled in the Upper Yard. Later that afternoon a statement issued by Collins announced that 'the Members of the Provisional Government received the surrender of Dublin Castle at 1.45pm today. It is now in the hands of the Irish nation.'

This was neither the start nor the end of the British evacuation. Across the city the demobilisation of British forces had already begun, with troops and stores being moved to the Dublin docks in preparation for their return sailing home. The demobilisation was a massive undertaking. It was not just the question of how to remove the large number of troops that had built up in Ireland during the War of Independence, but how to unravel a formal British military presence in the country that stretched back to the seventeenth century. In every county there were barracks that had been occupied by British forces, and supplies of everything from food and uniforms to guns and ammunition were stored in massive quantities. In addition, defensive structures that had been installed during the War of Independence had to be dismantled, with barbed wire and sandbags needing to be removed from townlands across the country. Much of what could not be removed was sold. Less than a week after the Treaty's ratification, and before the formal handover of Dublin Castle, *The Irish Times* reported on 'a sale of barbed wire, boxes and odds and ends at the naval base, Kingstown … The sandbags have not yet been removed from the pier and other places, but there is an air of packing up.' A fortnight later, in the same newspaper, an auctioneers and valuers in Maryborough, Co. Laois, was advertising the sale of 'military effects' from the local barracks and internment camp. Up for grabs were 'stores' and 'reserve rations' that included 1,100 hair mattresses and bolsters, and several tons of barbed wire and corrugated iron. Not long after, further south, in Templemore, prospective purchasers were able to acquire all this and more, including candles, cutlery, cooking ranges, chairs, blankets, pillows, dinner tables, lamps, glasses, shovels, soaps, wash-hand stands and weighing machines. The unexpressed yet obvious conclusion to be drawn was clear: the emptying of British-occupied military barracks was to cover both people and possessions. It was to be a complete operation.

The first barracks to be evacuated by British troops was at Clogheen, Co. Tipperary, at the end of January 1922, and at the beginning of February a large crowd gathered to cheerfully observe the departure of the last of the detested Auxiliary Division from its Dublin base at Beggars Bush Barracks. Although it was understood that a total exodus could not be affected overnight – it was, after all, an enormous logistical undertaking – the British government was nevertheless anxious to move as quickly as possible so as to impress on the Irish people that the Anglo-Irish Treaty meant the delivery of real and substantive change. In practice, this meant that as smaller barracks were emptied, most troops moved to Cork, the Curragh or into Dublin to await shipment home, while others were transferred to service in Northern Ireland. The main route out of Ireland for British forces was through Dublin and its port, with 60% of the evacuation taking place through the city. Coupled with this withdrawal was the disbandment of the RIC, which commenced in March 1922 and was completed within two months. Once the 7,000-strong force had been stood down, it was replaced by the police force of the Provisional Government, the Civic Guard, later renamed An Garda Síochána. Many former members of the RIC moved to Northern Ireland and joined the newly formed RUC, while large numbers chose retirement and moved to Britain with their families. An annual pension fund for former RIC members of £1.5 million was made available, which was guaranteed under the terms of the Treaty and paid for by the Free State.

The first barracks to be evacuated by British troops was at Clogheen, Co. Tipperary, at the end of January 1922.

If all of this wasn't an onerous enough undertaking, the deteriorating political climate during 1922 made matters more demanding for both the Provisional Irish and British governments. Following the occupation of the Four Courts by anti-Treaty forces from 14 April and the outbreak of the Civil War on 28 June, British authorities endeavoured to proceed with their evacuation without becoming embroiled in the Irish struggle over the terms of the Treaty. As spring progressed and the fissures in nationalism deepened, General Macready moved the bulk of the remaining British troops towards Dublin to keep them at a distance from any potential flashpoints. Indeed, by the time the Civil War had begun, there were no British forces remaining in Connacht or Munster, and the RAF had departed, except for a small contingent at Collinstown and an emergency landing strip in the Phoenix Park. Beyond that, what remained were the troops stationed at the so-called Treaty ports and in the greater Dublin area. In all, Macready held back over 5,000 troops in Dublin in case they were needed, should the Provisional Government's authority falter.

Even so, the extent of the British disentanglement from the twenty-six counties was evident everywhere, and the signs of separation were not confined to events on the island of Ireland. A fortnight before the Civil War began, on 12 June, the colours of the six Irish regiments in the British Army – the Royal Irish Regiment, the Connaught Rangers, the South Irish Horse, the Prince of Wales's Leinster Regiment, the Royal Munster Fusiliers and the Royal Dublin Fusiliers – were presented to King George V at Windsor Castle. It was a ritual, if heavy-hearted, act of disbandment. Detachments from all six regiments were present, and in accepting their colours King George declared, 'As your King, I am proud to accept this trust. But I fully realise with what grief you relinquish these dearly-prized emblems; and I pledge my word that within these ancient and historic walls your colours will be treasured, honoured, and protected as hallowed memorials of the glorious deeds of brave and loyal regiments.' Although their colours would be hung permanently on the grand staircase near to Windsor's St George's Hall, the ceremony was an emotional one for those in attendance. Men wept at what was, historian Heather Jones has observed, a 'powerful performance of monarchical retreat'. For these victorious veterans of the Great War, Jones

A copy of an address made by King George V at Windsor Castle on the occasion of disbandment of the Irish regiments following the creation of Irish Free State. These were given, in this case, to the men of the Prince of Wales's Leinster Regiment (Royal Canadians).

British troops, some of them members of the Royal Irish Rifles, chalk their goodbyes onto a wall at North Wall in December 1922. Others chalked messages onto the ships on which they would sail across the Irish Sea reading 'Farewell Dublin' and 'Don't Splash'.

remarked, the handing back of their regimental colours in London 'embodied their Irish defeat'.

Towards late 1922, the scale of British withdrawal was underscored by the fact that, for the first time since 1919, there was no public parade involving representatives of the British Army in Dublin's Armistice Day commemorations. Indeed, by then, only 364 officers and 6,254 personnel from other ranks were still situated at various locations in Dublin. A month later, their exodus began: on 10 December, the same day as General Macready attended the handover of the vice-regal lodge to the Irish Free State Army, Richmond Barracks was evacuated, with the three departing British infantry battalions marching to the North Wall to board ships for home. By 17 December the remaining nurses of the King George V Hospital had departed for Northern Ireland by train, and the last seven airmen who had manned an emergency landing strip at

Phoenix Park had flown to Britain. On that day, too, the final eighteen properties owned by the British War Department were handed over to the Irish authorities, including the General Headquarters. The final act for General Macready was to bid farewell to the 135 ex-servicemen who had decided to remain at the Royal Hospital in Kilmainham, before inspecting exiting troops on Sarsfield Quay. Macready was then driven to Kingstown to board his ship, the HMS *Dragon*, which, accompanied by HMS *Wolsey* and HMS *Venomous*, set sail following a seventeen-gun salute.

Departed, too, was Lord FitzAlan, Ireland's last lord lieutenant, who had returned to England before his office was finally wound up as the Irish Free State Constitution became law in early December. Indeed, on the very day after the Constitution took effect, FitzAlan was in Chichester in England, where he attempted to cast the British retreat not as imperial defeat but as a measure of British benevolence, an act of generosity which he hoped the new Irish State would repay. 'We could have conquered Ireland quite easily,' he proclaimed, but said there would have been continued bloodshed and atrocities and after thirty years, 'the whole thing would have to be done over again'. Instead, and by way of an alternative, FitzAlan declared that 'England' had decided upon 'an experiment' in Ireland that was 'well worth trying'. His remarks to his English audience suggested that the hope he had previously expressed for a peaceful and prosperous Irish future was just that – an expression of hope rather than confidence in the prospects for the new state and those leading it.

As it transpired, the experiment worked on many levels. There would no British return to the twenty-six counties and, in time, the troops who had been left in occupancy of the so-called Treaty ports would leave as well. In Dublin's Phoenix Park, meanwhile, the vice-regal lodge became home to a new governor general and later to a president of a full Republic. And yet, in the grounds of the grand residence, FitzAlan had, before returning to resume his life across the Irish Sea, planted two copper beeches to sit alongside other commemorative trees, including a Wellingtonia that Queen Victoria had seeded during her royal visit to Ireland in 1861. Whether it was ever considered in such terms or not, the symbolism of this act suggested that, whatever about ridding the new Free State of the essentials of British rule, the roots of British influence in Irish life would continue to run deep.

Wading Through Irish Blood:
Civil War, 1922–23

THE IRISH WAR of Independence ended in messy imperfection. It ended in compromise.

The British administration and its army would, as Arthur Griffith had promised to the Dáil, be driven out of much of Ireland, but without replacement by the venerated Republic. A new Irish Free State would be created, but on an island that was still partitioned, and with republican forces split on the character of the settlement reached in the Anglo-Irish Treaty that had been signed in London on 6 December 1921. Arguments for and against that Treaty were played out in passion-filled Dáil Éireann debates, which ran from mid-December 1921 to early January the following year. There were reasonable and compelling arguments presented on both sides, with pro-Treaty TDs keen to emphasise both the freedoms won and opportunities presented in a settlement that, Michael Collins famously remarked, would provide a stepping-stone to the 'ultimate freedom that all nations desire and develop to'. Opponents of the Treaty, in contrast, could see only that which had been conceded and how far from the ideal of the Republic the Treaty fell, which explained their focus on issues like the 'oath' and the status of the governor general. These they considered betrayals of the Republic that had been proclaimed at Easter 1916 and reaffirmed with the establishment of Dáil Éireann in 1919. 'I took an Oath to the Irish Republic, solemnly, reverently, meaning every word,' Kathleen Clarke, widow of executed 1916 leader Thomas, announced. 'I shall never go back from that.'

> **Arguments for and against that Treaty were played out in passion-filled Dáil Éireann debates.**

Clarke was nevertheless in the minority – if only just. When, finally, the TDs cast their votes on 7 January 1922, the majority swung in favour of the deal, sixty-four to fifty-seven. This vote was hardly emphatic. It did not, however, precipitate a rush to renewed conflict. Civil war was certainly not the reflex response to the Treaty; instead, it unfolded gradually, shaped by events beyond the country as well as by all too obvious divisions within it. The fractures witnessed in the Dáil soon surfaced in an array of nationalist and republican organisations. Splits occurred in Sinn Féin, in Cumann na mBan and the IRA, the rising political temper exemplified by the St Patrick's Day speech of Éamon de Valera in Thurles, where he warned that the unfinished business of the Irish Volunteers might see them 'wade through Irish blood', specifically that of members of the Irish government and their soldiers. And yet, a large measure of restraint went hand in glove with such incendiary rhetoric, slowing the slide into internecine strife.

In fact, over five months passed between the conclusion of the Treaty debates and the onset of civil war. During that time Rory O'Connor led a group of anti-Treaty forces into occupation of the Four Courts in Dublin, and a general election was held, prior to which Éamon de Valera and Michael Collins attempted to maintain a facade of unity: together they negotiated a 'pact' whereby Sinn Féin would run both pro- and anti-Treaty candidates with a view to forming a coalition government afterwards. The election took place – reaffirming the majority support for the Treaty – but no coalition materialised. What ensued instead was urban warfare, ignited not by any event in Ireland, but by one at Eaton Place in London. This was where Longford-born Field Marshal Sir Henry Wilson, then an MP and chief security advisor to the new Northern Ireland government, resided, and where he was shot on 22 June 1922. The two men later hanged for killing the Irish-born former Chief of the Imperial General Staff were London-born and based members of the IRA: Commandant Reggie Dunne and

A pro-Treaty poster and anti-Treaty leaflet reflecting the very different ideas on what the Treaty meant for the opposing sides.

Volunteer Joe O'Sullivan. Both, like Wilson, were veterans of the First World War, in which O'Sullivan had lost a leg.

The assassination of Wilson caused consternation in London, and British Prime Minister David Lloyd George wrote immediately to Michael Collins informing him that his government's ambiguous treatment of the IRA could no longer be tolerated. Nor, the British Prime Minister insisted, could Rory O'Connor be left in control of the Four Courts to orchestrate 'enterprises in murder'. As a result, on 28 June, six days after the shooting of Wilson and just four after the announcement of the election results, the National Army – as the pro-Treaty forces were then known – began bombarding the Four Courts.

> On 28 June, the National Army – as the pro-Treaty forces were then known – began bombarding the Four Courts.

This was the start of a civil war that would be fought in phases. The first was a brief bout of large-scale fighting in Dublin, following which the focus shifted to anti-Treaty strongholds in Munster, including the cities of Limerick and Waterford. By August 1922, however, the urban phase of the Civil War, its outcome then certain, had ended, with government forces establishing a firm control. This was to be succeeded by a protracted, low-level guerrilla campaign by anti-Treaty republicans, whose government opponents could, over time, draw upon more (and paid) manpower and significantly larger volumes of equipment, generous supplies of which – arms and ammunition – were provided by the old British enemy.

Not everyone rushed to join the fray, however. A Neutral IRA was established in December 1922 for those unwilling to be drawn to either side of a bitter divide. The labour movement steered a similar middle course, going so far as to hold a general strike against militarism in April 1922 in an effort, ultimately futile, to stay the drift towards civil war. Others simply opted to prioritise issues and interests different to those preferred by the determined fighting factions. It was, for instance, the defence of fair wages and broader workers' rights that drove postal workers to take strike action in September 1922, the first major industrial dispute of the Free State era, albeit one the Provisional Government chose, in the context of wider disorder, to characterise as an act of disloyalty meriting a repressive response, rather than as a legitimate pursuit of labour interests in a democratic society.

Then there were those for whom the passions aroused by civil war were secondary to those they held for sport and entertainments, such as concerts and cinema, markers of a social normalcy that occasionally jarred with the single-minded combatants. In March 1923, in order to highlight the execution and mistreatment of IRA prisoners by the new Free State government, anti-Treatyites issued a proclamation ordering an indefinite period of 'national mourning' during which all forms of amusement, entertainment and sport were to be abandoned. The proclamation came with a campaign of intimidation, such as occurred when the Dublin Brigade of the IRA wrote to the secretary of Howth Golf Club to remind him that non-observance of the golf ban would result in 'drastic action' being taken against the club.

Measured against international comparisons, the Irish Civil War, then in its endgame, was both shorter and far less bloody than those experienced elsewhere. However, this shouldn't obscure the devastations involved, the brutalities inflicted or the bitter legacies left. A generation of political leaders was killed, yet the names of Michael Collins, Cathal Brugha, Liam Lynch, Liam Mellows and Harry Boland are just a few among an estimated 1,600 who lost their lives. This was a scale of human loss dwarfed by that of the Irish involved in the First World War, and it compared with a death toll of 2,850 men, women and children killed across the entirety of the Irish revolutionary period from 1916 to 1921.

Contained as it was, there is nevertheless still something about civil wars that sets them apart, and no side emerged from the Irish experience with reputations unscathed. With dreadful deeds done on both sides, there was, as historian John Borgonovo has remarked, 'enough shame to go around'. The disruptions of war were undoubtedly used by some as an opportunity to settle scores or advance personal agendas, and, as a growing body of new research has documented, members of the pro- and anti-Treaty forces were guilty of perpetrating acts of extreme sexual violence against women, up to and including gang rape. Violence against civilians was widespread, as was the destruction of property, including the homes of elected representatives and the 'big houses' of the old Anglo-Irish ascendancy, attacks begun during the War of Independence that, for no obvious strategic purpose, increased dramatically throughout the Civil War.

Decrying the lamentable drift of events in October 1922, the Irish Catholic bishops – supporters of the Provisional Government – issued a pastoral letter defending the denial of sacraments to violent anti-Treaty republicans

After the anti-Treaty forces in the Four Courts surrendered, fighting continued on O'Connell Street. After several days of intense fighting, Dublin was secured by the National Army.

and denouncing as un-Catholic, immoral, 'criminal and suicide' the ongoing campaign against the civil authority. While a number privately communicated their unease, the bishops were not given to such fierce public pronouncements when it came to the excesses of the Free State and National Army. The former would enact repressive public safety laws and execute without due process far more republicans – eighty-one of them – than the British had previously done. At Ballyseedy, Co. Kerry, in reprisal for heavy local casualties in its own ranks, the National Army committed one of the worst atrocities of the entire revolutionary decade: in March 1923 Free State troops tied nine prisoners to a landmine and blew it up, leaving only a single survivor – Stephen Fuller – who was blown clear of the site by the force of the blast. It was left to a group of women to pick up the bits of what was left of Fuller's colleagues. Sally Sheehy, one of them, recalled gathering the 'remains of the dead bodies, brains, clothes'.

Two months later, with a ceasefire rather than a decisive victory, the Civil War – an 'eleven-month squabble' as one historian has characterised it – ended. Its effects were nevertheless felt for generations within families, communities and, of course, in the politics of the state it had helped to both secure and stain. Among the combatants and survivors was the anti-republican Todd Andrews, who later remarked, 'In Civil War, alas, there is no glory. There are no monuments to victory or victors, only to the dead.' There were – and are – monuments all the same, erected at different times by different groups and scattered across the country, from roadsides (as in the case of Ballyseedy) to a desolate Wicklow mountain, where a small commemorative stone cross marks the spot where the badly broken body of anti-Treaty officer Noel Lemass was found buried in October 1923, months after his abduction in the summer of that year. Throughout a lengthy political career that would see him rise to the position of taoiseach in the independent state, Seán Lemass would choose not to talk publicly about the circumstances of his brother's death.

> 'In Civil War, alas, there is no glory. There are no monuments to victory or victors, only to the dead.'

But for all that there was a reluctance to speak about events of the Civil War, historian Síobhra Aiken has shown the ways in which veterans – men and women – used Irish- and English-language literature to pierce the silence with their memoirs, novels and poetry. Applicants under successive Military Service Pensions Acts – writers of a different kind – also attested to the physical, material and emotional ravages of a civil war that echoed through the generations – and not only in Ireland. Thousands of applicants wrote from overseas, among them a large number of anti-Treaty IRA veterans who chose exile in the United States over life in a Free State they had at once helped forge and fight against. In their totality, these military pension application files are as much a record of post-revolutionary disappointment and damaged and broken lives as they are a chronicle of what people did, when and where. In all their rich detail and bureaucratic blandness, they read as a sometimes sad and inglorious endnote to a decade of revolutionary upheaval – much, indeed, like the Civil War.

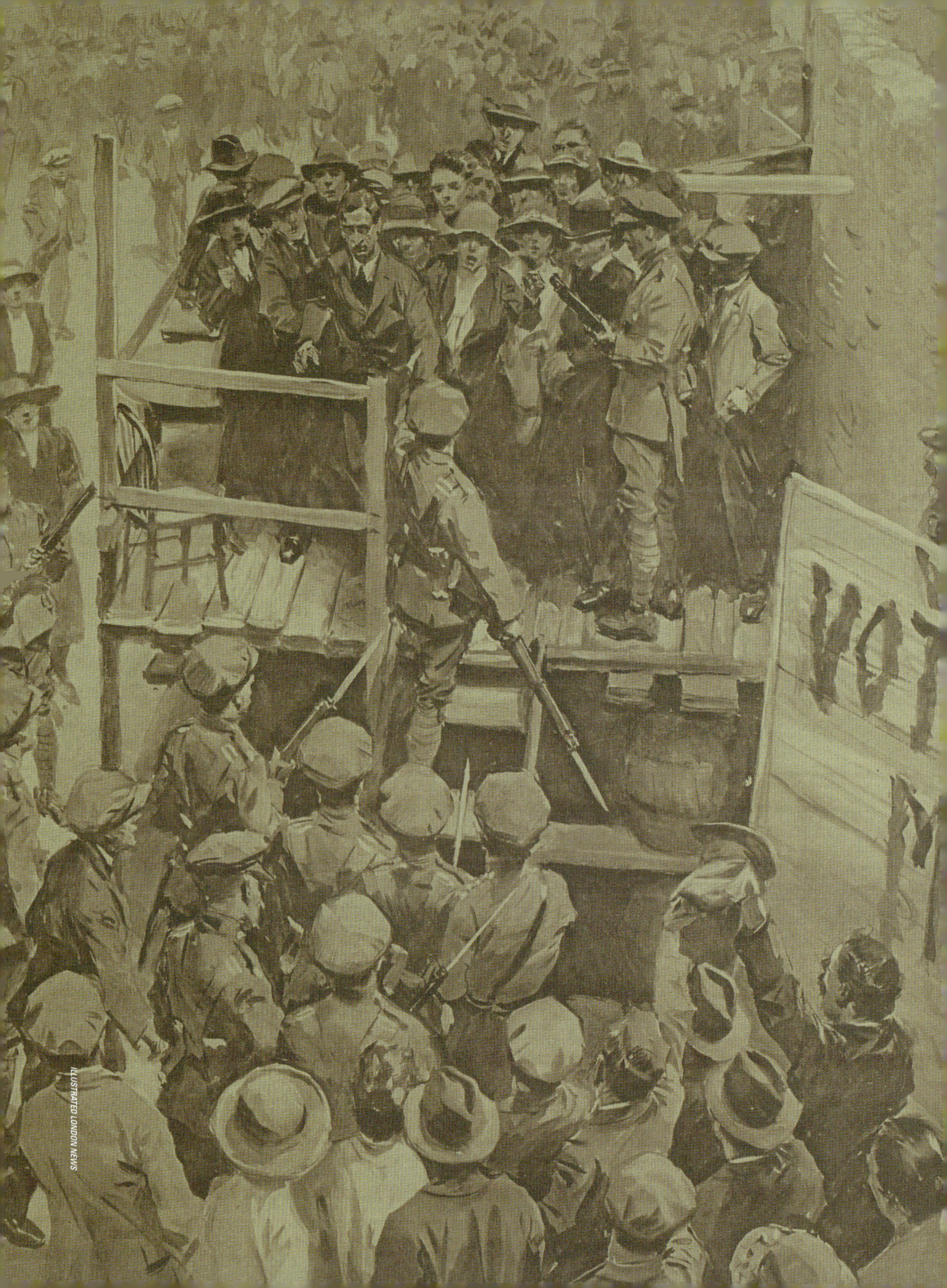
VOT

1923

'Seven years of intense effort have exhausted our people. Their sacrifices and their sorrows have been many ... they are weary and need a rest. A little time and you will see them recover and rally again to the standard.'

Éamon de Valera
24 MAY

1923

1 JAN
President W.T. Cosgrave says the first New Year's Day in Saorstát Éireann is a cause for celebration. He expresses the hope that 1923 will deliver peace, order and Irish unity.

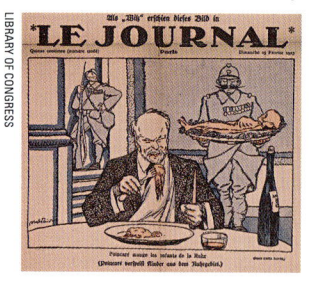

△ **11 JAN**
France, led by Premier **Raymond Poincaré**, and Belgium invade the resource-rich Ruhr region in response to unpaid reparations from Germany. They occupy coal mines, factories, railways and steel works.

20 JAN
Eleven republican prisoners in three locations (Limerick, Tralee and Athlone) are executed, reflecting an escalation in the use of this policy by the Irish Free State government.

26 JAN
Long queues of young men form outside recruitment stations in Dublin in response to an urgent appeal for new recruits to the National Army. These stations are open between the hours of 10 a.m. and 4 p.m.

Rathfarnham Residence of President W.T. Cosgrave Destroyed in Arson Attack

Dublin, 15 January – The country residence of the President of the Executive Council, William T. Cosgrave, was gutted in an arson attack on 13 January.

The house, Beechpark, is situated in Ballyboden, a mile and half from Rathfarnham, and nobody was in occupancy at the time. The incendiaries took great care to ensure that an early alarm could not be raised to save the property, cutting the telephone wires in the area.

President Cosgrave has told reporters that he was not surprised by the attack. The property had been purchased in 1919, but Mr Cosgrave had not lived there for more than eight months as he had initially been 'on the run' during the War of Independence.

The fire at Beechpark was discovered at 6.30 a.m. by a young man living some distance away, who placed a phone call to the Rathmines Fire Brigade. By 7.30 a.m. President Cosgrave, accompanied by Commandant Joseph O'Reilly, was at the site to supervise the salvage operation. Except for a few items of furniture saved by a caretaker, who had been in bed in an adjoining building when the fire was started, many of the contents of the house were destroyed, including artefacts of considerable historical interest – a large collection of manuscripts and letters from most of the men who had taken part in the 1916 Rising, and letters and documents belonging to the late President Arthur Griffith and Michael Collins.

President Cosgrave visits the ruins of his house at Beechpark.

French Troops Move to Occupy German Ruhr Region Amid Claims of a Reparations Default

The Ruhr, 16 January – The French army has in recent days moved to take occupation of the Ruhr region of Germany.

The French Premier, Raymond Poincaré, has defended the action in the French chamber on the grounds that Germany had defaulted from its reparations responsibilities under the Versailles Treaty in terms of coal and wood deliveries.

Monsieur Poincaré said that France did not desire to act outside the Treaty of Versailles and had only entered Essen and the Ruhr to defend the joint interests of the Allies. He added, too, that France was not acting alone but with the support of Belgian and Italian engineers.

Germany has decreed the Franco-Belgian action as a breach of the treaty, which, it claims, makes no allowance for territorial sanctions. It is being reported that the German government will, once the French occupation becomes established, declare the peace treaty to be broken and will no longer negotiate with the Reparations Commission.

The Ruhr represents the heart of the German coal industry and, so far, the French have been met with only passive resistance. A half-hour stoppage of all work in Essen was observed in protest at the occupation, and miners in the region have refused to work overtime. There have also been reports of bouts of patriotic German singing and anti-French demonstrations.

Speaking in Washington, the US Ambassador to Britain, George Harvey, has said that there is 'no telling what may result from the occupation of the Ruhr, and nobody can tell from day to day what is going to happen'.

In early 1923 the German government, represented here by Chancellor Wilhelm Cuno, faced the anger of its citizens over what they perceived as the unfair terms of the Treaty of Versailles, and the threats of the French to invade the Ruhr on the grounds that the Germans were in default in paying reparations.

1923

31 JAN
The Irish Labour Party moves a Dáil motion to condemn the government's 'policy and practice of reprisals as immoral, unjust, and unlawful'.

4 FEB ▷
Eight British soldiers and the son of a ferryman lose their lives in a boating tragedy in Dundrum Bay, Co. Down. The soldiers, belonging to the **Royal West Kent** and Cheshire regiments, as well as a Royal Engineer, had been attempting to make their return to Ballykinlar Camp where they were stationed when the ferryboat capsized.

The front of the German magazine **Simplicissimus** *with a caption translating to 'Charges for alleged crimes committed by French occupying forces in the Battle of the Ruhr'.*

1923

8 FEB
General Richard Mulcahy, Commander-in-Chief of the National Army, offers an amnesty to anti-Treaty IRA members willing to surrender by 18 February. It follows a call by captured IRA commander Liam Deasy, who thereby avoided execution, for an 'immediate and unconditional surrender of all arms and men'.

10 FEB
Ireland lose their first international rugby match of the year to England before 20,000 spectators at Leicester. Defeated by 23 points to 5, *The Irish Times* reports that 'Our team was outclassed in all departments.'

▽ 16 FEB
After discovering the historic site the previous November, British archaeologist Howard Carter unseals the burial chamber of the 'Boy Pharaoh' **Tutankhamun** in Egypt. King Tut had ruled over Egypt from about 1336–1327 BC and nobody had seen inside his final resting place for over 3,000 years.

14 More Executed By Free State Following Military Tribunals

The policy of the Irish Free State executing its political opponents continues

Dundalk, 23 January – A statement issued by the General Headquarters of the Irish Army at Portobello Barracks notes that three more men were executed yesterday morning at Dundalk Barracks.

The three men were all found guilty of possessing arms and ammunition without the proper authority at Dowdallshill, Dundalk, on 7 January 1923. They have been named as James Melia, Thomas Lennon and Joseph Ferguson.

The news from Dundalk comes within days of the revelation that a further 11 men had been executed at Athlone, Tralee and Limerick. An official report issued by the army HQ at Portobello Barracks confirmed the details of these executions.

A de Valera campaign leaflet addressed to the electors of Clare featuring two of those executed in Limerick on 20 January, Cornelius McMahon and Patrick Hennessy.

Labour Party Condemns Free State Policy of Reprisals as Uncivilised

Dublin, 1 February – The Labour Party yesterday moved a motion calling upon Dáil Éireann to condemn the 'policy and practice of reprisals as immoral, unjust, and unlawful' and 'that it ought not to be tolerated in a civilised community'.

The party's leader, Mr Thomas Johnson, explained that the motion was being put forward in response to a worrying proclamation that had appeared in yesterday's morning newspaper, purportedly coming from Major General D. Hogan, General Officer of the Dublin Command. The proclamation was in regard to the kidnapping of Senator John Bagwell, who is general manager of the Great Northern Railways.

Bagwell was seized from his home in Howth by armed forces and removed to an unknown destination. A warning was then issued that should

Senator Bagwell's captors fail to release him unharmed in the next 48 hours, punitive action would be taken against several associates in the conspiracy who were already in custody.

In his reply to this statement, Mr Johnson remarked that this would mean punitive action would be taken not against the culprit but against 'other people, who are presumed to have known something about this conspiracy'. Mr Johnson continued, 'I want to say that no civilised people, and no Legislature of a civilised State can defend this doctrine of reprisals, and that is what is meant here. Somebody commits an offence, and somebody else must suffer for it, because, forsooth, the Executive arm is not capable of bringing to justice, or what purports to be justice, the offenders.'

Since the issuing of the proclamation and the discussion around it in the Dáil, Senator Bagwell has been set free. He was picked up unharmed by passing motorists on a road near Swords and brought to the city, where he had a lengthy interview with President Cosgrave.

Senator John Bagwell (left) with Thomas Grattan in December 1922.

Stricter Film Censorship Requires Appointment of National Censor, Free State Minister Told

Dublin, 10 February – A stricter regime of film censorship is coming to the Irish Free State and will be supported, if necessary, by legislation, the Minister for Home Affairs, Kevin O'Higgins, has said.

Mr O'Higgins was responding to a statement on the evils of cinema that had been presented to him by a deputation representing the Irish Vigilance Association, Priests' Social Guild and the Catholic, Protestant, Episcopalian and Presbyterian Churches in Ireland.

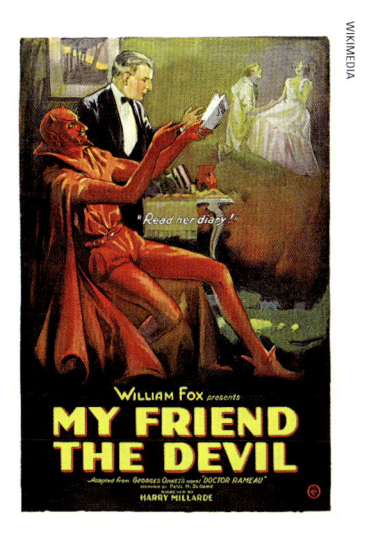

Films such as My Friend the Devil *outraged Irish audiences and complaints were made about such films.*

1923

3 MAR ▽
The first issue of *Time* magazine is published in the United States.

4 MAR
Limerick's hurlers become All-Ireland champions and the first recipients of the Liam McCarthy Cup after defeating Dublin before an attendance of 19,000 at Croke Park, which included President William T. Cosgrave and other members of the Free State government. Owing to the disruptions and delays of recent years, this was the All-Ireland final for 1921.

6 MAR
Five members of the National Army are killed at Knocknagoshel, Co. Kerry, after triggering a booby-trapped mine when inspecting an arms dump. In response, it is determined that in future anti-Treaty prisoners should clear potentially mined roads: 'The tragedy of Knocknagoshel must not be repeated.'

REVOLUTIONARY TIMES 1913–23

1923

7 MAR
Nine republican prisoners are tied in a circle around a mine, which is then exploded by National Army troops at Ballyseedy Cross, Co. Kerry. Blown clear by the blast and presumed dead, Stephen Fuller is the sole survivor.

17 MAR
Belfast-based Alton United surprise Dublin side Shelbourne to win the FAI Cup final at Dalymount Park on a 1–0 scoreline.

19 MAR
Irish agriculture is in a much more depressed state in 1923 than it was in 1912, Richard Wilson, a Farmers' Party TD for Kildare–Wicklow, tells the State-established Agricultural Commission. The TD was speaking on behalf of the Irish Farmers' Union (IFU).

3 APR
Lily Graham establishes a new British record in Birmingham by dancing continuously for 24 hours and 5 minutes. Graham was accompanied by a dance partner, the first of whom had to be replaced after collapsing at the 19-hour mark.

With over 150 picture houses in Ireland – 31 of them in Dublin city and its suburbs – and a daily attendance of over 20,000 people, the statement claimed that it was 'evidently undesirable that our people should be accustomed to see and applaud scenes of murder, robbery, violence of every kind, offensive suggestiveness, sexual immorality, and yet such scenes are often set before them in our picture houses in Dublin and throughout Ireland'.

The deputation argued that the existing system of censorship was unsatisfactory to the point that there was no censorship at all in many parts of Ireland. In Dublin, the system was alleged to have completely broken down, with films shown without ever being presented to the censors.

Many members of the same deputation met last year with Dublin Corporation to raise similar concerns about the inadequacy of the current system of film censorship, a meeting which followed months after the Municipal Council itself had adopted a resolution – passed on 1 May 1922 – calling on Dáil Éireann to appoint a Board of Film Censors for Ireland. On this occasion, the various deputations urged the appointment of a national censor and a supporting staff of full-time officials. The idea is that no film could be shown anywhere in Ireland without a licence declaring that it had been passed by the national censor.

To meet the operating costs of this scheme, the deputation proposed that funding come from either the amusement tax or a special levy on the valuation of theatres.

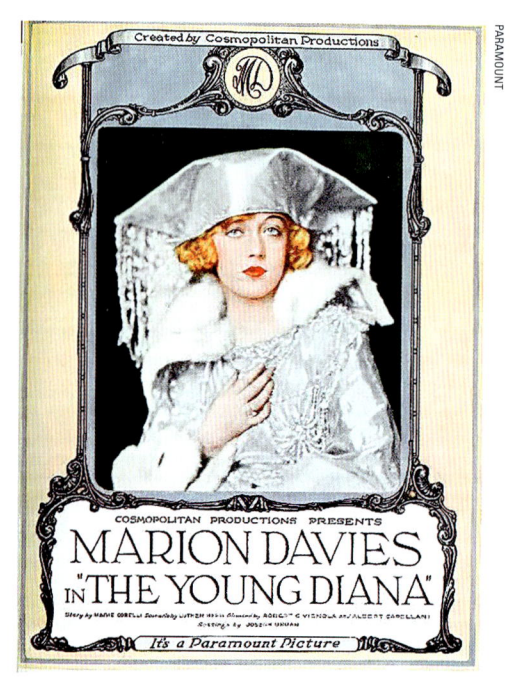

Poster for The Young Diana.

1923

Anti-Treaty prisoners at Passage West being rounded up and led to Cork Gaol by Free State troops. Wives and children of the prisoners look on, waving them goodbye.

Eight Killed in Ballyseedy Mine Explosion as Kerry Fatalities Rise

Ballyseedy, 8 March – In Kerry, eight anti-Treaty prisoners were killed after being blown up by a mine attached to a barricade they had been ordered to clear.

A statement issued by National Army headquarters claims that a party of their troops travelling from Tralee to Killorglin encountered a barricade of stones on a roadway at Ballyseedy. Rather than remove the barricade themselves, the statement says that the troops returned to Tralee and came back with a number of prisoners, who were directed to remove the obstruction. As they did, a trigger-mine apparently concealed in the barricade exploded.

Following an incident the previous day at Knocknagoshel where five members of the National Army were killed by a trap-mine, General Paddy O'Daly ordered that in the future it would be left to prisoners to lift all mines and clear all dumps and barricades.

Kerry has been at the centre of some of the most violent Civil War disturbances in recent weeks. In the south of the county – in the wake of the Ballyseedy mine explosion – a further four prisoners were killed when a mine exploded as a barricade was being cleared north-east of the town of

6 APR
Éamon de Valera meets papal envoy Monsignor Salvatore Luzio, who was dispatched to Ireland in March by Pope Pius XI in order to examine conditions and try to find a basis for peace.

10 APR ▷
IRA Chief of Staff **Liam Lynch** is fatally wounded when shot by Free State soldiers in the Knockmealdown Mountains. He is succeeded by Frank Aiken.

REVOLUTIONARY TIMES 1913–23

1923

17 APR
Cumann na nGaedheal is officially launched as a political party at a conference held in the Mansion House on Dublin's Dawson Street.

17 APR
The General Council of the Tailteann Games decides to further postpone its festival, originally planned for the summer of 1922, until the first fortnight of August 1924. It is agreed that the following year's programme will feature an extended music section, as well as wrestling, gymnastics, literature and motor-car racing.

27 APR
Éamon de Valera issues a proclamation declaring readiness to negotiate an immediate cessation of hostilities on the basis of certain stated principles. An accompanying order, signed by IRA Chief of Staff Frank Aiken, directs commanding officers to 'arrange the suspension of all offensive operations as from noon Monday, April 30th'.

◁ **2 MAY**
The remains of anti-Treaty TD **Laurence Ginnell** are interred in his native Delvin, Co. Westmeath, after his death in a Washington hotel on 17 April.

Cahirciveen. The incident occurred in the wake of a two-hour engagement involving National Army troops and Irregulars, which ended in the capture of seven of the latter, alongside arms, ammunition and equipment.

The sole National Army survivor of the Knocknagoshel mine explosion has been named as Volunteer Joseph O'Brien. Private O'Brien was discovered with both his legs shattered at the knees and only attached to him by skin and muscle. Both legs were immediately amputated on his arrival at hospital in Tralee. It is understood that Private O'Brien has also suffered serious damage to his face and eyes.

Wexford Mansion of Free State Senator Destroyed by Fire

Gorey, 12 March – The beautiful Co. Wexford mansion owned by Senator Sir Thomas Esmonde was destroyed by fire on 9 March.

The destruction was deliberate. A force of approximately 50 raiders entered the magnificent house at night through one of its lower windows.

The Senator was not in residence at the time of the attack as he left for London a month ago on business in the company of his daughter. However, his brother, Colonel Esmonde, formerly of the Royal Dublin Fusiliers, was present, as were five servants. They were given ten minutes to get ready, after which they were taken to an outbuilding under armed guard.

The mansion was set alight using petrol poured over furniture and through the many rooms. Gas bombs were also used, with the huge flames emitted visible for miles around, attracting, amongst others, National Army troops at nearby Gorey. By the time they arrived at the scene, however, the raiding party had left.

Ballynastragh House, with about 40 rooms and its distinctive, imposing tower, has been a well-known local landmark since it was remodelled in the 1860s.

Ballynastragh House c.1826.

1923

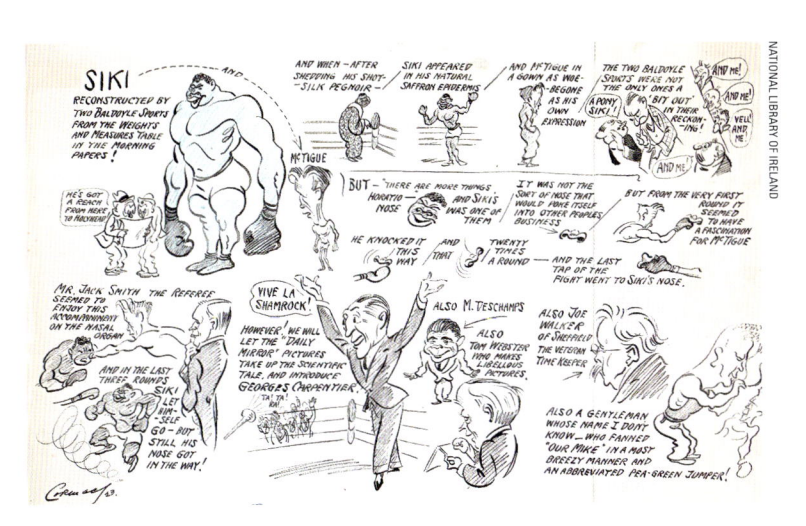

Illustration depicting the 1923 World Light Heavyweight Championship boxing match that took place in La Scala Opera House, Prince's Street, Dublin, on St Patrick's Day, 1923.

Irishman Wins World Boxing Title on St Patrick's Night in Dublin

Dublin, 19 March – It was a St Patrick's Day to remember for Clareman Mike McTigue, who defeated Senegalese boxer Louis Mbarick Fall – 'Battling Siki'– to secure the World Light Heavyweight Title at the La Scala Theatre in Dublin.

The fight took place amidst heavy security, a consequence of the ongoing Civil War and, more particularly, the recent republican 'proclamation' demanding an end to all sports and amusements.

The security concerns were justified. Not far from the venue where the fight took place, at the rear of the Pillar Picture House on Sackville Street, a landmine exploded causing widespread damage, with two children receiving injuries from falling glass. The reverberations were felt the length of Sackville Street.

The city was thronged with foreign visitors attending the fight at the La Scala. Press representatives from all over the world were in attendance, as was the former world champion, the famous Frenchman Georges Carpentier, and his manager. Carpentier, who was introduced to the crowd before the fight, sensationally lost his title last year to the Senegalese Siki. Another boxer who was introduced to the crowd was Frank Moran, the American who, like Carpentier, fought the legendary Jack Johnson some years ago.

On this occasion, it was a New York-based Irishman and a Senegalese who held top billing, with the fight – after 20 unspectacular rounds with no knock-out blows – ultimately decided by the referee. 'McTigue wins on points,' came the announcement, to the delight of a home crowd, which leapt to its feet and started chanting, 'McTigue, McTigue, McTigue.'

2 MAY
It is reported that a collapse in the collection of rates, owing to a campaign of opposition to payment, has left Leitrim County Council in a state of insolvency.

5 MAY
Forty-eight Dublin Fire Brigade men begin strike action after refusing to accept a reduction of wages that had been agreed between Dublin Corporation and other trade union representatives.

9 MAY △
Pope Pius XI hosts an audience in the Vatican with British royals King George V and Queen Mary.

11 MAY
'We in Ulster have been brought up to regard Sunday as a day of rest,' Sir James Craig tells the Northern Ireland Parliament as he introduces a new Intoxicating Liquor Bill. It provides, *inter alia*, for Sunday closing and the abolition of off-licences in premises where other business is carried on.

1923

13 MAY
10,000 people attend a James Connolly commemoration on a rain-swept Sackville Street in Dublin. The principal speaker, James Larkin, recently returned from America, uses the occasion to appeal for peace.

△ **22 MAY**
Stanley Baldwin becomes British Prime Minister.

24 MAY
A dump arms order is issued by Frank Aiken, with an accompanying message from Éamon de Valera. This marks the end of the Civil War.

30 MAY
Two Galway men, Michael Murphy and Joseph O'Rourke, are executed in Tuam Military Barracks for their involvement in an armed robbery of the Munster and Leinster Bank at Athenry. The men, both from Ardrahan, protest that there was no political dimension to the robbery and that their actions were rooted in a dispute over land.

As victor, the Clareman becomes not only the World Light Heavyweight Champion, but also the Heavyweight Champion of Europe. He also claims £1,500 of the £2,000 purse.

'Wild women' Drive Republican Resistance, Journalist Claims

22 March, Dublin – The key for defeating anti-Treaty forces in the ongoing Civil War is to target the 'wild women' who drive the republican resistance, a special correspondent for the London-based *Morning Post* newspaper has claimed.

In a report that has been reprinted in the *Belfast News Letter*, the Dublin-based correspondent asserts that it is the women who 'inspire, organise, plan, recruit, carry messages and weapons, spy, steal, deliver threatening notices, distribute the *Republican Bulletin* and perform all the essential tasks without which Liam Lynch and his acolytes would be as "helpless as babies in a bath"'.

This perspective was offered in response to the recent wave of arrests of republican women.

The *Morning Post*'s correspondent argues that if the government can manage to find prison accommodation for these republican women – Mountjoy is currently reported to have six people per cell – then it would prove a much more effective weapon in combating the campaign against the state than arresting several thousand republican youths. Unlike the women, it is suggested that these youths are 'futile creatures – for the most part quite incapable of organisation or leadership'.

Bridie O'Mullane in Cumann na mBan uniform c.1918. Bridie was the organisation's Director of Publicity and Propaganda during the Irish Civil War.

Day One of Ireland's New Customs Border

Dublin, 2 April – Customs barriers came into operation yesterday – April Fool's Day – on the island of Ireland, meaning that, for the first time, all persons travelling between Northern Ireland and the Irish Free State by road or rail are liable to be searched. The new arrangements marked the emergence of the Irish Free State as fiscally autonomous.

To gauge the impact of the new rules on the travelling public, a special correspondent of *The Irish Times* journeyed from Holyhead to Bessbrook via Dublin and reported the trip to have been uneventful. On the train north, he reported that it was the intention to check baggage between

Goraghwood or Bessbrook and Portadown when the train is moving, so as to avoid delays. At Dundalk station, meanwhile, a large group of staff from the Free State inland revenue department was observed preparing to undertake checks on the first train from Belfast.

Returning to Dublin by road, the reporter was questioned at an imperial customs station near Newry, but not at a Free State customs post. The Newry customs post was described as a neat octagonal tin pagoda housing three officials, only one of whom on this occasion was wearing a uniform.

In advance of the customs arrangements taking effect, there was a major increase in the traffic volumes along border areas, notably from Derry city to Donegal and in the Strabane and Lifford areas. Indeed, such was the level of activity that the Derry and Lough Swilly Railway Company ran an extra train to clear the load before the midnight introduction of the customs frontier. Donegal traders are believed to have sufficiently stocked up on many items to last a couple of months. However, it was the high number of cars that were being delivered into the Free State that was most striking.

There were similar scenes in Dublin: several additional steamers were deployed to deliver the large quantities of supplies from England into the Free State in advance of the new regulations taking effect.

There remains much uncertainty among businesses as to the impact the customs barriers will have on trade. In a letter to the Dublin Chamber of Commerce, President Cosgrave's private secretary noted that Mr Cosgrave fully realised that the 'introduction of the new customs regime must inevitably be attended with a certain amount of difficulty, but he feels that he can rely on the trading community to do what they can to obviate unnecessary delay, and that the Customs authorities will grant all possible facilities to traders in the passage of their goods out of Customs custody'.

Civil War Ends with Order to Dump Arms

'Further sacrifice of life would now be in vain', anti-Treaty forces told

Dublin, 29 May – The Irish Civil War seems to have come to an end.

An order to dump all arms has been issued by Mr Frank Aiken, Chief of Staff, to his anti-Treaty forces. This instruction was accompanied by a general order from Mr Éamon de Valera advising that 'Further sacrifice of life would now be vain' and that a continuance of the armed struggle would be 'unwise in the national interest and prejudicial to the future of our cause'.

1923

1 JUN
General Richard Mulcahy, Commander-in-Chief of the National Army and Minister for Defence, announces plans to drastically reduce the size of the army. It is proposed that the number of soldiers be reduced from 49,000 to between 28,000 and 30,000 by the end of the year.

3 JUN ▽
For the first time in 300 years, benediction of the holy sacrament is given inside the gates of the historic castle at **Cashel**, on the occasion of the annual Corpus Christi procession.

12 JUN
'I burned the Castle that night at 10 o'clock as a result of a despatch I received.' A former IRA leader, Thomas Clifford from Tralee, confesses to a London court of his role in burning the historic Ballyheigue Castle in Co. Kerry in May 1921. The court was hearing a case brought by the castle's owner, Jeremiah Leen, against Lloyd's underwriters on a policy of insurance.

1923

17 JUN
Dublin footballers defeat Mayo to win the deferred All-Ireland final for 1921.

21 JUN
A small wooden cross is erected by National Army soldiers at Béal na Bláth, the site where Michael Collins was killed in August 1922.

3 JUL
Noel Lemass, an anti-Treaty officer, is abducted as he walks along Wicklow Street in Dublin. His badly beaten body – he was also shot three times in the head – is discovered in the Dublin Mountains nearly four months later, on 12 October.

5 JUL
The Right Reverend Dr Robert Miller tells the annual synod of the diocese of Cashel and Emly that the Protestant minority in the Irish Free State is asking for no special privileges but seeks only to pursue their 'ordinary work free from anxiety as to ourselves and our property'.

10 JUL
A Dáil debate on the Public Safety (Emergency Powers) Bill 1923 is told, by Thomas Johnson, leader of the Labour Party, that the proposed legislation is worse than previously experienced British repression.

The orders were dated to 24 May and documents containing the full texts of both were captured and subsequently released to the press by the government's publicity department. Both Mr Aiken and Mr de Valera acknowledge, in the former's words, that the 'enemies of the Republic have for the moment prevailed', but there is no concession of defeat, and the message remains one of defiance and pride from the anti-Treaty side.

To the 'Soldiers of the Republic, Legion of the Rearguard', Mr de Valera's order acknowledged the toll that recent years had taken on Irish society. 'Seven years of intense effort have exhausted our people. Their sacrifices and their sorrows have been many ... they are weary and need a rest. A little time and you will see them recover and rally again to the standard. They will then quickly discover who have been selfless and who selfish – who have spoken truth and who falsehood. When they are ready, you will be, and your place will be again as of old with the vanguard.'

Battle of Boyne Landmark Destroyed in Targeted Explosion

Louth, 3 June – An obelisk erected in 1736 on the site of the Battle of the Boyne of 1690 was completely destroyed in a mine explosion.

The limestone granite monument, erected with the support of public contributions from 'several' Protestants across Ireland and Britain, had borne the inscription: 'Sacred to the glorious memory of King William III.' It destroyed a roadway adjacent to the bridge pier, such was the force of its fall.

Having once stood 30 feet higher than Nelson's Pillar, only its rocky base remains, and a pile of masonry lies on the nearby road. Had the huge obelisk column fallen onto the bridge, the likelihood is that it too would have been destroyed. Even so, the completeness of the destruction suggests serious planning on the part of those responsible.

Holes were apparently bored deep into the rock foundations of the monument for the mines to be set inside. It is likely that time fuses were also used.

The first stone of the obelisk had been laid in 1736 by Duke of Dorset and Lord Lieutenant of Ireland Lionel Sackville.

The obelisk that commemorated the Battle of the Boyne before and after it was blown up.

1923

New Land Bill to Create a 'Nation of Peasant Proprietors'

London, 24 July – New land legislation will help create a 'nation of peasant proprietors', the Dáil has been informed.

The Land Bill 1923, which was accepted by all parties and which passed through the report stage in the Dáil yesterday, has been hailed by Mr Darrell Figgis TD as both a 'very great achievement' and a 'very great landmark', not least because it was built on the principle of establishing a 'nation of peasant proprietors'.

Mr Patrick Hogan, the Minister for Agriculture, said that the Dáil recognised the rights of property, and it was for that reason it was preparing to pay a 'certain amount' for the land that it was proposing to confiscate.

The Irish Bill has also been discussed extensively in the UK's House of Lords, where the Duke of Devonshire, Secretary of State for the Colonies, admitted that the Land Bill would 'affect a great many landlords very severely'.

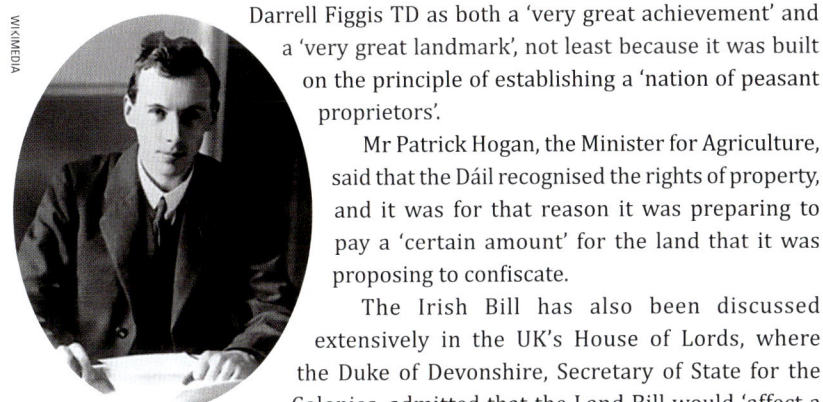

Patrick Hogan TD.

Memorial Unveiled to Dead Leaders Described as 'the architect and the master-builder of our nation'

Dublin, 14 August – A new memorial to two 'dead leaders' – President Arthur Griffith and General Michael Collins – was unveiled on Leinster Lawn on Dublin's Merrion Street yesterday.

They were, President Cosgrave said, the 'architect and master builder of our nation'. A ceremony to publicly reveal the temporary cenotaph to the men who 'gave their lives in doing their duty to Ireland' was held yesterday on the first anniversary of the month of their respective deaths and before an attendance of ministers, members of the Dáil and Seanad, public bodies and a large military contingent.

The Griffith-Collins Cenotaph, Leinster Lawn.

19 JUL △
With more hotels, the Dublin coastal suburb of **Killiney** could become a 'second Monte Carlo', a local councillor tells the *Irish Independent*.

19 JUL
A 22-year-old woman is brutally assaulted in Terenure. The woman is discovered unconscious, after being beaten and tied to a lamppost near the entrance of Terenure College. Three men, one of whom is on bail, are subsequently arrested.

24 JUL
The first motor car to be completely manufactured and assembled at the Ford Motor Plant at the Marina Works in Cork takes to the streets of Cork city.

2 AUG
President of the United States Warren G. Harding, 57, dies suddenly at San Francisco's Palace Hotel. He is automatically succeeded in office by his vice-president, Calvin Coolidge.

REVOLUTIONARY TIMES 1913–23

1923

6 AUG
The opening of the ILP&TUC is disrupted by unruly scenes outside the Mansion House. A principal purpose of the protest was to highlight the cause of anti-Treaty prisoners and internees.

△ **13 AUG**
Gustav Stresemann becomes Chancellor and Foreign Minister in Germany. His coalition government survives only until November.

14 AUG
Ninety-nine miners are killed by an explosion at a coal mine in Kemmerer, Wyoming.

14 AUG
A 23-year-old man is killed and five others wounded after shots are fired at a licensed premises hosting a dance at Kealkil, near Bantry, Co. Cork. The building was surrounded by National Army soldiers prior to the shooting.

17 AUG
The Dublin Horse Show draws to a close at the RDS in Ballsbridge. Over 50,000 spectators attend across the four days of the show.

In attendance, too, were members of the Griffith and Collins families.

The cenotaph was covered top to bottom in a white cloth before the ceremony and its unveiling was performed by President Cosgrave, whose arrival, alongside the governor general, signalled the commencement of the ceremony.

Designed by Mr George Atkinson, RHA, and situated in a position of considerable prominence, the memorial is made of wood and covered with expanded metal lathing and cement. At its centre the monument features a Celtic Cross, with simple pylons on either side of it, while at its front are medallion portraits of the dead leaders.

Delivering an oration in advance of the unveiling, President Cosgrave said that the cenotaph was a 'symbol of Ireland's reverence and sorrow, of Ireland's pride and gratitude, to the memory of two heroic men'.

Earlier in the day a memorial Mass was celebrated at the Pro-Cathedral, and in military barracks throughout the country the occasion was marked by special parades of troops, which were organised for the same hour as the ceremonies in Dublin.

'They are coming for me, boys' – De Valera Dramatically Arrested at Ennis Election Rally

Ennis, 16 August – There were dramatic scenes in Ennis yesterday, where Éamon de Valera was arrested by soldiers of the National Army while he was addressing an election rally.

According to an official report issued by army headquarters, the arrest of the anti-Treaty leader and former president of Sinn Féin took place after shots were fired at Free State (National) troops from the direction of the speakers' platform. 'A rifle was shot out of the hands of one of the soldiers,' the report claimed. 'The troops fired in the air, following which the crowd dispersed, and the arrest was effected.'

The taking prisoner of Mr de Valera, a candidate for the constituency of Clare, where he came to political prominence in a by-election in 1917, is certain to raise political temperatures in advance of the forthcoming election.

Mr de Valera had been speaking to an enthusiastic crowd from a platform erected on O'Connell Square at the time of his arrest. He had begun his address in Irish, before switching to English and launching into a passionate refutation of some of the government claims that have been levelled at their anti-Treaty political opposition.

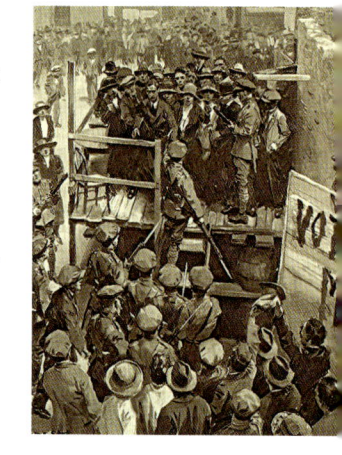

Éamon de Valera is cheered by supporters before being taken into custody.

'They spoke to you when we couldn't come to you to tell you the truth. They spoke to you, and said that we were anarchists and that we were out for destruction. We come here, and I come here to tell you that I have never stood for destruction. I have never stood for brother's hand being raised against brother's hand.'

Mr de Valera added, to loud cheers from the crowd, that if the people of Ireland stood together and were united, they could achieve 'complete independence'.

Before he could proceed any further, Mr de Valera saw the National Army troops approach the platform, to which he declared, 'The soldiers are coming ... They are coming for me, boys.'

There followed scenes of chaos as shots were fired and people stampeded their way to safety. Mr de Valera, it is understood, has been taken to Limerick, where he remains in custody.

Election '23 – Pro-Treaty Cumann na nGaedheal to be Largest Party in New Dáil

Labour loses ground, while Independents perform well

Dublin, 3 September – As it was in the third and last Dáil, the pro-Treaty party, now known as Cumann na nGaedheal, will be the largest in the incoming fourth Dáil.

Even before the counting of votes had been completed under the proportional representation system, the make-up of the new Dáil had become clear, and with it the winners and losers from a general election where many constituencies had been redrawn and where more seats were being fought over.

1923

17 AUG
'A recommendation to include instruction in the Irish language in the curricula of schools in Northern Ireland is denounced by two unionist MPs,' the *Belfast News Letter* reports. 'If parents wish their children to learn Irish or any other useless language they should pay for it out of their own pockets, but it should not be a charge upon either the tax or rate payer.'

27 AUG
Polling day in the general election. W.T. Cosgrave's Cumann na nGaedheal party wins 63 seats, with Éamon de Valera's Sinn Féin claiming 44.

31 AUG △
Fear about the future peace and stability of Europe grows after the forces of Italian Prime Minister **Benito Mussolini** occupy the Greek island of Corfu. It follows the murder of an Italian general and four members of his staff who were engaged, under international authority, in determining the boundary between Greece and Albania.

1923

1 SEP
The Great Kanto Earthquake devastates large parts of two Japanese cities, Tokyo and Yokohama, with massive loss of life. In the days that follow, the Irish Free State expresses its 'profound sympathy' to the government and people of Japan.

5 SEP
World-famous Irish tenor John McCormack is conferred with the Freedom of the City of Dublin. The decision to confer the civic honour upon McCormack was taken at a meeting of Dublin Corporation on 3 September.

9 SEP
Before an attendance of 26,119 at Croke Park, Kilkenny defeats Tipperary on a 4–2 to 2–6 scoreline to win the delayed 1922 All-Ireland Hurling Championship title.

10 SEP
The Irish Free State is admitted into the League of Nations with the unanimous approval of the representatives of 46 nations at a meeting in Geneva. Admission confirms international recognition of the Free State's status.

During the 1923 election campaign, Cumann na nGaedheal staged a rally in St Stephen's Green. On the platform are W.T. Cosgrave, Kevin O'Higgins, Eoin MacNeill and other leading figures in the party.

For both the government and the main republican opposition, there have been seat gains and losses across the various constituencies, but Cumann na nGaedheal will be satisfied that, after all the upheavals of the last year, the result is already being presented, as one early press report has put it, as an 'unqualified endorsement to their policy and programme'.

However, on consideration of the final count and seats, the reality is less clear-cut. It is notable that anti-Treaty republican or Sinn Féin candidates have secured a significant number of seats – surpassing their performance from last June – and are clearly the second-largest electoral bloc.

Without question, the most disappointed party emerging from this election will be Labour, which had won 17 of 18 seats it had contested in the June 1922 election and now returns with just 14 seats in an enlarged chamber.

1923 general election handbill for Sinn Féin.

The Farmers' Party likewise had a disappointing day at the polls. While their representation in the next Dáil will be greater than it was in the last, it is still going to be much lower than they might have anticipated and many would have expected.

In terms of seat distribution, the final running totals for the respective parties are as follows (the figures in brackets are seats won in June 1922 for the 128-member third Dáil): Cumann na nGaedheal 63 (58); anti-Treaty Sinn Féin 44 (36); Labour 14 (17); Farmers 15 (7); Independents 17 (10).

Ireland Accepted into League of Nations at Geneva Ceremony

Geneva, 11 September – 'Our freedom is recognised by the nations of the world,' President William T. Cosgrave told a press representative following Ireland's acceptance into the League of Nations in Geneva yesterday.

A report of the Sixth Commission of the League of Nations, which recommended Ireland's admission, was approved unanimously by the representatives of 46 nations. Delegates of each nation were called in alphabetical order to give their approval, to which each and every one responded with a 'Yes', leaving it to the President, Cosme de la Torriente y Peraza of Cuba, to proclaim Ireland elected.

There followed a storm of applause, after which the President of the League invited the Irish delegates – President Cosgrave, Professor Eoin MacNeill and Mr Desmond Fitzgerald – to take their places, the Irish table being placed between that of Haiti, New Zealand and Norway.

When invited to address the Assembly, President Cosgrave spoke first in Irish, announcing that the delegates of Saorstát Éireann, from its Parliament and government, had come to participate in the great work of the League. When turning to English, he spoke at greater length, beginning, pointedly, by stating that it was 'on behalf of Ireland, one of the oldest and yet one of the youngest nations', that he thanked the Assembly for the unanimous acceptance of Ireland's application and that she now 'entered into a new bond of union with her sister nations, great and small, who are represented in this magnificent world gathering'.

In emphasising Ireland's pacific ambitions, the President asserted that it was Ireland's 'earnest desire' to co-operate with fellow members in efforts to 'avert the ancient evils of warfare and oppression'.

On the conclusion of President Cosgrave's speech, the Irish table in the Assembly hall was surrounded by well-wishing representatives from other nations, the Latin-American delegates among the most enthusiastic. Last night, while still in Geneva, President Cosgrave told a special representative of the *Irish Independent* that 'our status is defined, we now begin to receive the universal consideration to which we are entitled by the position we have won'.

1923

17 SEP ▷
Children are starving because of the political imprisonment of their fathers and the consequent loss of family income, newly elected TD **Caitlín Brugha** tells a public meeting in Waterford.

17 SEP
Hundreds of homes and businesses are destroyed and thousands are left homeless as fires, driven by hot, dry winds, rip through the university district of Berkeley, California.

19 SEP
The fourth Dáil meets for the first time and re-elects William T. Cosgrave as president.

27 SEP
Mussolini's Italian forces begin to evacuate Corfu, but there is anger in Greece at being forced to pay Italy a large indemnity.

29 SEP
A British mandate for Palestine, drawn up in 1920, comes into effect. The mandate formalises British rule in the region and provides for the establishment of a Jewish national homeland in Palestine.

1923

1 OCT
The Imperial Economic Conference meets in London, with the Irish Free State represented for the first time. 'The troubles and difficulties of our present situation and the circumstances surrounding it make my immediate association with the Conference less than I would wish,' William T. Cosgrave remarks in his opening statement.

◁ **4 OCT**
Mike McTigue, who became Light Heavyweight Boxing Champion of the World in Dublin, sensationally loses his crown to an 18-year-old challenger, William Lawrence 'Young' Stribling, in Georgia, USA, but the referee reverses this decision within the hour and declares the fight a draw.

10 OCT
Lord Edward Carson cuts the sod on the construction of the Silent Valley reservoir project in the Mourne Mountains, which aims to secure the water supply for Belfast's expanding industry and growing population with an intended storage capacity for 3,000 million gallons of water.

Death to the Irish Pub? Catholic Temperance Reformers Urge a Slashing of Pub Numbers

Dublin, 26 September – Cut the number of pubs by half and impose restrictions on opening hours, including Sunday closing. This is what the Catholic hierarchy regards as a moderate programme of reform, as a number of bishops have given their endorsement to the Catholic Total Abstinence Federation's plan for temperance reform. This plan was outlined at a well-attended meeting in Dublin's Mansion House last night, alongside a demand that it be immediately adopted by the Free State government.

In setting out the Federation's programme last night, its President, the Rev. Dr Coffey, said that its leading feature was its 'moderation', a term also used in a number of the endorsements that were issued by prominent Catholic bishops.

Last night's meeting was informed that there were approximately 17,000 public houses in Ireland, which equated to something like one for every 200 people. It was therefore not too much, Canon Lyons, parish priest of Ardee, remarked, to ask that half of these pubs be wiped out.

A Catholic Total Abstinence League medal.

Germany Edges Towards 'Revolution' Amidst Economic Chaos and a Rise in Extremist Nationalism

Bavaria, 2 October – Martial law was proclaimed across Germany amidst growing nationalist unrest and a declaration by the government of Bavaria that the Treaty of Versailles was no longer binding.

According to a special correspondent with the *Evening Standard* newspaper, events in Germany are moving in the direction of a serious crisis. 'Everybody in the country foresees a revolution,' the correspondent claims. 'No one knows a way out. Deep pessimism is universal … a revolutionary outbreak in Germany would of course have far-reaching effects and would impact across the continent.'

The Bavarian government has issued a statement claiming that the Treaty of Versailles had been 'broken by the Invading Powers', a reference to the invasion by French and Belgian troops of the Ruhr region in January this year as a means of extracting reparations.

In an effort to maintain order within its own state, the Bavarian government has banned all political meetings and moved additional troops into Munich, the Bavarian capital, from other districts. This follows a refusal on the part of Herr Adolf Hitler, who is being described as the 'would-be Mussolini of Bavaria', to give an assurance that, if granted approval to hold meetings of his National Socialist group, that they would be conducted in an orderly manner.

The Bavarian Premier, Dr Von Knilling, is nevertheless confident that extremist demonstrations will be kept in check and has appointed Dr Von Kahr as Commissioner General precisely because of his influence with nationalist organisations in the region. Since then, Herr Hitler has issued a 'proclamation' to the effect that he was opposed to the present dictatorship and in favour of autonomy for Bavaria within the Reich. Bavaria is the second largest state in Germany, with a population of over seven million people.

Munich was central to the initial attempts by Hitler to rise to power, as symbolised by his failed Beer Hall Putsch in November 1923. The mythology of early Nazi action would become part of the party's later propaganda including this 1943 reprint of the words attributed to Albert Schlageter: 'the banner must stand, even if the man falls'.

Re-opening of Mallow Viaduct Heralded as a Sign of Returned Normality

The rebuilt bridge, destroyed during the Civil War, is the first major piece of government reconstruction

Mallow, 6 October – The re-opening yesterday of the Mallow viaduct over the River Blackwater has been hailed by President Cosgrave as a sign of a return to normal conditions.

It is also the first major work of reconstruction to be completed by the Free State government. The new structure, a triumph of modern engineering, carries the railway line across the Blackwater at a height that affords the traveller a commanding view of the countryside around, and of the town of Mallow, which is positioned within the valley.

The presence of President Cosgrave underscored the significance of the event, as did the presence of his fellow Cabinet members: Mr Ernest Blythe, the new Minister for Finance; General Richard Mulcahy, Minister for Defence; Mr J.J. Walsh, Postmaster General; and Mr Michael Hayes, Ceann Comhairle of the Dáil.

1923

13 OCT
Minister for Home Affairs Kevin O'Higgins addresses the annual conference of the Irish Catholic Truth Society. He delivers a paper entitled 'The Catholic Layman in Public Life'.

13 OCT
Republican prisoners in Mountjoy Prison, seeking unconditional release, begin a hunger strike that spreads to other jails. About 8,000 prisoners end up joining the strike.

17 OCT
The Sinn Féin Ard-Fheis recommits to securing international recognition for an independent Irish republic. The Ard-Fheis also discusses the issues of prisoner releases, the Catholic Church's attitude to republicans and the release of documents relating to the negotiations of the Anglo-Irish Treaty in December 1921.

17 OCT
'I have got a wife for every man that has come to me,' a Co. Monaghan matchmaker tells a Clones court. His case, seeking recovery of allegedly unpaid expenses, is dismissed by the judge.

25 OCT
Attorney General Hugh Kennedy, KC, is returned as TD for Cumann na nGaedheal at the South Dublin by-election.

1923

26 OCT
Delegates attending a meeting of the FAI in Dublin are told there is no immediate prospect of a unified Irish football administration.

29 OCT
Mustafa Kemal Atatürk, commander of the Ottoman forces during the Gallipoli campaign of 1915, is unanimously elected the first president of the Republic of Turkey.

30 OCT
The *Irish Independent* reports that there is widespread alarm in education circles after it is disclosed that the Free State government plans to cut the salaries of national schoolteachers by 10%.

◁ **8–9 NOV**
Adolf Hitler and members of the Nazi party launch an abortive coup against the Weimar Republic in Germany. It becomes variously known as the '**Munich Putsch**' or the 'Beer Hall Putsch'.

15 NOV
In an attempt to curb Germany's hyperinflation crisis, the Rentemark is introduced as the country's interim currency.

A view of the old ten-arch bridge in Mallow – this is how the viaduct looked before its destruction in August 1922.

The original viaduct, which was destroyed by anti-Treaty forces in August 1922, had been built using 10,000 tons of masonry in ten arch spans. This has now been replaced by a new steel viaduct, the construction of which has been hampered by labour disputes in Cork. The reopening of the viaduct is considered not only critical to the local economic life of Mallow and Cork, but to industries in the whole Munster region.

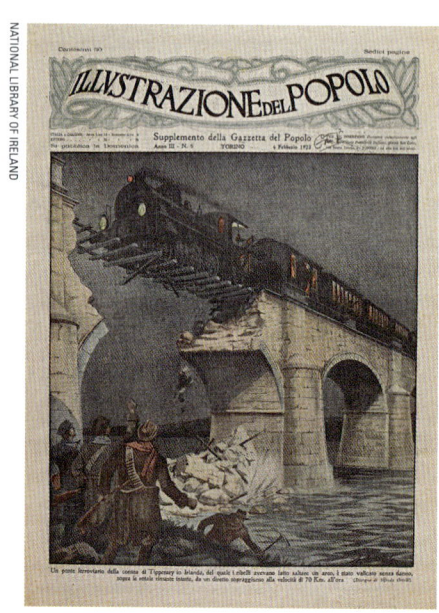

Destruction of railway bridges was one of the tactics used by the anti-Treaty IRA to disrupt the ability of the Free State to function. This illustration of a similar attack in Tipperary featured on the cover of Illustrazione del Popolo.

Thousands Join Hunger Strikes Across Irish Prison System

Government takes hard line and refuses to contemplate political prisoner releases

Dublin, 30 October – About 8,500 prisoners are now believed to be on hunger strike across the Free State's crisis-afflicted prisons.

The spread of the hunger strikes inside the prisons has led to protests and demonstrations outside. Speaking at a meeting outside Mountjoy, at which the release of all the prisoners was demanded, Maud Gonne MacBride declared that should one prisoner die, she would herself go on hunger strike until their release was realised. MacBride urged other mothers to join with her, if needed, in starting a hunger strike on the doorsteps of Free State ministers.

The Free State government has, nevertheless, been unyielding in the face of the looming prison crisis. Speaking last week in Dublin, President Cosgrave insisted that there would be no unconditional release of prisoners and that those in jail were there because neither life nor property was safe when they were at large.

President Cosgrave also claimed that the 'hunger strike' was a fraud, alleging that brown bread and pastilles had been found in the pockets of some prisoners. At the same time, and somewhat in contradiction with this claim, Mr Cosgrave declared that should a prisoner die, it would be his own fault and not the government's.

The front cover of Le Petit Journal illustré, *28 October 1923, depicts hunger strikers in Mountjoy refusing food from prison officers.*

1923

20 NOV
Republican prisoner and Cork native Denis Barry dies after 34 days on hunger strike. Barry had been removed from Newbridge internment camp to the Curragh Military Hospital in an unconscious condition the day before his death.

23 NOV
Another republican hunger striker, Andy O'Sullivan (38), dies shortly after being removed from Mountjoy to hospital. Originally from Denbawn, Co. Cavan, he had worked as an agricultural instructor in the Mallow area and served with the 5th Battalion, Cork 4th Brigade during the War of Independence.

29 NOV ▷
The prime minister of New Zealand, **William Massey**, visits Northern Ireland. Born near Limavady and hailed as a 'distinguished Ulsterman', Massey delivers a lecture to the Belfast Chamber of Commerce at the Ulster Hall.

10 DEC
W.B. Yeats receives the Nobel Prize for Literature at a ceremony in Stockholm.

Remembering 1923
a hundred years on

RTÉ films *Ireland 100: An Old Song to be Sung*, one of the last events of the Decade of Centenaries. This two-hour long concert, which was subsequently broadcast on RTÉ television, featured an array of Irish musical performers and touched not only on events from the period 1913–23, but also on an array of issues and institutions that flowed from the foundation of an independent Irish state. Nuala O'Connor, executive producer, explained how the idea for the show had been to reflect, through performance, songs, words and music, 'an appreciation of where we have come from, of what we have come through as a people and a state, and of our experiences living through the twentieth and the first quarter of the twenty-first century'.

30 October 2023

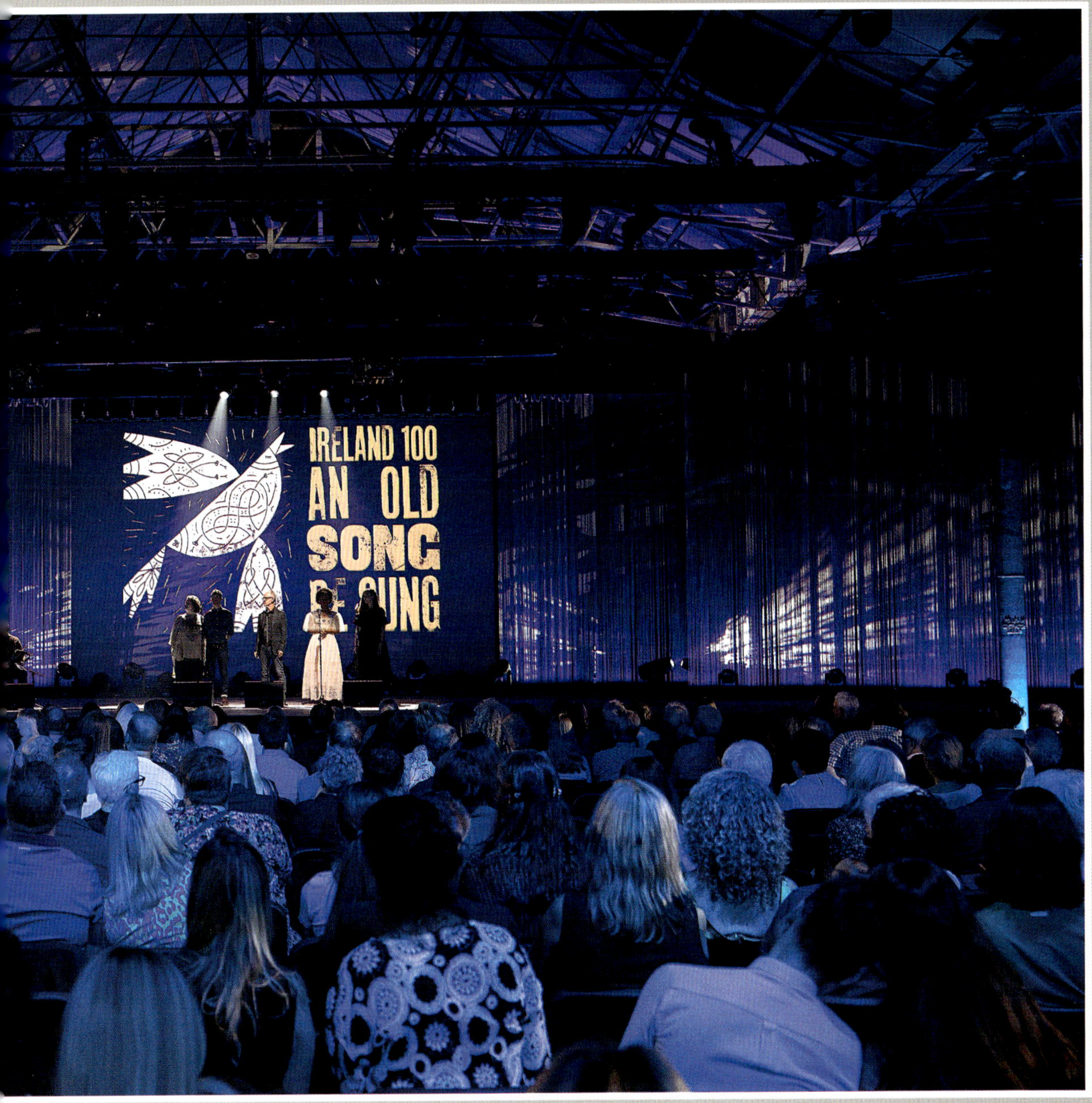

RICH GILLIGAN

Status and Statehood:

Securing Ireland's Place Among the Nations of the World

THE MEETING IN Dublin's Gresham Hotel to establish an Irish Olympic Committee (IOC) in April 1920 had as much to do with politics as it did sport. Irish athletes had competed with remarkable success at every modern Olympic Games since their revival in 1896, but never under the flag of their own country, instead taking part under the British flag or that of the nation to which they had emigrated. The founding of the IOC aimed to change that: its goal was to secure the right to Irish representation from the International Olympic Committee at the Antwerp games later that year. Before travelling to Belgium to present Ireland's Olympic claims in person, the IOC's first president, J.J. Keane, sought the support and services of the Dáil's overseas representatives. However, his efforts ended in failure, falling foul of the conservatism – and political prejudices – of an International Olympic Committee whose decision-making was controlled by a small coterie of member-states that included the UK.

The overlap of Ireland's Olympic claims with the rise of Sinn Féin and its assertion, following the 1918 election, of Irish sovereignty in the tangible form of Dáil Éireann was no accident. What Ireland was attempting in the sporting sphere was a mirror of what was already being tried politically: the securing of international recognition for a separate, independent Ireland. A sovereign Irish republic had, of course, been proclaimed in front of the GPO in Dublin at Easter 1916, and the seeking of a wider support for that status had been endorsed at Sinn Féin's Ard-Fheis in October 1917, but the global context in which Irish self-determination would be considered was radically altered by the fallout from the First World War. Empires had collapsed, new states and republics had been established in Austria, Czechoslovakia and Hungary by late 1918, with more to follow, and a peace conference had

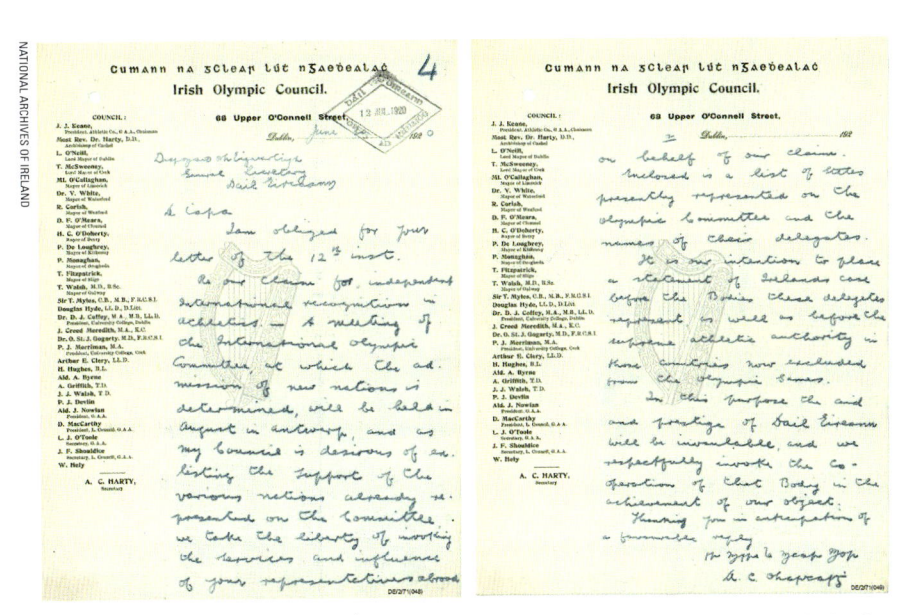

A.C. Harty seeks the support of Dáil Éireann's representatives abroad in pressing the case for Ireland's 'independent international recognition in athletics', June 1920.

been convened for Paris in January 1919 to set the foundations for a new international order.

Among the 'big powers' represented in Paris was the United States, whose President, Woodrow Wilson, had earlier outlined his vision for a post-war world rooted in his 'fourteen points' – a set of principles that had at their core the concept of national self-determination. This, of course, was the very basis of Sinn Féin's 1918 election manifesto and its claims to international legitimacy. Unlike pre-war Irish nationalism, which was fixated on Home Rule, London and the machinery of British politics, Sinn Féin's activity incorporated a more international focus. Sinn Féiners understood themselves as operators on a global stage and acted accordingly. When, for instance, Dáil Éireann met for the first time on 21 January 1919 at Dublin's Mansion House – just three days after the opening of the Paris conference – it theatrically presented as one of its foundational documents a 'Message to the Free Nations of the World', which, invoking Wilsonian rhetoric and asserting Irish antiquity and distinctiveness, urged 'every free nation to uphold her [Ireland's] national claim to complete independence as an Irish Republic'.

As its careful choreography intended, this first – and very public – session of the Dáil was geared less to those in attendance than to the outside world, and news of its deliberations circulated widely in the international press. But simply exhorting support for Irish independence did not mean that the cause itself was actually advanced. It was notable, therefore, that Foreign Affairs was among the first ministries established by the Dáil (under Count George Plunkett, father of one of the executed 1916 leaders) and that the French-speaking TD, Seán T. O'Kelly, was swiftly dispatched to Paris to establish an office (where he was later joined by George Gavan Duffy), their primary purpose being to present the case on the ground for Irish entry to the peace conference. This, in essence, was Ireland's first diplomatic mission. It didn't succeed.

The problem for Ireland was that it was seeking severance not from one of the defeated, disintegrating empires (Austro-Hungarian, German or Ottoman) but from Britain, one of the big, victorious powers, which actively worked to scupper the efforts of the Irish delegation in Paris. No help was forthcoming from the United States either: for all that Woodrow Wilson's talk of 'self-determination' had helped fill Sinn Féin's rhetorical sails, the American President was reluctant to tackle the Irish question, on the basis, he maintained, that it was an internal British matter.

The 'big four' (L–R): Prime Minister David Lloyd George, Premier Vittorio Orlando, Premier Georges Clemenceau, and President Woodrow Wilson at the Peace Conferencein Paris, 27 May 1919.

The failure of the Irish delegates to get a hearing in Paris – always a remote prospect, O'Kelly had quickly concluded – led to a shift in the Dáil's approach. A presence in Paris was maintained, but diplomatic efforts broadened, with the establishment of a consular network of envoys, official and unofficial, across Europe and beyond. In London, for instance, Art O'Brien was established as the permanent Irish representative and he combined work on behalf of the Dáil with directing the affairs of the Irish Self-Determination League (similar leagues sprouted in Canada, Australia and New Zealand); in Madrid, Máire O'Brien led the dissemination of Dáil propaganda; Nancy Wyse-Power, daughter of Ladies Land League and suffrage campaigner, Jennie, established a foothold in Berlin; George Gavan Duffy, after a spell in Paris, became Sinn Féin envoy in Rome. The peripatetic TD Dr Patrick McCartan travelled to Moscow in a doomed attempt to muster Russian support, while further afield in South America, the Irish propagandist effort was led by Eamonn Bulfin, Laurence Ginnell and Patrick Little.

Seán T. O'Kelly, Mary Kate O'Kelly (née Ryan), and Harry Boland at Kingsbridge Station en route to Paris in early 1919.

This is not an exhaustive list. There were other envoys, other foreign missions and diaspora-led campaigns, such as the race conventions held in Philadelphia, Melbourne and Buenos Aires from 1919. Significant, too, was the protracted presence in the United States of the President of Sinn Féin and Dáil Éireann, Éamon de Valera, who was absent from Ireland for much of the War of Independence following his dramatic escape from Lincoln Prison in February 1919. De Valera departed for America, land of his birth, in June of that year and didn't return to Ireland until December 1920: in the intervening eighteen months, he toured extensively, received rapturous receptions in stadiums and theatres, and helped both to raise funds for the fledgling republic – in the form of Dáil 'bond certificates' – and whip up a wave of publicity around Ireland's independence demand.

De Valera's gruelling American adventure was not without difficulties, however: announced to US audiences as 'President of the Irish Republic', a title he did nothing to disavow, issues of money, personality and political strategy led to a falling out with significant Irish-American figures. De Valera's determination to influence the programmes of the Democratic and Republican parties in advance of the November 1920 US presidential election, for instance, led him to ignore advice from the influential and politically experienced Judge Daniel Colohan, the effect of which was that neither party committed any mention of Ireland to their campaign platforms. That presidential election – comfortably won by republican Warren G. Harding – underscored the extent to which, in American politics, Irish issues were always subordinate to domestic political considerations, allowing a relieved British ambassador to the US to crow that 'for the first time on record, an electoral campaign has been conducted in the United States without the political "crimes" of England being dragged into the fray'.

Any yet there was no shortage of international attention on those 'crimes'. The excesses of British policy in Ireland in the second half of 1920 – repression and reprisals – were widely publicised in the international press, in part a measure of the effectiveness of the Dáil's network of envoys, but a consequence, too, of the work of the Dáil's publicity department and the credibility accorded its output, particularly the factsheet-style *Irish Bulletin*, by foreign correspondents. The seventy-four-day hunger strike of Lord Mayor of Cork Terence MacSwiney, which ended in his death in Brixton Prison in October 1920, also reverberated worldwide: the drawn-out, dreadful drama of MacSwiney's sacrifice was closely followed by a rapt international media, catalysing organised protests and expressions of sympathy and support. From the United States, for instance, the Jamaican-born nationalist leader, Marcus Garvey, sent a message, early in the hunger strike, to Brixton's prison chaplain. 'Convey to McSwiney [*sic*] sympathy of 400,000,000 Negroes,' it read. But it wasn't only the actions of MacSwiney that impressed Garvey: he, like anti-imperialists in Egypt and India, saw in the Irish separatist struggle a cause akin to his own and an example of how to advance ideas of black liberation across Africa, the Caribbean and, of course, the United States.

When the Anglo-Irish war ended in truce and the Anglo-Irish Treaty followed it in December 1921, Garvey was quick to give it his blessing. In a message

Marcus Garvey, the Jamaican-born nationalist leader.

to lead negotiator Arthur Griffith, he offered congratulations on his 'masterly achievement of partial independence for Ireland' and exclaimed, 'Long live the Irish Free State.' But just as the Treaty divided the Dáil – it conferred upon the twenty-six counties the status of a 'Dominion' within the Empire as opposed to a republic free of it – so too did those divisions manifest among those who had theretofore spearheaded Sinn Féin's overseas diplomatic efforts, some going so far as to now devote themselves to denying legitimacy to the new Irish Free State overseas.

The international community determined otherwise. The Irish Free State came into force on 6 December 1922 – the first anniversary of the signing of the Treaty – and the following year, on 10 September, it became a member of the League of Nations, the inter-governmental organisation established out of the First World War to promote international co-operation, peace and security. Entry into the League was, as one approving contemporary chronicler put it, 'an express and clear recognition by the world at large of our distinct nationhood and of our newly established freedom and autonomy'. But the Free State that joined the League of Nations was nowhere mentioned in the accession speech delivered in Geneva by William T. Cosgrave, President of its Executive Council. Instead, Cosgrave made repeated reference to 'Ireland', the partition of which would acquire a more permanent than provisional appearance in 1925 when a boundary commission, born out of the Treaty, failed to result in an adjustment of territorial boundaries to Irish nationalists' satisfaction.

With the Irish Free State's internationally recognised border now fixed, the state grasped every opportunity to emphasise that everything was not as it appeared and that it retained a right to represent the whole island. The Olympic Games were one such opportunity. So, when, in 1928, the IOC came looking for £1,000 to support its participation at the 1928 Olympic games – a separate Irish team had first participated in Paris four years earlier – the Irish government weighed up the pros and cons of doing so. In the end, the money was agreed, with the Department of Finance swayed by the fact that the Irish team would represent 'not merely' the Irish Free State, but Ireland 'as a whole'. Even for a cash-strapped, cost-conscious Department of Finance, the politics of anti-partition took precedence as 'no opportunity', it was determined, was to be lost in emphasising 'amongst the nations the essential unity of Ireland'.

From the Cultural Revival to the Nobel Prize

WHILE IMPRISONED in Gloucester Prison in January 1919, Arthur Griffith penned a memo suggesting the ways in which Dáil Éireann might shape its approach to the Paris Peace Conference, which began that month. In a wide-ranging document, Griffith suggested that Ireland should 'Mobilise the poets. Let them address Wilson and let them remind him in their best verse that he has the opportunity and the duty of giving the world true peace and freedom. Let them exhort him to stand firm and win a great victory for man than any that has been won for centuries [sic]. Let them remind him that the peoples look to him as to the man of hope, that all his ideals fail if Ireland is permitted to remain enclosed.' In the event no poets were dispatched to Paris to represent Dáil Éireann, and US President Woodrow Wilson remained unmoved by the Irish cause of self-determination. Griffith's notion of mobilising the poets is instructive, however, of the power of the Irish cultural revival and the galvanising role it played during the Irish revolutionary period.

In December 1923, just seven months after hostilities in the Irish Civil War had ended, W.B. Yeats was awarded the Nobel Prize for Literature. The prize citation stated that 'his always inspired poetry … in a highly artistic form gives expression to the spirit of a whole nation'. In Yeats' acceptance speech, which he titled 'The Irish Dramatic Movement', he offered his view that 'the modern literature of Ireland, and indeed all that stir of thought which prepared for the Anglo-Irish War, began when Parnell fell from power in 1891'. The split in the Home Rule movement that followed from charges of adultery against

… 'his always inspired poetry … in a highly artistic form gives expression to the spirit of a whole nation'.

W.B. Yeats, photographed in his Nobel Prize-winning year.

Parnell, and the subsequent distancing of the Catholic hierarchy from his leadership, gave the cultural revival, which was already in existence, renewed impetus and importance. In the political vacuum that would exist until John Redmond's leadership of the Home Rule cause began in 1900, and against the backdrop of the Land Wars and the defeat of the Second Home Rule Bill in 1893, the revival gave expression and a voice to an Irish cultural nationalism. In its entirety, the cultural revival, as P.J. Mathews and Declan Kiberd noted, 'generated not only a remarkable crop of artists of world significance, but also a range of innovative political thinkers and activists, among the most influential that Ireland has produced'.

The cultural revival had its roots in a broader movement that had begun in the mid-nineteenth century, with an initial focus on the Irish language. In 1877 the Society for the Preservation of the Irish Language was formed in Dublin, which would split in 1880, when a further organisation, the Gaelic Union (Aontacht na Gaeilge), was formed. Active in the Gaelic Union was Michael Cusack, who would go on to form the GAA in 1884, and the scholar Douglas Hyde. In November 1892 Hyde gave a lecture to the National Literary Society, which he titled 'The Necessity for De-Anglicizing Ireland' and in which he argued that the power and ubiquitous nature of British culture in Irish life had led to the near destruction of an indigenous culture. Hyde believed that the best way of resisting this alien culture was to fully embrace the use of the Irish language. To that end he formed, in July 1893, the Gaelic League (Conradh na Gaeilge) as a vehicle to promote and teach the language. Hyde was the first president of the League and his co-founder, the scholar Eoin MacNeill, its first secretary. MacNeill would also be the first editor of the League's newspaper, *An Claidheamh Soluis,* from 1899. The Gaelic League was successful in building its membership. Within a decade it had a network of over 400 branches across the country and, by lobbying the education system, had Irish introduced to the curriculum of over 1,300 schools by 1903.

A 1943 stamp commemorating Douglas Hyde and the Gaelic League.

The cultural revival was a much larger and broader force than one built solely around the language issue. As Marjorie Howes and Joe Valente have argued, 'looking at the Revival, we can discern that its various branches grew into a network of interactive relationships without any overarching centre of authority or intentionality'. This is an important way of understanding the cultural revival in Ireland and its reach into a plethora of different interest groups. As Howes and Valente explained, 'nothing like a bureau of revivalism existed or could have existed. Its constituent organizations, like the GAA, the Gaelic League, the creamery movement, the Irish Literary Theatre, etc., pursued their own aims in relative autonomy from the others and modulated in accordance with their own feedback mechanisms, each of which affected and was affected by the others in a fashion that could not have been and yet must seem, in retrospect, purposeful.'

In his Nobel Prize acceptance speech Yeats acknowledged the work of the wider cultural revival and that of Hyde and the Gaelic League, but in the context of the range of interests that the revival would cover, Yeats recalled that he 'had begun a movement in English, in the language in which modern Ireland thinks and does its business'. Yeats, along with Lady Augusta Gregory, was one of the great driving forces behind the foundation of the Abbey Theatre as Ireland's National Theatre. The process had begun in 1899 with the foundation of the Irish Literary Theatre (by Yeats, Gregory and Edward Martyn), which staged its plays in the Gaiety Theatre and the Antient Concert Rooms, as well

FROM THE CULTURAL REVIVAL TO THE NOBEL PRIZE

as the parallel work of William and Frank Fay and their Irish National Dramatic Company. The latter was important for its staging of plays by Irish writers, such as Yeats' *Cathleen Ni Houlihan* in 1902. In 1903 the arrival of Annie Horniman in Dublin, whom Yeats had known in London, was critical in providing the financial support that brought the Abbey into being. The theatre opened in December 1904 and its opening nights featured plays by Yeats, Lady Gregory and John Millington Synge.

Yeats had argued that a national theatre and the ability to stage live performances was critical, as the public read little and so enthusiastically embraced the spectacle of the theatre. While the Abbey Theatre did prove popular, it existed in a perpetually precarious financial state and drew the ire of its audiences when it staged Synge's *The Playboy of the Western World* in 1907 and George Bernard Shaw's *The Shewing-Up of Blanco Posnet* in 1909. Despite its problems, the Abbey was concrete evidence of the cultural revival and one that attracted many nationally minded men and women through its doors. At the Abbey the Irish watched Irish plays and, as Yeats would note in his Stockholm speech in 1923, 'indeed the young Ministers and party politicians of the Free State have had, I think, some of their education from our plays'.

A poster for plays by Yeats, Gregory and Synge in the Abbey Theatre in December 1904 and January 1905.

The cultural revival was a success insofar as it led to the creation of organisations such as the Gaelic League, the Abbey Theatre and the GAA. Also, through a renewed interest in history, literature, the language and folklore, many Irish people began to understand, appreciate and connect with a sense of national identity. The cultural revival was important in nationalising the population's thinking, and in political form no doubt assisted the Home Rule movement during the 1910s and, from 1917, the rise of Sinn Féin. As Mathews and Kiberd noted, there was an 'extraordinary reawakening of intellectual life and the rebirth of civic action in Ireland, decades after a devastating famine, and in the wake of the political implosion which followed the Parnell era'. Joep Leerssen, in understanding the language and sporting components of the revival as mass movements, noted that, 'the Gaelic League also proved a great nationalist mobiliser for the population at large, alongside sports associations such as the Gaelic Athletic Association'. So the cultural revival had a far wider impact than simply revitalising and growing organisations dedicated to literature, the language and sports.

As these organisations and the movements were national in their reach, they soon came to the attention of advanced nationalists. In the context of the politicisation of the cultural revival, Leerssen remarked that 'these associations as well as Griffith's Sinn Féin were quickly infiltrated and dominated by radicals sympathising with or being members of the Irish Republican Brotherhood: Patrick Pearse foremost amongst them.' Pearse had joined the Gaelic League in 1896, and by 1903 he was the editor of *An Claidheamh Soluis*. He was an advocate of the language and an accomplished poet and critic, who propagated the ideas of the cultural revival at his school, St Enda's. In November 1913 Pearse attended the inaugural meeting of the Irish Volunteers, and a month later had been sworn in as a member of the IRB. Of those signatories of the Proclamation executed at the end of the Easter Rising, three - Pearse, Joseph Mary Plunkett and Thomas MacDonagh - were published poets and active in the Gaelic League.

> The political radicalism that would culminate in the Rising of 1916 had its roots in the nationalistic thinking inherent in the cultural revival.

The political radicalism that would culminate in the Rising of 1916 had its roots in the nationalistic thinking inherent in the cultural revival. But the organisations of the revival, such as the Gaelic League or the GAA, were not the sole drivers towards political radicalisation. Throughout the period a wide range of civic organisations sprang up in Ireland that gave voice to an array of causes, including feminism, nationalism, socialism, suffrage and trade unionism. It was the ideas verbalised by all these movements that sought a new vision of Ireland, which, when coupled with the spirit of the cultural revival, lit the touchpaper in a relatively small number of people that would lead to the militarism of the Easter Rising.

In its entirety, the cultural revival encompassed many different activities. Alongside the language activism of the Gaelic League and the drama staged by the Abbey Theatre, there were parallel revival movements in folk music (the Feis Ceoil from 1897), the visual arts (with painters such as Paul Henry and the sculptor Oliver Sheppard) and crafts (Cuala Press from 1908 and the Dun Emer Guild from 1902). Throughout its existence the revival period witnessed the publication of some of Ireland's finest literature. Much of the work was fictional or based around historical themes, but there was much that was political in intent, such as the works of Mary Colum, James Connolly, Maud Gonne, Alice Milligan and Patrick Pearse, and those which addressed the question of women's rights and suffrage by Hannah Sheehy Skeffington, Mary MacSwiney and Constance Markievicz. The literary work of the revival embraced, among others, Yeats' *The Celtic Twilight* and Douglas Hyde's *Love Songs of Connaught* in 1893, George Sigerson's *Bards of the Gael and the Gall* in 1897, and Gregory's *Cuchulain of Muirthemne* and Gregory and Yeats' *Cathleen Ni Houlihan* in 1902, and it concluded, as Ireland began life as an independent state, with the publication in Ireland of James Joyce's *Ulysses* in 1922, Liam O'Flaherty's *The Informer* in 1925 and Sean O'Casey's *The Plough and the Stars* in 1926. The work of the 1920s, through Joyce's modernism and O'Flaherty's and O'Casey's inclusion of the violence inherent in the period since 1916, marked a turn away from the forms and motifs of the revival.

When Yeats died in 1939, the British-born poet W.H. Auden wrote, 'In Memory of WB Yeats', which included the lines: 'Mad Ireland hurt you into poetry. / Now Ireland has her madness and her weather still, / For poetry makes nothing happen'. The cultural revival had stalled before Yeats died. For all its idealism and its transformative effect on Ireland, the state that came into being after the Civil War was very different from the one the revival had imagined. It was divided by the bitterness of the Civil War, the failure to create a republic, and the partition of Ireland. It would also be a state in which the conservative forces of Catholicism would dominate and cultural freedom and innovation would be strangled. As Roy Foster concluded of the ending of the revival, 'But inartistic puritanism characterised the values proclaimed by the new Irish Free State from 1922, reducing the memory of Revivalism to an ersatz-Gaelic prettiness and pietistic didacticism.' Despite the ending of the revival as a vibrant and broad-focused force in Irish society, the remarkable body of art and literature that was produced and the crowds that still fill Croke Park every summer bear testimony to the power and legacy of the revival period.

> 'Mad Ireland hurt you into poetry. / Now Ireland has her madness and her weather still, / For poetry makes nothing happen'.

Selected Further Reading

Books and Articles

Adams, R.J.C., *Shadow of a Taxman: Who Funded the Irish Revolution* (Oxford, 2022)

Aiken, Síobhra, *Spiritual Wounds: Trauma, Testimony and the Irish Civil War* (Dublin, 2022)

Beiner, Guy, 'A Short History of Irish Memory in the Long Twentieth Century' in Thomas Bartlett (ed.), *The Cambridge History of Ireland,* Vol. IV: 1800 to the Present (Cambridge, 2018), pp. 708-25

Borgonovo, John, *The Dynamics of War and Revolution: Cork City, 1916-1918* (Cork, 2013)

Bowman, Timothy, *Carson's Army: The Ulster Volunteer Force, 1910-22* (Manchester, 2007)

Campbell, Fergus, *Land and Revolution: Nationalist Politics in the West of Ireland 1891-1921* (Oxford, 2005)

Connolly, Linda (ed.), *Women and the Irish Revolution: Feminism, Activism, Violence* (Dublin, 2020)

Crowley, John, Ó Drisceoil, Donal, Murphy, Mike and Borgonovo, John (eds), *Atlas of the Irish Revolution* (Cork, 2017)

Cunningham, John and Dunne, Terry (eds) *Spirit of Revolution: Ireland from Below, 1917-1923* (Dublin, 2024)

Daly, Mary E. (ed.), *Roger Casement in Irish and World History* (Dublin, 2005)

Daly, Mary E. and O'Callaghan, Margaret (eds), *1916 in 1966: Commemorating the Easter Rising* (Dublin, 2007)

Destenay, Emmanuel, *Shadows from the Trenches: Veterans of the Great War and the Irish Revolution, 1918-1923* (Dublin, 2021)

Dolan, Anne, *Commemorating the Irish Civil War: History and Memory, 1923-2000* (Cambridge, 2003)

Dolan, Anne and Crowe, Catríona (eds), *'A very hard struggle': Lives in the Military Service Pensions Collection* (Dublin, 2023)

Dolan, Anne and Murphy, William, *Michael Collins: The Man and the Revolution* (Cork, 2018)

Dooley, Terence, *Burning the Big House: The Story of the Irish Country House in a Time of War and Revolution* (New Haven, 2022)

Dungan, Myles, *Irish Voices from the Great War* (Dublin, 1995)

Dungan, Myles, *Four Killings: Land Hunger, Murder and Family in the Irish Revolution* (London, 2021)

Earner-Byrne, Lindsey, *Letters of the Catholic Poor: Poverty in Independent Ireland, 1920-1940* (Cambridge, 2017)

Evershed, Jonathan, *Ghosts of the Somme: Commemoration and Culture War in Northern Ireland* (Notre Dame, 2018)

Fanning, Ronan, *Fatal Path: British Government and Irish Revolution* (London, 2013)

Ferriter, Diarmaid, *A Nation and Not a Rabble: The Irish Revolution 1913-23* (London, 2015)

Ferriter, Diarmaid, *Between Two Hells: The Irish Civil War* (London, 2021)

Ferriter, Diarmaid and Riordan, Susannah (eds), *Years of Turbulence: The Irish Revolution and Its Aftermath* (Dublin, 2015)

Fitzpatrick, David, *Politics and Irish life, 1913-1921: Provincial Experience of War and Revolution* (Cork, 1998)

Fitzpatrick, David, *Harry Boland's Irish Revolution* (Cork, 2003)

Fitzpatrick, David (ed.), *Terror in Ireland: 1916-1923* (Dublin, 2012)

Foster, Gavin M., *The Irish Civil War and Society: Politics, Class and Conflict* (Basingstoke, 2015)

Foster, Roy, *Vivid Faces: The Revolutionary Generation in Ireland 1890-1923* (London, 2015)

Foy, Michael T., *Michael Collins's Intelligence War: The Struggle Between the British and the IRA, 1919-1921* (2008)

Frawley, Oona (ed.), *Women and the Decade of Commemorations* (Bloomington, 2021)

Friemann, Gretchen, *The Treaty: The Gripping Story of the Negotiations that brought about Irish Independence and led to Civil War* (Dublin, 2021)

Gallagher, Niamh, *Ireland and the Great War: A Social and Political History* (London, 2020)

Gannon, Darragh and McGarry, Fearghal (eds), *Ireland 1922: Independence, Partition and Civil War* (Dublin, 2022)

Gibney, John and O'Malley, Kate, *The Handover: Dublin Castle and the British Withdrawal from Ireland, 1922* (Dublin, 2022)

Gillis, Liz and McAuliffe, Mary, *Richmond Barracks 1916: "We Were There". 77 Women of the Easter Rising* (Dublin, 2016)

Gray, Peter and Purdue, Olwen (eds), *The Irish Lord Lieutenancy: c. 1541-1922* (Dublin, 2012)

Grayson, Richard, *Belfast Boys: How Unionists and Nationalists Fought and Died Together in the First World War* (London, 2009)

Grayson, Richard, *Dublin's Great Wars: The First World War, the Easter Rising and the Irish Revolution* (Cambridge, 2018)

Grayson, Richard and McGarry, Fearghal (eds), *Remembering 1916: The Easter Rising, the Somme and the Politics of Memory in Ireland* (Cambridge, 2016)

Hopkinson, Michael, *Green against Green: The Irish Civil War* (Dublin, 1988)

Hopkinson, Michael (ed.), *The Last Days of Dublin Castle: The Mark Sturgis Diaries* (Dublin, 1999)

Hopkinson, Michael, *The Irish War of Independence* (Dublin, 2002)

Horne, John (ed.), *Our War: Ireland and the Great War* (Dublin, 2010)

Horne, John and Madigan, Edward (eds), *Towards Commemoration: Ireland in War and Revolution, 1912-1923* (Dublin, 2014)

Jeffery, Keith, *Ireland and the Great War* (Cambridge, 2011)

Jeffery, Keith, *1916: A Global History* (London, 2015)

Jones, Heather, *Violence Against Prisoners of War in the First World War: Britain, France and Germany, 1914-1920* (Cambridge, 2011)

Kiberd, Declan and Mathews, P.J., *Handbook of the Irish Revival: An Anthology of Irish Cultural and Political Writings 1891-1922* (Dublin, 2015)

Laffan, Michael, *The Partition of Ireland 1911-1925* (Dundalk, 1983)

Laffan, Michael, *The Resurrection of Ireland: The Sinn Féin Party, 1916-1923* (Cambridge, 1999)

Laird, Heather, *Commemoration* (Cork, 2018)

Lane, Leeann, *Rosamond Jacob: Third Person Singular* (Dublin, 2010)

Lane, Leeann, *Dorothy Macardle* (Dublin, 2019)

Maguire, Martin, *The Civil Service and the Revolution in Ireland, 1912-1938: 'Shaking the blood-stained hand of Mr Collins'* (Manchester, 2008)

Mannion, Patrick and McGarry, Fearghal, *The Irish Revolution: A Global History* (New York, 2022)

McAuliffe, Mary, *Margaret Skinnider* (Dublin, 2020)

McCullagh, David, *De Valera*. Vol. 1: Rise 1882-1932 (Dublin, 2017)

McGarry, Fearghal, *The Rising: Ireland Easter 1916* (Oxford, 2010)

McGreevy, Ronan, *Wherever the Firing Line Extends: Ireland and the Western Front* (Dublin, 2016)

McWilliams, Ellen, *Resting Places: On Wounds, War and the Irish Revolution* (Belfast, 2023)

Meleady, Dermot, *John Redmond: The National Leader* (Dublin, 2013)

Milne, Ide, *Stacking the Coffins: Influenza, War and Revolution in Ireland, 1918-19* (Manchester, 2018)

Mitchell, Arthur, *Revolutionary Government in Ireland: Dáil Éireann, 1919-22* (Dublin, 1995)

Moore, Cormac, *Birth of the Border: The Impact of Partition in Ireland* (Dublin, 2019)

Morrison, Eve, *Kilmichael: The Life and Afterlife of an Ambush* (Dublin, 2022)

Murphy, William, *Political Imprisonment and the Irish, 1912-1921* (Oxford, 2014)

Nic Dháibhéid, Caoimhe, Bew, Paul and Coleman, Marie (eds), *Northern Ireland 1921-2021: Centenary Historical Perspectives* (Belfast, 2022)

O'Connor, Emmet, *Syndicalism in Ireland, 1917-1923* (Cork, 1988)

O'Connor, Emmet, *James Larkin* (Cork, 2002)

O'Connor, Emmet, *A Labour History of Ireland, 1824-2000* (Dublin, 2011)

O'Leary, Brendan, *A Treatise on Northern Ireland*. Vol. 1: Colonialism (Oxford, 2020)

Orr, Philip, *The Road to the Somme: Men of the Ulster Division Tell Their Story* (Belfast, 2008)

Ó Tuathaigh, Gearóid (ed.), *The GAA and the Revolution in Ireland 1913-1923* (Cork, 2015)

O'Halpin, Eunan and Ó Corráin, Daithí, *The Dead of the Irish Revolution* (New Haven, 2020)

Parkinson, Alan F., *A Difficult Birth: The Early Years of Northern Ireland 1920-1925* (Dublin, 2020)

Pennell, Catriona, *A Kingdom United: Popular Responses to the Outbreak of the First World War in Britain and Ireland* (Oxford, 2012)

Quinn, James, and White, Lawrence William (eds), *1916 Portraits and Lives* (Dublin, 2015)

Stover, Justin, *Enduring Ruin: Environmental Destruction During the Irish Revolution* (Dublin, 2022)

Toibín, Micheál, *Enniscorthy: History & Heritage* (Dublin, 1988)

Townshend, Charles, *The Republic: The Fight for Irish Independence* (London, 2013)

Townshend, Charles, *The Partition: Ireland Divided, 1885-1925* (London, 2021)

Valente, Joseph and Howes, Marjorie (eds), *The Irish Revival: A Complex Vision* (Syracuse, 2023)

Walker, Brian, *Irish History Matters: Politics, Identity and Commemoration* (Stroud, 2019)

Walker, Stephen, *Ireland's Call: Irish Sporting Heroes Who Fell in the Great War* (Dublin, 2015)

Walsh, Fionnuala, *Irish Women and the Great War* (Cambridge, 2020)

Ward, Margaret, *Fearless Woman: Hanna Sheehy Skeffington, Feminism and the Irish Revolution* (Dublin, 2019)

Wills, Clair, *Dublin 1916: The Siege of the GPO* (London, 2010)

Yeates, Padraig, *A City in Wartime: Dublin 1914-1918* (Dublin, 2011)

The *16 Lives* series published by O'Brien offers biographies of all those executed in 1916.

The *Irish Revolution* series published by Four Courts and edited by Mary Ann Lyons and Daithí Ó Corráin offers a history of each county during the revolutionary period.

Other Resources

Major online and digitisation projects for the period included *1914-1918 Online: International Encyclopedia of the First World War*, https://encyclopedia.1914-1918-online.net/home.html, which was led by the Friedrich-Meinecke-Institute of Freie Universität Berlin. In Ireland the Military Archives of the Irish Defence Forces digitised and made available the witness accounts of the Bureau of Military History Collection, which covered the 1913-21 period, and the Military Service Pension Collection, which includes pension applications and associated correspondence for those active in the period 1916-23: www.militaryarchives.ie/en/home/. The National Library of Ireland has also digitised private papers and other materials from its collection and made them available online at www.nli.ie. Likewise, the National Archives of Ireland has digitised key collections such as the Dublin Metropolitan Police Movement of Extremists Files, 1915-16, the Reports of Court Martial Proceedings, 1916, and the records of the Property Losses (Ireland) Committee, 1916 (PLIC), which was established to assess claims for damages to buildings and property as a result of the destruction caused by the 1916 Rising. These collections and others are free to access on the National Archives of Ireland's Decade of Centenaries website: (https://centenaries.nationalarchives.ie/centenaries/ and are helpfully accompanied by bespoke search engines. The National Archives is also partner with the Royal Irish Academy in the important *Documents in Irish Foreign Policy* project (www.difp.ie), the latter also providing a home for the wonderful *Dictionary of Irish Biography* (www.dib.ie), which provides accessible, authoritative and scholarly biographies not only on key figures from the revolutionary era but from across the broad sweep of Irish history. Both the *DIFP* and the *DIB* are fully searchable online, as is a sample of 10,000 artefacts from its historical, military and Easter week collections on the National Museum of Ireland's website.

A major portal for the role of women during the revolutionary period, Mná 100, which contains an array of contextual and archival pieces, is available at www.mna100.ie. Maynooth University's *Letters of 1916-23* is a digital collection of private letters that were sent during the period and cover day to day life, as well as commentary on the political changes taking place: https://letters1916.ie. Trinity College Dublin's *Beyond 2022* is a virtual reconstruction of the Record Treasury of the Public Record Office of Ireland, which was destroyed during the War of Independence: www.virtualtreasury.ie. The Derry-based Nerve Centre led the innovative Creative Centenaries project, the website of the which (www.creativecentenaries.org) showcases the work of Northern Ireland's creative sector in responding to the Decade of Centenaries. Included are digital toolkits for community groups and the heritage sector, ibooks, graphic novels, animated histories, and a wealth of other resources which will continue to educate and inform long after the current centenary cycle has passed.

Alongside publishing *Century Ireland*, the RTÉ website has established itself as an important online hub for historical content and analysis on the revolutionary decade through its RTÉ Brainstorm initiative and its partnership with the UCC's *Atlas of the Irish Revolution* and *Irish Civil War Fatalities* projects. Complementing these, special mention is merited for Tommy Graham's *History Ireland* website (www.historyireland.com), which includes recordings from its popular hedge schools series, as well as John Dorney's website (www.theirishstory.com), which has published a large body of short- and long-form articles on Irish history, but with a particular focus on the revolutionary period.

Finally, there has, over the course of the decade, been a keen focus in the press, in edited collections and academic journals on the process and experience of commemoration, which not only illuminate many of issues and controversies that arose over the course of the recent decade, but which are sure to serve as vital reference works for future scholars of commemorations policy and practice and Irish social memory. Notable among these are a special edition of the *Éire-Ireland* journal, published in 2022 and edited by Sara Dybris McQuaid and Fearghal McGarry. In addition, the *History Workshop Journal* (2018) published an article by Peter Leary on 'Negotiating Ireland's 'Decade of Centenaries in the new Age of Brexit', while Caoimhe Nic Dháibhéid's 'Historians and the Decade of Centenaries in modern Ireland' appeared in *Contemporary European History* in 2023. Meanwhile, the National University of Ireland published in print and online Guy Beiner's lecture 'Forgetting in the Decade of Commemorations: New Directions for Irish Historical Research', which was delivered in connection with to his awarding of the NUI's Irish Historical Research prize in 2019. Variations on these themes were also explored as part of President Michael D. Higgins's stimulating seminar series of historical cultural and philosophical reflections, *Machnamh 100*, which was held at Áras an Uachtaráin between December 2020 and November 2022. The fruits of this initiative make for fascinating viewing and reading and can be accessed on the website of the Irish President at https://president.ie/en/presidential-seminars/machnamh-100.

List of Illustrations

Courtesy of the Board of Trinity College Dublin: p. 99; p. 144; p. 175; p. 181; p. 183.

Courtesy of the GAA Museum at Croke Park: p. 92; p. 241; p. 292.

Courtesy of Imperial War Museum, p. 100, Art.IWM PST 13602; p. 101, Q 33222.

Courtesy of Kilmainham Gaol/OPW: p. 151.

Courtesy of the Library of Congress: p. 2, LC-B2-2841-16; p. 41, LC-DIG-ggbain-15801; p. 50, LC-B2-3686-4; p. 55, LC-USZC4-10981; p. 57: LC-B2-3287-9; p. 61, POS-WW1-GtBrit, no. 262; p. 64, LOT 2495; p. 72, LC-DIG-ppmsca-55686; p. 79, LC-DIG-ppmsc-09867; p. 88, LC-DIG-pga-12423; p. 90, D568.3.H3; p. 107, LC-DIG-ggbain-20341; p .113, LC-USZC4-10985; p. 123, LC-DIG-ggbain-24108 p. 125, LC-USZC4-2926; p. 130, LC-USZC4-2928; p. 146, LC-USZC4-3802; p. 148, LC-USZC4-12719; p. 153, 00280658984; p. 154, LC-USZC4-595; p. 164, LC-DIG-ppmsc-07950; p. 167, LC-DIG-ppmsc-07950; p. 190, LC-USZC4-11540; p. 199, LC-USZC4-12169; p. 203, LC-DIG-anrc-00493; p. 203, LC-USZC4-1126; p. 211, LC-DIG-anrc-17962; p. 211, LC-DIG-anrc-00488; p. 215, LC-DIG-ppmsca-55643; p. 219, LC-DIG-ds-12367; p. 236, LC-DIG-pga-02438; p. 244, LC-DIG-ppmsca-41422; p. 264, LIC-DIG-ggbain-28298; p. 274, LC-USZ62-59601; p. 279, LC-USZ62-11221; p. 281, LC-DIG-npcc-02649; p. 338, LC-DIG-ds-00785; p. 348, LC-DIG-pga-04153; p. 352, National Jukebox; p. 352, LC-USZ62-104776; p. 376, LC-DIG-pga-10542; p. 377, LC-USZ62-105690; p. 382, LC-DIG-ggbain-31070; p. 397, LC-DIG-ppmsc-09882, p. 398, LC-USZ62-105684; p. 395, LC-USZ62-85345; p. 402, LC-USZ61-1854.

Reproduced by kind permission of the Director of the National Archives of Ireland: p. 37; p. 40; p. 46; p. 150; p. 314; p. 399.

Courtesy of the National Library of Ireland: p. 4, NPA SHE33; p. 11, EPH F273; p. 13, NPA DHYA; p. 17, MS 15,673/8/2; p. 20, KE 76; p. 21, MS 17,503/27; p. 37, L_ROY_01732, p. 42, MS 41,494/2/1; p. 43, NPA POLF11; p. 43, CDB57; p. 44, MS. 9469, p. 53, LB 05 i 17; p. 54, INDH12C; p. 55, EPH G11; p. 56, L_ROY_08907; p. 78, LB 05 17; p. 83, LB 05 17; p. 84, MS 47719; p. 85 POOLED 2749/2; p. 86, IND H 0576; p. 89, KE 234; p. 93, L_CAB_03930; p. 102, EPH E378; p. 114, NPA PROC; p. 115, EPH F338; p. 116, NPA DOCE3; p. 121, EPH F233; p. 122, MS 44,337/1/3; p. 124, NPA CAS56B; p. 131, NPA DOCH3; p. 131, MS 49,491/2/524; p. 135, PD C56; p. 136, PD PEAR-PA (2) III; p. 138, EPH C613; p. 148, POOLEWP 1137; p. 157, Eas 1700; p. 159, Ke 126, p. 159, NPA POLF4; p. 160, EPH A319; p. 160, Ke 132; p. 162, POOLEWP 2679; p. 163, NPA ASH; p. 165, NPA POLF4; p. 169, POOLEWP 0552; p. 179, EPH A176; p. 183, D 146; p. 190, PD E17; p. 191, EPH A128; p. 191, EPH C473; p. 195, INDH192B; p. 198, EPH E28; p. 199, EPH A440; p. 201, NPA SHEA21; p. 204, EPH E7; p. 205, NPA INP; p. 206, EPH A665; p. 207, EPH B44; p. 217, MS 17,651/5/7; p. 224, NPA DOCG40; p. 226, D173; p. 226, NPA DAIL; p. 227, MS 17,658/1/4; p. 229, D173; p. 231, INDH54; p. 235, KE 210; p. 235, KE 121; p. 237, PD2159 TX (20) 90; p. 238, EAS_1767; p. 239, MS 17,651/5/7; p. 242, LB 05 I 17; p. 249, NPA PHOP14; p. 250, D139; p. 252, MS 10,433/9/7; p. 253, EPH A190; p. 256, D146; p. 257, INDH70; p. 260, MS 5,848/22; p. 265, D146, p. 265, EPH G100; p. 267, LB 05 i 17; p. 280, P_WP_2891; p. 293, HOG 161; p. 297, NPA POLF191; p. 298, HOGW 118; p. 300, PD 4309 TX 242; p. 302, NPA POLF264; p. 303, HOGW 124, p. 305, HOGW 47; p. 305, HOGW 73; p. 307, HOG 167; p. 310, NPA MKN8; p. 310, PD 2159 TX (54) 2; p. 311, NPA DOCB16; p. 312, BEA46; p. 313, INDH382; p. 316, INDH401 p. 318, INDH108; p. 323, HOGW 184; p. 329, INDH89; p. 331, HOGW 105; p. 336, HOG 234; p. 337, NPA BEG; p. 338, HOGW 135; p. 339, NPA DEV25; p. 340, NPA CIVP4; p. 340, MS 27,624; p. 341, HOGW 87; p. 341, HOGW 98; p. 342, NPA CEA119; p. 344, NPA POLF220; p. 345, EPH F295; p. 347, EPH E219; p. 347, EPH C840; p. 349, EPH D188; p. 350, EPH G71; p. 350, HOG 230; p. 350, PD 3067 TX 21; p. 350, NPA CIVP8; p. 351, HOG 85; p. 353, HOG 145; p. 353, PD 4309 TX 145; p. 354, MS48, 086/1; p. 357, D145, p. 357, HOGW 36, p. 357, PD3104 TX 19; p. 361, HOGW 32; p. 366, INDH122; p. 369, EPH G18; p. 372, HOGW 60; p. 381, HOGW 11; p. 381, INDH559A; p. 383, PD 4309 TX (1) 13; p. 385, HOG 196; p. 387, NPA POLF92; p. 389, INDH556; p. 389, PD4309TX 213; p. 390, KEN6; p. 390, EPH C200; p. 394, EAS_0907; p. 394, PD C63; p. 395, PD C85; p. 401, INDH63; p. 405, INDH3464.

Courtesy of Military Archives, Ireland: p. 268, BMH-CD-208-2-1; p. 300, DP8916 John James Phelan.pdf.

Courtesy of Pearse Museum/OPW: p. 36, p. 47.

Acknowledgements

This book is borne out of an online project, *Century Ireland*, that began life in 2013 and ran over the course of eleven years. It was an enormous undertaking, conceived as a partnership between a research team based at Boston College in Dublin, RTÉ and Ireland's national cultural institutions, and many people duly contributed to the project.

At the core of the project were our own researchers, writers and content producers, and it is no exaggeration to say that *Century Ireland*, and consequently this book, could never have developed in the way they did without the talent and commitment of a team that, at various times, included Ben Shorten, Matt Stapleton, Alyson Gray and Ellen King.

But our efforts were also supported by a wider community of postgraduate student interns, whose collaboration with *Century Ireland* was a product of our relationships with University College Dublin (UCD) and Trinity College, Dublin (TCD), and specifically with postgraduate courses they have run on media history, public history and cultural heritage. Our particular thanks here to Professor Paul Rouse and Dr Conor Mulvagh at UCD, and to Dr Georgina Laragy in TCD.

At Dublin City University, meanwhile, Dr William Murphy was a huge source of support and advice which extended to a generous willingness to read these pages in draft form.

From the very outset of the *Century Ireland* project, Catríona Crowe, then of the National Archives of Ireland, and Ed Mulhall, then of RTÉ, were astonishingly generous in sharing the wisdom of their experience and giving freely of their time to act as archival and editorial advisors. Catríona was also one of our first filmed interviewees, while Ed contributed some of the website's standout long reads on the relationship between politics and literature throughout this period.

At Boston College our very sincere thanks are due to Thea Gilien, Claire McGowan, David Quigley and John Burke for their support, and our colleagues in Irish Studies and at the Burns Library, who provided regular advice and a range of material that supported the website.

Century Ireland was funded throughout its lifetime by the Department of Tourism, Culture, Arts, Gaeltacht, Sport and Media, and we are grateful for the support of the various ministers we worked under, namely Jimmy Deenihan,

Heather Humphreys, Josepha Madigan and Catherine Martin. We were also assisted within the department by Sinead Copeland, Orlaith Lochrin, Niall Ó Donnchú and Rónán Whelan. John Concannon, who headed up Ireland 2016, was another enthusiastic supporter of, and advocate for, the project.

Our partners in the library and archive world were amazing, so many thanks to the National Library of Ireland, the National Archives, National Museum of Ireland, National Gallery of Ireland, Dublin City Gallery: The Hugh Lane, Dublin City Library and Archives, University College Dublin, Galway University, the *Dictionary of Irish Biography*, Irish Film Institute, Villanova University, Public Record Office of Northern Ireland, The Nerve Centre, Derry, Beyond 2022 at Trinity College, and Global Ireland. Cécile Chemin at the Military Archives was a pleasure to work with, as was Stephen MacEoin in the early phase of the project. We are, nevertheless, particularly keen to acknowledge the assistance of Katherine McSharry, Lar Joye, Brenda Malone and Zoe Reid, who throughout the lifespan of the project lent us their keen eye on library and archive collections and how best they might be accommodated within our project.

RTÉ was our media partner and hosted the *Century Ireland* website, which was built by Emmet Dunne, Ed Kelly and their team at Kooba, and developed with the advice received from Mark Hennessy and Neil Lyden at RTÉ.

The relationship with RTÉ was crucial to making *Century Ireland* a truly public history project, and critical to the building of that relationship was the enthusiasm and professional commitment of the aforementioned Ed Mulhall, Lorelei Harris, Glen Killane, Declan McBennett and Yetti Redmond – all of them bringing to the project the very best of public service values.

Throughout, we made extensive use of RTÉ Archives content and are grateful to Liam Wylie and Colm Talbot for their consistent engagement with, and support for, the project. In what was a model of the collaborative spirit underpinning *Century Ireland*, we worked in 2014 on a series, *Talking WW1*, which aired on RTÉ and was used extensively by *Century Ireland*, as well as by the National Library of Ireland as part of its own First World War exhibition. That series was made possible with the help of the RTÉ News editorial and technical teams, but most especially David McCullagh and Larry Dalton. In a later series of interviews, we were helped by many of the same crew but with Bryan Dobson in the role of informed and effectively probing interviewer. We also worked with RTÉ's *Nationwide* team, in particular Donal Byrne and Anne-Marie O'Callaghan, who were of great support, as was John O'Regan, who oversaw the coverage of big state ceremonials that signposted the decade. Meanwhile,

Claire Coffey and the good people at the RTÉ News Channel added a new and innovative dimension to our public outreach by broadcasting daily *Century Ireland* headlines of what was making the news 100 years ago.

The project would not have existed were it not for the work of academics in universities across Ireland and beyond, who happily published on, or agreed to being interviewed for, our website. Needless to say, they are too numerous to mention all by name, yet Dr Darragh Gannon and Professor Fearghal McGarry merit special mention for their work on the Global Irish Revolution, which was widely platformed on *Century Ireland*. So too does Ruth Hegarty at the Royal Irish Academy, with whom we collaborated on bringing the beautiful and scholarly *Ireland 1922* book to online audiences over the course of a twelve-month period in 2022.

Turning a vast, decade-long online project into a book would not have been possible without the pleasurable stewardship provided by the team at Merrion Press, most notably Conor Graham, Wendy Logue and Patrick O'Donoghue. The design work on the book, a massive undertaking, was initially developed by Peadar Staunton before being taken on by Alba Esteban Segura.

At home, no less than at work, we are fortunate to be surrounded by talented and wonderful people and we are grateful for the love and support of our families – Moynagh, Ellen and Samson; Sophie, Olivia and Tomás.

Finally, the *Century Ireland* project was started as a digital project and remains fully and freely accessible to online audiences. Our hope for this book is that it does justice to the ambition and spirit of that project, and honours the work of everyone who was involved.

Mike Cronin
Mark Duncan
July 2024